Data Modeling Master Class

A Best Practices Approach to Understanding and Applying Fundamentals Through Advanced Modeling Techniques

Steve Hoberman
Steve Hoberman & Associates, LLC
me@stevehoberman.com
www.stevehoberman.com
www.technicspub.com

Published by:
Technics Publications, LLC
966 Woodmere Drive
Westfield, NJ 07090 U.S.A.
me@stevehoberman.com
www.technicspub.com

Cover design by Mark Brye

The publisher offers discounts on this book when ordered in quantity for special sales. For more information, please contact:

Technics Publications Corporate Sales Division
966 Woodmere Drive
Westfield, NJ 07090 U.S.A.
me@stevehoberman.com
This book is printed on recycled acid-free paper.

ISBN, print ed. 978-1-9355041-6-0
First Printing First Edition 2008
First Printing Second Edition 2011
First Printing Third Edition 2011
Printed in the United States of America

Library of Congress Control Number: 2011935783

Data Modeling Master Class

The Master Class is a complete course on requirements elicitation and data modeling, containing four days of practical techniques for producing solid relational and dimensional data models. After learning the styles and steps in capturing and modeling requirements, you will apply a **best practices approach** to building and validating data models through the Data Model Scorecard®. You will know not just how to build a data model, but also how to build a data model **well**. Three case studies and many exercises reinforce the material and enable you to apply these techniques in your current projects.

By the end of the course, you will know how to...

1. Apply requirements elicitation techniques including interviewing and prototyping
2. Explain data modeling constructs and employ the "6 Questions" approach to ensure model precision
3. Demonstrate reading a data model of any size and complexity with the same confidence as reading a book
4. Validate any data model with key "settings" (scope, abstraction, timeframe, function, and format) as well as through the Data Model Scorecard®
5. Practice finding structural soundness issues and standards violations
6. Build relational and dimensional subject area, logical, and physical data models
7. Recognize situations where abstraction would be most valuable and situations where abstraction would be most dangerous
8. Use a series of templates for scoping and validating requirements, and for data profiling
9. Express how to write clear, complete, and correct definitions
10. Describe the two reasons an enterprise data modeling project can fail, and the factors that must be in place for the enterprise data model to succeed

About Steve

Steve Hoberman is the most requested data modeling instructor in the world. Introduced at over 50 international conferences as everything from a "data modeling guru" to "data modeling rock star", Steve balances the formality and precision of data modeling with the realities of building software systems with severe time, budget, and people constraints. In his consulting and teaching, he focuses on templates, tools, and guidelines to reap the benefits of data modeling with minimal investment. He taught his first data modeling class in 1992 and has educated more than 10,000 people about data modeling and business intelligence techniques since then, spanning every continent except Africa and Antarctica. Steve is the author of five books on data modeling, including the bestseller *Data Modeling Made Simple*.

- **Abstraction**. Part of the logical data modeling process and is usually performed after normalizing. Abstraction brings flexibility to your logical data models by redefining and combining some of the data elements, entities, and relationships within the model into more generic terms.
- **Accumulating measure**. Monitor progress of a business process. Frequently the amount of days required to complete a certain business process step are tracked, such as Remaining Days Count or Settlement Days Count.
- **Aggregate**. A table which contains the resolution of a one-to-one relationship.
- **Alternate key**. The one or more data elements that uniquely identify a value in an entity and that is not chosen to be *the* unique identifier.
- **Application Subject Area Model (ASAM)**. The ASAM is a subject area model of a defined portion of a particular application. The ASAM can be for either a proposed or existing application. Many BSAMs are the first step in large development efforts (first understand the business before you understand the application), and therefore the BSAM is usually the starting point for the ASAM.
- **Behavioral dimension**. A dimension that is created based upon measurements. Measurement ranges are grouped together in the dimension, such as by sales amounts or performance. Ideal when the users recognize the same set of bands, and they are stable.
- **Bridge table**. A table which resolves a many-to-many relationship from the dimension to the meter. In other words, a given meter instance may need to refer to more than one dimension instance. Bridge tables can be shown as the typical resolution of a many-to-many on a logical, but may need a different physical structure depending on reporting tools.
- **Business Subject Area Model (BSAM)**. The BSAM is a subject area model of a defined portion of the business. The scope can be limited to a department or function such as manufacturing or sales. It can be as broad as the entire enterprise or industry. The BSAM focuses on a business area, not a particular application.
- **Candidate key**. The one or many data elements that uniquely identify a value in an entity. Candidate keys are either primary or alternate keys.
- **Cardinality**. The symbols on both ends of a relationship that define the number of instances of each entity that can participate in the relationship. It is through cardinality that the data rules are captured and enforced. The domain of values to choose from to represent cardinality on a relationship is limited to three values: zero, one, or many. *Many* (some people read it as *more*) means any number greater than one.
- **Comparison Subject Area Model (CSAM)**. The CSAM is a subject area model that shows the relationships between two or more ASAMs. It is used primarily for impact analysis and issue resolution. CSAMs build on two or more ASAMs, in which one or more ASAMs represent an existing application environment and (optionally) one or more ASAMs represent proposed changes to an environment.

- **Conformed dimension**. Built with the organization in mind, instead of just a particular application, to support drill across queries and enterprise consistency. Conformed dimensions do not need to be identical with each other, they just need to be from the same superset. Conformed dimensions allow the navigator the ability to ask questions that cross multiple marts.
- **Data element**. A property of importance to the business whose values contribute to identifying, describing, or measuring instances of an entity.
- **Data model**. A set of symbols and text which describes an information landscape.
- **Data Model Scorecard®.** A set of 10 categories for validating the quality of a data model.
- **Degenerate dimension**. A dimension whose data element(s) have been moved to the fact table. A degenerate dimension is most common when the original dimension contained only a single data element such as a transaction identifier.
- **Denormalization**. The process of selectively violating normalization rules and reintroducing redundancy into the model. This extra redundancy can reduce data retrieval time and produce a more user-friendly model.
- **Dependent entity**. Also known as a weak entity, a dependent entity is an object of interest to the business that depends on one or many other entities for its existence. The entities that a dependent entity depends on can be independent entities or other dependent entities. A dependent entity is depicted as a rectangle with rounded edges.
- **Dimension**. Subjects whose only purpose is to add meaning to the measures. Dimensions are either hierarchies or lookups.
- **Domain**. The complete set of all possible values that a data element can be assigned.
- **Drill across**. Navigation from one dimensional model to another dimensional model.
- **Drill down**. When the context for the measure goes from higher level to lower level. For example, needing to see the measures at a month level and then at a day level.
- **Drill up**. When the context for the measure goes from lower level to higher level. For example, needing to see the measures at a day level and then at a month level.
- **Elicitation**. To draw forth or bring out. "Eliciting requirements" is a more collaborative term than "gathering requirements".
- **Enterprise Data Model (EDM)**. A subject-oriented and integrated data model representing all of the data produced and consumed across an entire organization. Subject-oriented means that the concepts on a data model fit together as the CEO sees the company, as opposed to how individual functional or department heads see their view of the company. Integration means that all of the data and rules in an organization are depicted once and fit together seamlessly.
- **Entity**. Something of interest to the business. An entity is a collection of information about something that the business deems important and worthy of capture. An entity is a who, what, when, where, why, or how.
- **Family Tree**. A spreadsheet which documents the lineage for each data element in the data model.
- **Fact**. *See measure.*

- **Factless fact**. A fact table that does not contain any facts. Factless facts count events by summing relationship occurrences between the dimensions.
- **Fold Up But Easily Separate (FUBES)**. A denormalization technique where tables are combined yet there is still the ability to access individual instances from each of the entities.
- **Foreign key**. A data element that provides a link to another entity.
- **Grain**. A meter's lowest level of detail. It should be capable of answering all of the business questions within the scope of the dimensional model.
- **Grain Matrix**. A spreadsheet, which captures the levels of reporting for each fact or measurement. It is the spreadsheet view of an initial design, which could result in a star schema.
- **Hierarchy**. An arrangement of items (objects, names, values, categories, etc.) in which the items are represented as being "above," "below," or "at the same level as" one another.
- **Independent entity**. Also known as a kernel entity, an independent entity is an object of interest to the business that does not depend on any other entity for its identification. Each occurrence of an independent entity can be identified without referring to any other entity on the model. An independent entity is depicted as a rectangle.
- **Inversion Entry (IE)**. A non-unique index (also known as a secondary key).
- **Junk dimension**. A dimension containing all the possible combinations of a small and somewhat related set of indicators and codes.
- **Logical Data Model (LDM)**. A representation of a detailed business solution.
- **Measure**. A data element that a set of business users need to 'see', and which can also be mathematically manipulated. Gross Sales Amount is an example of a measure.
- **Metadata**. Text that describes what the audience needs to see.
- **Meter**. An entity containing a related set of measures. It is not a person, place, event, or thing, as we would expect on the relational model. Instead, it is a bucket of common measures. Common measures as a group address a business concern, such as Profitability, Employee Satisfaction, and Sales. The logical meter becomes one or more physical fact tables.
- **Model**. A set of symbols and text used to make a complex concept easier to grasp.
- **Network**. A many-to-many relationship between entities (or between entity instances).
- **Normalization**. The process of building the relational data model. It is a formal process of asking business questions where in the resulting data model "Every data element depends upon the key, the whole key, and nothing but the key."
- **Physical Data Model (PDM)**. A representation of a detailed technology solution.
- **Primary key**. The one or more data elements that uniquely identify a value in an entity and that is chosen to be *the* unique identifier.
- **Relationship**. The line connecting two entities. On a relational data model the line represents a business rule and on a dimensional data model the line represents a navigation path.

- **Snapshot measure**. Monitor the impact of events created from a business process, such as Account Balance Amount, Ozone Layer Thickness, and Average Survey Question Score. It is (at least theoretically) possible to produce snapshot measures by summing transaction measures. For example, to determine the Account Balance Amount we can sum the results of all individual account transactions such as deposits and withdrawals.
- **Slowly Changing Dimension (SCD)**. A reference subject area where there is a need to maintain history. That is, when values of a reference subject area get updated, there are three ways to manage this change. Type I means no history, Type 2 is all history, and Type 3 is some history.
- **Snowflake**. A physical dimensional modeling structure where each set of tables is implemented separately, very similar in structure to the logical dimensional model.
- **Star schema**. A physical dimensional modeling structure where each set of tables that make up a dimension is flattened into a single table.
- **Subject Area Model (SAM)**. A representation of the business at a very high level. It is a very broad view containing only the basic and critical concepts for a given scope.
- **Subtyping**. Grouping together the common properties of entities while retaining what is unique within each entity.
- **Summarization**. A table which contains information at a higher level of granularity than exists in the business.
- **Surrogate key**. A unique identifier of a table. The surrogate key is usually a system-generated counter.
- **Transaction measure**. Monitor events created from business processes, such as Order Quantity, Customer Count, and Gross Sales Amount. An important property of transaction measures is that they are fully additive across all dimensions.
- **View**. A virtual table. It is a "view" into one or many tables or other views that contain or reference the actual data elements. A view runs the SQL to retrieve data at the point when a data element in the view is requested.
- **Wayfinding**. Encompasses all of the ways in which people and animals orient themselves in physical space and navigate from place to place. Urban planner Kevin A. Lynch coined the term in his 1960 book Image of the City, where he defined wayfinding as "a consistent use and organization of definite sensory cues from the external environment".

TABLE OF CONTENTS

Module 0

Foundation

Topic	Page
Data model explanation	0-3
Data model and modeler characteristics	0-11
Data model settings	0-17
Model components	0-31
Data Model Scorecard® overview	0-63

Data model explanation

Fun with data

Steve Hoberman
President
me@stevehoberman.com
Visit www.stevehoberman.com
10 Main St | New York, NY 10021 | 212-555-1212
Steve Hoberman & Associates, LLC

WALK AROUND MAGIC CHILDREN'S PARTIES
THE AMAZING ROLANDO
MAGIC FOR ALL OCCASIONS
BillSmith@TheAmazingRolando.com
732-555-1212 BILL SMITH

findsonline.com
Internet Auction Experts
Steve@findsonline.com
Jenn@findsonline.com
Steve and Jenn
(973) 555-1212

Jon Smith
Raritan River Club
FINE FRESH SEAFOOD
Fax (908) 555-1212
Banquet 554-1212
Reservations@RaritanRiverClub.com
58 Church Avenue
New Brunswick, NJ 08901
(908) 333-1212

Org name	Phone #				

Five possible business rules

1. A contact must have at least one phone number.
2.
3.
4.
5.

Data model explanation

Fun with data

BACKGROUND

A spreadsheet groups data in columns. There is a column for last name, another for first name, and so on. A data model takes this idea a step further, showing not only the column headings but also the way in which the headings relate to each other. For example, a data model will show not only "first name" and "last name," but also their individual properties and the rules that exist between first name" and "last name".

I once opened the drawer in my nightstand (a scary proposition, as it had not been cleaned since the mid-1980s) and grabbed a handful of business cards. I laid them out and picked four that I thought would be the most fun to model. I chose my current business card; a business card from an internet business that my wife and I tried to start years ago when dot-com was hot; a business card from a magician who performed at one of our parties; and a business card from one of our favorite dining establishments. I changed the names and contact information to protect the innocent and reproduced these on the facing page.

FUN WITH DATA

Review these four business cards and convert them to a spreadsheet. Then write down at least 5 possible business rules that constrain these spreadsheet columns. And this is a data model!

WHY THIS EXERCISE?

- **Process**. The thinking process applied to producing the model is just as important in most cases as the end deliverable. You find yourself asking lots of questions or making lots of assumptions.
- **Creativity**. There are numerous modeling notations (including spreadsheets), some being more intuitive, precise, and extensible than others. Which notation would your audience best understand?
- **Just like the real world!** You might have taken shortcuts with this exercise because of time and information limitations.

Data model explanation

Definition

Model = A set of symbols and text used to make a complex concept easier to grasp to provide a valuable wayfinding tool

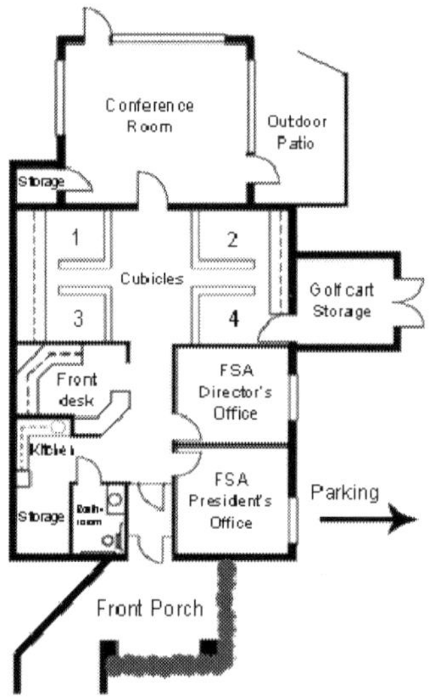

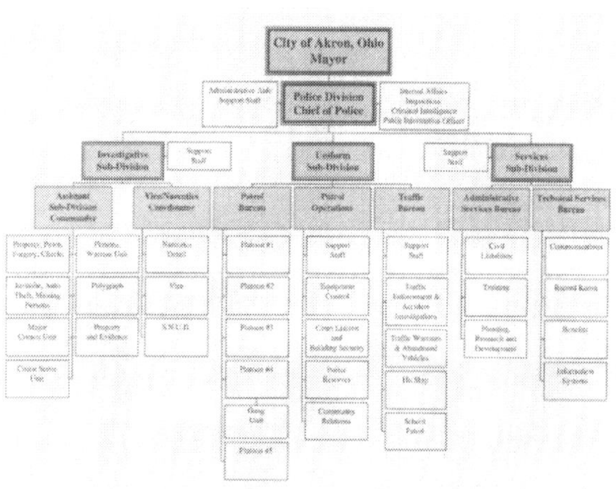

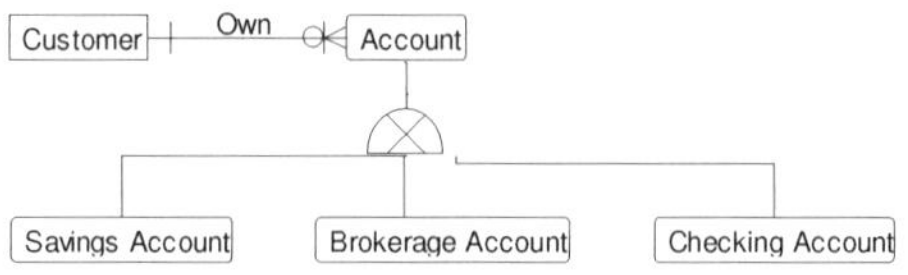

- Each Customer can own one or many Accounts.
- Each Account must be owned by one Customer.
- Each Account can be a Savings, Brokerage, or Checking Account.

Data model explanation

Definition

WAYFINDING

Wayfinding encompasses all of the ways in which people and animals orient themselves in physical space and navigate from place to place. Urban planner Kevin A. Lynch coined the term in his 1960 book Image of the City, where he defined wayfinding as "a consistent use and organization of definite sensory cues from the external environment". Historically, wayfinding refers to the techniques used by travelers over land and sea to find relatively unmarked and often mislabeled routes. These include but are not limited to dead reckoning, map and compass, astronomical positioning and, more recently, global positioning. *Wikipedia*

The ability to transform "cognitive maps" gained from personal experience into symbolic visual representations provided humans with a powerful cooperative advantage. Maps enabled us to share wayfinding experiences and geographic knowledge, thereby extending our communal ability to explore wider and wider regions without becoming afraid or getting lost. *Peter Morville, Ambient Findability*

MODEL DEFINITION

A model is a set of symbols and text used to make a complex concept easier to grasp. The world around us is full of obstacles that can overwhelm our senses and make it very challenging to focus only on the relevant information needed to make intelligent decisions. A map helps a visitor navigate a city. An organization chart helps an employee understand reporting relationships. A blueprint helps an architect communicate building plans. The map, organization chart, and blueprint are all types of models that represent a filtered simplified view of something complex.

DATA MODEL DEFINITION

A data model uses symbols and text to help developers and analysts better understand a set of data elements and their business rules. An increase in understanding the data leads to an improved communication level within the organization and therefore a more flexible and stable application environment.

Data model explanation

Favorite modeling quotes and some poetry

The soul never thinks without a picture.
Aristotle

Modeling is a tool for coping with problems of largeness.
Tom DeMarco

Where is the wisdom? Lost in the knowledge.
Where is the knowledge? Lost in the information.
T.S. Eliot

Where is the information? Lost in the data.
Where is the data? Lost in the database.
Joe Celko

Start where you are. Use what you have. Do what you can.
Arthur Ashe

A message to mapmakers: highways are not painted red, rivers don't have county lines running down the middle, and you can't see contour lines on a mountain.
William Kent, Data and Reality

Who wants to be the Data Architect?

A diagram is a sentence in a graphical language.
Daniel Moody

It's like a story!

Data model explanation

Favorite modeling quotes and some poetry

MOTIVATING WORDS

There are so many great quotes that capture the value of pictures and in simplifying the complex world around us using pictures.

DATA MODELING POETRY, BY LEONARDO NETTO, DATA ARCHITECTURE, TELUS

A piece of craftsmanship built and not bought
born amid a storm of conflicting ideas and unplanned thoughts
with ultimate almost utopic aim but noble to be fought
to bring perfect balance to the future,
learned from what past taught
hoping the art will long last, but prepared if not!

Data model explanation

Data model purpose

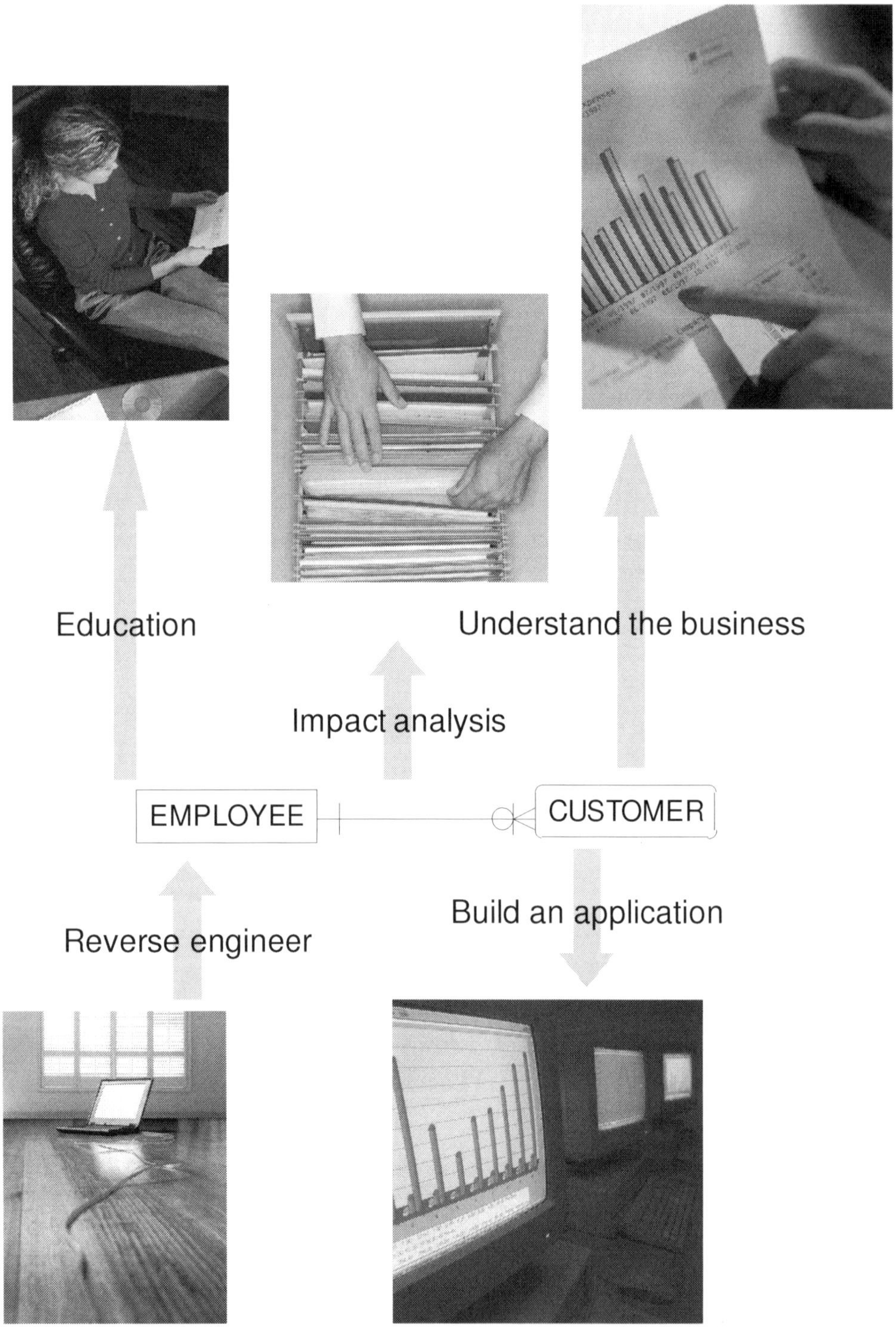

Data model explanation

Data model purpose

BACKGROUND

Traditionally, data models have been built during the analysis and design phases of a project to ensure that the requirements for a new application are fully understood and correctly captured before the actual database is created. There are, however, other uses for modeling than simply building databases. Among the uses are the following:

- **To understand an existing application**. We can derive a data model from an existing application by examining the application's database and building a data model of its structures. The technical term for the process of building data models from existing applications is 'reverse engineering'. The trend in many industries is to buy more packaged software and to build less internally; therefore our roles as modelers are expanding and changing. Instead of modeling a new application, the data modeler may capture the information in existing systems, such as packaged software.
- **To perform impact analysis**. A data model can capture the concepts and interactions that are impacted by a development project or program. What is the impact of adding or modifying structures for an application already in production? One example of impact analysis would be to use data modeling to determine what impact modifying its structures would have on the purchased software.
- **To understand a business area**. As a prerequisite to a large development effort, it usually is necessary to understand how the business works before you can understand how the applications that support the business will work. Before building an order entry system, for example, you need to understand the order entry business process.
- **To educate team members**. When new team members need to come up to speed or developers need to understand requirements, a data model is an effective explanatory medium.

Data model characteristics

Communication

Communication during the data modeling process

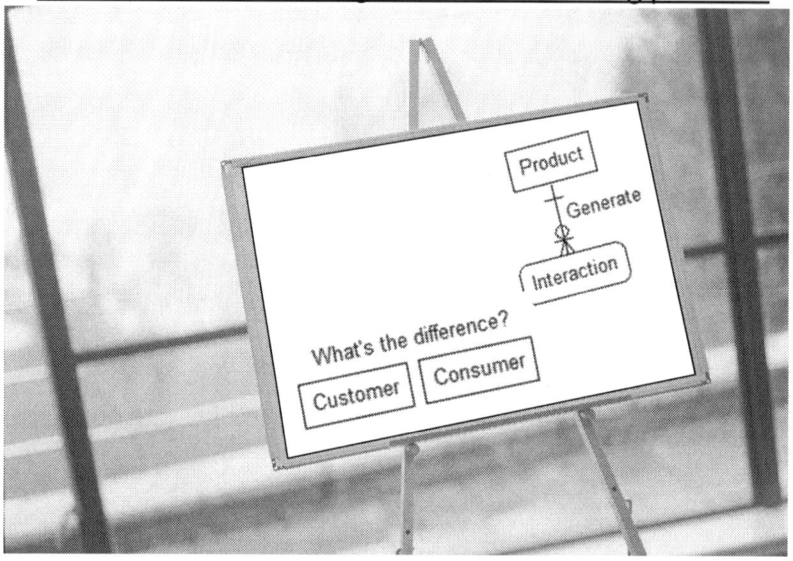

Communication using the finished data model

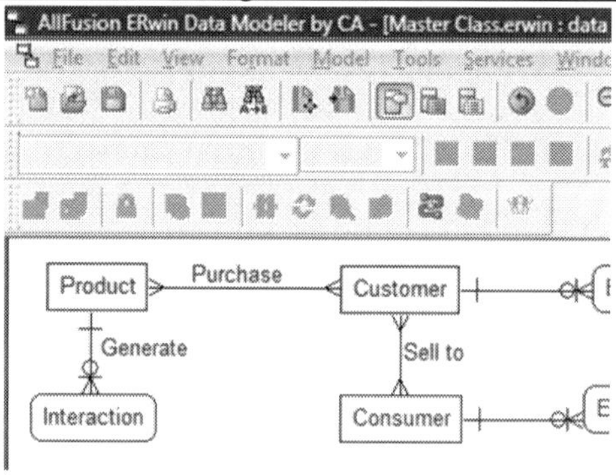

Communication with different audiences

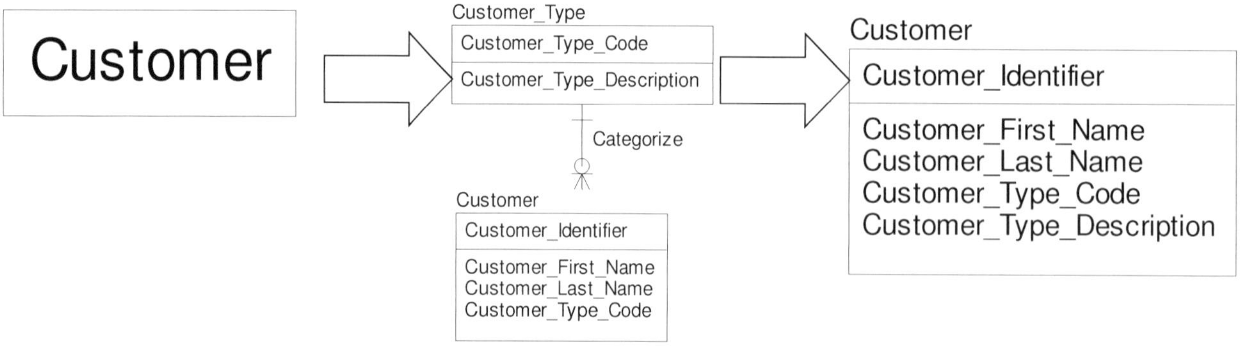

Data model characteristics

Communication

BACKGROUND

Communication is the primary reason we build data models. People who need to understand the content the models represent usually have various levels and types of experience. The model is the bridge to understanding. Regardless of whether we are trying to understand how key concepts in a business relate to one another or the workings of a 20-year-old order-processing system, the model becomes an ideal mechanism for explaining information.

DURING THE MODELING PROCESS

During the process of building data models, we are forced to analyze data and data relationships. We have no choice but to acquire a strong understanding of the content of what is being modeled. Much knowledge is gained as the persons involved in the modeling process challenge each other about terminology, assumptions, rules, and concepts. During the process of modeling an existing application that represents the recipes of manufactured items, I was amazed to witness team members with years of experience debate whether an ingredient differed from a piece of raw material.

AFTER THE MODELING PROCESS

The completed data model is the medium for discussion on what to build in an application, or more fundamentally, how something works. Before I started working at a large manufacturing company, my soon-to-be manager gave me a large book containing a set of data models for the company. I read this book several times, becoming familiar with the key concepts in the business and their business rules. On my first day on the job, I already knew much about how the business worked. When my colleagues mentioned terms specific to the company, I already knew what they meant.

COMMUNICATION WITH DIFFERENT AUDIENCES

I recently built a data model to capture consumer interactions within snack food. The key business user and I built a high-level model showing the subjects that are relevant for the project. The model helped with scoping the project, understanding key terms, and building a rapport with the business. This model became the mechanism with which we bridged our understandings of key terms such as *consumer*, *product*, and *interaction*. Several months later, I used a much more detailed model of the same consumer-interaction information to inform the report developers of exactly what was expected to appear on each report along with all the necessary selection criteria.

Data model characteristics

Formalization

99

The Customer Identifier
is the identifier for the customer

N/A

-1

Employee is someone
who breathes oxygen

Data model characteristics

Formalization

BACKGROUND

Formalization means that there is a single, precise interpretation of every symbol and term on the model. The data modeling symbols representing rules can be read only one way. You might argue with others about whether the rule is accurate, but that is a different argument. In other words, it is not possible for you to view a symbol on a model and say, "I see A here" and for someone else to view the same symbol and respond, "I see B here."

POOR DEFINITIONS WEAKEN PRECISION

There are two situations however, that can degrade the precision of a data model. If the definitions behind the terms on a data model are nonexistent or poor, multiple interpretations become a strong possibility. Imagine a business rule on our model that states that an employee must have at least one benefits package. If the definition of *employee* is lacking, we may wonder, for example, whether this business rule includes job applicants and retired employees.

DUMMY VALUES WEAKEN PRECISION

The second situation occurs when we introduce data that are outside the normal set of data values that we would expect in a particular data grouping. An old fashioned trick for getting around the rigor of a data model is to expand the set of values that a data grouping can contain. For example, if a rule on a model specified that a business card must have at least one phone number to exist, a clever person who wanted to get around this rule could easily expand the values of the phone numbers to include "other" or "99" or "not applicable." Such a value tied to a business card would maintain the rule that a business card have at least a single phone number, even if that phone number were really not applicable, which implies that a business card could contain zero phone numbers.

Data modeler characteristics

Important skills

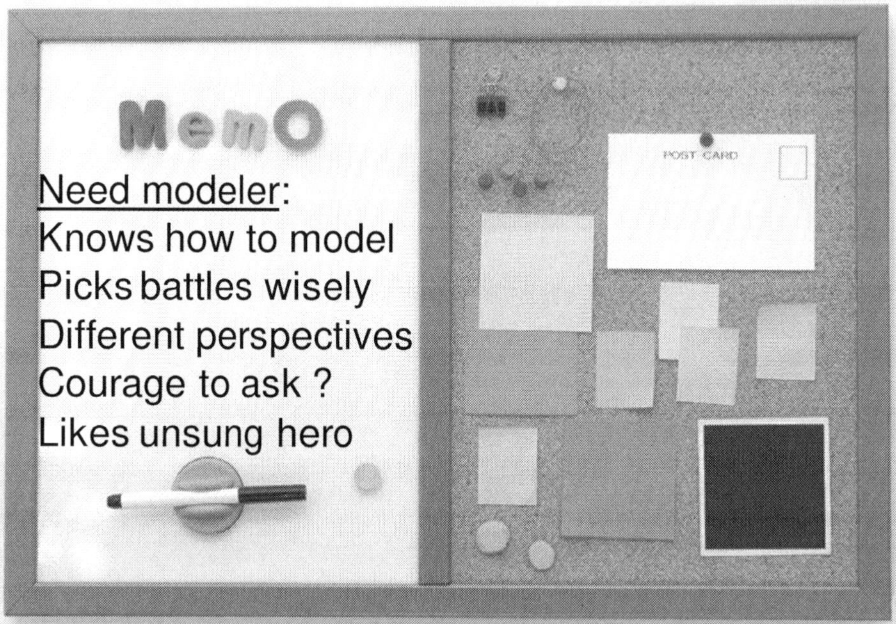

The Lone Ranger Fantasy

When the clients don't show their appreciation, pretend that they're stunned by your performance – but never forget that it's your fantasy, not theirs.

Gerald Weinberg, The Secrets of Consulting

Data modeler characteristics

Important skills

BACKGROUND

Besides knowing how to build models, there are several other essential skills the modeler must have.

PICKS BATTLES WISELY

There are going to be discussions and arguments that the modeler will need to decide whether they are worth the battle. Sometimes for example, forcing a project team to rename all of their non-compliant data element names a week before production can isolate the modeler and the modeling team. Even though it is the right thing to do, is it the right thing to do in a particular situation? Pick your battles wisely!

DIFFERENT PERSPECTIVES

There are several different perspectives the modeler must have during the modeling process. Having both a project and program view can sometimes be conflicting and it will be important for the modeler to understand where to make the tradeoffs. The same holds true for an ivory tower versus real world view. What might be right in a textbook may not be practical for a particular application.

COURAGE TO ASK QUESTIONS

Even if the modeler risks exposing a lack of understanding on her part or on the parts of IT or the business, the modeler has the courage to ask questions. Asking questions is the primary method of gathering knowledge.

OK WITH UNSUNG HERO ROLE

If the modeler does everything right, she should get no credit whatsoever. This is a little bit of an exaggeration, but what is meant is that if the model meets the requirements and is fairly flexible, there should be no surprises and the modeling activity can become a non-event (which is a really good thing!). Consider this quote from an actual senior manager email:

"Congratulations to successfully achieving another milestone on our process and system transformation journey. The impact of any Data project gets largely ignored, especially if it almost becomes a 'non-event' to the business. Congratulations again to you and the entire team."

Data model settings

Overview

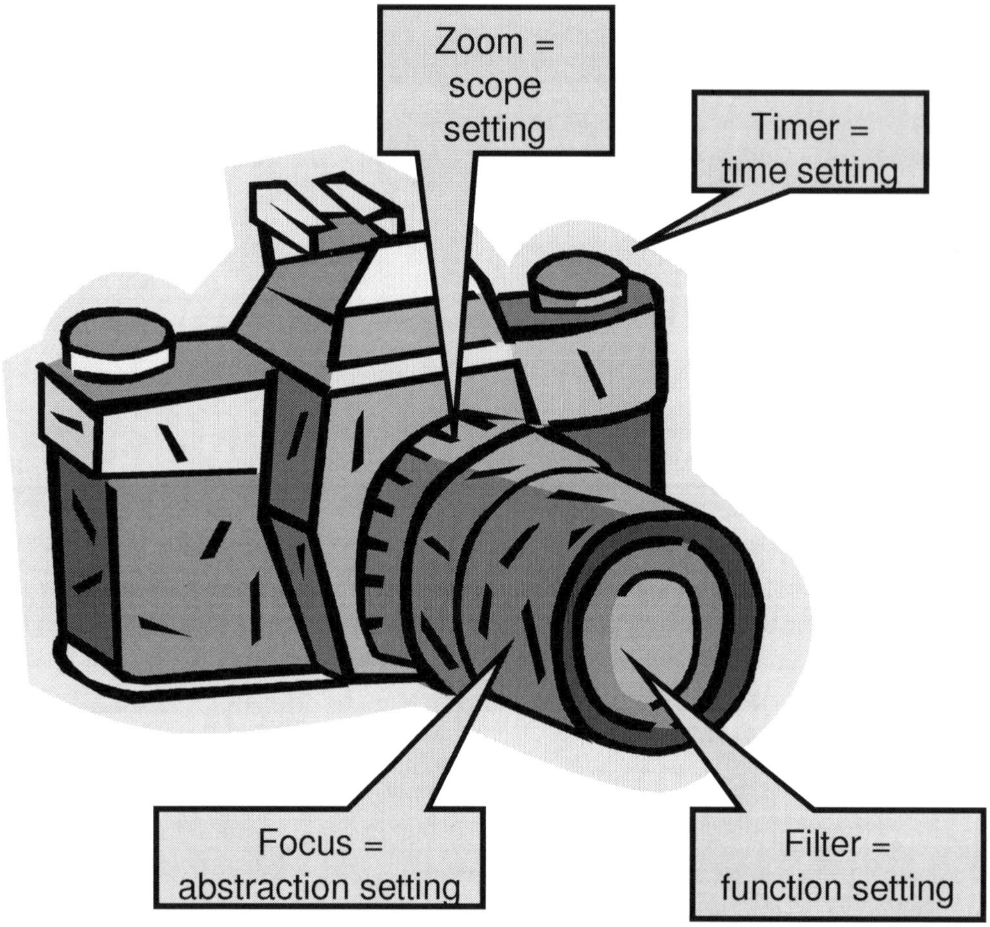

Plus don't forget your film!

Which setting is right for your model? As with photographing the sunset, it depends on the purpose. Match the goals of your model with the appropriate model settings.

Data model settings

Overview

CAMERA HAS SETTINGS

A camera has many settings available to take the perfect picture. Imagine facing an awesome sunset with your camera. With the same exact sunset, you can capture a very different image based on the camera's settings such as the focus, timer, and zoom.

MODEL HAS SETTINGS

There are four settings on a camera that translate directly over to the model: zoom, focus, timer, and filter. A model is characterized by one setting value from each setting. Which setting is right for your model? As with photographing the sunset, it depends on the purpose.

YOU CAN USE THIS TOOL TO...

Ensure you are building the right model for the task, and also to assess other models and challenge the modelers with good questions based on these settings.

SETTINGS OVERVIEW

The zoom setting on the camera allows the photographer to capture a broad area with minimal detail, or a detailed area without much context. Similarly, the scope setting for the model varies how much you see in the picture as well. The focus setting on the camera can make certain objects appear sharp or blurry. Similarly, the abstraction setting for the model can use generic concepts such as Party and Event to "blur" the distinction between concepts. The timer allows for a real time snapshot or a snapshot for some time in the future. Similarly, the time setting for the model can capture a current view or a "to be" view sometime in the future. The filter setting can taint the appearance of the entire picture to produce a certain effect. Similarly, the function setting for the model taints the model with either a business or application view.

FILM IS IMPORTANT TOO!

Plus, the type of film you use is important! A proof sheet shows all of the images on a single piece of paper (subject area), the negative has the raw format of the image (logical), and the output can be any number of formats including paper film, slide, etc. (physical).

Data model settings

Scope

Department (Project)	Sales data mart Trading application Reservations system Enhancement to existing app
Organization (Program)	DW ODS CRM EDM
Industry	Healthcare Telecommunications Banking

Data model settings

Scope

SCOPE

We can model a relatively small amount of information for a business process, such as order processing. Typically the scope for projects fall into either entire departments, the organization or the industry.

DEPARTMENT (PROJECT)

The most common type of modeling assignment has project-level scope. We are asked to model an operational or business intelligence area with the final goal being to have a successful application at the end of the development process.

ORGANIZATION (PROGRAM)

A program is a large centrally-organized initiative that contains multiple projects. For example, a data warehouse or operational data store are program-level initiatives that each contain many projects. Becoming more common is the enterprise scope. We are modeling an entire organization and at times even information outside the organization such as competitor or regulator information. These can be very complex and require long-term modeling assignments.

INDUSTRY

There is much work underway in many industries to share a common data model. Industries such as health care and telecommunications have consortiums where data modeling common structures are being developed. Having such a common structure makes it quicker to build applications and easier to share information across organizations.

Data model settings

Abstraction

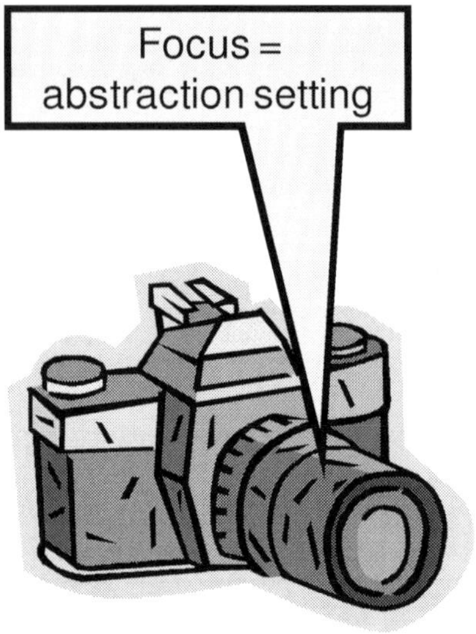

<u>In the business clouds</u> ○Only generic business terms	Party Event Document
<u>In the database clouds</u> ○Only generic database terms	Object Table Entity
<u>On the ground</u> ○Minimal generic terms ○Mostly concrete business terms	Customer Product Employee

Data model settings

Abstraction

ABSTRACTION

Similar to how the focus on a camera allows you to make the picture sharp or fuzzy, the abstraction setting for a model allows you to represent "sharp" (concrete) or "fuzzy" (generic) concepts. Abstraction brings flexibility to your data models by redefining and combining some of the data elements, entities, and relationships within the model into more generic terms. Abstraction is the removal of details in such a way as to broaden applicability to a wide class of situations while preserving the important properties and essential nature from concepts or subjects.

IN THE BUSINESS CLOUDS

At this level of abstraction, only generic *business* terms are used across the model. The business clouds model hides much of the real complexity within generic concepts such as Person, Transaction, and Document. In fact, both a candy company and insurance company can look very similar to each other using business cloud entities.

IN THE DATABASE CLOUDS

At this level of abstraction, only generic *database* terms are used across the model. The database clouds model is the easiest level to create, as the modeler is "hiding" all of the business complexity within database concepts such as Entity, Object, and Attribute.

ON THE GROUND

This model uses a minimal amount of business and database cloud entities, with a majority of the entities representing concrete business terms such as Student, Course, and Instructor. This model takes the most time to create of the three varieties. It also can add the most value towards understanding the business and resolving data issues.

Data model settings

Time

<u>Today</u> oCurrent view	"A price is the same across all restaurants."
<u>Tomorrow</u> oEnd of year, 5 years out, 10 years out oCoincides with big change oIdealistic view	"A price can vary based on restaurant."

Data model settings

Time

TIME

Similar to how the timer on a camera allows you to photograph a future scene, the time setting for a model allows you to represent a future "to be" view on a model. A model can represent how a business works today or how a business might work sometime in the future.

TODAY

A model with the today setting captures how the business works today. If there are archaic business rules, they will appear on this model even if the business is planning on modifying them in the near future. In addition, if an organization is in the process of buying another company, selling a company, or changing lines of business, a today view would not show any of this. It would only capture how the business works today.

TOMORROW

A model with the tomorrow setting can represent any time period in the future. Whether end of the year, five years out, or 10 years out, a tomorrow setting represents an ideal view of the organization. When a model needs to support an organization's vision or strategic view, a tomorrow setting is preferred. I worked on a university model that represented an end of year view, as that would be when a large application migration would be completed. Note that most organizations who need a tomorrow view, first have to build a today view to create a starting point.

Data model settings

Function

<u>Business</u> Business terminology and rules	The business calls it 'classification' and 'classification value'
<u>Application</u> Application terminology and rules	SAP/R3 calls it 'characteristic' and 'characteristic value'

Data model settings

Function

FUNCTION

Similar to how a filter on a camera can change the appearance of a scene, the function setting for a model allows you to represent either a business or functional view on the model. Are we modeling the application's view of the world or the business' view of the world? Sometimes they can be the same (or very close to the same).

BUSINESS

This view uses business terminology and rules. The model represents an application independent view. It does not matter whether the organization is using SAP or Siebel, the business will be represented in business concepts.

APPLICATION

This view uses application terminology and rules. It is a view of the business through the eyes of an application. If the application uses the term 'Object' for the term 'Product', it will appear as Object on the model and be defined according to how the application defines the term, not how the business defines it.

Data model settings

Format

<u>Subject area (Proof sheet)</u>
High level business solution
Scoping tool
Only basic and critical concepts

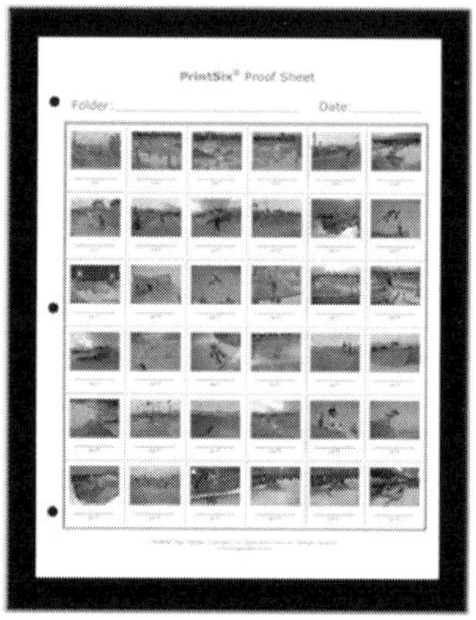

<u>Logical (Negative)</u>
Detailed business solution
Normalization and abstraction
Dimensionality
"Essence"

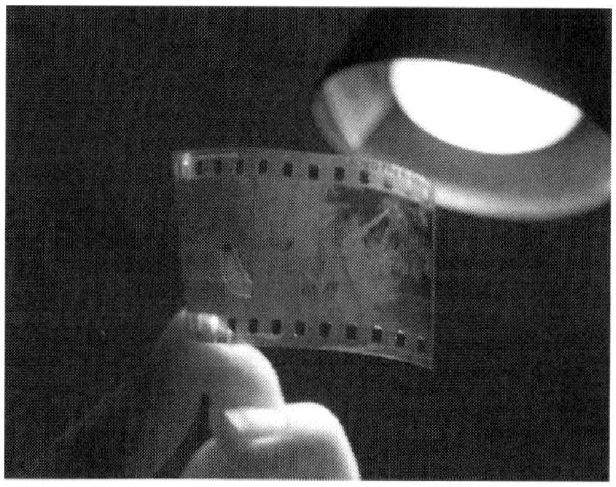

<u>Physical (Output)</u>
Detailed technical solution
Denormalization, indexing, views, and partitioning
Star schema and snowflake
"Incarnation"

Data model settings

Format

FORMAT

Similar to how the zoom on a camera allows you to focus on a small part of a scene or pan out to capture all of the details, the format setting for a model allows you to represent some or all of the details on a model. The format setting adjusts the level of detail for a model, making the model either at the very broad and high level subject area view, or the more detailed logical or physical views. Some organizations have a combination of subject area, logical, and physical models, depending on model purpose.

SUBJECT AREA

A subject area model (SAM) represents the business at a very high level. It is a very broad view containing only the basic and critical concepts for a given scope.

LOGICAL

A logical data model (LDM) represents a detailed business solution. In our relational world, the business solution takes the form of a normalized model. Normalization is the process of ensuring every data element on a data model is single-valued and depends completely and only on the primary key. In our dimensional world, the business solution takes the form of a meter surrounded by dimensions, some of which are hierarchies.

PHYSICAL

A physical data model (PDM) represents a detailed technology solution. It is optimized for a specific context (such as software, hardware, or data). A physical data model resembles its logical data model, the exception being the addition of performance techniques such as denormalization, indexing, views, and partitioning. The same logical data model can look completely different depending on how it has been optimized. The same order logical data model for example, will have completely different order processing and sales reporting physical data models. Order processing involves lots of inserts and updates, and sales reporting involves lots of retrieval, and therefore different physical data modeling techniques will be used.

Data model settings

Some fun!

Scenario	Scope	Abstraction	Time	Function	Format
Capture the details for the current book ordering process to be used as an evaluation tool to select a vendor package. Need to include orders across all sales channels.	__Dept __Org __Industry	__Bus Clouds __DB Clouds __Ground	__Today __Tomorrow	__Bus __App	__SAM __LDM __PDM
Study the technical design of a proposed vendor package to determine which fields are needed for sales reporting.	__Dept __Org __Industry	__Bus Clouds __DB Clouds __Ground	__Today __Tomorrow	__Bus __App	__SAM __LDM __PDM
Capture all of the business requirements for a brand new sales reporting system focusing only on consumer-direct (that is, sales made directly to individuals).	__Dept __Org __Industry	__Bus Clouds __DB Clouds __Ground	__Today __Tomorrow	__Bus __App	__SAM __LDM __PDM
Explain this brand new sales reporting system to the business sponsor who does not have a technical background.	__Dept __Org __Industry	__Bus Clouds __DB Clouds __Ground	__Today __Tomorrow	__Bus __App	__SAM __LDM __PDM
Explain an existing data dictionary tool to agile developers who will need to extract definitions for the sales reporting system.	__Dept __Org __Industry	__Bus Clouds __DB Clouds __Ground	__Today __Tomorrow	__Bus __App	__SAM __LDM __PDM

Data model settings

Some fun!

BACKGROUND Check off what you think is the most appropriate settings for each of these scenarios.

TIP Always consider the audience and why the model is being built.

Model components

Entity

What?

Who?

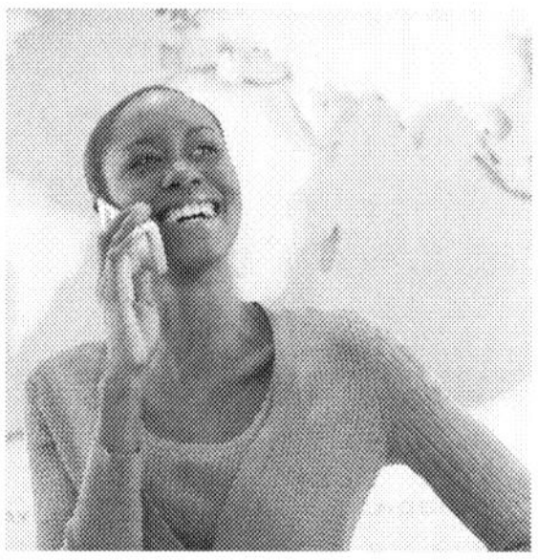

An entity is a collection of information about something that the business deems important and worthy of capture. An instance is an entity value.

Where?

When?

Why?

How?

Model components

Entity

BACKGROUND

An entity is something of interest to the business. *Entity* is a noun. An entity is a collection of information about something that the business deems important and worthy of capture. An entity is a who, what, when, where, why, or how. Each of these categories have slightly different behavior and dependencies. Here are some examples of each of these:

Who?	Party and role, person, organization, employee, customer, vendor, student, Hotmail account owner
What?	product, service, raw material, finished good, course, song, photograph
When?	time, date, year, calendar, fiscal period, minute
Where?	location, mailing address, distribution point, website URL, file where documents are stored, IP address
Why?	transaction, order, return, complaint, compliment, inquiry
How?	document, invoice, contract, agreement, account, speeding ticket

ENTITY DEFINITIONS

Here are some experts' definitions for the term entity:
Peter Chen (1976): "A thing which can be distinctly identified."
C.J. Date (1986): "Any distinguishable object that is to be represented in the database."
Thomas Bruce (1992): "Any distinguishable person, place, thing, event, or concept about which information is kept."

ENTITY INSTANCE

Entity instances are the occurrences or values of a particular entity. The entity *customer* can have instances Bob, Joe, Jane, and so forth. The entity *account* can have instances for Bob's checking account, Bob's savings account, Joe's brokerage account, and so on.

DETAIL

An entity can be at a subject area, logical, or physical level of detail. For an entity to exist at a subject area level, it must be both basic and critical to the business. Entities at a logical level follow the rules of normalization or dimensionality. At a physical level, the entities are relational database tables.

Model components

Independent vs. dependent entities

Independent (Kernel): Stands on its own

Dependent (Weak) : Requires reference to at least one other entity for its identification

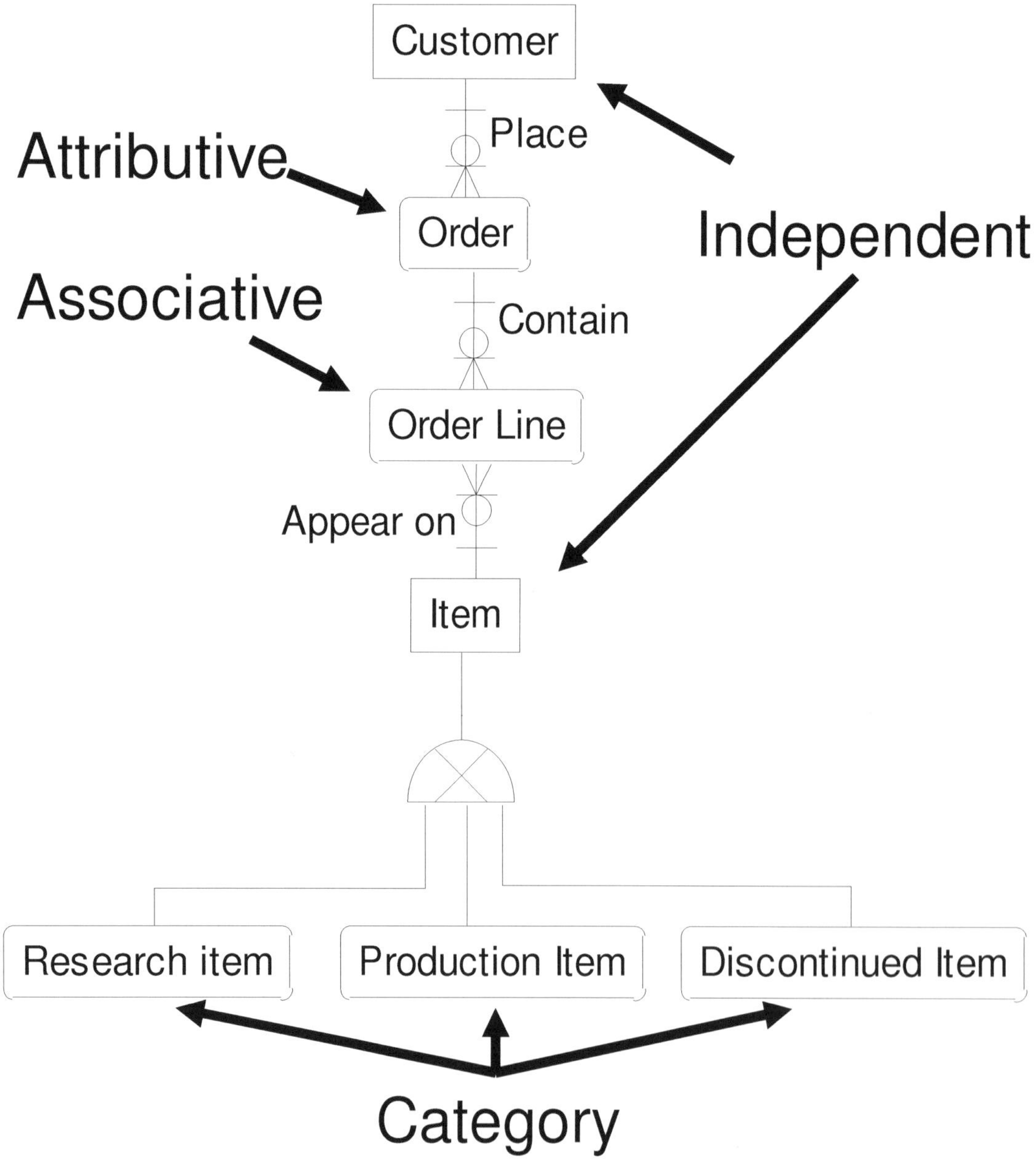

Model components

Independent vs. dependent entities

INDEPENDENT

Also known as a kernel entity, an independent entity is an object of interest to the business that does not depend on any other entity for its identification. Each occurrence of an independent entity can be identified without referring to any other entity on the model. An independent entity is depicted as a rectangle. On the facing page, both Customer and Item are independent entities.

DEPENDENT

A dependent entity is an object of interest to the business that depends on one or many other entities for its existence. The entities that a dependent entity depends on can be independent entities or other dependent entities. A dependent entity is depicted as a rectangle with rounded edges. There are three main types of dependent entities: attributive, associative, and category. It is important to distinguish independent from dependent, and then within dependent these three types of dependent entities because it forces the analyst to ask more questions when eliciting requirements, and it allows the modeler to communicate more within the data model.

ATTRIBUTIVE

An attributive entity (also known as a "characteristic" entity) depends on only one other entity: its parent entity. Part of what makes the attributive entity unique is what completely makes the parent entity unique.

ASSOCIATIVE

An associative entity depends on two or more entities. As with the attributive entity, the associative entity is a child entity. At least part of what makes it unique comes from other entities (its parents). Uniquely identifying an instance of an associative entity requires, at a minimum, the sum of the primary keys from the participating entities.

CATEGORY

Category entities are known by a number of names: subtyping, supertyping, generalization, and inheritance. I'll use the term *subtyping* throughout the course. Subtyping is grouping together the common properties of entities while retaining what is unique within each entity. The concept of subtyping can exist at subject area or logical levels of modeling. At the physical level, we need to resolve subtyping into one of several structures.

Model components

Subtyping

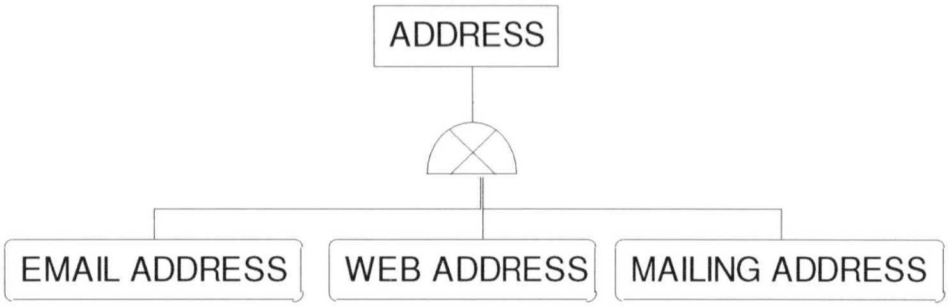

Non-overlapping

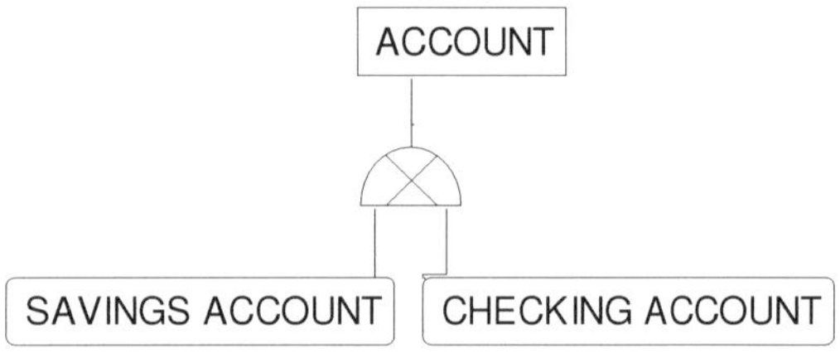

Overlapping

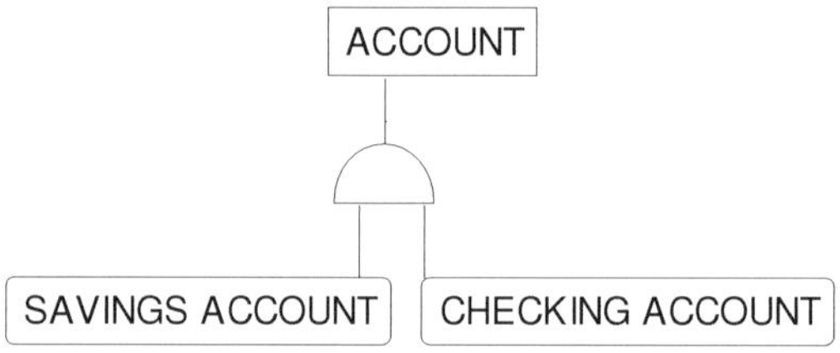

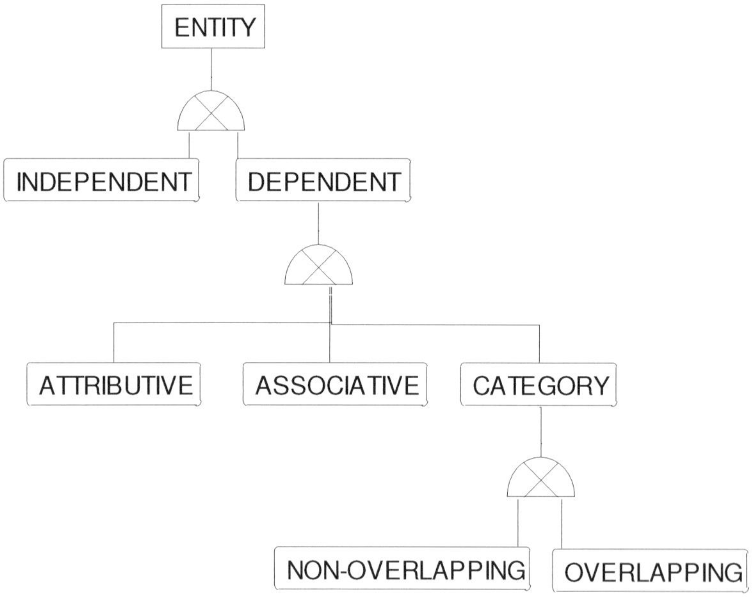

Model components

Subtyping

BACKGROUND

Subtyping is grouping together the common properties of entities while retaining what is unique within each entity. On the facing page, *Address* can be an *e-mail address*, *Web address*, or *mailing address*. *Address* is the supertype, and *e-mail address*, *Web address*, and *mailing address* are the subtypes.

The subtyping relationship exists between the supertype and each of its subtypes. There is no relationship implied by the subtyping symbol between the subtypes, except insofar as these subtypes share the same set of properties. If there is a relationship between *e-mail address* and *Web address*, it will need to be shown as well. The subtyping relationship implies that all the properties from the supertype are inherited by the subtype. In addition to its own properties, *e-mail address* also has those of *address*.

OVERLAPPING VS NON-OVERLAPPING

Two types of subtypes are used in the information engineering (IE) notation: non-overlapping and overlapping. *Non-overlapping*, or *exclusive*, means that an instance of an entity supertype can be any of the subtypes but cannot be more than one of them. *Overlapping*, or *inclusive*, means that an instance of an entity supertype can be one or many of the subtypes.

The subtyping symbol on the facing page with an *X* within it represents non-overlapping. This is the default in the information engineering notation, and therefore the most frequently occurring. An *account* can be a *savings account* or a *checking account*, but not both. In the second example, the subtyping symbol without the *X* represents overlapping: an *account* can be a *savings account*, a *checking account*, or both. When the subtype is overlapping, therefore, Bob could have an account with the characteristics of both a savings and a checking account.

SUBTYPING FUN

The subtyping diagram on the facing page communicates the relationships between the different types of entities.

Model components

Data element

A data element is a property of importance to the business whose values contribute to identifying, describing, or measuring instances of an entity.

Employee

- ✓Employee Identifier
- ✓Employee Last Name
- ✓Employee First Name
- ✓Employee Hire Date
- ✓Employee Signed Employment Contract
- ✓Employee Drivers License Photo

Model components

Data element

BACKGROUND

A data element is a property of importance to the business whose values contribute to identifying, describing, or measuring instances of an entity. The data element *claim number* uniquely identifies each claim. The data element *student last name* describes the last name of each student. The data element *gross sales amount* measures total sales.

DETAIL

As with entities, data elements can exist at subject area, logical, and physical levels. A subject area must be a concept both basic and critical to the business. We do not usually think of data elements as subject areas, but they can be subject areas. When I worked for a telecommunications company, *telephone number* was a data element so important to the business that it was represented as a subject area on a number of high-level subject area models.

A data element (aka attribute) on a logical data model is atomic and at times generic. *Atomic* means that the data element contains one and only one piece of business information and cannot be broken down any further without losing business meaning. For example, we would not have one logical data element containing city, state, and zip code, but three. The process of normalization would have imposed this rule. *Generic* means that when there is a need for additional flexibility, we create more encompassing data elements. In our example with the business card, we may decide to have data elements called *phone number* and *phone type code* that can represent different types of phone numbers, such as fax and mobile. We may decide to have a *party name* instead of a *person name* and a *company name*. We may decide to have a *postal code* instead of a *zip code*.

Column or *field* is the term used when referring to a property of the entity specific to the database. This is how the data element is represented in the actual database software.

Model components

Domain

> The complete set of all possible values that a data element contains is called a domain. It could be a format, range or list.

Order Status Code: Char(1)

Order Status Code: {O,S,R,C}

Today's Date <= **Order Delivery Date** <= (Today's Date + 3 months)

Corporate Unit Code: {01, 02, 03, 04, 05, 99}

Order Comments Text: Varchar(250)

Book cover: {*.jpg, *.pdf, *.tiff}

150 < **Image quality dots per inch** <= 300

Model components

Domain

BACKGROUND

The complete set of all possible values that a data element contains is called a domain. A data element never can contain values outside of its assigned domain, which is defined by specifying the actual list of values or a set of rules. *Employee gender code*, for example, can be limited to the domain of (*female, male*).

Employee hire date initially can be assigned the rule that its domain contain only valid dates, for example. Therefore, this can include values such as

- February 15th, 2005
- 25 January 1910
- 20030410
- March 10th, 2050

Because *employee hire date* is limited to valid dates, it does not include February 30th, for example. We can restrict a domain with additional rules. For example, by restricting the *employee hire date* domain to dates less than today's date, we would eliminate March 10th, 2050. By restricting *employee hire date* to YYYYMMDD (that is, year, month, and day concatenated), we would eliminate all the examples given except for 20030410. Another way of refining this set of values is to restrict the domain of *employee hire date* to dates that fall on a Monday, Tuesday, Wednesday, Thursday, or Friday (that is, the typical workweek).

PURPOSE

Domains are very useful for a number of reasons including:

- The data model communicates even more
- Greater consistency within and across applications
- Improves data quality by checking against a domain before inserting data
- Greater efficiency in building new models and maintaining existing models

Model components

A Key helps you find entity instances

Class Identifier	Student Identifier	Semester Identifier	Final Grade
123	44	39	C
45	44	39	B
123	32	39	B
123	44	40	A

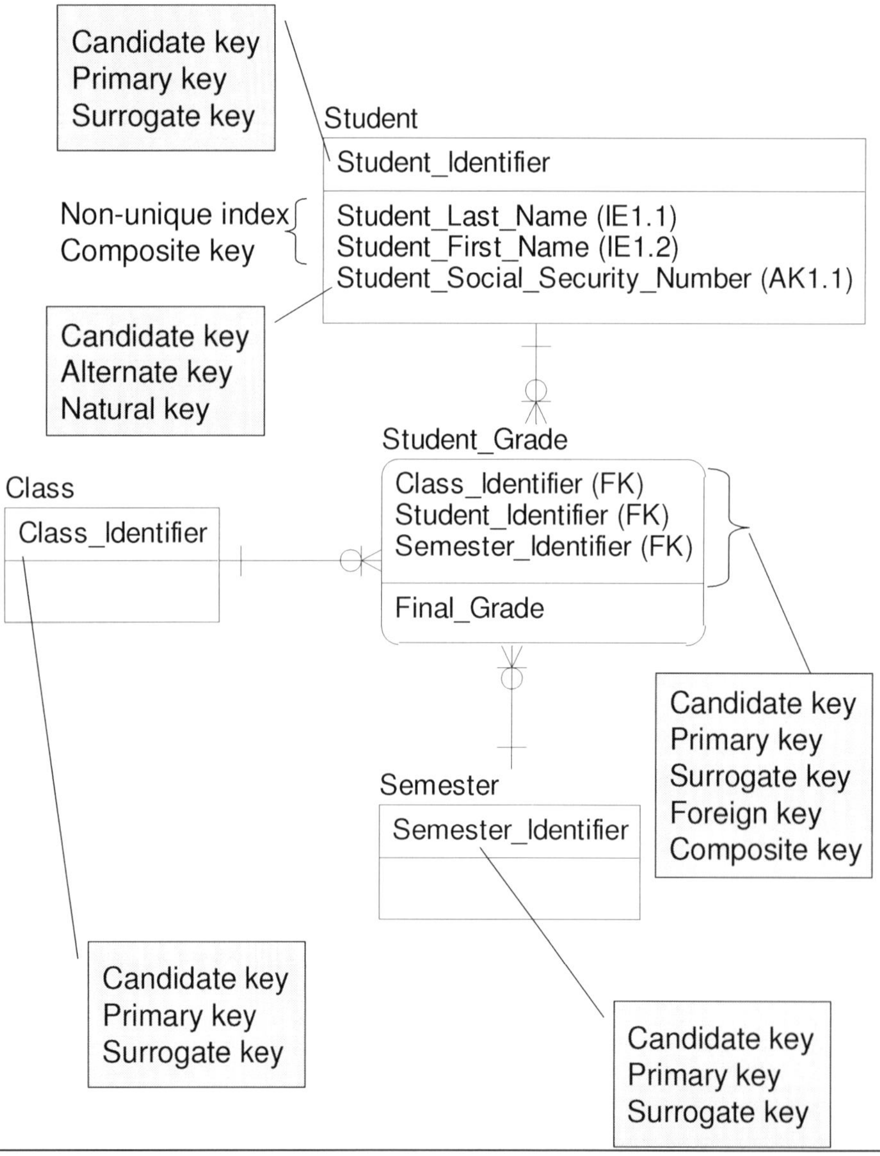

Model components

A Key helps you find entity instances

BACKGROUND

A data element becomes a key or non-key upon assignment to an entity. A key data element partly or fully identifies an entity instance, and/or partly or fully references a unique instance from another entity. By *partly*, I mean that a data element is part of a key, in which case there is more than one data element that makes up the entire key. The term *composite key* is used when there is more than one data element that makes up the key. Non-key data elements include all those that are not a key or part of a key.

A candidate key represents the one or many data elements that uniquely identify a value in an entity. Candidate keys are either primary or alternate keys. A primary key represents the one or more data elements that uniquely identify a value in an entity and that is chosen to be *the* unique identifier, as opposed to an alternate key that also uniquely identifies entity occurrences but is not chosen as the unique key. Both primary and alternate keys must be unique, minimal, and stable (that is, the values can't change over time).

The reason for selecting one unique identifier over another (that is, designating one set of data elements as the primary key and another set as the alternate key) is efficiency or value stability or privacy. Alternate keys tend to embody what the business feels is truly unique about the entity.

FOREIGN KEY

A foreign key is a data element that provides a link to another entity. When a relationship is created between two entities, the entity on the "many" side of the relationship inherits the primary key from the entity on the "one" side of the relationship. The foreign key allows for navigation between structures.

Model components

Surrogate key explanation

A substitute for a natural key, used by IT to facilitate integration and introduce database efficiencies. It is usually a meaningless integer counter.

If no natural key, no surrogate key (virtual key)

Always define alternate keys when using surrogate keys

Context can distinguish a surrogate from a natural key

Model components

Surrogate key explanation

BACKGROUND

A surrogate key is a unique identifier of a table. A surrogate key is an integer whose meaning is unrelated to its face value. (In other words, you can't look at a month identifier of 1 and assume that it represents January.) The surrogate key is usually a system-generated counter. Surrogate keys should not be visible to the business. They remain behind the scenes to help maintain uniqueness, allow for more efficient navigation across structures, and facilitate integration across applications. Context is also important: one application's surrogate key could be another application's natural key.

DEFINE AN ALTERNATE KEY WHEN USING A SURROGATE

- **Reduces the chances of bad data getting in.** You cannot load the same natural key twice.
- **Helps with processing records (distinguish inserts from updates).** We can easily check by seeing if the alternate key already exists. If it does, do an update. If it does not, do an insert.
- **Forces the modeler to understand what *really* makes a record unique.** It is very easy to slap on a counter and continue on our way. What requires more analysis and therefore increases our understanding of the entity, is to identify the business data elements that make the record unique. If no business AKs exist, use system AKs.

VIRTUAL KEY

There might be times however, when it is not possible to assign an alternate key when using a surrogate key. If there is truly no way to uniquely identify an entity instance, then we can't use the term *surrogate key*. This is because a surrogate key is a substitute for the actual key, and if we don't have an actual key then we don't have a surrogate key. We use the term *virtual key* in this situation. A virtual key is used when there is no unique way to identify an entity instance.

Model components

Surrogate key pros and cons

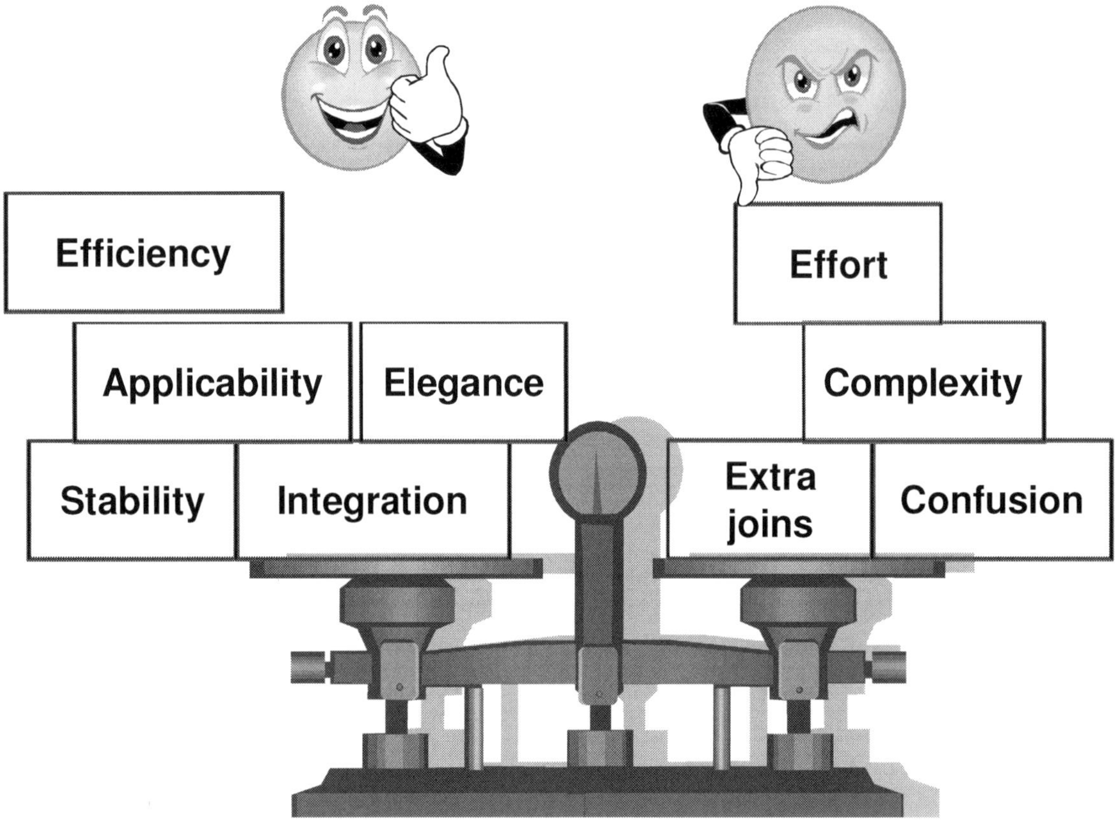

Model components

Surrogate key pros and cons

PROS

- **Stability**. If the logic is made available, natural key values can change without impacting lots of foreign key values. Make sure the logic is there though, as if not, a new record would be created instead of updating an existing record.
- **Integration**. The surrogate key must be unique within the scope of what we would like to integrate. If Customer Location and Warehouse Location each had their own surrogate key counter (overlapping key values), we could not bring them together under a single surrogate key. Note also that this is not data integration, but structure integration.
- **Applicability**. Even if no business values are available, we could still put something in such as "Not applicable", "Error in lookup", "Forever", or "It hasn't happened yet".
- **Efficiency**. It is easier to manipulate a single data element than a composite key or string key.
- **Elegance**. There is something quite slick about having a single data element to identify a row. It gives the appearance that the designer has their act together. Especially when there is complicated logic to determine when to use certain data elements as alternate keys.

CONS

- **Have to join to another table.** The surrogate key creates a layer of isolation, which if the reporting tool does not hide from the user, the user will need to understand and know how to make the join to get the real data.
- **Confusion**. We already have so many keys to worry about in our applications, especially integration areas such as our data warehouse. Also we can easily lose sight of the real keys or start attributing meaning to surrogate key values. If users have access to the surrogate keys, they might confuse them with other ids. Reserving the KEY classword for surrogate keys can help.
- **More development effort and complexity (less maintenance effort).** There is more work involved in generating the surrogate keys and using them as foreign keys in child entities.

To surrogate key, or not to surrogate key

Here is when to choose a natural key over a surrogate key:

To surrogate key, or not to surrogate key

BACKGROUND

As a data modeling expert in your company, you are frequently being asked modeling advice. On your way to the coffee machine one day, a project team manager stops you and explains: "Our team is working hard to document business rules, yet we feel we are lacking a number of IT rules. For example, what are the rules around when we should use a natural key over a surrogate key? Some members of my team want to have a surrogate key on every table, whereas other members want to only use the natural keys. When should you choose a natural key over a surrogate key?"

CHALLENGE

How would you respond?

Model components

Relationship

> A rule is an instruction about how to behave in a specific situation. A static rule is represented on a model via a relationship.

- Static Rules
  - Structure
    - Each product can appear on one or many order lines.
    - Each order line must contain one and only one product.
    - Each student must have a unique student number.
  - RI
    - An order line cannot exist without a valid product.
    - A claim cannot exist without a valid policy.
    - A student cannot exist without a valid student number.
- Action Rules
    - Freshman students can register for at most 18 credits a semester.
    - A policy must have at least three claims against it to be considered high-risk.
    - Take 10% off an order if the order contains more than five products.

Model components

Relationship

BACKGROUND

In its most general sense, a rule is an instruction about how to behave in a specific situation. The following are examples of rules that we have set or rules that have been set for us:

- Your room must be cleaned before you can go outside and play.
- If you get three strikes, you are out and it is the next batter's turn.
- The speed limit is 55 mph.

When we build an application, setting rules means defining constraints on what the application (and therefore the user) can and cannot do. Rules are visually captured on our data models through relationships.

STATIC VS ACTION RULES

At the highest level, a rule can be either a static rule or an action rule. Static rules are instructions on how data relate to one another. Action rules are instructions on *what* to do when data elements contain certain values. There are both structural and referential integrity (RI) static rules. Structural rules (also known as cardinality rules) define the quantity of each entity instance that can participate in a relationship. For example:

- Each product can appear on one or many order lines.
- Each order line must contain one and only one product.
- Each student must have a unique student number.

RI rules focus on ensuring valid values:

- An order line cannot exist without a valid product.
- A claim cannot exist without a valid policy.
- A student cannot exist without a valid student number.

Action rules are instructions on *what* to do when elements contain certain values, which usually take the form of 'if-then' statements:

- Freshman students can register for at most 18 credits a semester.
- A policy must have at least three claims against it to be considered high-risk.
- Take 10% off an order if the order contains more than five products.

In our data models, we can represent and enforce static rules, yet for the most part only represent the data to support action rules. That is, we cannot enforce action rules on a data model. Note that there are always exceptions, and the creative modeler can leverage subtyping or database views to represent action rules.

Model components

Cardinality

Example 1

	Yes	No
Can a Customer own more than one Account?	✓	
Can an Account be owned by more than one Customer?		✓
Can a Customer exist without an Account?	✓	
Can an Account exist without a Customer?		✓
Do I need to know the Customer to bring back their Account(s)?		✓
Do I need to know the Account to bring back its Owner(s)?		✓

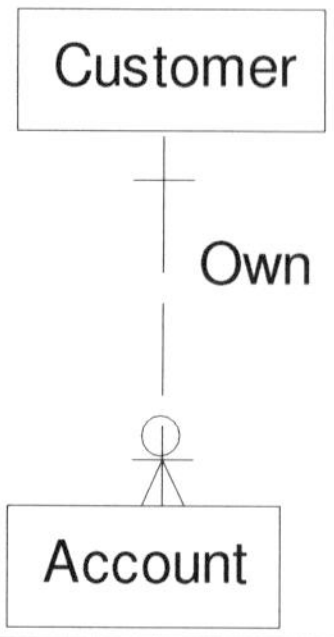

Example 2

	Yes	No
Can a Customer own more than one Account?	✓	
Can an Account be owned by more than one Customer?		✓
Can a Customer exist without an Account?	✓	
Can an Account exist without a Customer?		✓
Do I need to know the Customer to bring back their Account(s)?	✓	
Do I need to know the Account to bring back its Owner(s)?		✓

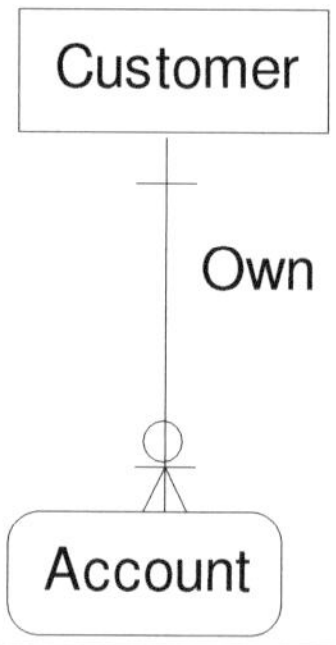

Example 3

	Yes	No
Can a Customer own more than one Account?		✓
Can an Account be owned by more than one Customer?		✓
Can a Customer exist without an Account?	✓	
Can an Account exist without a Customer?		✓
Do I need to know the Customer to bring back their Account(s)?		✓
Do I need to know the Account to bring back its Owner(s)?		✓

Your model:

Example 4

	Yes	No
Can a Customer own more than one Account?	✓	
Can an Account be owned by more than one Customer?	✓	
Can a Customer exist without an Account?		✓
Can an Account exist without a Customer?		✓
Do I need to know the Customer to bring back their Account(s)?		✓
Do I need to know the Account to bring back its Owner(s)?		✓

Your model:

Model components

Cardinality

BACKGROUND

Cardinality represents the symbols on both ends of a relationship that define the number of instances of each entity that can participate in the relationship. It is through cardinality that the data rules are captured and enforced. The domain of values to choose from to represent cardinality on a relationship is limited to three values: zero, one, or many. *Many* (some people read it as *more*) means any number greater than one. We can't specify an exact number (other than through documentation), as in "A car has four tires." We can only say, "A car has many tires."

Each side of a relationship can have a combination of zero, one, or many. Through the specification of one or many, the structural portion of the cardinality represents the quantity of each entity instance in the relationship. The RI portion of the cardinality focuses on ensuring valid values through the specification of zero or one.

6 QUESTIONS

To be precise, every relationship requires asking 6 questions on participation, optionality, and identification. If for example, a requirement takes the form of "A Customer has Accounts", we need to ask the following questions:

- Participation
  - Can a Customer own more than one Account?
  - Can an Account be owned by more than one Customer?
- Optionality
  - Can a Customer exist without an Account?
  - Can an Account exist without a Customer?
- Identification
  - Do I need to know the Customer to bring back their Account(s)?
  - Do I need to know the Account to bring back its Owner(s)?

IDENTIFYING

A relationship is either identifying or non-identifying. An identifying relationship means that one of the participating entities is a dependent entity. That is, one of the entities is at least partly dependent upon the other entity for its identification. We cannot identify the child entity without using, at least in part, the parent's primary key. This type of relationship is shown with a solid line.

NON-IDENTIFYING

In a non-identifying relationship, the child entity does not need the parent entity's primary key for its identification. It still may be mandatory that the child contain the parent's primary key, but it is not identifying. This type of relationship is shown with a dotted line.

Model components

Hierarchy

Hierarchy example (most general)

- An Order may contain one or many Order Lines.
- An Order Line must belong to one Order.

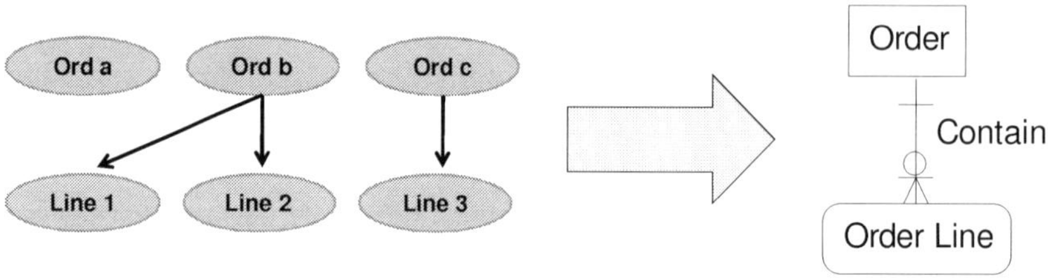

Build the data model capturing this hierarchy
(HINT: Subsumptive = Subtype)

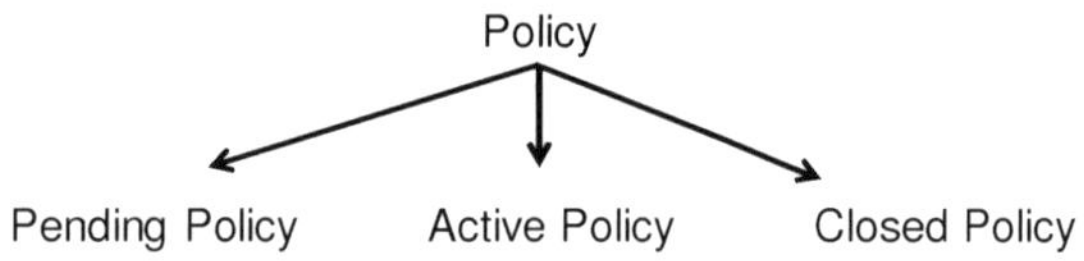

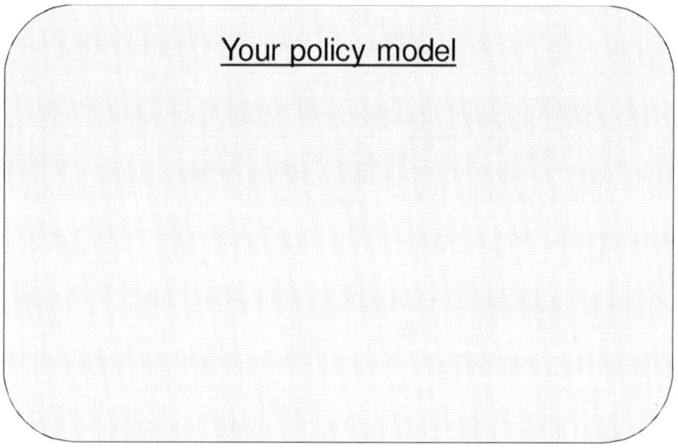

Build the data model capturing this sales structure

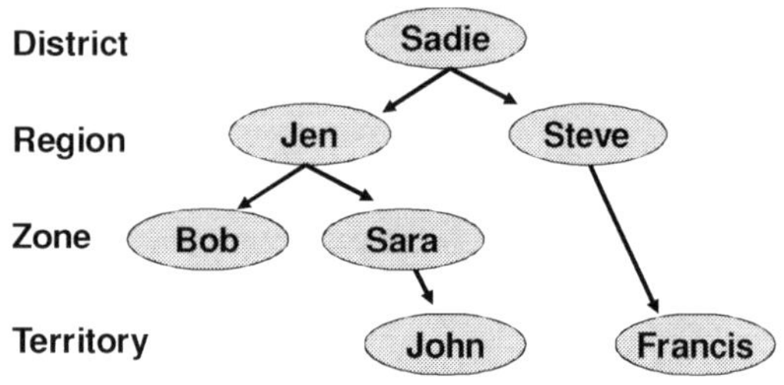

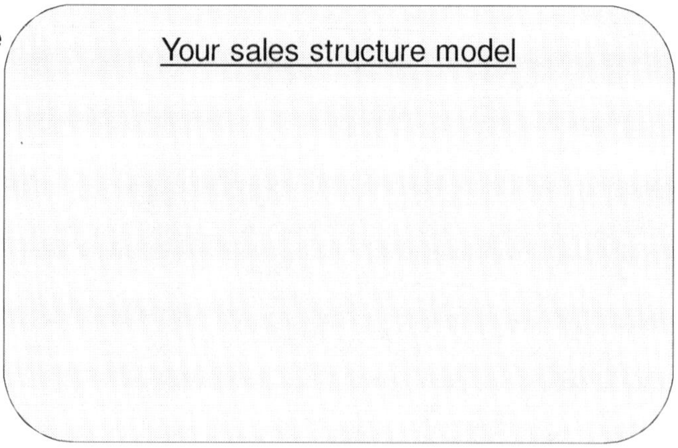

Model components

Hierarchy

BACKGROUND

A hierarchy is an arrangement of items (objects, names, values, categories, etc.) in which the items are represented as being "above," "below," or "at the same level as" one another. Abstractly, a hierarchy is simply an ordered set or an acyclic graph. A hierarchy can link entities either directly or indirectly, and either vertically or horizontally. The only direct links in a hierarchy, in so far as they are hierarchical, are to one's immediate superior or to one of one's subordinates. Wikipedia

Defining a hierarchy within the context of data modeling, it is a relationship between entities (or entity instances) where one entity (the child), can be related to at most one of the other entity (the parent).

TERMINOLOGY

Degree of branching refers to the number of direct subordinates or children an object has (equivalent to the number of vertices a node has). Hierarchies can be categorized based on the "maximum degree", the highest degree present in the system as a whole. Categorization in this way yields two broad classes: linear and branching.

In a **linear** hierarchy, the maximum degree is 1. In other words, all of the objects can be visualized in a lineup, and each object (excluding the top and bottom ones) has exactly one direct subordinate and one direct superior. In a **branching** hierarchy, one or more objects have a degree of 2 or more (and therefore the maximum degree is 2 or higher). Wikipedia

MOST COMMON TYPES

The most general type of hierarchy is the one-to-many relationship on a data model. Other common types include subsumptive hierarchy (aka taxonomic or IS-A) and compositional hierarchy. Subsumptive is represented most commonly through subtyping on a data model. Compositional hierarchies are the most used structures for dimensions.

Model components

Network

- A many-to-many relationship between entities (or between entity instances)

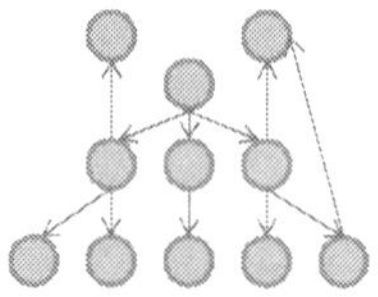

  - A Project must be assigned to many Employees.
  - An Employee must work for many Projects.

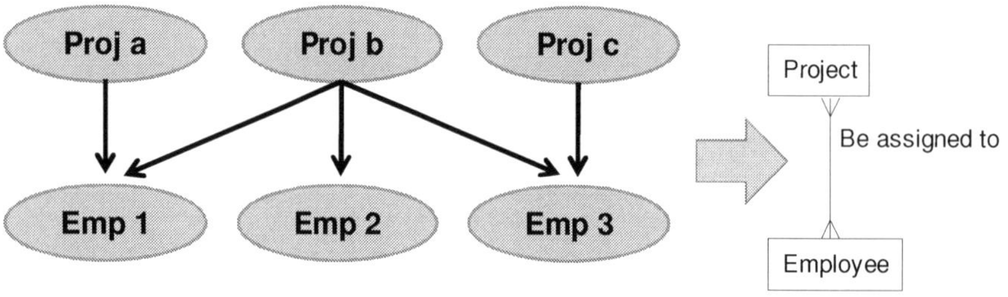

Build the data model that captures all of the materials required to make a finished product

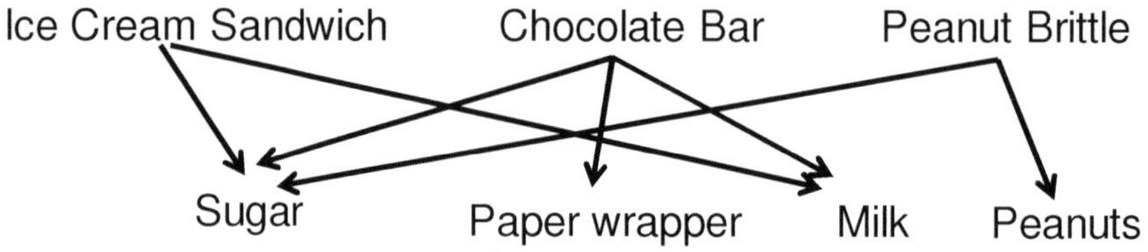

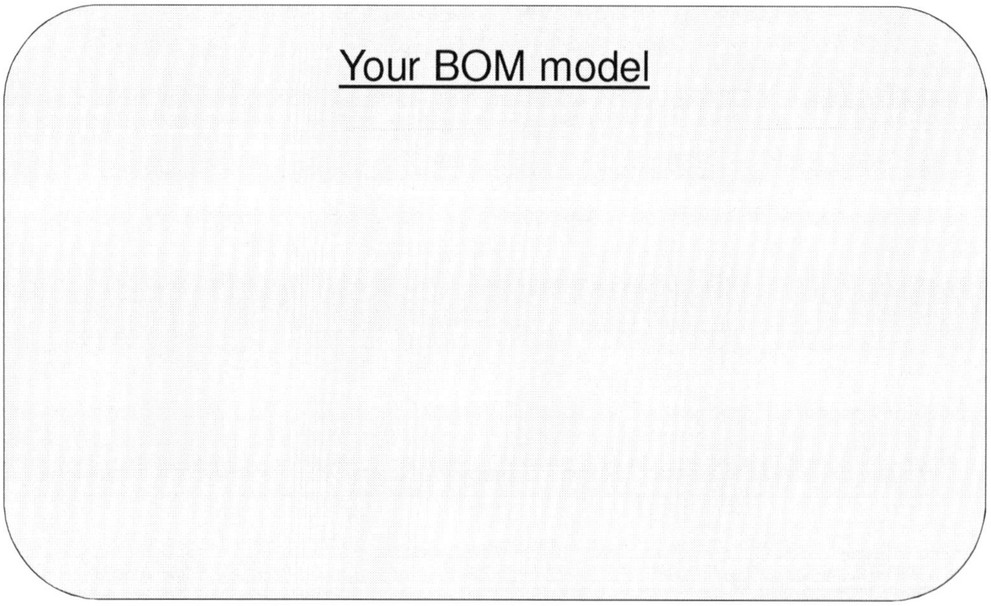

Model components

Network

BACKGROUND

A network is a many-to-many relationship between entities (or between entity instances).

EMOTION

Data modelers have a love-hate relationship with recursion. On the one hand, recursion makes modeling a complex structure a relatively painless procedure. On the other hand, some consider using recursion to be taking the easy way out of a difficult modeling situation. There are many rules that can be obscured by recursion. *Bill of materials*, for example, contains many complex rules that could lead the modeler to subtype *product* into *raw material*, *ingredient*, and so on, and show all the rules between these entities. Those in favor of recursion argue that you may not be aware of all the rules and that recursion protects you from having an incomplete model. The recursion adds in a level of flexibility that ensures that any rules not previously considered are also handled by the model. It is therefore wise to consider recursion on a situation-by-situation basis.

Model components

Relationship labels

contain work for own initiate categorize apply to	has have associate participate relate be	Is

What do you think the 'reason' is in this relationship?

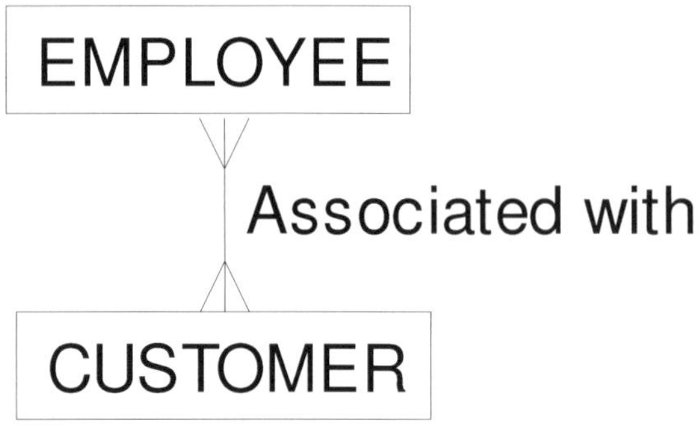

Model components

Relationship labels

BACKGROUND

Labels are the verbs that appear on the relationship lines. Labels allow us to describe a rule directly on the model. Labels should be as descriptive as possible.

THE VALUE OF LABELS FROM WILLIAM KENT, DATA AND REALITY

"A relationship is an association among several things, with that association having a particular significance. For brevity, I will refer to the significance of an association as its 'reason'. There is an association between you and your car, for the reason that you own it. There's an association between a teacher and a class, because he teaches it. There's an association between a part and a warehouse, because the part is stored there."

GOOD LABELS

Here are some examples of good label names:

- contain
- work for
- own
- initiate
- categorize
- apply to

BAD LABELS

Always avoid the following words as label names, as they provide no additional information to the reader (you can use these words in combination with other words to make a meaningful label name; just avoid using these words by themselves):

- has
- have
- associate
- participate
- relate
- be
- is (ok to use though when reading from subtype to supertype)

Fun reading a data model

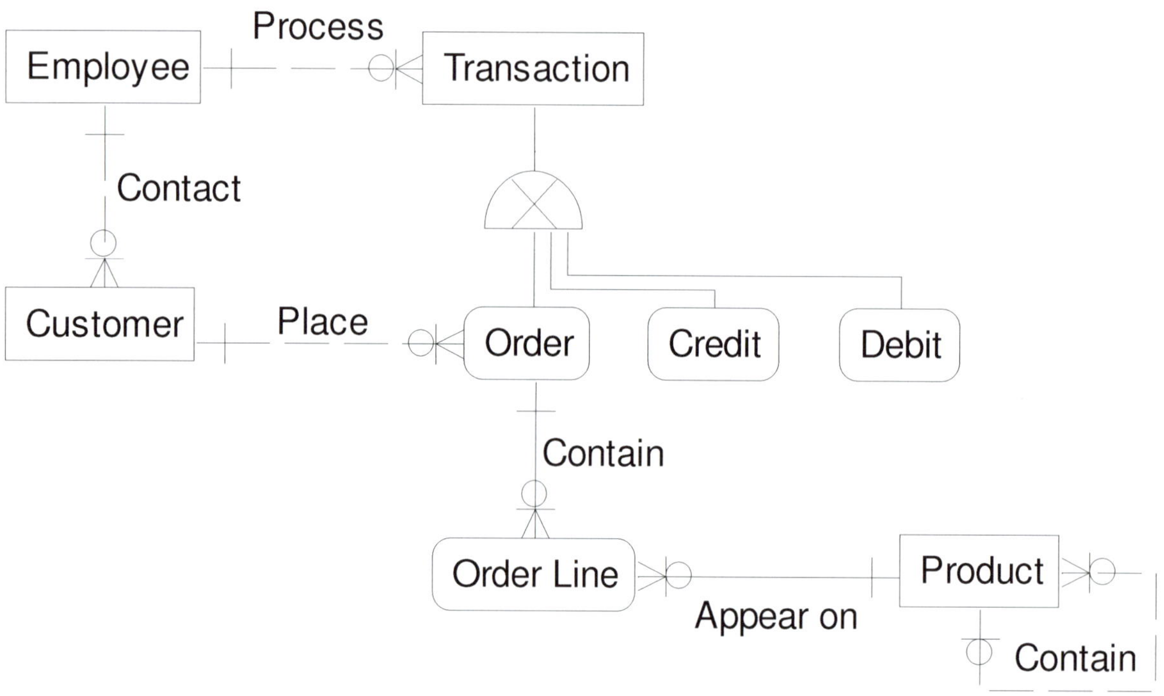

Fun reading a data model

BACKGROUND

Read the story in the model on the facing page. Use the word 'Each' and start at the one side of the relationship (or the supertype). Once you are comfortable reading this model, extend it by adding at least one new relationship and entity.

The corner office

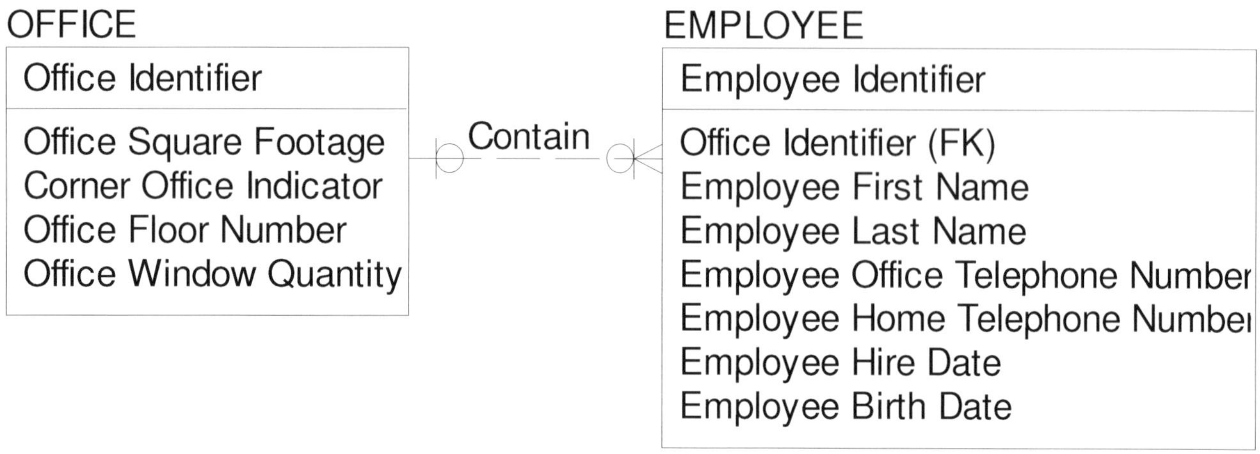

Here is the model with Office First Occupied Date included:

The corner office

BACKGROUND

You are working on a logical data model, a subset appearing on the opposite page. The relationship states:

- Each Office can contain many Employees.
- Each Employee may reside in one Office.

You need to add the data element **Office First Occupied Date** to this model.

Office First Occupied Date is the official date as recorded in the Human Resources database as to when a person first took residence in an office. It must be a business day (that is, not a weekend day or holiday).

The business expert in this area provides you with the following 3 rules:

- Office First Occupied Date is a mandatory field for each employee that has an office.
- Only managers have an office and all managers have an office.
- A manager has one and only one office.

CHALLENGE

Modify this model to accommodate this new data element and these 3 business rules.

PURPOSE

How far can you go to enforce that a data element be populated?

Data Model Scorecard® Overview

Importance of data model quality

Model these 2 business rules:
1. A Student can take many Classes.
2. An Instructor can teach many Classes.

How would you model these rules?

Leverage

1. Bob the Student is the same person as Bob the Instructor.
2. A Class can be team taught.
3. A Student can be an Applicant who has not taken any classes yet.

Data quality

1. How many people are on campus this semester?
2. How many Students teach Classes?
3. How many Instructors are not teaching Classes this semester?

"Big Picture"

Our data warehouse has a single view of 'Class'. We need to integrate systems that have something called 'Course' with other systems that call something 'Class' with other systems that call something 'Session'.

Data Model Scorecard® Overview

Importance of data model quality

LEVERAGE

Using given resources in such a way that the potential positive or negative outcome is magnified. Wikipedia.

All of the development including interface, extract, screen designs, and functionality are built upon the database design. The database design is built from the data model. Therefore the data model can make or break an entire application. Once an application is built upon a good data model, it becomes easier to support and expand, leading to a long and stable application life. A poor data model is the exact opposite, possibly taking a shorter time to develop but shifting the time and cost to support which will outweigh the cost of development in a short time and eventually lead to the demise of the application.

The key reason for giving special attention to data organization is leverage in the sense that a small change to a data model may have a major impact on the system as a whole. Data Modeling Essentials

DATA QUALITY

The degree of excellence of data. Factors contributing to data quality include: the data is stored according to their data types, the data is consistent, the data is not redundant, the data follows business rules, the data corresponds to established domains, the data is timely, the data is well understood, the data satisfy the needs of the business, the user is satisfied with the validity of the data and the information derived from that data, the data is complete, and there are no duplicate records. CSUMB Online Glossary

Although the data model can't represent all business rules, it can enforce quite a bit through referential integrity (RI). What it does enforce in terms of data rules can dramatically improve data quality and catch many data errors before they are loaded into the application. Also clear and concise definitions can help people make better decisions, and raise possible issues before development begins. Naming standards help people understand the content of an entity or data element by its name. For example, following the guidelines of one Subject, zero, one, or more Modifiers, and one Classword, help make data elements more easily understood.

"BIG PICTURE"

Although a model might be built to support a particular application, the terminology and structures on the model should have a level of consistency across the enterprise. This helps create a single version of the truth or "Big Picture" for an organization.

Data Model Scorecard® Overview

Traditional data model review methods

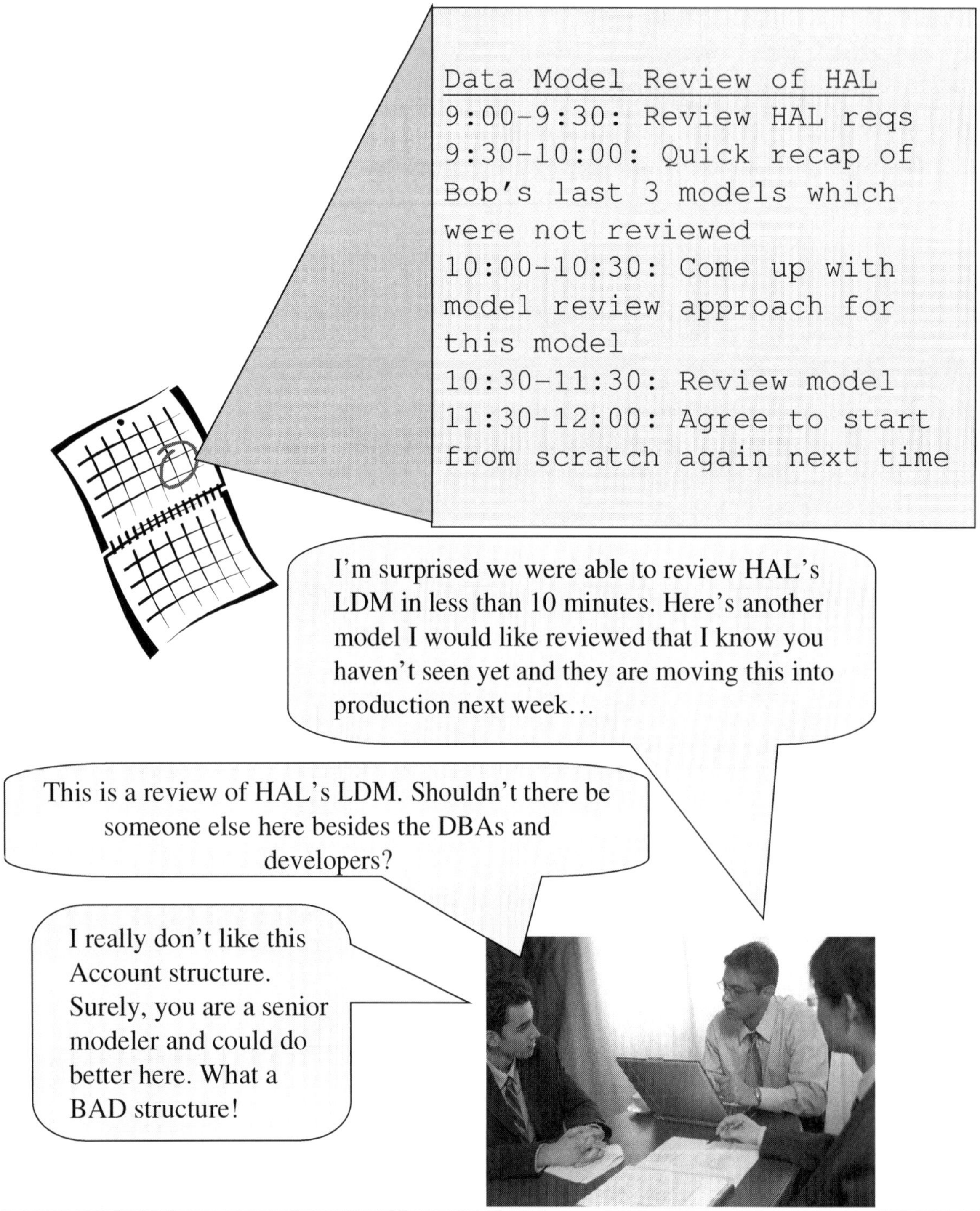

Data Model Scorecard® Overview

Traditional data model review methods

APPROACH

A majority of model reviews tend to be organized and performed with minimal structure and formality. There is usually missing a set of activities that are reusable across model reviews, and checklists are also missing which are used for verification during the review process. In addition, many models escape from being reviewed. Those models that are reviewed usually are reviewed inconsistently with other models because the same process is never followed twice.

AUDIENCE

Due to missing a standard review process and checklist, many organizations fail to include the right people in the review. For example, I have been in logical data model reviews where there were only technical people present (DBAs and developers) and no one from the business or functional side.

TIMING

Reviews need to happen as early as possible and usually more than one review needs to occur for each model. I have been in too many situations where I received a comment such as this from the project manager: "Can you take a quick look at our data model? We are going into production next week and were told we need your blessing before we go live." Also, during a model review, action items to change the model can come up that require another review to ensure the changes happened correctly and to review the model again in its entirety after the changes have been made. It is important to timebox a review so that it does not reach the point of diminishing returns. Also, if too many people are in the room it will be counterproductive, and if too few people are in the room it will not be considered a complete review.

JUDGMENT & EMOTION

A model should not be considered "good" or "bad". Judgment needs to be removed from the model and so does emotion. I was once in a model review where the modeler left the room in tears. At another time I was having one of my models reviewed and someone in the room actually stood up on the table and looked down at me explaining with a fair amount of emotion what she did not like about my model. It is best for team rapport and model quality to be objective when reviewing a model.

Data Model Scorecard® Overview

Scorecard characteristics

1. Acknowledges strengths and makes recommendations

Data Model Scorecard™ review of HAL application

…

25. "There is a perfect balance of abstraction on the model because…"

…

125. "A surrogate key requires an alternate key. On this entity you might consider the alternate key to be…"

2. Objective and externally-defined

3. Easy to apply and customize

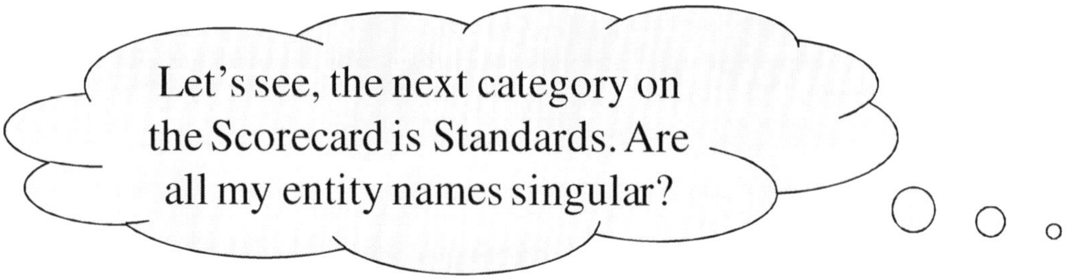

4. Supports all types of models

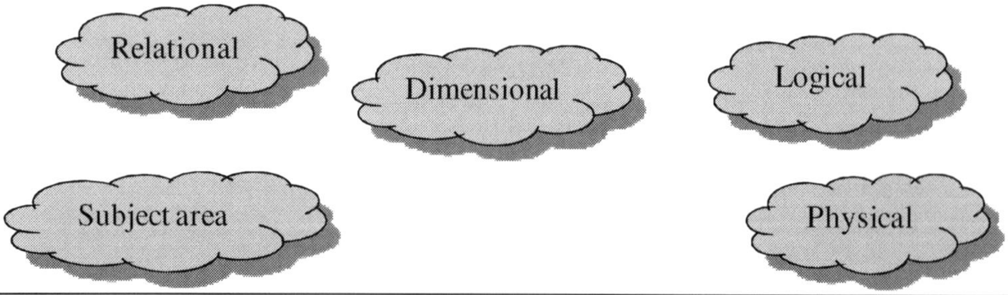

Data Model Scorecard® Overview

Scorecard characteristics

BACKGROUND

Aim, wind, and gravity influence an arrow's trajectory, much the same way as deadlines, skills, and experience influence a data model's trajectory, strongly impacting whether a model will reach its target of accuracy, longevity, practicality, and consistency. The archer's score can be quickly calculated and we can easily see the success or failure of her work. This is where the analogy ends however, because there is no standard way of measuring the strengths and weaknesses of our models, leaving much up to interpretation, perception, and the test of time. After years of reviewing hundreds of data models, I have formalized a set of data model quality criteria into what I call the Data Model Scorecard®. The Scorecard contains 10 clear and distinct criteria for validating a data model. The scorecard has four main characteristics that make it an invaluable tool.

ACKNOWLEDGE STRENGTHS AND RECOMMEND AREAS FOR IMPROVEMENT

It is important to just not focus on what could be better, but to also focus on the strengths of a model. The Scorecard highlights strengths, giving specific examples of what was done using best design practices. It also makes recommendations on areas for improvement, along with detailed recommendations that can be made directly to the model.

OBJECTIVE AND EXTERNALLY-DEFINED

I have participated in model reviews where modelers take the review personally and comments take the form of "I don't like what you did here..." or "You are still not getting this structure right..." We need to step back from the 'I' and 'You', and critique the model with an external and objective perspective. Team rapport remains intact as you as the reviewer are not criticizing their model, but rather this objective and external scale believes there are areas for improvement. The Scorecard uses a points system and several metrics for measuring model quality.

EASY TO APPLY AND CUSTOMIZE

The scorecard was designed for even those new to modeling to critique their own models and models of their colleagues. It should be incorporated into a methodology as a final checkpoint before the model is considered complete.

SUPPORTS ALL TYPES OF MODELS

The Scorecard is designed to be used for all model levels of detail: subject area, logical, and physical. It also supports both relational and dimensional modeling.

Data Model Scorecard® Overview

Scorecard template

#	Category	Total score	Model score	%	Comments
1	How well do the characteristics of the model support the type of model?	10			
2	How well does the model capture the requirements?	15			
3	How complete is the model?	15			
4	How structurally sound is the model?	15			
5	How well does the model leverage generic structures?	10			
6	How well does the model follow naming standards?	5			
7	How well has the model been arranged for readability?	5			
8	How good are the definitions?	10			
9	How consistent is the model with the enterprise?	5			
10	How well does the metadata match the data?	10			
	TOTAL SCORE	100			

Scorecard example (plus a 50 page document!)

#	Category	Total score	Model score	%	Comments
1.	How well do the characteristics of the model support the type of model?	10	10	100%	Lots of processing data elements
2.	How well does the model capture the requirements?	15	14	93%	Revisit some AKs
3.	How complete is the model?	15	15	100%	Legacy system mapping
4.	How structurally sound is the model?	15	10	67%	Null AKs
5.	How well does the model leverage generic structures?	10	10	100%	Perfect use of abstraction
6.	How well does the model follow naming standards?	5	4	80%	Great standard for table naming
7.	How well has the model been arranged for readability?	5	4	80%	Incorporate a subject area model
8.	How good are the definitions?	10	9	90%	Very comprehensive definitions
9.	How consistent is the model with the enterprise?	5	5	100%	Great rapport with business
10.	How well does the metadata match the data?	10	10	100%	Handles changing natural account numbers
	TOTAL SCORE	**100**	**91**		

Data Model Scorecard® Overview

Scorecard template

BACKGROUND

Each of the 10 categories has a total score that relates to the value your organization places on the question. Remember, just as in any assessment, the total must be 100. The model score column contains the results of how a particular model scored. For example, if a model received 10 on "How well does the model capture the requirements?" then that is what would go in this column. The % column stores the model score in category divided by the total score in category. For example, receiving 10 out of 15 would lead to 66%. The comments column contains any pertinent information to explain the score in more details or to capture the action items on what is required to fix the model. The last row contains the total score, and this can be tallied up or averaged for each of the columns to arrive at an overall score.

EXAMPLE

The model that was reviewed in this example received a score of 91. Category 4 was a strong area for improvement and categories 6 and 7 also contain areas for improvement. There was a 50 page document that accompanied this Scorecard. This document explained the results in detail. Both strengths and areas for improvement were explained in detail through a complete set or representative set of examples. For example, Category 2 lost some points because this model was missing some alternate keys. In the accompanying document, those entities missing alternate keys were listed as well as those entities with suspect alternate keys.

YOU CAN USE THE DATA MODEL SCORECARD® – READ LEGAL STUFF

Steve Hoberman & Associates, LLC hereby grants to companies a non-exclusive royalty free limited use license to use the Data Model Scorecard® solely for internal data model improvement purposes. The name 'Steve Hoberman & Associates, LLC' and the website 'www.stevehoberman.com' must appear on every document referencing the Data Model Scorecard®. Companies have no right to sublicense the Data Model Scorecard® and no right to use the Data Model Scorecard® for any purposes outside of company's business.

Data Model Scorecard® Overview

How well do the characteristics of the model support the type of model?

MODEL TYPE

Scope for subject area models

- *Are all subject areas basic and critical?*
- *Are you touching business complexity?*
- *Is it clear what is in and out of scope?*

Content for logical data models

- *Is it application and technology independent?*
- *Fully normalized or fully dimensionalized?*
- *Does it represent a business solution?*

Context for physical data models

- *Has performance, security, and development tool requirements been considered and incorporated?*
- *Does it represent a technical solution?*
- *Has it been "cautiously modified"?*

Relational vs. Dimensional

- *Has dimensional been used only when business users need to see metrics at different levels of granularity?*
- *Has relational been used for all other scenarios?*

Data Model Scorecard® Overview

1. How well do the characteristics of the model support the type of model?

EXPLANATION

This question ensures that the model type (subject area, logical, or physical – and then either relational or dimensional) of the model satisfies the criteria for this level of detail. In general terms, the subject area model should contain a well-defined scope, the logical data model should be application-independent and represent a business solution, and the physical data model should be tuned for performance, security, and consider development tool constraints (e.g. cube technology, database limitations, etc.). The physical data model should represent a technical solution. A dimensional model is built when there is a need to play with numbers and a relational is built for everything else.

PURPOSE

To meet the expectations of scope, content, or context.

CHALLENGE

The modeler and reviewer need to understand the definition of each model type. Especially tricky is the definition of a logical data model. Should a logical be limited to a relational normalized structure or can it also be dimensional? Also, during crunch times it is possible that one model might be created to represent both logical and physical views for example, and this can complicate the grading of this category. I once heard this type of model referred to as a "physio-logical" model.

SUBJECT AREA

Each subject area must be basic and critical. This means that they are core to the group being modeled, and without this concept the business being modeled would be very different or possibly non-existent. Customer, Product, and Employee are all examples of subject areas.

LOGICAL

If a logical data model is relational, it should be fully normalized. If a logical is dimensional, every hierarchy level should be shown and there should only be a single meter. It needs to be completely independent of software, hardware, and network, representing a business solution.

PHYSICAL

The physical data model represents context. Will the logical data model work with a given set of software, hardware, and network? If there are opportunities to improve performance, space management, and security, for example, the model should be cautiously modified to allow it to work more efficiently.

Data Model Scorecard® Overview

2. How well does the model capture the requirements?

Each Customer can own many Accounts. Each Account must be owned by one and only one Customer. This means you can't have joint accounts. Is this true Sally the Steward?

Data Model Scorecard® Overview

2. How well does the model capture the requirements?

EXPLANATION

This is the "correctness" category. That is, we need to understand the content of what is being modeled. This can be the most difficult of all 10 categories to grade, the reason being that we really need to understand how the business works and what the business wants from their application. If we are modeling a *sales data mart*, for example, we need to understand both how the invoicing process works in our company, as well as what reports and queries will be needed to answer key sales questions from the business.

PURPOSE

We need to ensure our model represents the data requirements, as the costs can be devastating if there is even a slight difference between what was required and what was delivered. Besides not delivering what was expected is the potential that the IT/business relationship will suffer. The model needs to meet business expectations.

CHALLENGE

What makes this category even more challenging is the possibility that perhaps the business requirements are not well-defined, or differ from verbal requirements, or keep changing usually with the scope expanding instead of contracting.

Data Model Scorecard® Overview

3. How complete is the model?

- Confirms all requirements are in the model, and nothing extra
- Includes meta data (e.g. definitions, stewardship, AKs)

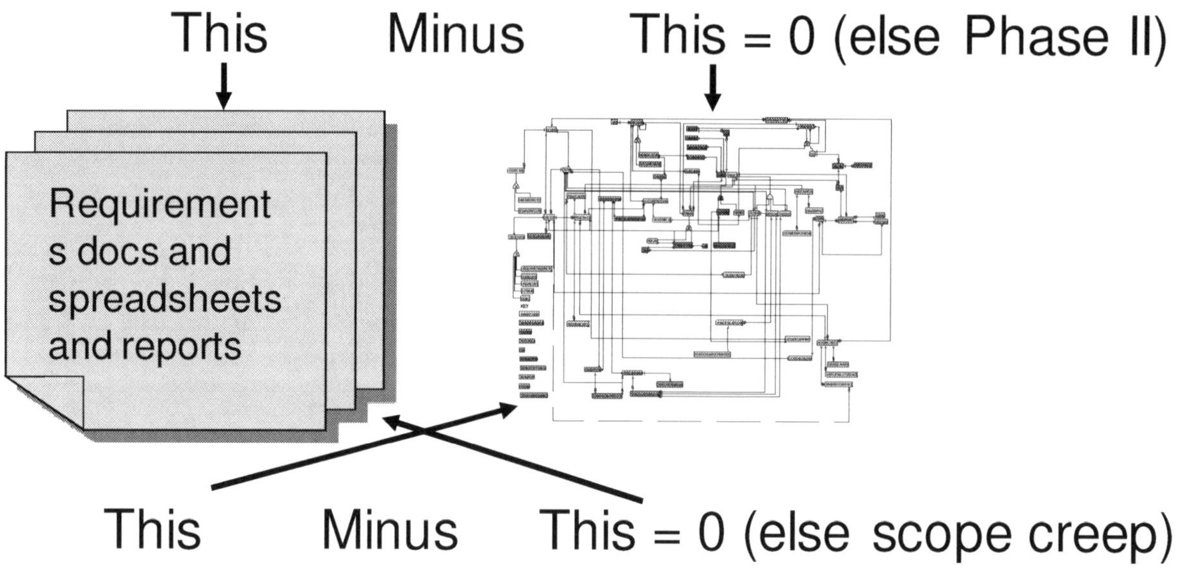

Data Model Scorecard® Overview

3. How complete is the model?

EXPLANATION

This category checks for data model components that are not in the requirements or requirements that are not represented on the model. If the scope of the model is greater than the requirements, we have a situation known as "scope creep." This means that we are planning on delivering more than what was originally required. This may not necessarily be a bad thing, as long as this additional scope has been factored into the project plan. If the model scope is less than the requirements, we will be leaving information out of the resulting application, usually leading to an enhancement or "phase 2" shortly after the application is in production. For completeness, we need to make sure the scope of the project and model match, as well as ensuring all the necessary metadata on the model is populated.

Regarding metadata, there are certain types that tend to get overlooked when modeling, such as definitions, stewardship (defined by Anne Marie Smith as "responsibility without authority"), and alternate keys. These types of metadata along with ones that are mandatory parts of our model such as data element name and format information need to be checked for completeness in this category.

Ensures the scope of the model matches the scope of the requirements. You can validate the correctness category and this category in parallel, as the red flags and proactive measures are very similar.

PURPOSE

To meet the scope of the requirements.

CHALLENGE

It can be difficult to grade this category without written signed off requirements and without a metadata checklist which contains the types of metadata that are required and those that are optional.

Data Model Scorecard® Overview

4. How structurally sound is the model?

- Data Modeling 101
- Many violations flagged by our modeling and database tools
- Ensures that the model follows good design principles

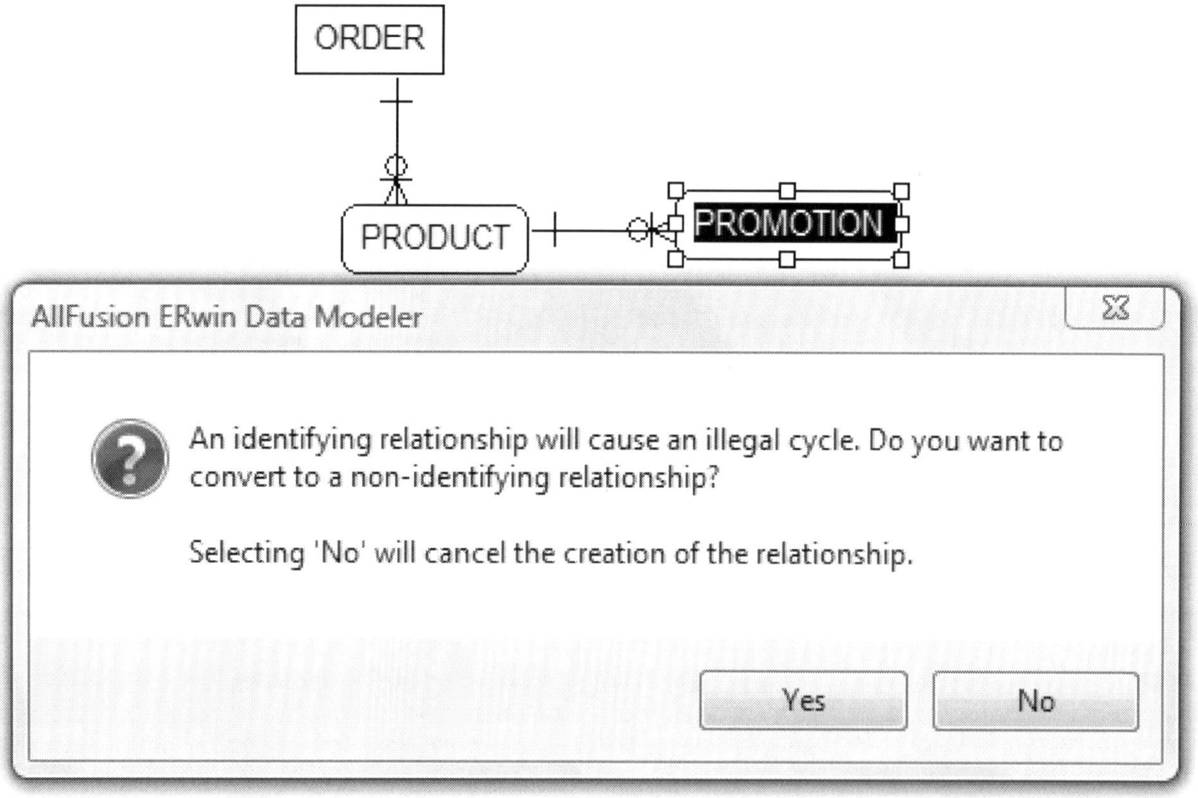

Data Model Scorecard® Overview

4. How structurally sound is the model?

EXPLANATION

This is the "Data Modeling 101" category. This category validates the design practices employed to build the model. We don't need to necessarily understand the content of the model to score this category. Just the structure. Many of the potential problems from this category are quickly and automatically flagged by our modeling and database tools. Examples include prohibiting having two data elements with the same exact name in the same entity, a null data element in a primary key, and certain reserved words in data element and entity names. This category ensures that the model follows good design principles independent of content.

PURPOSE

To minimize relational database issues.

CHALLENGE

There could be structural soundness issues that escape the human eye, or are very tedious to check for. For example, ensuring that if the same data element appears more than once on the same model, it has the same format across the model.

Data Model Scorecard® Overview

5. How well does the model leverage generic structures?

Gauges the use of generic data element, entity, and relationship structures

Location = Customer Location + Plant Location + …

Ensures the correct level of generic concepts are applied on the model

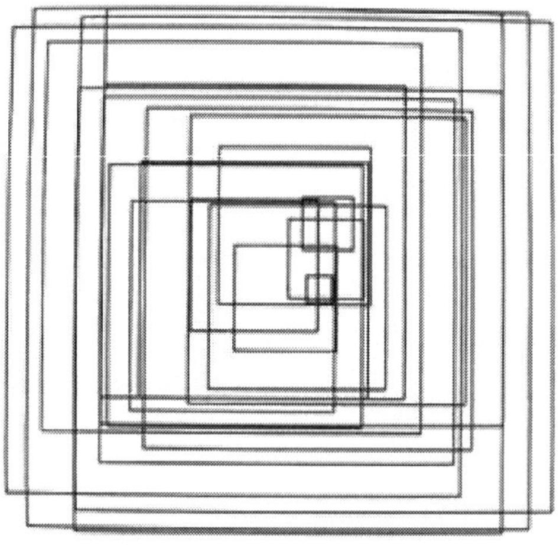

Data Model Scorecard® Overview

5. How well does the model leverage generic structures?

EXPLANATION

This category gauges the use of generic data element, entity, and relationship structures. One of the most powerful tools a data modeler has at their disposal is abstraction, the ability to increase the types of information a design can accommodate using generic concepts. Going from Customer Location to a more generic Location for example, allows the design to more easily handle other types of locations, such as warehouses and distribution centers. This category ensures the correct level of abstraction is applied on the model.

PURPOSE

To have the right level of flexibility.

CHALLENGE

You need to know how to phrase “what if” scenarios, and find people in the business who can answer these questions.

Data Model Scorecard® Overview

6. How well does the model follow naming standards?

Naming standards

- Ensure structure integration
- Increase team understanding across areas

3 categories

1. Structure
2. Term
3. Syntax
   - Plural or singular
   - Hyphens, spaces, or Camelback
   - Upper case, initial upper case, or lower case

Data Model Scorecard® Overview

6. How well does the model follow naming standards?

EXPLANATION

Correct and consistent naming standards are extremely helpful for knowledge transfer and integration. New team members who are familiar with similar naming conventions on other projects will avoid the time to learn a new set of naming standards. This category focuses on naming standard structure, abbreviations, and syntax.

STRUCTURE

Structure includes the components of a name. A popular standard for data element structure is one Subject Area, zero, one, or many Modifiers, and one Class Word. A subject area is a concept that is basic and critical to the business. A modifier qualifies this subject area and a class word is the high-level domain for a data element. Examples of class words are Quantity, Amount, Code, and Date.

TERM

Term includes proper spelling and abbreviation. An abbreviations list can be used to name each logical and physical term. Organizations should have a process in place for efficiently creating new abbreviations if a term cannot be found on a list. The process should be carefully managed to prevent different abbreviations being created for the same or similar term, and for creating the same abbreviation for completely different terms.

SYNTAX

Syntax includes whether the term should be plural or singular, whether hyphens, spaces, or Camelback (i.e. initial upper case with no spaces in between words such as customerLastName) should be used, and case (i.e. upper case, initial upper case, or lower case).

PURPOSE

Ensures structure integration. Efforts to bring together information from multiple systems will be less painful if the data elements are named consistently across projects. Besides this integration benefit, it can also increase team understanding across areas and reduce the amount of time it takes for new members to come up to speed.

CHALLENGE

Weighing consistency vs. correctness. Write and enforce grandfathering rules on earlier standards.

Data Model Scorecard® Overview

7. How well has the model been arranged for readability?

Proper layout ensures your model is easy to read so that the other scorecard categories can be accurately measured

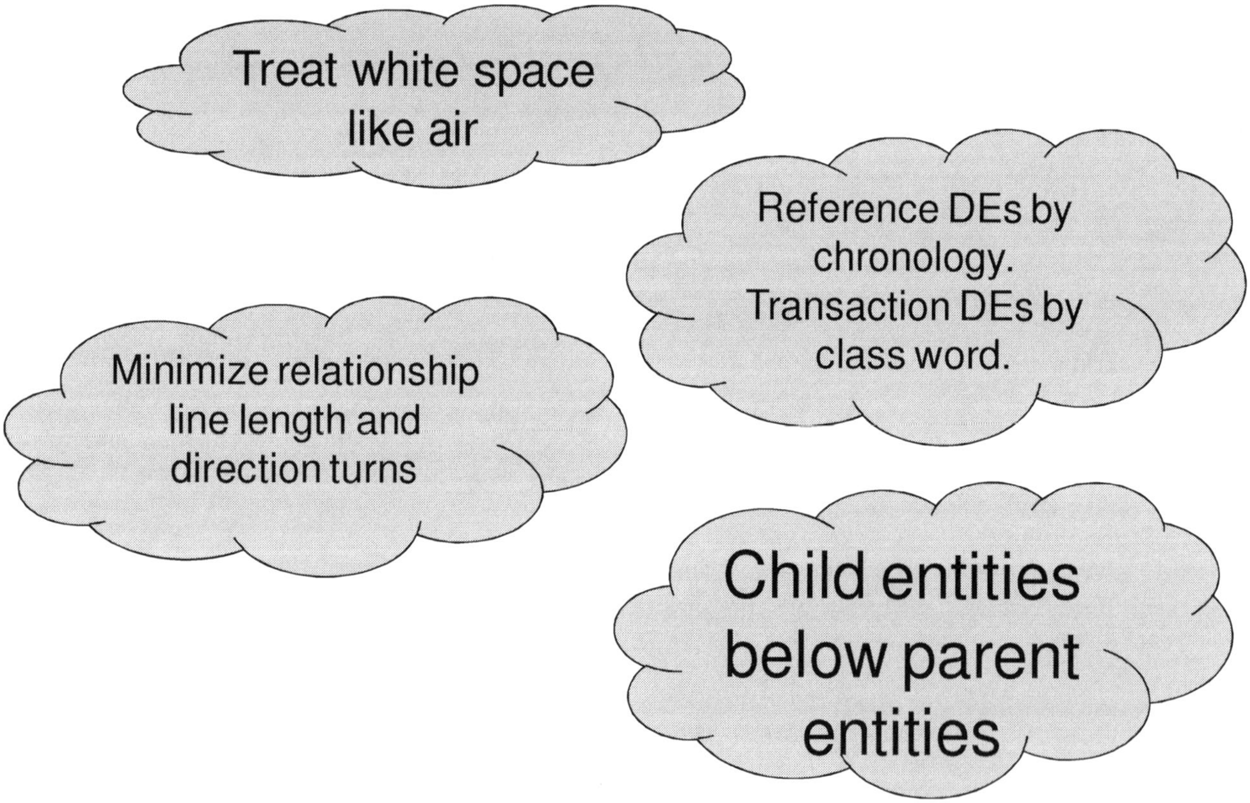

Data Model Scorecard® Overview

7. How well has the model been arranged for readability?

EXPLANATION

This question checks to make sure the model is visually easy to follow. Readability needs to be considered at a model, entity, data element, and relationship level.

At a model level, I like to see a large model broken into smaller logical pieces. I also search for the "heart" of the model. That is, upon looking at a data model, which part of the model are your eyes naturally attracted toward? This tends to be an entity or entities with many relationships to other entities, similar to the hub on a bicycle tire with many spokes to the outside rim of the tire. This "heart" needs to be carefully positioned so that the reader can identify it early on and use this as a starting point to walk through the rest of the model.

At an entity level, I like to see child entities below parent entities. Child entities being on the many side of the relationship, and parent entities on the one side of the relationship. So if an *order* contains many *order lines*, *order line* should appear below *order*.

At a data element level, I like to see some logic applied regarding the placement of data elements within an entity. For example, on reference entities such as *customer* and *employee*, it is more readable to have the data elements listed in an order that makes sense for someone starting at the beginning of the entity and working down sequentially. For example, *city name*, then *state name*, then *postal code*. For transaction entities such as *order* and *claim*, I have found it more readable to group the data elements into class words, such as all amount data elements grouped together.

At a relationship level, I try to minimize relationship line length, and the number of direction changes a relationship line makes. I also look for missing or incomplete relationship labels, if labels are appropriate on the model. The larger the model, the less useful it is to display labels as the extra verbiage can make the model harder to read.

PURPOSE

Ensures your model is easy to read so that the other scorecard categories can be accurately measured.

Data Model Scorecard® Overview

8. How good are the definitions?

DEFINITIONS

Entity and data element definitions should be clear, complete, and correct

A Customer is a person or organization who obtains our product for resale. The Customer normally obtains the product through purchase. An example of a customer who does not purchase our product is the Salvation Army, which receives the product for free as a charity organization. A person or organization must have obtained at least one product from us to be considered a Customer. That is, Prospects are not Customers. Also, once a Customer, always a Customer so even Customers that have not obtained anything in 50 years are still considered Customers. The Customer is different than the Consumer, who purchases the product for consumption as opposed to resale.

Examples:
Walmart
Bob's Grocery Store
Military Base 1332

Data Model Scorecard® Overview

8. How good are the definitions?

EXPLANATION

This category includes checking all definition to make sure they are clear, complete, and correct. Clarity means that a reader can understand the meaning of a term by reading the definition only once. Completeness ensures the definition is at the appropriate level of detail, and that it includes all the necessary components such as derivations and examples. Correctness focuses on having a definition that totally matches what the term means, and is consistent with the rest of the business.

PURPOSE

Ensures no doubt exists about the contents of data elements and the relationships between entities. Doubts and misinterpretations lead to model ambiguity.

CHALLENGE

You will need to find business people from outside your department or project to validate the definitions.

Data Model Scorecard® Overview

9. How consistent is the model with the enterprise?

Does this model complement the "Big Picture"?

Big Picture sources

- Enterprise model
- Packaged software (e.g. ERP solutions)
- Industry data models
- Industry consortiums
- Common thought

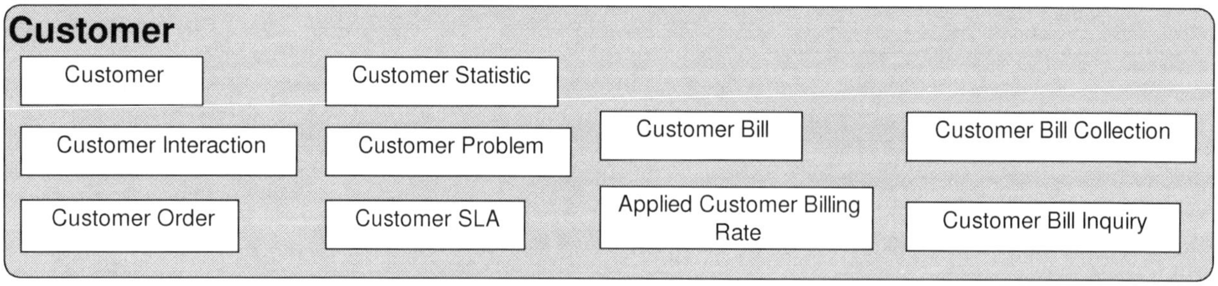

Data Model Scorecard® Overview

9. How consistent is the model with the enterprise?

EXPLANATION

Does this model complement the "big picture"? The structures that appear in a data model should be consistent in terminology and usage to structures that appear in related data models, and with the enterprise model if one exists. This way there will be consistency across projects.

PURPOSE

Ensures the information is represented in a broad and consistent context, so that one set of terminology and rules can be spoken in the organization.

CHALLENGE

Not all organizations have an enterprise data model. If no enterprise model exists, I look for widely accepted existing models for comparison, ERP models if they are accessible and intelligible, or universal models which are models that are built for a particular industry or function.

Data Model Scorecard® Overview

10. How well does the metadata match the data?

Determines how well the structure matches reality

What's really "under the hood"?

Metadata				Results				Validation (Y / N / ?)				
Name	Definition	Format	Null	First 10-25 distinct values	Percent null	Maximum length	Percent failed lookups	Meaning	Null	Length	Lookup	Com-ments
PRO_ITEM_REF_DB_ID	The unique identifier generated for a product.	Char(5)	N	12452 33855 85958 37580 38447 38936 33490 48476 38111	0	5	95	Y	Y	Y	?	Are you sure you are doing the lookup properly? Make sure you ignore the last character on each value in this data element when you do the lookup. This last character means something else. Call me if you need more of an explanation.

Data Model Scorecard® Overview

10. How well does the metadata match the data?

EXPLANATION

This category determines how well the data elements and their rules match reality. Does the data element Customer Last Name really contain the customer's last name, for example?

PURPOSE

Ensures the model and the actual data that will be stored within the resulting tables are consistent with each other, so to reduce surprises later on in software development.

CHALLENGE

This might be very difficult to do early in a project's life cycle because data can be difficult to access from the source system before development has begun. However, the earlier the better so you can avoid future surprises which can be much more costly.

Data Model Scorecard® Overview

Introducing the Scorecard into your organization

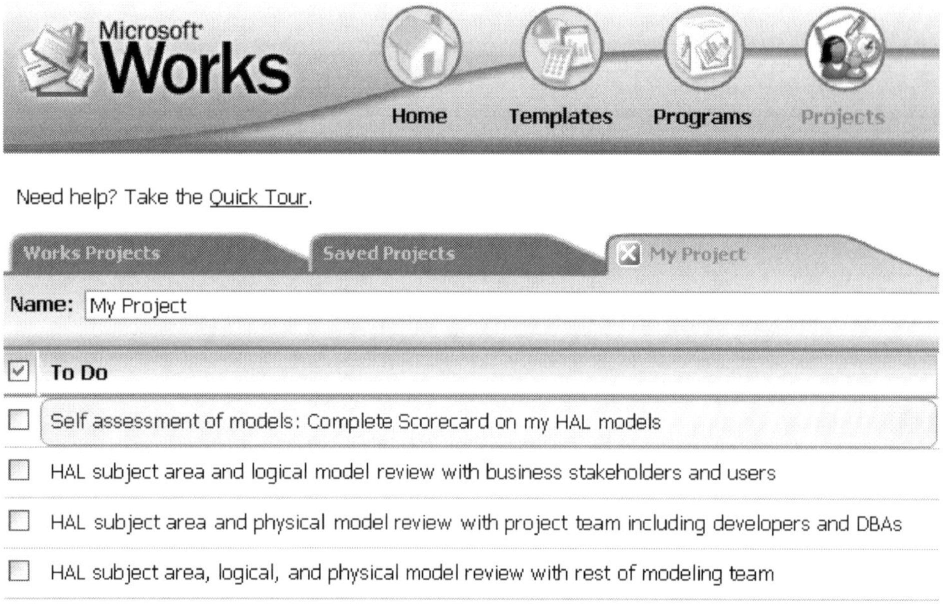

WPS Insurance Corporation Scorecard Template

#	Category	Total score	Model score	%	Comments
1.	How well does the model capture the requirements?	15		0%	
2.	How complete is the model?	15		0%	
3.	How structurally sound is the model?	15		0%	
4.	How well does the model follow naming standards?	15		0%	
5.	How good are the definitions?	10		0%	
6.	How consistent is the model with the enterprise?	10		0%	
7.	How well does the model leverage generic structures?	10		0%	
8.	How well has the model been arranged for readability?	5		0%	
9.	How well does the metadata match the data?	5		0%	
10.	How well has real world context been incorporated into the model?	0		0%	
	TOTAL SCORE	**100**			

Data Model Scorecard® Overview

Introducing the Scorecard into your organization

CHECKPOINT

A data model review should be a checkpoint that must be achieved before building the database and writing code. There are two types of reviews, those with the project team and those with other modelers. The purpose of the project team review is to ensure everyone is on the same page and has the same understanding of the data elements and rules to be implemented. The purpose of the review with other modelers is to ensure that modeling best practices and standards are adhered to, and to make sure you are not missing anything as sometimes eyes outside the project can help bring to the surface.

It is a good idea to spend a few minutes with the modeler or modeling team reviewing the Scorecard prior to building the models. This lets the modelers know the scale in which their models will be critiqued.

It might take some effort, but it is also worthwhile to incorporate the Scorecard milestones into your organization's project template. This way every new project already has the Scorecard review points defined and you will not have to spend time explaining why the Scorecard review needs to take place with each new project. Instead, it will become second nature as any other task on the project plan.

EXAMPLE

The example on the facing page is a customization of the Scorecard performed by Steve Doty at WPS Insurance Corporation.

FEEDBACK FROM GMAC

GMAC has applied the Scorecard and reports the following positive feedback:

- Sets expectations for the modeler.
- Reduce model iterations.
- Sharing resources across LOBs and countries is possible if using the same criteria.
- Provides meaningful metrics.
- Provides a measuring stick for existing applications. That is, provides a starting score for systems we know have designs that need work.

Data Model Scorecard® Overview

Scorecard challenges

- ☑ Resources
- ☑ Resistance to change
- ☑ Emotion
- ☑ Iteration
- ☑ Need to set ideal amount of time:

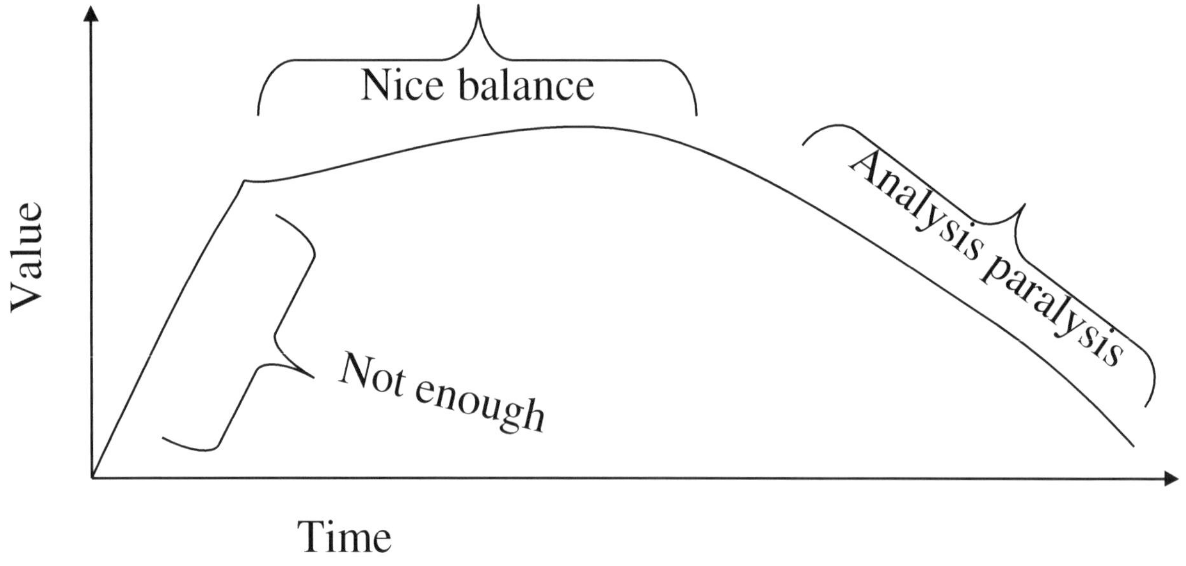

Data Model Scorecard® Overview

Scorecard challenges

RESOURCES

One of the challenges with reviewing the model with other modelers however, is that in today's lean and mean organizations, there aren't many people just doing modeling. Years ago, I worked in a group that had 9 data modelers full time. Later, I worked on a team that had 6 data modelers full time. Today where I work there aren't any full time data modelers! In situations like this, it is best to borrow some time from a modeler or a related project or perhaps your organization has a person who reviews models for best practice guidelines, at least part time.

RESISTANCE TO CHANGE

It took me over five years to convince project management to introduce a much-needed template into our methodology at a large manufacturing company. For many organizations it can be difficult to change.

EMOTION

It is critical that emotion be filtered out of the Scorecard work. It is very easy to get attached to the model and translate areas for improvement on the model with weaknesses of the data modeler. We should not connect the model with the modeler when applying the Scorecard.

ITERATION

It is important to have a follow up review of the model after initial review. This is so you can ensure recommendations to the model have been correctly applied and to have a second look at the model with the opportunity of identifying other areas for improvement that might have been missed during the first application of the Scorecard.

TIME

Whenever anyone asks me how long it will take to build a data model, my response is always "How much time do I have?" Modeling will take as much time as is allocated. If I am building a model for a Sales data mart for example, and I am given two weeks for the modeling I will finish the effort in two weeks. If I am given two months, I will finish the effort in two months. The same is true for the Scorecard; it will take as much time as allocated. Make sure you set enough time to provide valuable suggestions to the modeler but not too much time where analysis paralysis sets in.

Data Model Scorecard® Overview

Scorecard tips

☑Apply the Scorecard to one of your models first
☑Apply the Scorecard to all of your own models
☑Category #2 is the most difficult so spend the most time here
☑Focus on the model, not the modeler
☑Scorecard is the means, not the ends

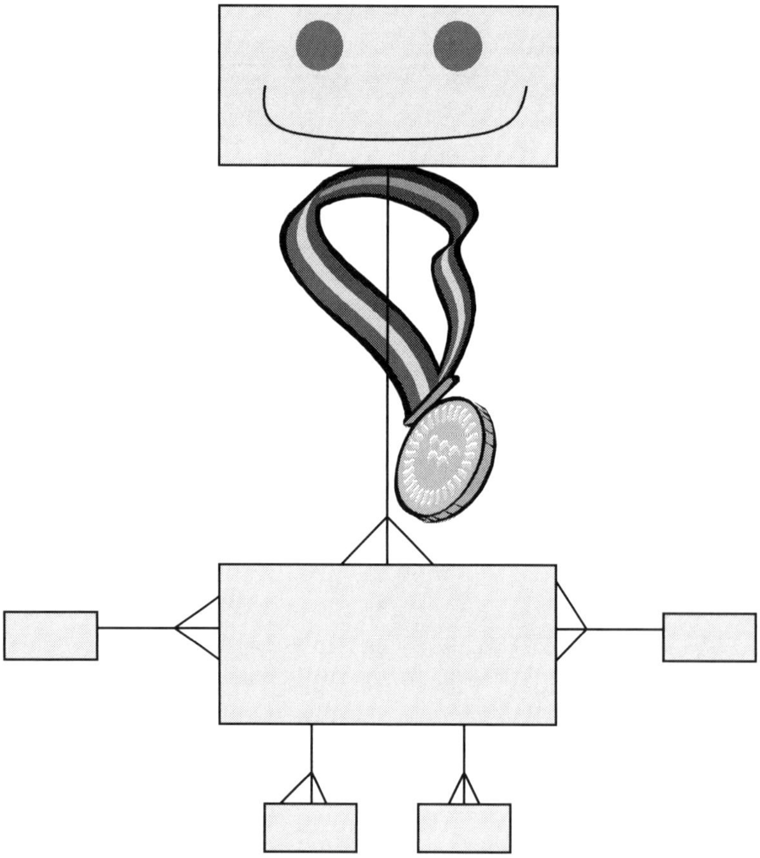

Data Model Scorecard® Overview

Scorecard tips

FIRST APPLY TO YOUR OWN MODEL

It is a good idea to apply it to one of your models before applying it to a colleague's model. This is so you can get comfortable with each of the categories and also think about the approach to deliver feedback so the modeler accepts instead of rejects the comments.

APPLY TO ALL OF YOUR OWN MODELS

This is so you can be ready to defend any Scorecard violations that you have done on purpose, and so you can identify any areas for improvement on your model before anyone else sees it.

BEWARE THE CORRECTNESS CATEGORY

The Correctness category (Category #2) requires understanding how the business works. When I come onsite to review models I spend most of my time learning about the organization, application, and model. I become familiar with terminology and business rules so I can to the best of my ability review this category.

FOCUS ON THE MODEL NOT THE MODELER

Make sure all of your energy is directed at the model and not the modeler. This allows you to see the structures without your own biases for the person who modeled the structures.

SCORECARD IS THE MEANS, NOT THE ENDS

The goal of applying the Scorecard is to produce a higher quality data model. Make sure all of the effort invested in every Scorecard is directed at improving data model quality and not in the Scorecard itself.

If we can define the end of the assignment as a hand-over rather than a sign-off, the question to the client changes from "do we need to do more to make it right?" to "are you able to take it from here?". Practically and psychologically, it will be easier to a get a "yes" to the second option.
Graeme Simsion, **About Working With Others** (Chapter 13) from **Data Modeling Made Simple**, 2nd Edition

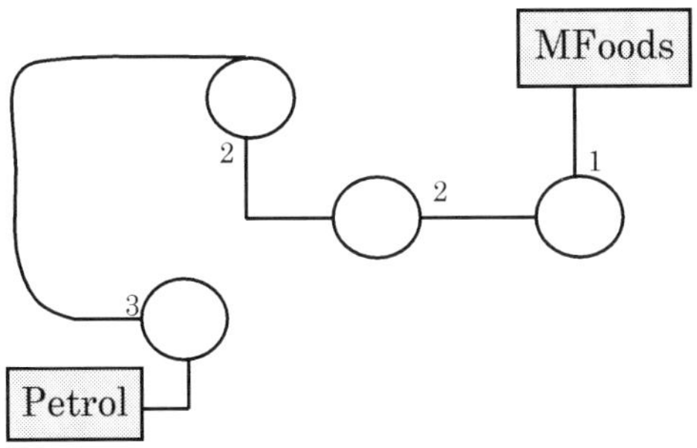

Module 1

Data Model Scorecard® Category #1: Model Type

Category Question: How well do the characteristics of the model support the type of model?

This module is your guide to: Understanding subject area, logical, and physical data models

Category overview

How well do the characteristics of the model support the type of model?

<u>Scope for subject area models</u>

- *Are all subject areas basic and critical?*
- *Are you touching business complexity?*
- *Is it clear what is in and out of scope?*

<u>Content for logical data models</u>

- *Is it application and technology independent?*
- *Fully normalized or fully dimensionalized?*
- *Does it represent a business solution?*

<u>Context for physical data models</u>

- *Has performance, security, and development tool requirements been considered and incorporated?*
- *Does it represent a technical solution?*
- *Has it been "cautiously modified"?*

<u>Relational vs. Dimensional</u>

- *Has dimensional been used only when business users need to see metrics at different levels of granularity?*
- *Has relational been used for all other scenarios?*

Category overview

How well do the characteristics of the model support the type of model?

EXPLANATION

This question ensures that the model type (subject area, logical, or physical – and then either relational or dimensional) of the model satisfies the criteria for this level of detail. In general terms, the subject area model should contain a well-defined scope, the logical data model should be application-independent and represent a business solution, and the physical data model should be tuned for performance, security, and consider development tool constraints (e.g. cube technology, database limitations, etc.). The physical data model should represent a technical solution. A dimensional model is built when there is a need to play with numbers and a relational is built for everything else.

PURPOSE

To meet the expectations of scope, content, or context.

CHALLENGE

The modeler and reviewer need to understand the definition of each model type. Especially tricky is the definition of a logical data model. Should a logical be limited to a relational normalized structure or can it also be dimensional? Also, during crunch times it is possible that one model might be created to represent both logical and physical views for example, and this can complicate the grading of this category. I once heard this type of model referred to as a "physio-logical" model.

SUBJECT AREA

Each subject area must be basic and critical. This means that they are core to the group being modeled, and without this concept the business being modeled would be very different or possibly non-existent. Customer, Product, and Employee are all examples of subject areas.

LOGICAL

If a logical data model is relational, it should be fully normalized. If a logical is dimensional, every hierarchy level should be shown. It needs to be completely independent of software, hardware, and network, representing a business solution.

PHYSICAL

The physical data model represents context. Will the logical data model work with a given set of software, hardware, and network? If there are opportunities to improve performance, space management, and security, for example, the model should be cautiously modified to allow it to work more efficiently.

Category overview

The six different model types

Level	Relational	Dimensional
Subject area (business need or scope)	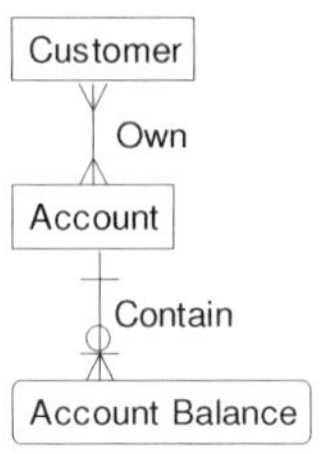	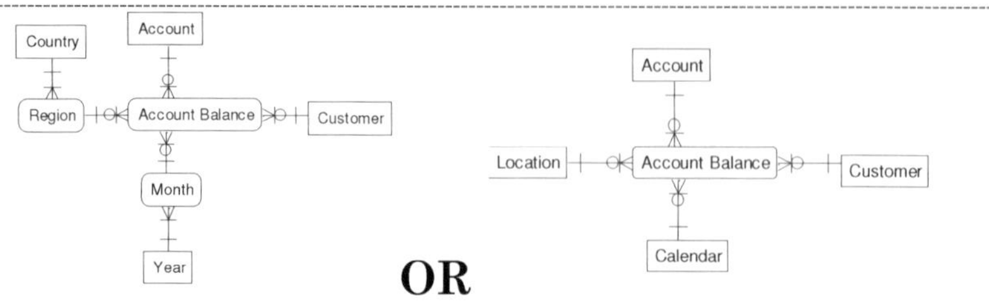
Logical (business solution)	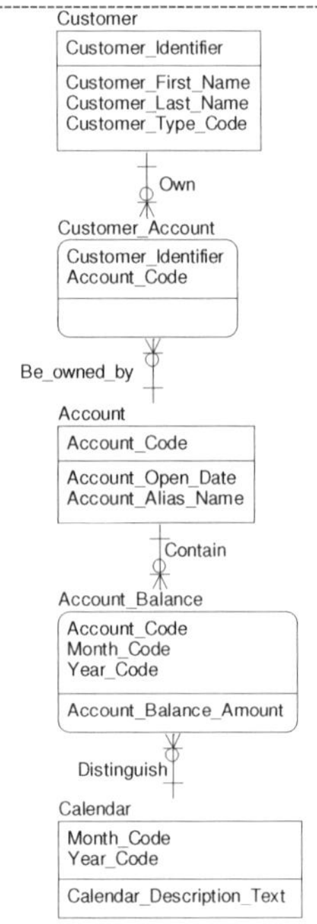	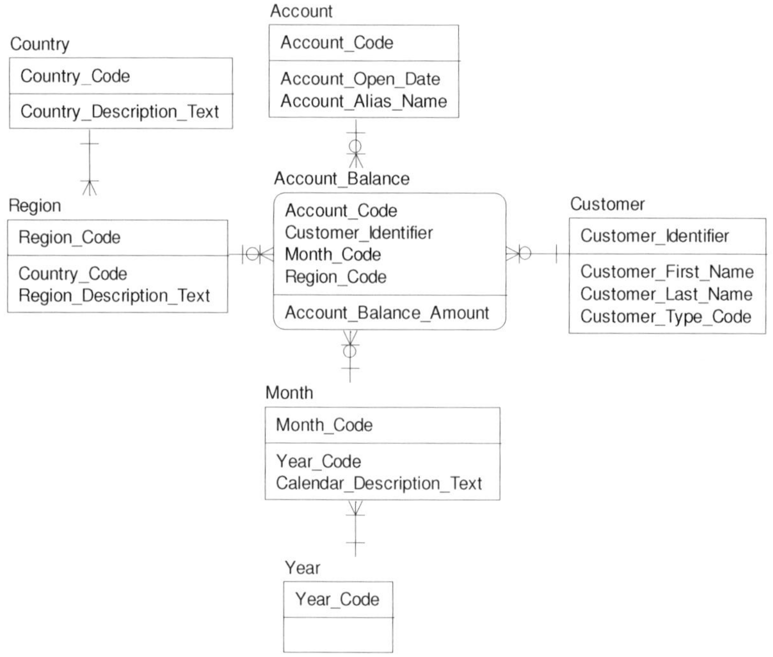
Physical (technical solution)	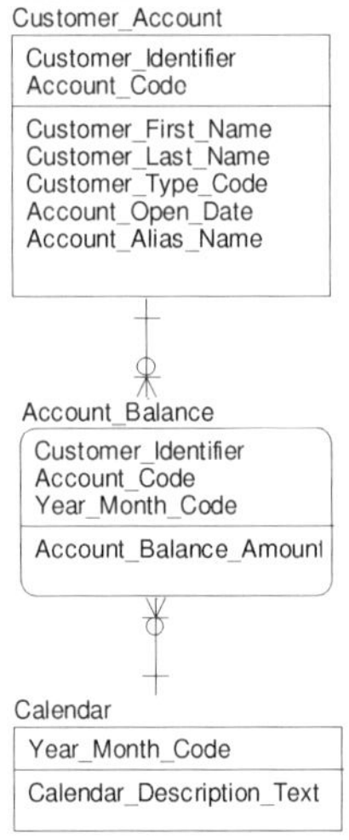	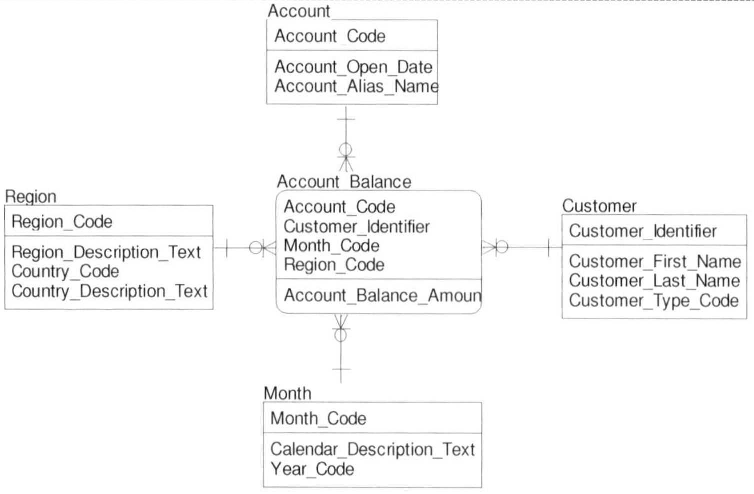

Category overview

The six different model types

BACKGROUND

Relational modeling is modeling business rules and dimensional modeling is modeling navigation paths.

SUBJECT AREA

High level, one inch equals 500 miles. We need to represent a very broad area on a "single piece of paper". Every entity and relationship must represent something basic and critical for that area we are modeling.

LOGICAL

Fully-attributed, yet independent of technology. Every data element is assigned to an entity either based on existence and participation business rules, or by what makes sense to monitor part of the business. This is the business solution.

PHYSICAL

The logical data model compromised for technology. In addition, the software, hardware, and network are important factors to consider in building a model that works. Often the logical structure is changed to improve application performance or storage efficiencies. This is the technical solution.

Level	Relational	Dimensional
Subject area	Broad scope concepts and rules	Broad scope metrics and slicing
Logical	Normalized	All metrics and levels shown
Physical	Denormalized, views, indexes, etc.	Star schema or snowflake

Subject area model

Subject area defined

A subject area is a concept that is both basic and critical to your audience.

Customer Product Employee Account	Real Estate Module Marketing Dept An index on Customer Last Name	Party Event Telephone # Lot # Calendar

Subject area model

Subject area defined

WHAT IS A SUBJECT AREA?

A subject area is a concept that is both basic and critical to your audience. "Basic" meaning that this term is probably mentioned many times a day in normal conversation. "Critical" meaning that the business would be non-existent or completely different without this concept. Some of the subject areas are easy to identify and include concepts that cross all businesses such as consumer, customer, employee, and product. Each of these subject areas will be shown in much more detail at the logical and physical phases of design. For example, the consumer area can be viewed as the logical entities Consumer, Consumer Association, Consumer Demographics, Consumer Type, and so on.

Subject areas in addition are audience-specific meaning that what is considered a subject area is sometimes dependent on the specific department, company, or industry. For example, what industry would phone number be considered a subject area? Also notice that at times a subject area might be more granular depending on the context. For example, a marketing department might consider Consumer Classification to be a subject area.

WHAT IS NOT A SUBJECT AREA?

Identifying the subject areas is not an easy activity. At the logical level we can lean on normalization to ensure we are at the right level of detail. At the physical level we know if as much as possible of the LDM is retained, <u>and</u> the database and reporting tool experts in your organization are satisfied with the would-be performance and other physical factors, you are at the right level. At a subject area level however, because a subject area is something that is basic and critical to a given audience, what is a subject area for marketing may not be a subject area for logistics and therefore it can be difficult to identify the right level of detail.

A good rule of thumb is to ask yourself whether the audience for this model would include this concept as one of the top 20 or 50 or 200 concepts in their business. This will rule out possibly those concepts that are too generic for a given audience, such as Party or Event. It will also rule out the physical constructs such as indexes, partitioning, and materialized views.

In addition, make sure subject areas are not departments or application modules. Subject areas such as Information Systems or Accounting are not modeling concepts but rather organization boundaries. In addition, software concepts such as SAP's modules of Manufacturing and Real Estate also are not subject areas.

Subject area model

Subject area model defined

A subject area model is a set of symbols and text that represents key concepts and the rules binding these key concepts for a defined business or application scope and for a particular audience. Aliases include CDM, subject model, business model.

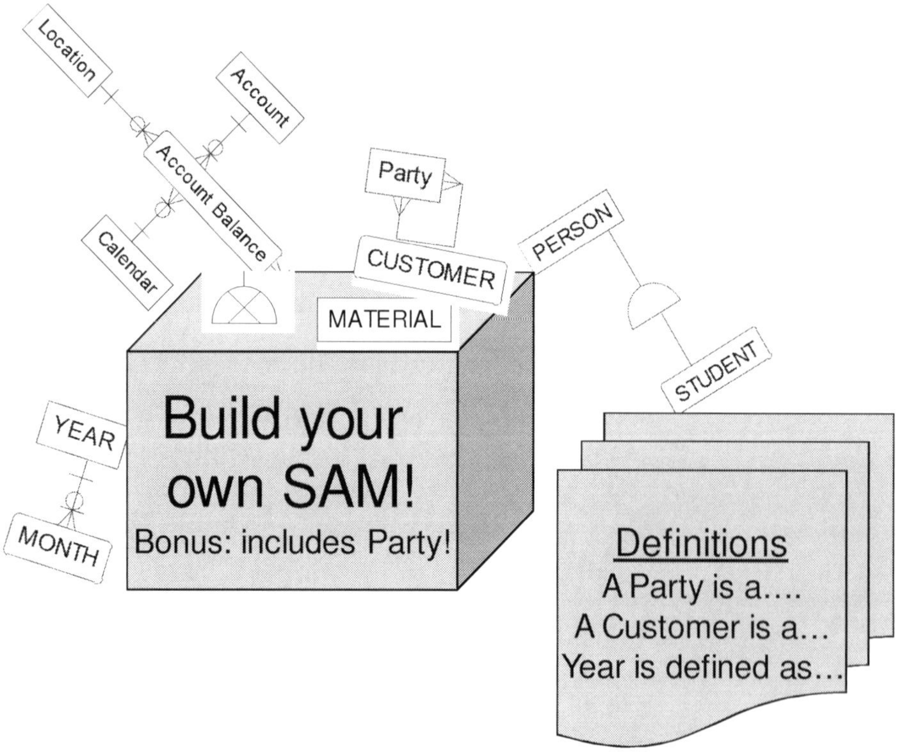

Subject area model

Subject area model defined

WHAT IS A SUBJECT AREA MODEL?

A subject area model is a set of symbols and text that represents key concepts and the rules binding these key concepts for a defined business or application scope and for a particular audience.

COMPONENTS OF A SUBJECT AREA MODEL

The subject area model follows a similar syntax that we have at the logical and physical data model levels:

- **Entity**: The concepts that are basic and critical to the business or application.
- **Relationship**: The business or application rules binding these concepts. The subject area model often includes subtyping structures.
- **Cardinality**: The participation rules defined on each relationship. Subject area models can contain many-to-many relationships (unlike logical and physical data models).
- **Definition**: A clear, correct, and complete explanation of the subject area. I believe that the definition is actually the most important component of a subject area model. Everyone can nod their heads and agree that a 'Customer' is basic and critical, but how many organizations do you know that can nod their heads on a single precise definition of Customer!

SUBJECT AREA MODEL ALIASES

The Subject Area Model sometimes goes by different names:

- **Conceptual Data Model (CDM).** I prefer not to use CDM for two reasons: Conceptual modeling is used to represent all of the modeling deliverables at a program level. This includes the subject area model but also includes other types of models such as a business question list. Also, the word 'Conceptual' seems like something you can't touch which smells like 'ivory tower' 'pie in the sky' and therefore is a waste of time to build.
- **Subject model.** I am sometimes torn between using subject area model and subject model. I see 'subject' however, being broader and more encompassing, such as Marketing or Manufacturing. A 'subject' includes 'subject areas'. Also subject area model gives us the neat acronym 'SAM'.
- **Business model.** I like this term very much, but sometimes a subject area model can legitimately represent an application, such as a subject area model of SAP/R3.

Subject area model

Importance of subject area modeling

I never knew a raw material and an ingredient were different concepts!

Why doesn't SAP provide a subject area model of their whole R3 system?

I started a week ago and this data warehouse is soooo complex!

What is the difference between a Product and an Offering?

This is amazing!!!

Subject area model

Importance of subject area modeling

PROVIDES BROAD UNDERSTANDING

The subject area model ties subject areas together, and is able to visually show the dependencies and rules between these subject areas. Because we are at the subject area level, it becomes easier to cover very broad areas. We can model entire departments or organizations, external concepts such as regulatory agencies or competitors, future architectures, etc.

DEFINES SCOPE AND DIRECTION

By visually showing subject areas and their business rules, we can more easily identify a subset of the model to analyze. For example, we can model the entire logistics department, and then scope out of this a particular logistics application that we would like to build.

OFFERS PROACTIVE ANALYSIS

By developing a subject area level understanding of the application, there is a strong chance we will be able to identify important issues or concerns that can save substantial time and money later on. Topics where prevention can occur include history requirements, functionality limitations, sourcing issues, etc.

"LOW HANGING FRUIT"

The subject area model takes a relatively minimal amount of time to build, and yet offers very large payoff in terms of business understanding and creating a solid foundation for design.

BUILDS RAPPORT BETWEEN IT AND BUSINESS

Building a subject area model together is a great way to improve relationships between business and IT. On one occasion, I and a key business user sketched out a Contact Data Mart subject area model which proved to build not just business understanding but also a strong relationship with this key user.

ACTUAL QUOTES

The facing page contains actual quotes from experiences with subject area models.

Subject area model

Variations of subject area models

		Relational	Dimensional
BSAM	Business Subject Area Model	✓	
ASAM	Application Subject Area Model	✓	✓
CSAM	Comparison Subject Area Model	✓	✓

BSAM

- Manufacturing
- Public utility
- Sales

ASAM

- Order Process System
- SAP Order Entry
- Sales Data Mart

CSAM

- SAP Order Entry Customization
- Order Entry Legacy vs. SAP
- Proposed Sales Data Mart within existing DW

Subject area model

Variations of subject area models

3 LEVELS

There are three types of subject area models, and I've coined acronyms for them that are easy to remember: the Business Subject Area Model (BSAM), the Application Subject Area Model (ASAM), and the Comparison Subject Area Model (CSAM). Each of these models serves a different purpose and often more than one type of model needs to be created. All three can be built using relational techniques, and the ASAM and CSAM can also be built dimensionally if the application is a data mart which allows the business to manipulate numbers.

BUSINESS SUBJECT AREA MODEL (BSAM)

The BSAM is a subject area model of a defined portion of the business. The scope can be limited to a department or function such as manufacturing or sales. It can be as broad as the entire enterprise or industry. Enterprise models tend to include external concepts such as government agencies, competitors, and suppliers. The BSAM focuses on a business area, not a particular application.

APPLICATION SUBJECT AREA MODEL (ASAM)

The ASAM is a subject area model of a defined portion of a particular application. The ASAM can be for either a proposed or existing application. Many BSAMs are the first step in large development efforts (first understand the business before you understand the application), and therefore the BSAM is usually the starting point for the ASAM. As an example, after creating the BSAM of the human resources department, we can now scope out of this an ASAM for an application tracking employee promotions.

COMPARISON SUBJECT AREA MODEL (CSAM)

The CSAM is a subject area model that shows the relationships between two or more ASAMs. It is used primarily for impact analysis and issue resolution. CSAMs build on two or more ASAMs, in which one or more ASAMs represent an existing application environment and (optionally) one or more ASAMs represent proposed changes to an environment. These are the most complicated of the three models to create, yet also provide a very large "wow" factor.

Subject area model

Business Subject Area Model (BSAM)

As a prerequisite to building the university's enterprise data warehouse, this BSAM was built to agree collectively on the terms and business rules, and then they could use this model as a scoping tool for deciding on which data mart to build first. Colors were used to identify the strategic source system for each subject area (e.g. red entities are sourced from PeopleSoft).

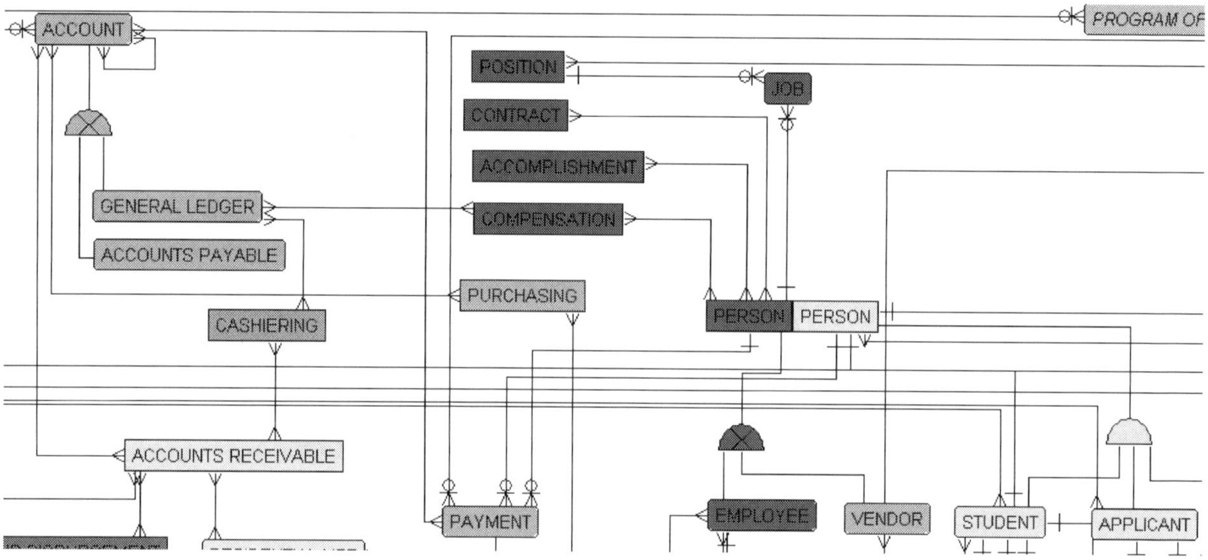

One who is enrolled or attends classes at a school, college, or university. A person engaged in study; one who is devoted to learning; a learner; a pupil; a scholar; especially, one who attends a school, or who seeks knowledge from professional teachers or from books; as, the students of an academy, a college, or a university; a medical student.

Subject area model

Business Subject Area Model (BSAM)

BACKGROUND

The BSAM is a subject area model of a section of the business. The section could be as narrow as a department or part of a department, or as broad as the entire organization, or even the entire industry including external concepts such as government agencies, competitors, and suppliers. The BSAM focuses on a business area, and not a particular application.

The BSAM is the most frequently built type of subject area model. Many times when we say we are creating a subject area model, we mean the BSAM. Before embarking on any large development effort, we first need to understand the business. If an organization needs a new claims-processing system, it needs to have a common understanding of claims and related subject areas. The BSAM can be created simply to understand a business area, or as a beginning to a large development effort, such as introducing third-party software into your organization.

WHEN TO BUILD A BSAM

A BSAM is most useful for any combination of the following situations:

- **Understanding a business area.** The most popular usage of the BSAM is to gain understanding into an area of the business. It could be the way the business works today or the way the business would like to work at some time in the future.
- **Designing an enterprise model.** An enterprise data model must initially be designed at the subject area level. Many times I recommend not getting any more detailed than the subject area level, due to the complexities and maintenance issues with hundreds of entities and thousands of data elements.
- **Starting a new development effort.** The BSAM is a very good place to start capturing the subject areas and business rules for a new application. All future subject area and logical data models are based on this initial model.

EXAMPLE

The model on the facing page is a university BSAM. It was built as a prerequisite to building the university's enterprise data warehouse. First business and IT needed to agree collectively on the terms and business rules (i.e. this model), and then they could use this model as a scooping tool for deciding on which data mart to build first in their data warehouse. Colors were used to identify the strategic source system for each subject area (e.g. red entities are sourced from PeopleSoft).

Subject area model

Application Subject Area Model (ASAM)

Relational ASAM

This Classifications SAP/R3 ASAM was built to explain this complex area to a broad audience, and for determining high level work effort for new classifications requirements.

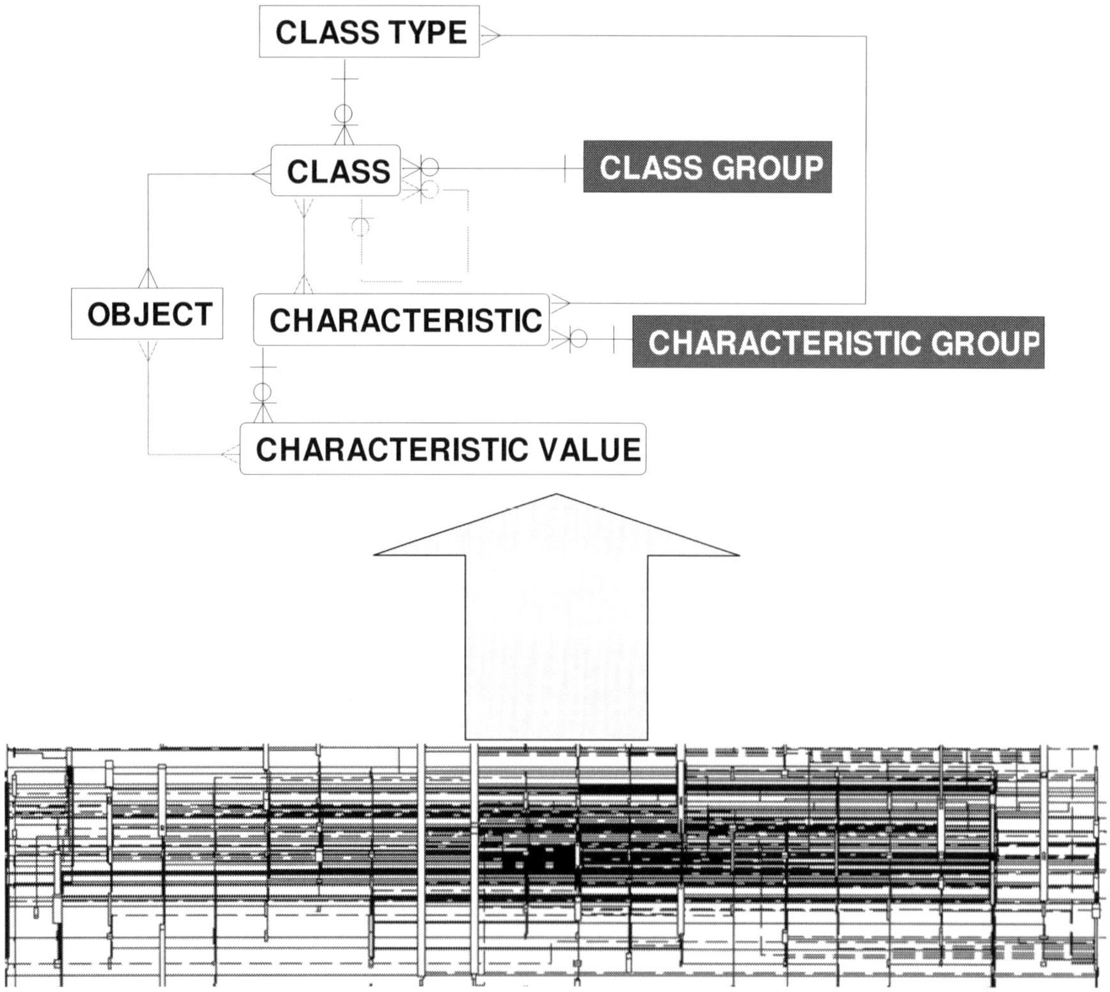

Subject area model

Application Subject Area Model (ASAM)

BACKGROUND

The ASAM is a data model containing the subject areas and business rules for a particular application. It can be a subset of the BSAM. As an example, after creating the BSAM of the human resources department, we can now scope out of this subject area our human resources application.

We build two types of applications, and therefore two types of ASAMs: relational and dimensional. Dimensional ASAMs are for data marts that focus on metric facts. Metric facts are numbers that monitor some aspect of the business. Relational ASAMs are for everything else. This includes operational systems, ERP systems, staging areas, data warehouses, operational data stores, and relational data marts.

WHEN TO BUILD AN ASAM

A BSAM is most useful for any combination of the following situations:

- **Understanding an application.** If you need to understand a current or proposed application, an ASAM is a great communication tool. An application might describe concepts using different terminology and enforcing different rules than the actual business area, and therefore this terminology and set of rules needs to be shown on the ASAM.
- **Starting a new development effort.** The ASAM should be completed ideally prior to logical design. This way terminology, rules, and definitions can be agreed upon prior to detailed project analysis. It will save time, money, and unpleasant surprises further down in the software lifecycle.

RELATIONAL EXAMPLE

The relational example on the facing page is an ASAM created from the classifications subject area in SAP/R3. In an effort to understand how SAP treats classifications (terminology, rules, and definitions), I created this model from studying screens, help files, and a large quantity of the underlying 350+ database tables. This model was used for education purposes as well as to gauge effort in making customizations and bespokes to the application.

Subject area model

Application Subject Area Model (ASAM)

Dimensional ASAM

This ASAM was built to confirm that IT correctly understood the business' high level reporting requirements for an Accessorial data mart.

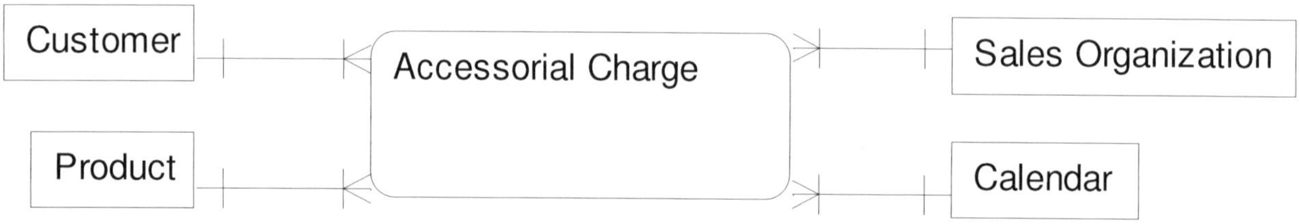

Subject area model

Application Subject Area Model (ASAM)

DIMENSIONAL EXAMPLE

The dimensional example on the facing page is an ASAM created based on accessorial charges within a manufacturing company. 'Accessorial' is defined as *A supplemental activity or material, outside normal handling and storage, that is billable in accordance with the clients' contract.* This data mart was used to answer questions such as "How many avoidable charges for a given time period were we charged by a given customer?"

Subject area model

Comparison Subject Area Model (CSAM)

This CSAM was built to explain how a proposed data mart would impact an existing data warehouse.

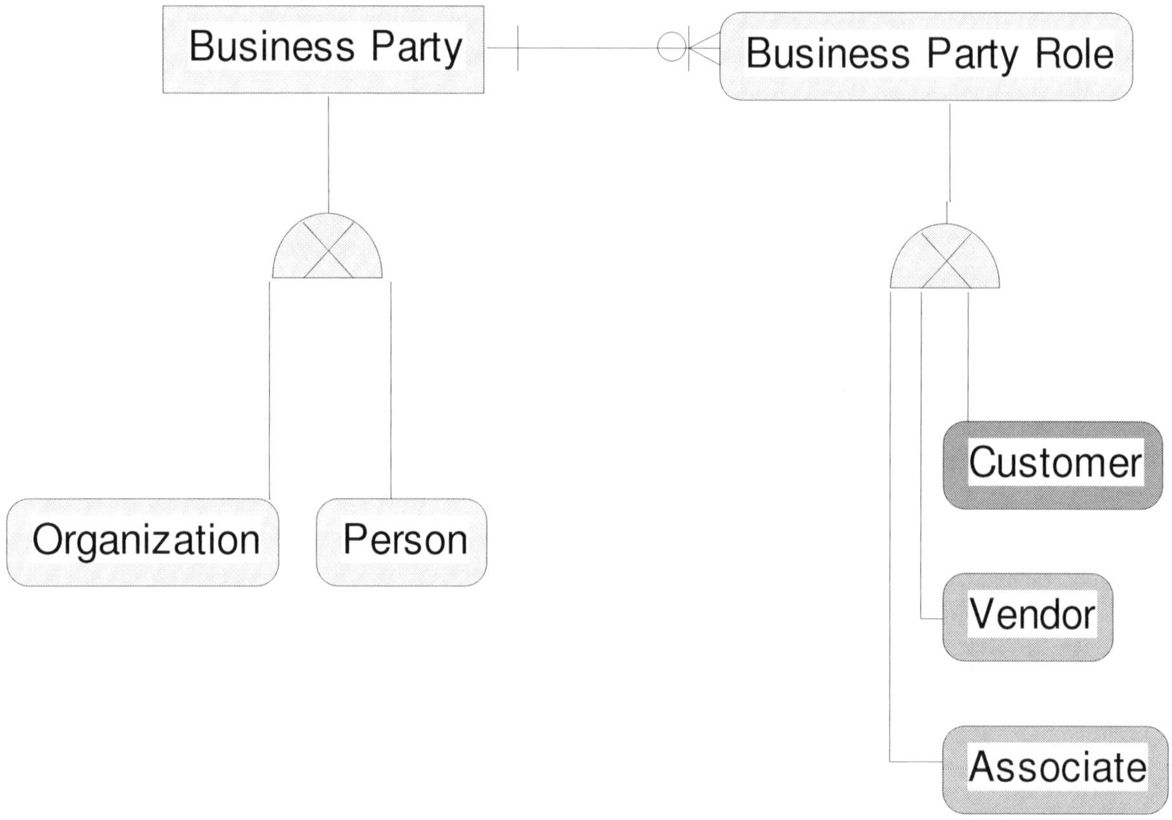

Subject area model

Comparison Subject Area Model (CSAM)

BACKGROUND

The CSAM is a data model comparing two or more ASAMs to see whether there are gaps or redundancies. It requires the most effort to build, but of the three types of subject area models it can provide the most benefits. It requires the most effort because there is more than one viewpoint to represent on a model. Usually more than one viewpoint leads to more than one interpretation of a subject area or rules. It takes time to identify these differences and resolve, or, at a minimum, document them.

WHEN TO BUILD A CSAM

- **Proposed data mart within current data warehouse architecture.** The CSAM will show how the new data mart requirements fit into what currently exists within the data warehouse.
- **Proposed new functionality to an existing operational or data mart application.** The CSAM will highlight the new functionality and show how it fits in with current functionality.
- **Replacing an application.** The CSAM can show the overlap at a subject area level when you are replacing an existing application with a new application. This is the same technique as replacing existing functionality, except we are doing this on a larger scale.
- **Customization to packaged software.** More and more we will be implementing packaged software, the most popular being Enterprise Resource Planning (ERP) and Customer Resource Management (CRM) applications. These expensive and very encompassing pieces of software need to be analyzed to see how they fit into the current environment. The CSAM will allow management to see the impact and overlap caused by introducing packaged software, hopefully before investing lots of money.

RELATIONAL EXAMPLE

The CSAM on the facing page shows how a proposed data mart would impact an existing data warehouse. Colors are used to indicate overlap level. Green is good, meaning that concepts the new data mart needs are already represented in the data warehouse. Red is bad, meaning the data mart needs information not yet present (or conflict with) information in the warehouse. Shades of yellow were used to indicate some level of overlap between mart and warehouse. This model was a large success for a project because it raised a key issue on Customer very early on in the project, and therefore saved substantial rework later on.

Subject area model

3 approaches to building a subject area model

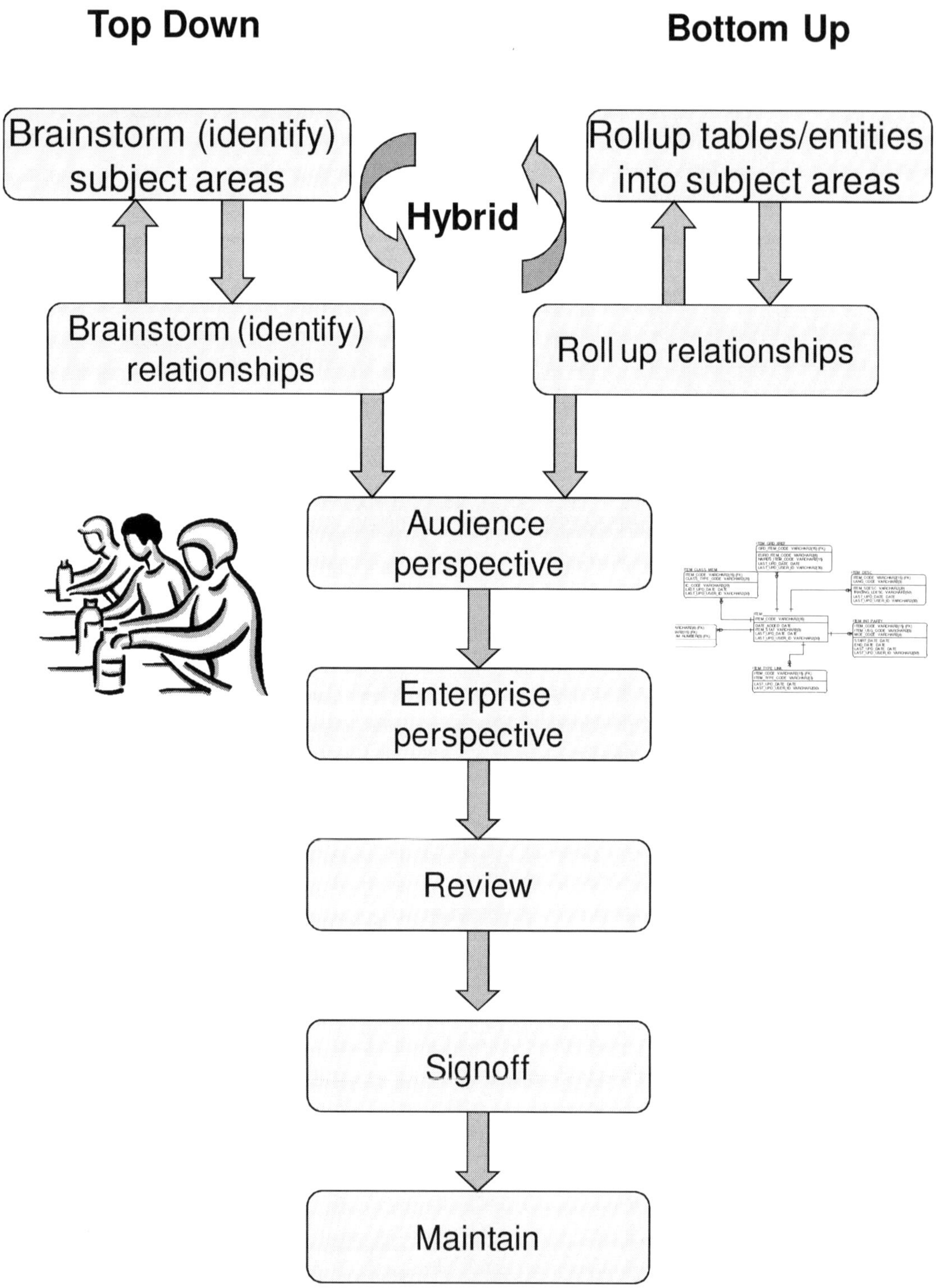

Subject area model

3 approaches to building a subject area model

BACKGROUND

There are three approaches to building a subject area model, and the approach taken depends on the available resources and the purpose of the model. If there are minimal business resources available and ample systems documentation, and the purpose of the model is to understand an existing application, a bottom-up approach is ideal. If a new system is being built from scratch and there are business experts eager to participate in the project, a top-down approach would be ideal. If a new system is being planned, or an upgrade to an existing system and business expertise is available and required, a hybrid approach is ideal.

BRAINSTORMING

In top-down and hybrid approaches, standard brainstorming techniques work quite well. I have found though, it is good to have something to start with, such as a generic model or a handful of subject areas you know will be on the list, such as Customer and Product. Remember, definitions are included here as well!

ROLLING UP

In bottom-up and hybrid approaches, we perform "data archeology" by examining sometimes hundreds of pages of documents and thousands of tables, and rolling them up into subject areas.

AUDIENCE PERSPECTIVE

This model needs to match the terminology of the business people involved in creating the model. Once they see their world in the boxes and lines, you can move on to the enterprise perspective.

ENTERPRISE PERSPECTIVE

Compare to an enterprise data model or common business knowledge or industry terms to ensure an enterprise perspective.

REVIEW

Make sure the model is reviewed for data modeling best practices as well as that it meets the requirements. If possible, apply the Data Model Scorecard®.

SIGNOFF

Easier said than done! Critical to the credibility of the model.

MAINTAIN

SAMs don't require the same frequency of maintenance as logical and physical, yet it still needs to be maintained to be valuable.

Subject area model

Subject area model challenges

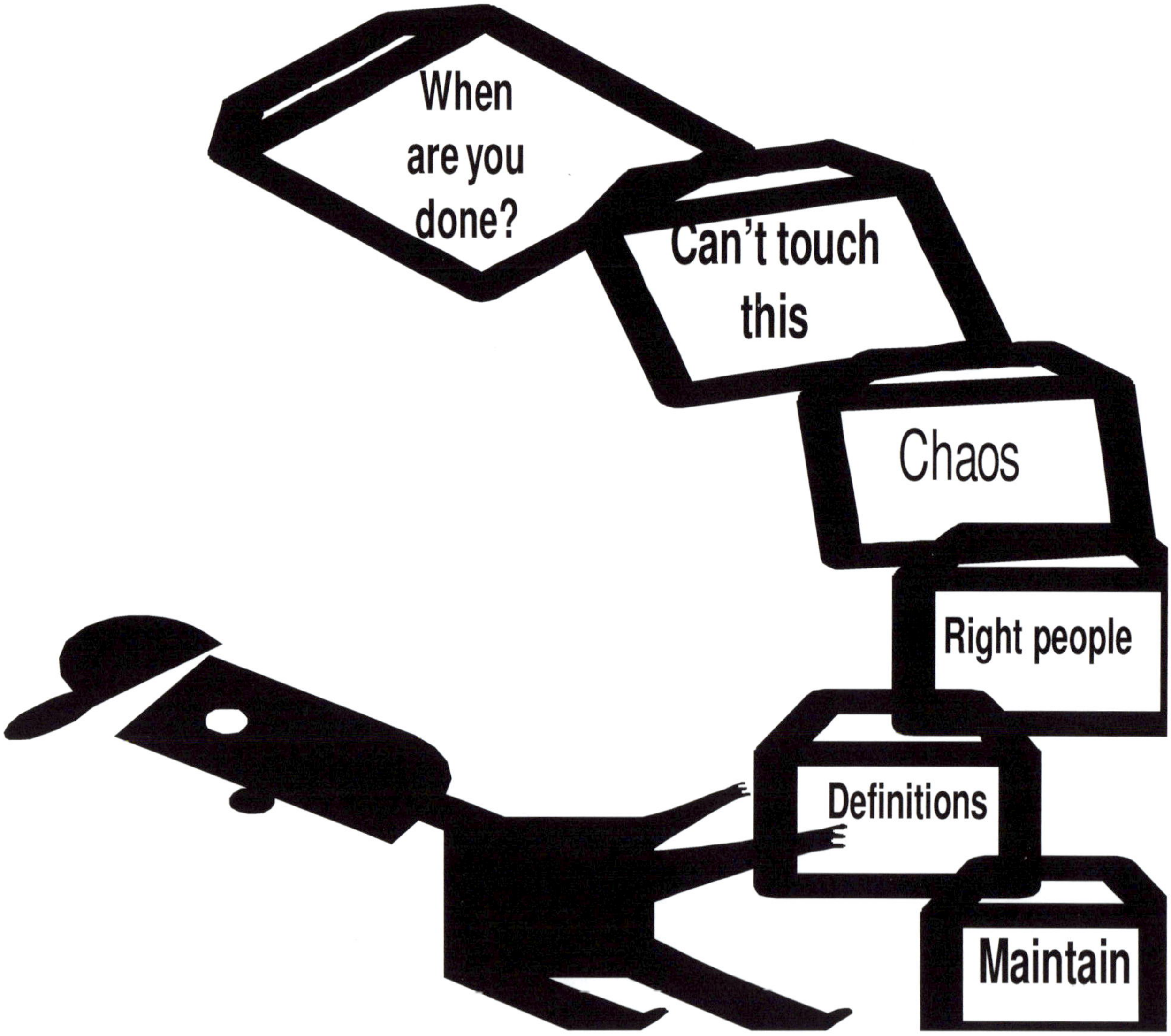

Subject area model

Subject area model challenges

WHEN ARE YOU DONE?

When you are building a database, you know you are done when the tables are built. But what about a subject area model? Because the level of detail on this model can vary, the team needs to know when to stop to avoid the model becoming too detailed or too nebulous (e.g. "Everything is a Thing"). Analysis/paralysis can stop the model in its tracks.

CAN'T TOUCH THIS!

The subject area model is not real like a physical data model or set of database tables are real. It is often not thought of as a necessity in developing a system. As long as there are database tables the system could work. Therefore in many cases this model is difficult to justify.

CHAOS

In many cases, subject area models are introduced when there is realization that things are totally out of control. I worked in one large company where a global SAP rollout continues to produce surprises "go live" weekend when different teams were unknowingly updating the same reports and structures. The management team knew they needed some type of big picture of SAP and the rollout environment. When subject area models become a reactive technique such as this, there is always a lot of tension and politics even before the first subject area is identified. Not the friendliest modeling environment!

RIGHT PEOPLE

Just like any project, it is important to have the right people involved. "Right people" in this context are those people who have the experience and enthusiasm to contribute to the models. Although at times people who don't have the experience (or the enthusiasm) will be the most important people you need to have in the room either because of perceived credibility to the project, or for political or budgeting reasons.

DEFINITIONS

Definitions can be extremely difficult to write at the subject area level. Subject area definitions typically cross functions and you will frequently run into situations where experts from different departments see the same terms differently.

MAINTAIN

It takes a minimal amount of effort to maintain the domain and subject area models, but they still need to be maintained. Even a short lapse of time where the models are forgotten can negate their usefulness.

Logical data model

The logical data model is the business solution

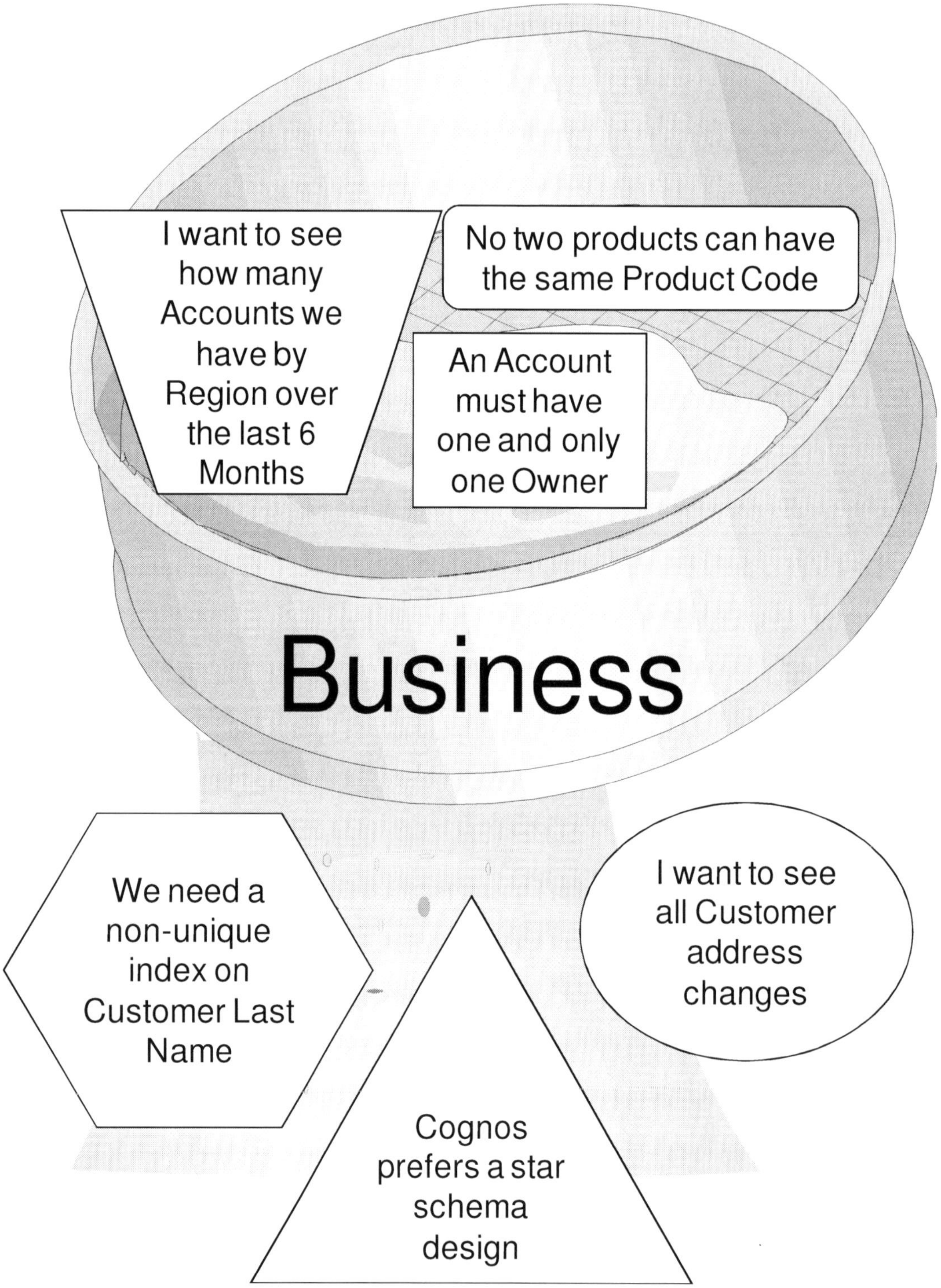

Logical data model

The logical data model is the business solution

DEFINITION

A logical data model (LDM) represents a detailed *business* solution. Business solution refers to focusing on solving a problem by understanding the characteristics of the data. The LDM is independent of technology. This means in capturing the business solution, we ignore all database and reporting software and hardware limitations. A logical data model of the order processing function for example, would look the same regardless of whether the application that is eventually built is built using IBM punch cards or Teradata!

RELATIONAL AND DIMENSIONAL

There are two types of logical data models: relational and dimensional. A logical relational model is a business solution of the data and rules of the *execution* of a business process. A logical dimensional data model is a business solution of the data and rules of the *evaluation* of a business process. Evaluation meaning the business is being monitored through metrics, such as Gross Sales Amount and Number of Customers.

WHAT IS LOGICAL?

Here are examples of what would be captured on an LDM:

- An Account must have one and only one Owner. (relational)
- I want to see how many Accounts we have by Region over the last 6 Months. (dimensional)
- No two products can have the same Product Code. (relational)
- I want to see Total Revenue by Customer, Product, and Region this Quarter as compared to last Quarter. (dimensional)

WHAT IS NOT LOGICAL?

Here are examples of what would <u>not</u> be captured on an LDM:

- We need a non-unique index on Customer Last Name, as this column will be retrieved often.
- Cognos prefers a star schema design so let's flatten each dimension into a single table.
- Microsoft Access will not be able to manage our Customer table so let's vertically partition contact details.
- I want to see all Customer address changes.

Logical data model

Logical relational data model

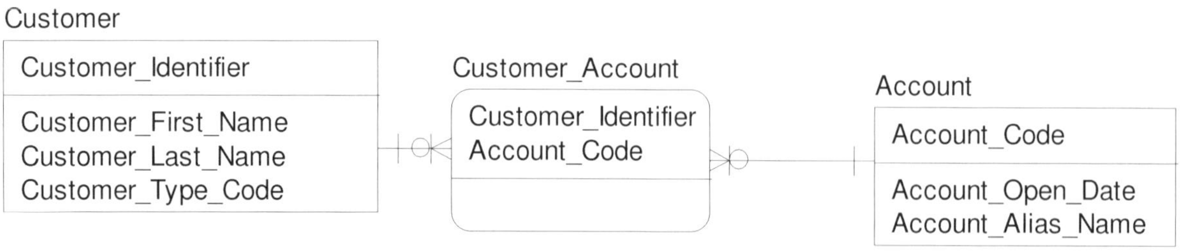

Logical data model

Logical relational data model

BACKGROUND

A logical relational model captures the business rules behind one or more business processes. This is the type of modeling that first came into being back in 1967 when Codd published his landmark paper distinguishing data from process. Relational models are heavily connected with mathematics. Set theory is the primary technique for building a logical relational data model. There are different levels of strictness within set theory, and each level represents another level of normalization, which will be discussed shortly.

A logical relational data model is a representation of the rules that govern the way in which a business process works. For example, a logical data model of claims processing would capture the data elements that are mandatory on an insurance claim and the data rules on who can file claims (for example, a policyholder can file zero, one, or many claims).

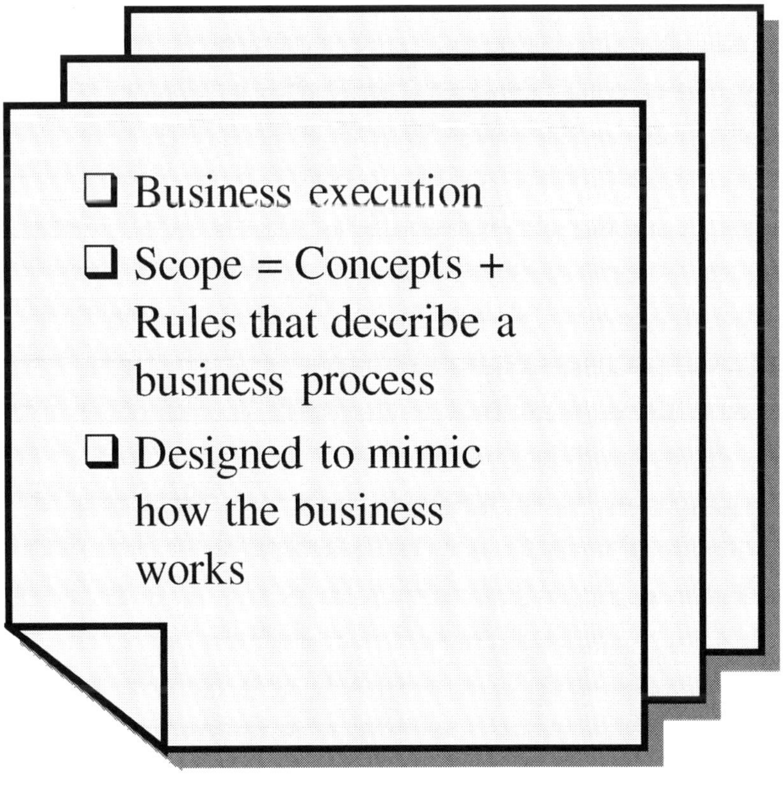

Logical data model

Logical dimensional data model

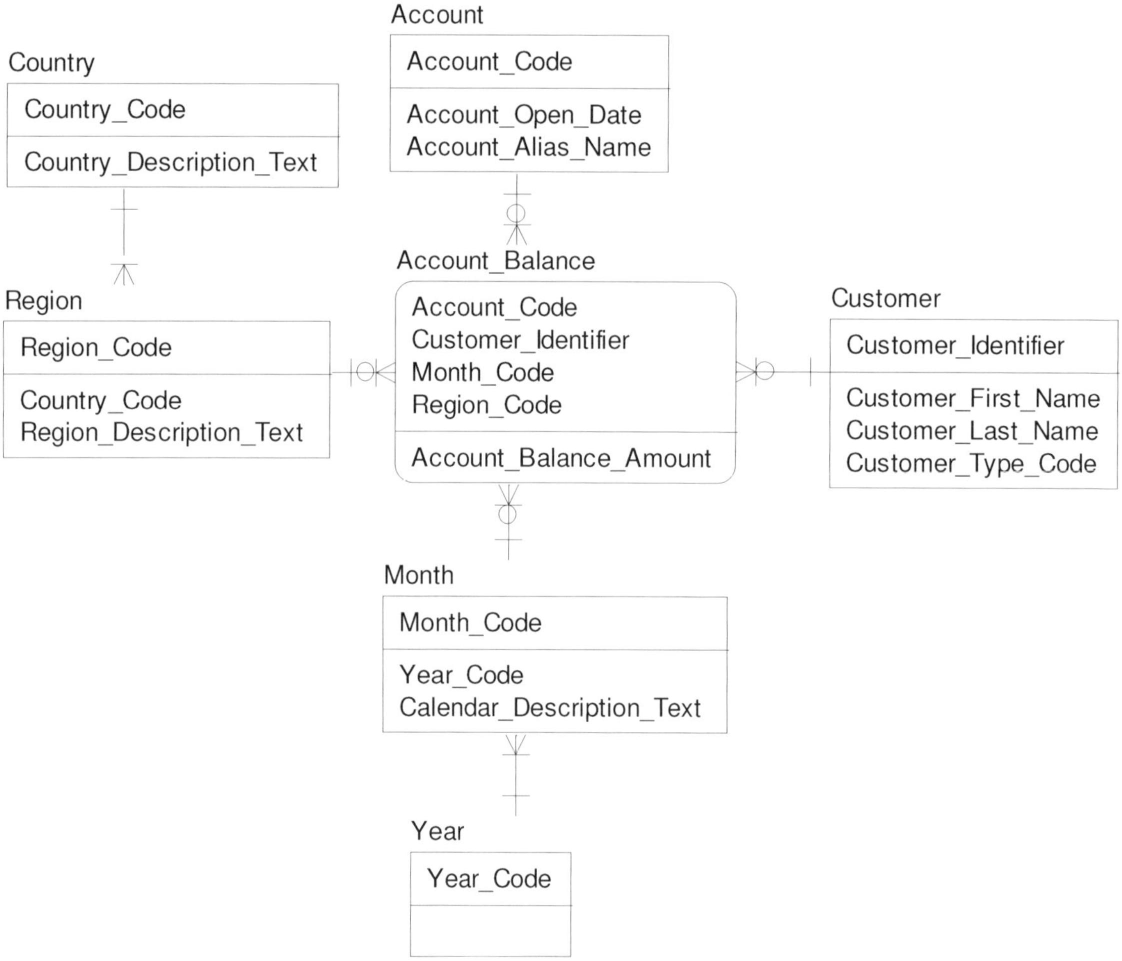

Logical data model

Logical dimensional data model

BACKGROUND

A logical dimensional data model is a business solution of the data and rules of the *evaluation* of a business process. Evaluation meaning the business is being monitored through metrics, such as Gross Sales Amount and Number of Customers.

A dimensional model is a data model whose only purpose is to allow efficient and user-friendly filtering, sorting, and summing of measures. The relationships on a dimensional model represent navigation paths instead of business rules as with the relational model. The scope of a dimensional model is a collection of related measures plus context that together address some business concern.

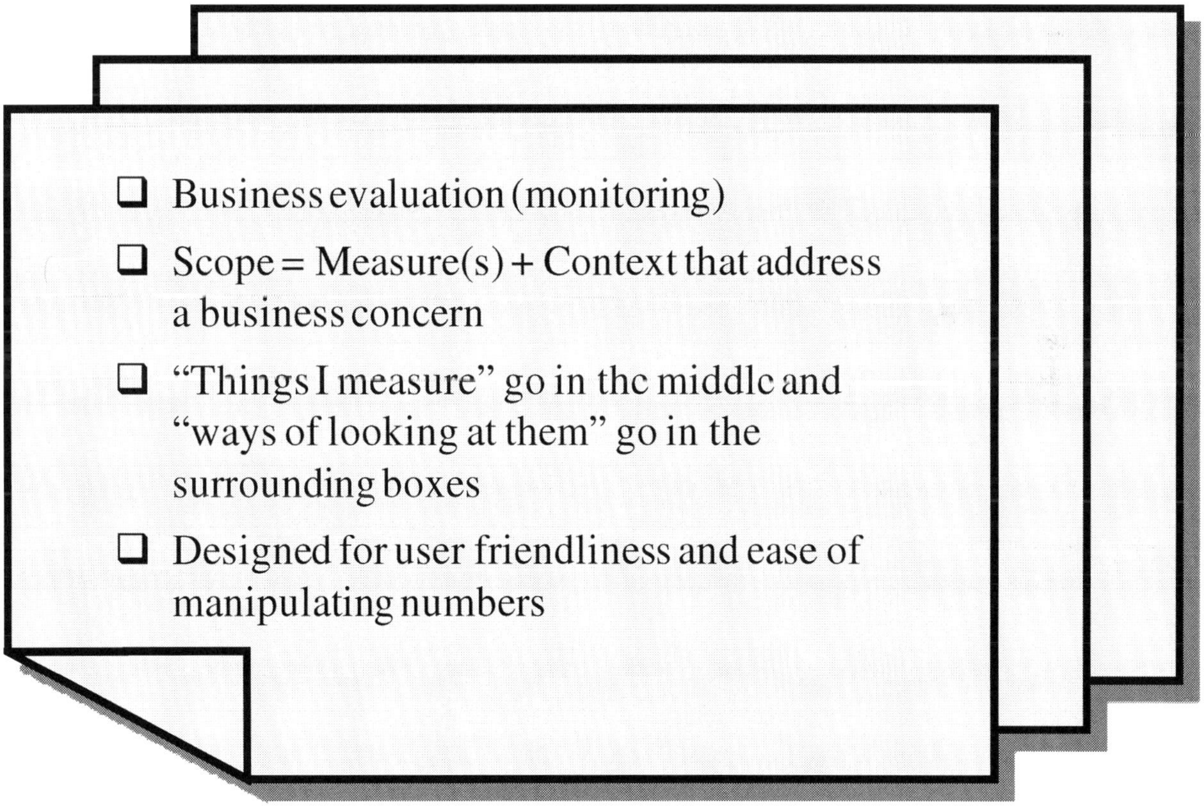

Logical data model

Dimensional model components

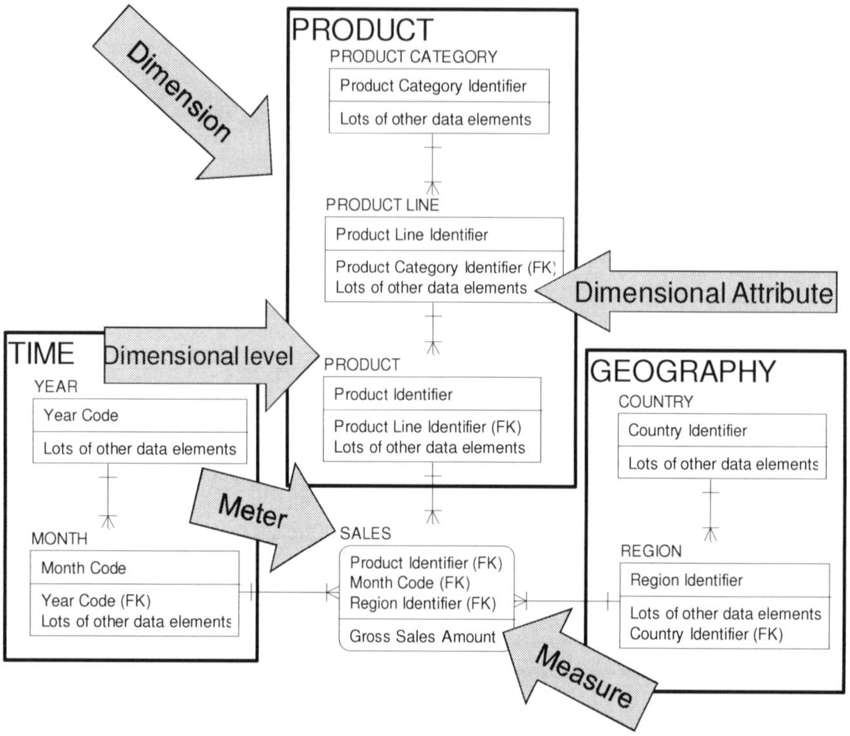

Requirements Statement	Measure(s)	Grain
I want to see total revenue by period, product, and region.		
Show me return amounts by order.		
What are gross sales of product brand for April?		
I need the percent change in member growth by demographics and month over the last five years.		
Get me the number of toys sold by child age appropriateness range, store number, and day of week.		

Logical data model

Dimensional model components

MEASURE

A measure is a data element that a set of business users need to 'see', and which can also be mathematically manipulated. Gross Sales Amount is an example of a measure.

METER

A meter is an entity containing a related set of measures. It is not a person, place, event, or thing, as we would expect on the relational model. Instead, it is a bucket of common measures. Common measures as a group address a business concern, such as Profitability, Employee Satisfaction, and Sales. The meter on the facing page is *Sales*. The meter is so important to the dimensional model that often the name of the meter is the name of the application.

DIMENSION

Things that get measured go in the middle and ways of looking at these things go in the surrounding boxes which are called dimensions. All the different ways of filtering, sorting, and summing measures are structured within dimensions. Dimensions are subjects whose only purpose is to add meaning to the measures. Dimensions are either hierarchies or lookups. *Gross sales amount* can be retrieved with any combination of month, product or region. Dimensions do not necessarily have to be hierarchies. Also, they usually appear in requirements statements after words such as 'by', 'for', and 'of'. If concepts are only related to each other through an event or transaction, then these concepts belong to separate dimensions.

DIMENSIONAL LEVEL

A dimensional level is one level within the hierarchy of a dimension, such as Country within the Geography dimension. Dimensional levels are created to allow easy drill up and down, and not built based on how the business works.

DIMENSIONAL ATTRIBUTE

The properties within a dimension, such as Country Code in the Country level of the Geography dimension. Note that sometimes numeric data elements can be dimensional attributes.

GRAIN

The grain is the meter's level of detail. It should be capable of answering all of the business questions within the scope of the dimensional model. It is generally a good practice to define the measures and grain as early as possible in the requirements process. The grain in this example is Month, Product, and Region.

Logical data model

Dimensional models are built for navigation

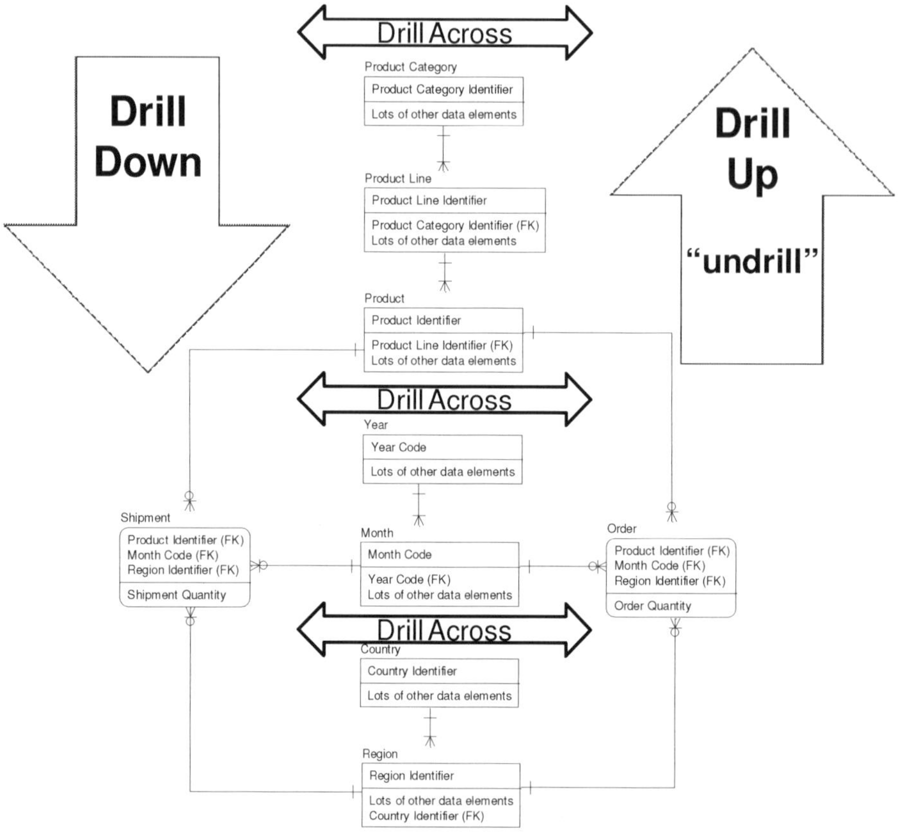

Requirements Statement	Drill Up, Drill Down, or Drill Across?
I want to see total revenue by period, product, and region. Then by country and year.	
What are gross sales of product brand for month? If I see a surprisingly low number I want to see gross sales by day.	
I need to see employee satisfaction by period, line of business and region. There is also a separate reporting initiative on employee productivity. I will eventually need to analyze the relationships between satisfaction and productivity.	

Logical data model

Dimensional models are built for navigation

DRILLING

Drilling is the process of changing the context of the measures. Changing the context means varying the dimensions that are used to view to measures, such as viewing the measures at a year level instead of at a month level, or at a region level instead of at a country level.

DRILLING DOWN

Drill down is when the context for the measure goes from higher level to lower level. For example, needing to see the measures at a month level and then at a day level.

DRILLING UP

Drill up is when the context for the measure goes from lower level to higher level. For example, needing to see the measures at a day level and then at a month level.

DRILLING ACROSS

Drill across is when there is a need to view measures from different dimensional models. The dimensions need to be built consistently to allow this type of analysis. Sometimes it is tempting to built relationships between meters or combine two or more meters into one. Be careful though – it is not worth the risk of erroneous results from measures that have no value for a given level of detail. For example, if there are order quantities yet no shipment quantities on a given day, what value would you put for shipment quantities? Zeros can cause confusion and the wrong results.

Logical data model

Measures monitor business processes

Transaction

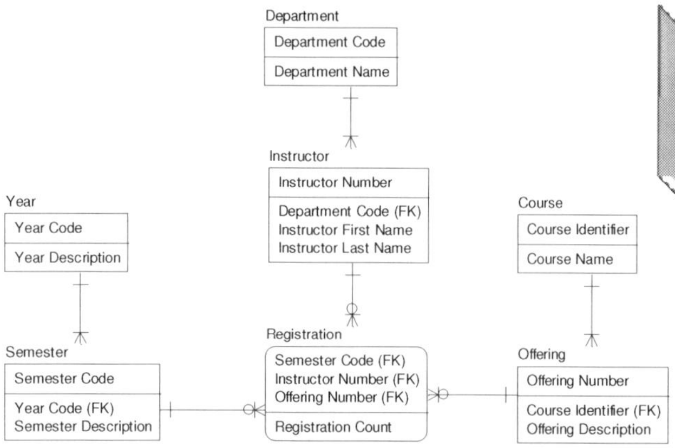

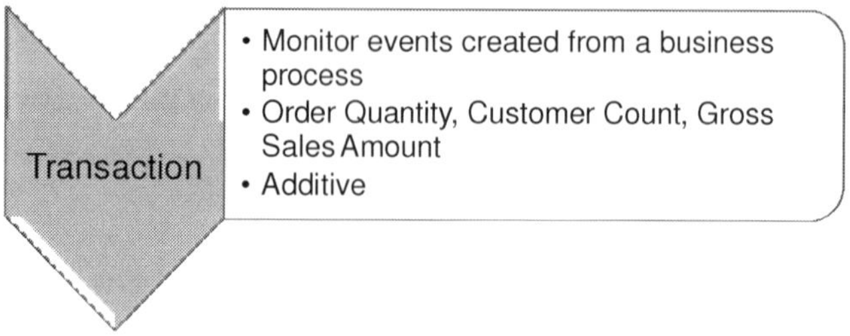

Snapshot

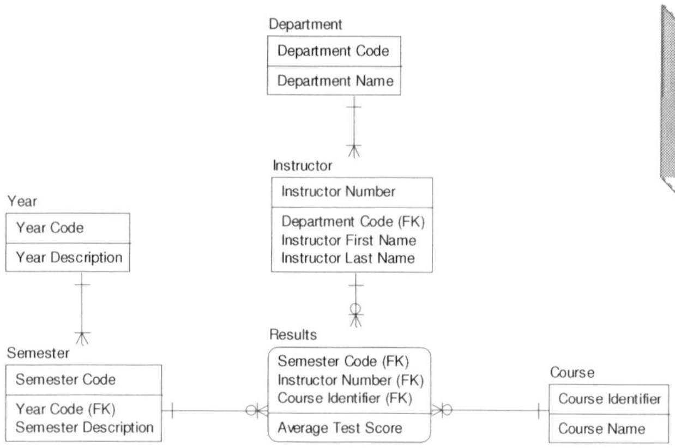

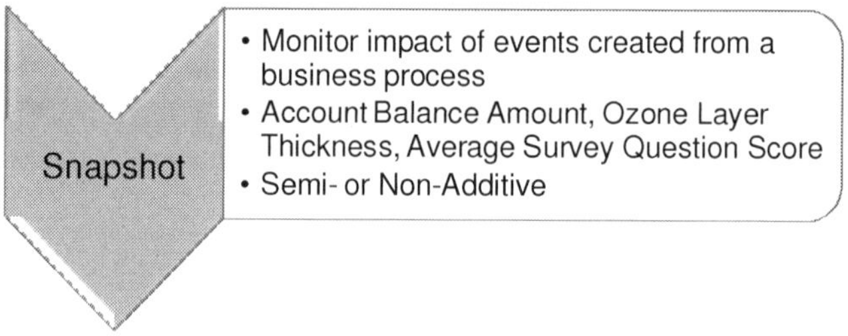

Accumulating

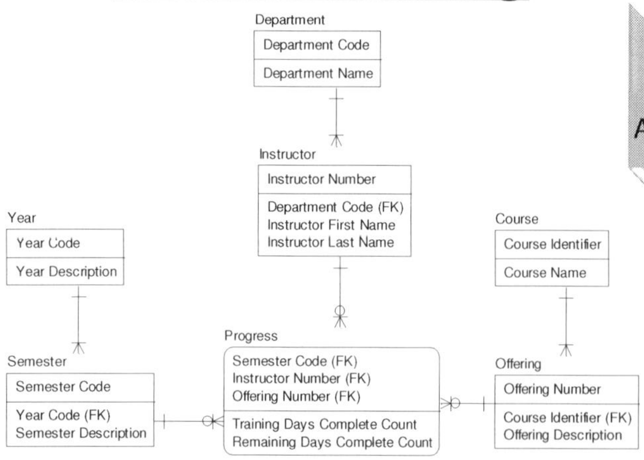

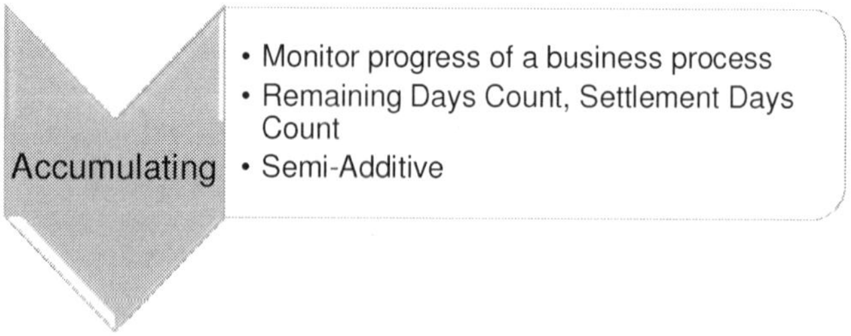

Logical data model

Measures monitor business processes

BACKGROUND

Measures monitor business processes in one of three ways: Transaction, Snapshot, or Accumulating. It is important to understand the difference between these three because they have very different behaviors which can impact reporting results.

TRANSACTION

Transaction measures monitor events created from business processes, such as Order Quantity, Customer Count, and Gross Sales Amount. In terms of business intelligence maturity, transaction measures are a great place to start. An important property of transaction measures is that they are fully additive across all dimensions. For example, we can add Order Quantities at a day level to produce a meaningful result at a month level.

SNAPSHOT

Snapshot measures monitor the impact of events created from a business process, such as Account Balance Amount, Ozone Layer Thickness, and Average Survey Question Score. It is (at least theoretically) possible to produce snapshot measures by summing transaction measures. For example, to determine the Account Balance Amount we can sum the results of all individual account transactions such as deposits and withdrawals. However, would it be possible to determine the Ozone Layer Thickness by summing the cumulative results of everything that can affect the thickness of the ozone layer? Not likely. Snapshot measures are semi- or non-additive. As much as we would like to for example, we cannot sum our Account Balance Amount over a period of months (but we can sum our Account Balance Amount across all of our accounts).

ACCUMULATING

Accumulating measures monitor progress of a business process. Frequently the amount of days required to complete a certain business process step are tracked, such as Remaining Days Count or Settlement Days Count. What is very interesting about accumulating measures is that they can be updated. For example, today there are five days left and tomorrow there might be four days left to complete a business process step. Accumulating measures are semi- or non-additive, as we cannot sum the days remaining today and days remaining tomorrow and get a meaningful result.

Logical data model

Dimensional modeling Do's

Do only build dimensional models for measures	Customer Count Top 50 Accounts Actual comments P & L statement
Do use relational for adhoc	"What products are for sale in the US?"
Do provide a richer grain if it will not impact performance, scope-creep, data quality validation, or user-friendliness	"Let's see, they want month level now, would they want day level a month from now?"
Do let creativity drive your dimensional structures	

Logical data model

Dimensional modeling Do's

DO ONLY BUILD DIMENSIONAL MODELS FOR MEASURES

Dimensional models should be built when there is a need to play with numbers. Metrics are data elements that can be mathematically manipulated, such as summed and averaged. The reason the dimensional model should be limited to numbers is because its design allows for easy navigation up and down hierarchy levels. By traversing hierarchy levels numbers need to be recalculated. For example, a Gross Sales Amount of $5 on a particular day might be $150 for a particular month in which that day belongs.

DO USE RELATIONAL FOR ADHOC

If there are no business requirements yet defined, dimensional models are difficult to build and will constrain the users. If the requirements are "Give me everything" or "I don't know what I want", it is a good practice to model relationally as this way the system has more flexibility. It is ok to use a dimensional structure however, when the adhoc requests are limited to the measures in a meter.

DO PROVIDE A RICHER GRAIN IF IT WILL NOT IMPACT PERFORMANCE, SCOPE-CREEP, DATA QUALITY VALIDATION, OR USER-FRIENDLINESS

This is a very controversial point among dimensional modelers. Do you design exactly for the questions the business needs answered, or do you add a more detailed grain to handle more detailed questions with the same measures? My belief is that it is ok to provide the richer grain as long as it does not impact performance (e.g. Will it take a lot longer to return results at a day level instead of at a month level?), scope-creep (e.g. Will the project take another month to finish because of the extra grain?), data quality (e.g. Will the business be responsible for checking an additional amount of data?), or user-friendliness (Is the dimensional model no longer easy to understand?).

DO LET CREATIVITY DRIVE YOUR DIMENSIONAL STRUCTURES

The relationships in a dimensional hierarchy do not have to mimic their relational counterparts. You can build dimensions to meet the way the business user thinks. For example, the concept of Lot includes product, shift, and plant. Yet in this example the business user wants to see Lot rolled up only under product.

Logical data model

Dimensional modeling Don'ts

Don't relate dimensions to each other	
Don't leave navigation paths empty	No optionality on relationships (lots of 99's!)
Don't mix grains	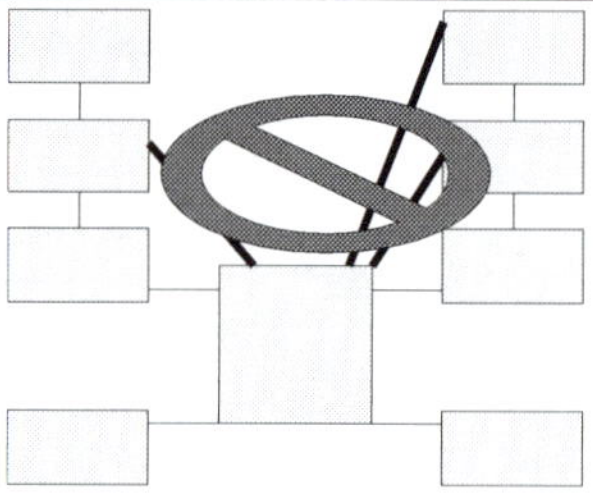
Don't combine relational and dimensional on same <u>logical</u> model	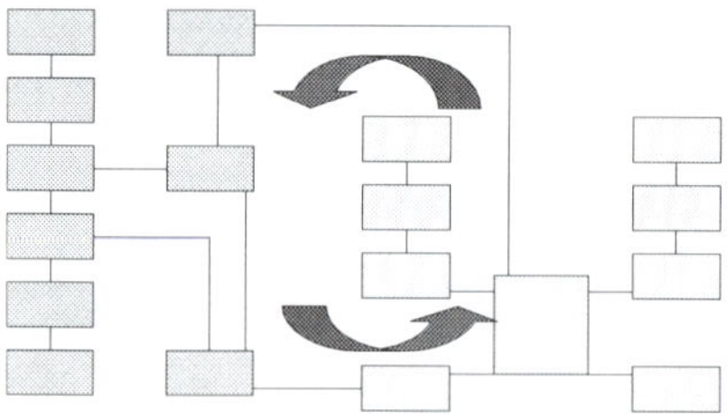

Logical data model

Dimensional modeling Don'ts

DON'T RELATE DIMENSIONS TO EACH OTHER

All relationships from dimensions must go through the meter. That is, you can never have relationships between different dimensions. You cannot show for example in the dimensional model on the facing page the rule capturing which products can be sold within which region, as this would require a relationship between *product* and *region*.

DON'T LEAVE NAVIGATION PATHS EMPTY

It is a good practice to avoid foreign key nulls on a dimensional model. If a specific Product does not roll up to a specific Product Line for example, using a default value instead of leaving the foreign key in Product empty will minimize reporting errors.

DON'T MIX GRAINS

Each meter must have a single grain. You want to avoid for example, relating both Product Line and Product to the Sales meter. The reason for this is when grains are mixed it becomes very easy to double and triple sum the measures. Creating summary tables or rolling up from Product to Product Line are better options.

DON'T COMBINE RELATIONAL AND DIMENSIONAL ON SAME LOGICAL MODEL

A logical model must be relational OR dimensional; it cannot have properties of both. When you get to the physical, one solution would be to combine them within the same schema. There are pros and cons though (like everything in the physical). Pros include meeting multiple needs within the same structure, cons include creating reporting complexity such as loops.

Logical data model

Additional dimensional modeling terminology

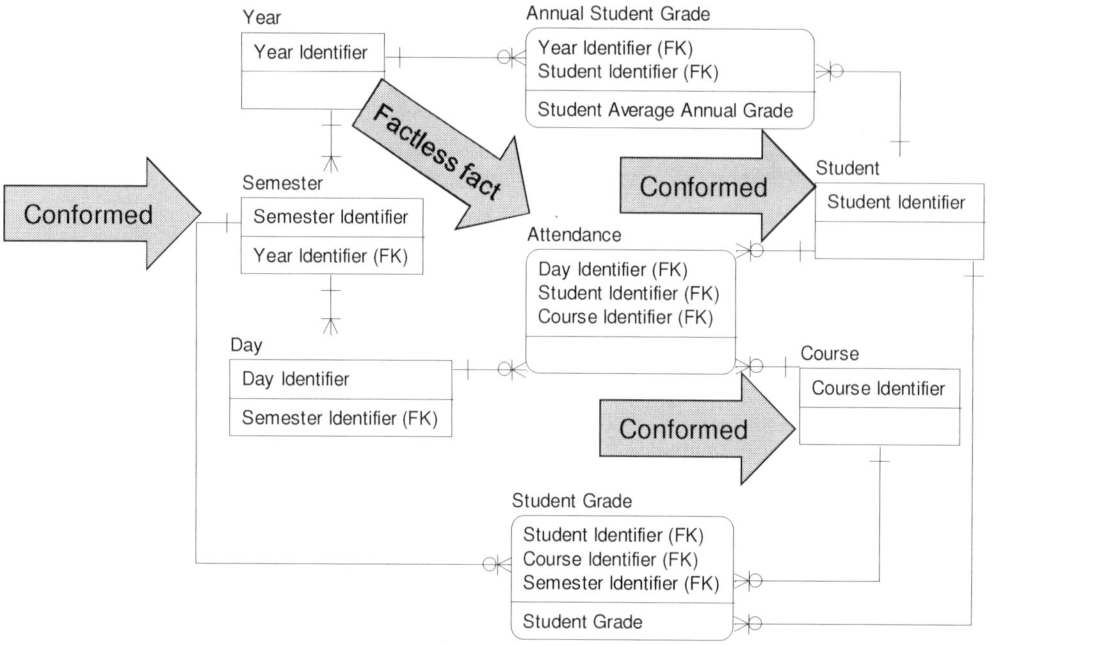

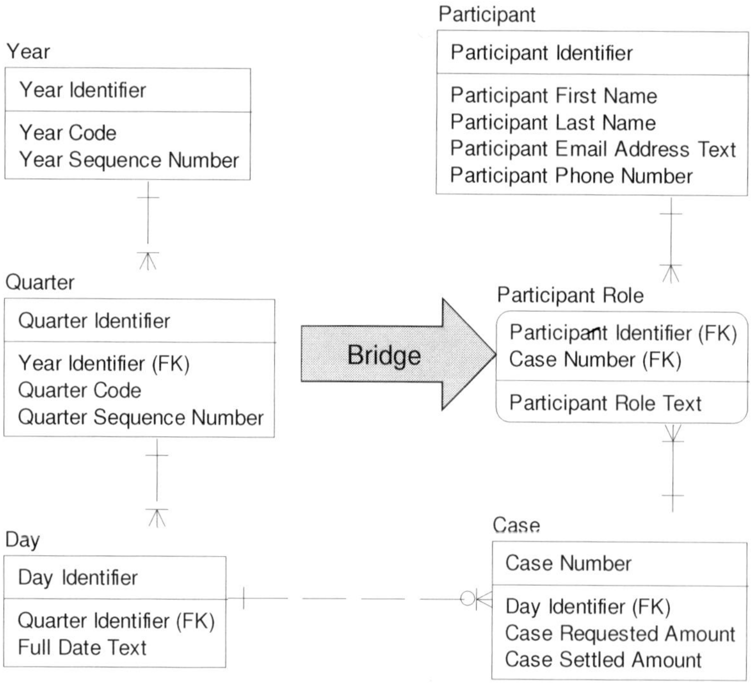

Logical data model

Additional dimensional modeling terminology

CONFORMED DIMENSION

Conformed dimensions share the same structure and content. They are built with the organization in mind, instead of just a particular application, to support drill across queries and enterprise consistency. Conformed dimensions do not need to be identical with each other, they just need to be from the same superset. Conformed dimensions allow the navigator the ability to ask questions that cross multiple marts.

FACTLESS FACT

A fact table that does not contain any facts is called a factless fact (good name, huh?). Factless facts count events by summing relationship occurrences between the dimensions. A factless fact in dimensional modeling has an associative entity as a counterpart on the relational modeling side. Usually on the physical dimensional model, there is a count measure added to the factless fact which always contains the value '1'. It is quicker to sum a field than it is easier to count relationship occurrences. Attendance is a factless fact on the facing page. It resolves the many-to-many-to-many relationship that exists between the dimensions.

BRIDGE TABLE

A bridge table resolves a many-to-many relationship from the dimension to the meter. In other words, a given meter instance may need to refer to more than one dimension instance. Bridge tables can be shown as the typical resolution of a many-to-many on a logical, but may need a different physical structure depending on reporting tools.

BEHAVIORAL DIMENSION

A dimension that is created based upon measurements. Measurement ranges are grouped together in the dimension, such as by sales amounts or performance. This type of dimension is ideal when the users recognize the same set of bands, and they are stable. "How many customers do we have with sales between \$500,000 and \$750,000?" Student Grade Point Average Range is an example of a behavioral dimension in the model below.

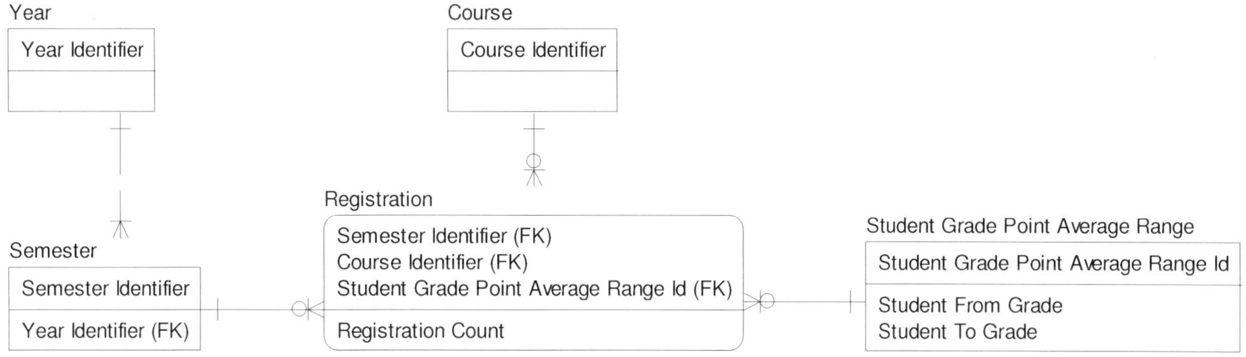

Logical data model

The early days of dimensional data modeling

DIMENSIONAL BATTLES

Two articles that are worthwhile reads:

- "A Dimensional Modeling Manifesto", by Ralph Kimball (www.dbmsmag.com/9708d15.html)
- "The Problem with Dimensional Modeling", by Bill Inmon (www.billinmon.com/library/articles/artdimmd.asp)

> The dimensional model is the only viable technique for achieving both user understandability and high query performance in the face of ever-changing user questions.
>
> Ralph Kimball, DBMS Magazine, August 1997

> The dimensional modelers have crafted a fine hammer. Now everything looks like a nail to them.
>
> Bill Inmon, DM Review, May 1998

> The data warehouse is nothing more than the union of all the data marts.
>
> Ralph Kimball, Dec 1997

> You can catch all the minnows in the ocean and stack them together and they still do not make a whale.
>
> Bill Inmon, DM Review, May 1998

Logical data model

More recent quotes on dimensional modeling

HISTORY OF DIMENSIONAL MODELING

Ralph Kimball played a major role in establishing dimensional modeling as an industry standard, but he did not invent dimensional modeling. Dimensional modeling has been around just as long as relational modeling. The terms 'fact' and 'dimension' for example, were first used in a joint research project that took place during the 1960s between General Mills and Dartmouth University. In the 1970s, AC Nielson and IRI were using these terms in their analytics environment, and Ralph first heard of these terms at AC Nielson in 1983.

Which is right, dimensional or relational?

I can do everything with Stars.

We want to use their Dealer dimension, but we see Dealer slightly differently...

Can you have both relational and dimensional structures in the same application?

We want the Inmon approach in the Kimball timeframe.

Ralph Kimball invented the fact and dimension concepts.

Logical data model

Relational modeling is all about normalizing

Logical data model

Relational modeling is all about normalizing

BACKGROUND

When I turned 12, I received a trunk full of baseball cards as a birthday present from my parents. I was delighted, not just because there may have been a Hank Aaron or Pete Rose buried somewhere in that trunk, but because I loved to organize the cards. I categorized each card according to year and team.

Normalization is a process of applying rules to render simple and stable something that is complex. I was normalizing the baseball cards according to year and team. We can normalize the data elements within our organizations, with a different set of rules yet with the same goal of simplifying and stabilizing something complex. Just as those baseball cards lay unsorted within that trunk, our companies have huge numbers of data elements spread throughout departments and applications. The rules applied to normalizing the baseball cards entailed first sorting by year, and then by team within a year. The rules for normalizing our data elements can be boiled down to sorting them according to their correct primary and foreign keys. The end result is a simple and stable view of how a business area or application works, or should work.

In analyzing the data elements for the correct primary and foreign keys, we are forced to understand the rules governing the way a business works. We analyze each data element in order to understand not only what it is, but also how it relates to every other data element in our model. By asking questions and finding answers, we develop a strong understanding of the content of the model.

To identify the correct primary and foreign keys, we need to apply a series of more granular rules. The rules are grouped into levels according to their specificity. Each level is considered a separate normal form, starting with first normal form, which is the least specific, and concluding with fifth normal form, the most specific.

The full set of normalization levels is the following:

- first normal form (1NF)
- second normal form (2NF)
- third normal form (3NF)
- Boyce/Codd normal form (BCNF)
- fourth normal form (4NF)
- fifth normal form (5NF)

If a model is in 5NF, it is also in 4NF, BCNF, and so on. That is, the higher levels of normalization subsume the lower rules.

Logical data model

Normalization benefits

Logical data model

Normalization benefits

STRONGER UNDERSTANDING

Normalization forces us to understand the content of what is being modeled. We learn how each data element relates to every other data element. Before normalization, we may have a fairly good understanding of a particular data element (such as its definition and domain), but we most likely lack knowledge about the way in which this data element relates to every other data element in the model.

GREATER APPLICATION STABILITY

Normalization leads to a model that mimics the way in which the business works. As the business goes about its daily operations, the application receives data according to the rules that govern the business. The model underlying the application has been structured with the knowledge that these rules can govern, and therefore the system runs smoothly as long as the rules in the business match the rules documented throughout the normalization process. If, for example, more than one person can own an account, the model—and, therefore, the application—will accommodate this fact.

LESS DATA REDUNDANCY

Each level of normalization removes a certain kind of *data redundancy* from the model. Data redundancy occurs when the same information appears more than once in the same model. As redundancy is removed, changing the data becomes a quicker process, because there is less of it to update or insert. If *person's last name* appears four times on a model and Mary's last name changes, the application would have to ensure that all four occurrences of Mary's last name get updated correctly.

BETTER DATA QUALITY

By reducing redundancy and by enforcing data rules through relationships, the data are less likely to get out of synch or violate business rules. Also, a considerable number of rules, therefore, are enforced on the model. If an account must have at least one account owner, the model will prevent accounts with invalid or missing account owners from occurring.

FASTER BUILDING OF NEW MODELS

Normalization ensures correct primary and foreign keys. As a result, data elements are assigned to their most appropriate entity. All data elements that require *account identifier* for uniqueness appear in *account*. There is a degree of common sense applied to the place in which data elements reside, and therefore it becomes easier to identify and reuse normalized structures on a new model. The result is more consistency across models and less time developing applications.

Logical data model

Normalization in a nutshell

Make sure every data element is single-valued and depends completely and only on its primary key.

Single-valued:

Person First Name Person Year of Birth	Valid Date Range Mailing Address	Phone Number Credit Card Number Postal Code

Dependency = a primary key value returns at most one value

☺ Customer Id '123' returns Customer Last Name 'Smith'

☹ Department Code 'A' returns both 'Accounting' and 'Sales'

Completely = minimal primary key

Only = no derived data

Logical data model

Normalization in a nutshell

IN ONE SENTENCE

Make sure every data element is single-valued and depends completely and only on its primary key. An easy (and humorous) way to remember this is with this slogan: "Every data element depends on the key, the whole key, and nothing but the key, so help me Codd!"

SINGLE-VALUED

A data element must contain only one piece of information. Sometimes it is easy to identify data elements that need to be split apart into two or more other data elements, and sometimes it can be tricky. Where it gets tricky is when the data element theoretically could be split apart, but does anyone from the business really ever need to see it in separate pieces? This is the important question to ask. Postal Code could be multi-valued for example, depending on your perspective of this field. The first digit in Zip Code for example, covers region. The next two digits specify a Facility (there are over 900 facilities in the United States).

DEPENDENCY

'Dependency' means that for a given primary key value, will it always return at most one of every data element that is identified by this key? If a Customer Identifier value of '123' for example, returns three Customer Last Names ('Smith', 'Jones', and 'Roberts'), this violates the dependency definition.

COMPLETELY

'Completely' means that the minimal set of data elements is present in the primary key. If for example, there are two data elements in an entity's primary key yet only one is needed for uniqueness, normalization requires this situation to be fixed.

ONLY

'Only' means that each data element must depend directly on the primary key and nothing else. For example, if derived data depends on the components of the data element and not directly on the primary key, this situation violates normalization.

Logical data model

Starting with chaos

Employee

Employee Identifier
Department Code

Phone Number 1
Phone Number 2
Phone Number 3
Employee Name
Department Name
Employee Start Date
Employee Vested Indicator

Logical data model

Starting with chaos

BACKGROUND

We have all put together puzzles at one time or another. After we open the box and dump out the pieces, the sight can be overwhelming: hundreds, maybe even thousands, of tiny pieces in a large pile. The pile is in a state of chaos. As we pick each piece up and examine it, we understand that its characteristics make it unique. We lack knowledge at this point about how these puzzle pieces connect with each other. We begin the process of fitting the pieces together and, after much effort, we complete our masterpiece. Each puzzle piece is in its proper place.

The term *chaos* can be applied to any unorganized pile, including data elements. We may have a strong understanding of each of the data elements, such as their name and definition. We lack knowledge about how the data elements fit together. We understand each piece of the puzzle, but we do not yet understand the connections between the pieces. In our example with the business card, how do the data elements *address* and *telephone number* connect? Just as we need to determine the appropriate place for each piece within our puzzle, we need to determine the appropriate place for each data element within our model.

EXAMPLE

The Employee example on the facing page is our starting point. We might have great definitions for each of these data elements but what is lacking is how they relate to each other. Hence the chaos.

Logical data model

Normalization – 1NF

Always a good idea to look at some data!

Emp Id	Dept Cd	Phone 1	Phone 2	Phone 3	Emp Name	Dept Name	Emp Start Date	Emp Vested Ind
123	A	973-555-1212	678-333-3333	343-222-1111	Henry Winkler	Data Admin	4/1/2001	N
789	A	732-555-3333	678-333-3333	343-222-1111	Steve Martin	Data Admin	3/5/1999	Y
565	B	333-444-1111	516-555-1212	343-222-1111	Mary Smith	Data Warehouse	2/25/2001	Y
744	A	232-222-2222	678-333-3333	343-222-1111	Bob Jones	Data Admin	5/5/2005	N

Employee

Employee
Employee Identifier Department Code
Employee Phone Number Organization Phone Number Department Phone Number Employee First Name Employee Last Name Department Name Employee Start Date Employee Vested Indicator

Logical data model

Normalization – 1NF

BACKGROUND

1NF states that every non-key data element must depend on its primary key. Another way of looking at 1NF is that for a given primary-key value, we can identify at most one of every data element that depends on that primary key. If a *customer identifier* value of 123 brings back both Smith and Jones as *customer last name* values, we have not identified the correct primary key.

Two activities will ensure that a valid primary key is assigned to each entity:

- Move repeating data elements to a new entity.
- Separate *multi-valued* data elements.

MOVE REPEATING DATA ELEMENTS TO A NEW ENTITY

A repeating data element occurs when two or more of the same data element exists within the same entity. Repeating data elements is bad, because data elements fix the number of values an entity instance can have. If a data element is repeated three times in an entity, we can have at most three occurrences of this data element for a given entity instance. We cannot have four and we waste space if we have only one or two. Therefore, we need to move the data element that is repeating to a new entity.

SEPARATE *MULTIVALUED* DATA ELEMENTS

Multi-valued means that within the same data element we are storing at least two distinct values. In other words, we need to ensure that each data element is atomic and contains only one value. For example, *name* may contain both a first name and last name. *First name* and *last name* can be considered distinct data elements, and therefore "John Smith" stored within *name* is multi-valued, because it contains "John" and "Smith."

EXAMPLE

In this example, we parsed first name and last name, and analyzed in more detail the phone numbers. We learn from the data that each of the phone numbers represent separate business elements, and are therefore not a repeating group.

NORMALIZATION IS REALLY JUST A FORMAL PROCESS OF ASKING BUSINESS QUESTIONS

- Does it make business sense to parse Employee Name?
- How about Phone Number? How about Emp Start Date?
- Is Phone Number really a repeating group? What is the significance of 1, 2, and 3?

Logical data model

Normalization – 2NF

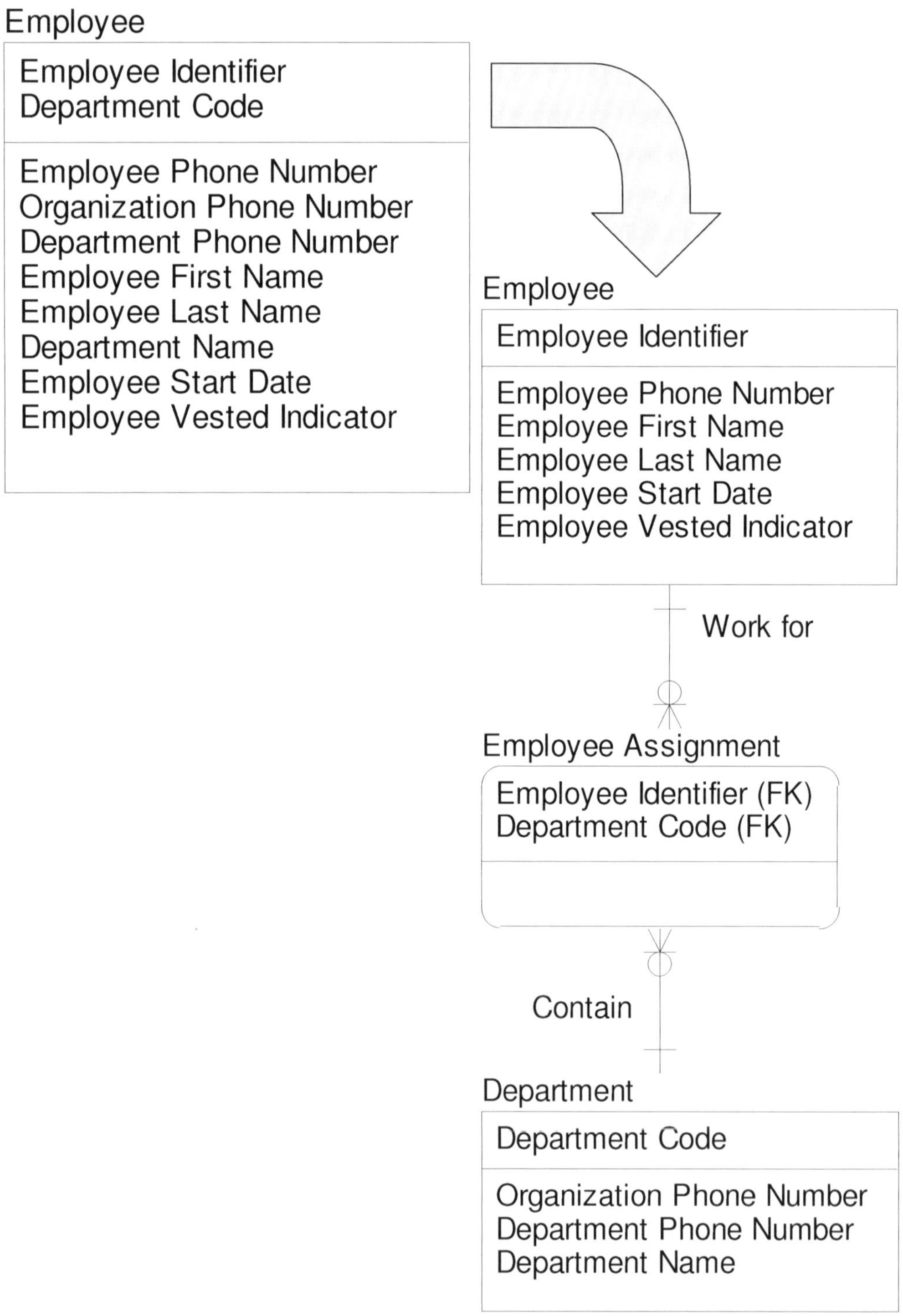

Logical data model

Normalization – 2NF

BACKGROUND

Our completely normalized model will have the correct set of primary and foreign keys, with each level of normalization adding rules to help us get closer to this goal. 2NF contributes to this goal by requiring each entity to have the minimal correct primary key—in other words, a minimal set of data elements to uniquely identify each entity instance.

In more formal terms, 2NF states that we must remove non-key data elements not dependent on the whole primary key. As we noted earlier, non-key data elements are all data elements except for primary, foreign, and alternate keys. A data element that depends on only part of the primary key is called a partial key dependency. We want to make sure our primary keys are correct, and we want to remove any partial key dependencies.

EXAMPLE

In this example we realize we don't have the minimal primary key, and therefore split apart Department from Employee.

QUESTIONS AT THIS STEP

- Can an Employee work for more than one Department?
- Is the Employee Start Date the date the Employee started work for the Organization or for the Department?

Logical data model

Normalization – 3NF

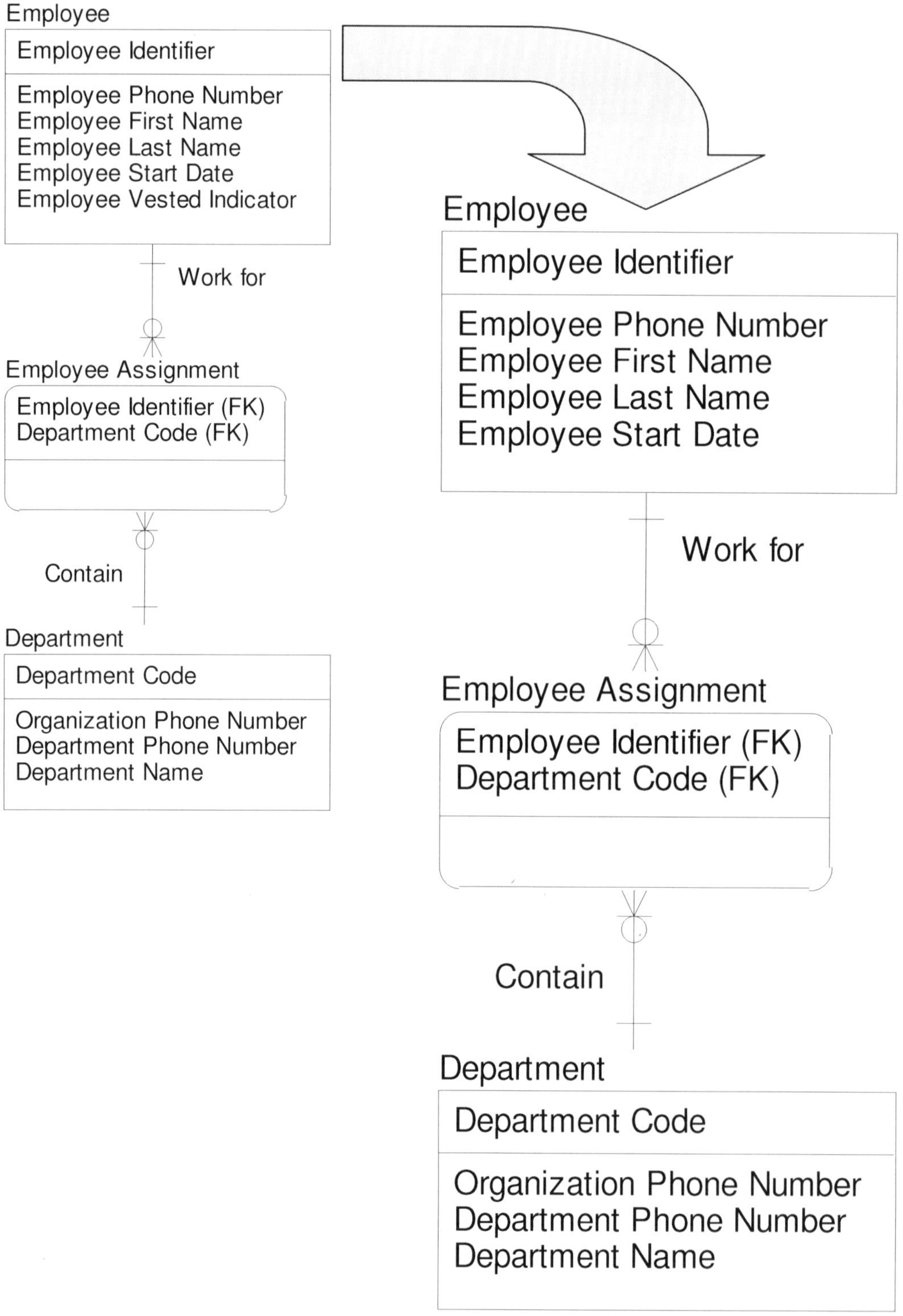

Logical data model

Normalization – 3NF

BACKGROUND

Even though there are higher levels of normalization than 3NF, many interpret the term "normalized" to mean 3NF. This is because the higher levels of normalization (that is, BCNF, 4NF, and 5NF) cover specific situations that occur much less frequently than the first three levels.

3NF requires the removal of hidden dependencies. Each non-key data element must be directly dependent on the primary key, and not directly dependent on any other non-key data elements within the same entity.

3NF violations usually fall into these two categories:

- derived data
- decodes embedded with codes in non-lookup entities

EXAMPLE

Assuming the Employee Vested Indicator is an easily derivable data element completely based on Employee Start Date, I removed it to make the model in 3NF.

QUESTION AT THIS STEP

How do you derive Employee Vested Indicator?

Logical data model

The Normalization Hike – 10 steps to the summit!

5NF **4NF**	10. Look for hidden business rules in the primary keys of entities with three or more identifying relationships
BCNF **3NF** **2NF**	9. Remove data elements not directly dependent on primary key 8. Remove data elements not dependent on whole primary key
1NF	7. Resolve many-to-many relationships 6. Remove repeating data elements 5. Separate multi-valued data elements 4. Validate initial rules 3. Refine scope 2. Sort data elements 1. Build a subject area model

Logical data model

The Normalization Hike – 10 steps to the summit!

JUST LIKE HIKING

There is a trail near our house we hike quite often. It takes time and effort to reach the summit, which is a beautiful lookout point over the surrounding towns and countryside. As data modelers, we go through a similar trek during every design. We start off at the bottom of a trail, ready for an adventure, with little understanding of how the data elements relate to each other. As we progress along the trail--huffing, puffing, and sweating--we get to higher elevations, and our view improves. We normalize--first normal form, second normal form, and third normal form--each additional degree of normalization taking us to a higher level of understanding. When we eventually arrive at fifth normal form, we have developed a complete understanding and appreciation of the application. The Normalization Hike is an informal set of rules for progressing to the lookout point in fifth normal form. One organization calls this mountain "Hober-Hill".

NORMALIZATION REALIZATION

Many years ago, I was normalizing trying to think through again how 2NF differs from 3NF. It suddenly occurred to me that it doesn't really matter what the difference is between 2NF and 3NF! What does matter is that model at the end is completely normalized. I started drafting informal (yet complete steps) to normalizing and I arrived at these 10 steps. The Normalization Hike's two main goals are:

- **Describe the levels of normalization in a succinct and practical way.** The Normalization Hike provides a less technical and theoretical explanation of normalization than your standard explanation. For example, this tool avoids words such as "determinate" and "join-dependency". There is no need in our finished design to distinguish 2NF from 3NF.
- **Provide the visual.** The Normalization Hike is a progression we go through whenever we do a design. Just like any long hike with a challenging destination, the more we progress along the trail, the greater our understanding and appreciation, and the more sweat and effort goes into arriving at the final normalized logical design. This visual is very effective for explaining the value of normalization and the effort that normalization requires.

REGARDLESS OF APPROACH

Whether you are starting with a list of source system data elements, a set of business requirements, or a completely clean slate, you can apply the Normalization Hike. Normalization is all about asking business questions – each level you go you ask more questions until there is complete business understanding.

Logical data model

One of my favorite topics: Desserts!

A.Menu subset

VANILLA BEAN CHEESECAKE

Cheesecake made with real vanilla beans, baked in a vanilla graham-cracker crust. Layered with white chocolate mousse and white chocolate shavings. Served with whipped cream and a fresh strawberry.

WARM APPLE CRISP

Apples simmered with cinnamon and brown sugar, then sprinkled with oatmeal crumbles. Topped with hot caramel sauce.

OREO® MADNESS

Two giant Oreo® cookies sandwiched with vanilla ice cream and topped with chocolate and caramel sauces.

Logical data model

One of my favorite topics: Desserts!

A. SAMPLE DATA

Let's say you are a data modeling consultant brought in to a large restaurant chain to better understand dessert buying habits across restaurants and regions. You are provided with a document containing three sections. Section A contains a sample menu showing desserts (see facing page). Section B contains the requirements which unfortunately are just three business questions that must be answered by the application that is built upon your model (see below). Section C contains a known list of data elements (see next two pages).

B. REQUIREMENTS

- List the best-selling three desserts by restaurant and region for the last six months.
- List the worst-selling three desserts by restaurant and region for the last six months.
- Which restaurant owner sells the most desserts?

C. DATA ELEMENTS

The list on the next two pages contains all of the data elements within the scope of the proposed application. This list could have come from examining existing applications (e.g. source system extract files) or it could have come from meetings with the business users. Looking at source systems first is a bottom up approach, and working with the business folks first is a top down approach. Take a few minutes to become familiar with these data elements, as we will carry this example through many sections.

We might have a good understanding of each of the individual data elements including their definition and format information, but still lack how each of the data elements relate to each other.

In a bottom-up modeling approach, this list would most likely come from source system files and tables. In a top-down modeling approach, this list would come from requirements documents and meetings with the business users.

Logical data model

Starting with Chaos – Data Element Listing

Name	Definition	Format	Null?
	Order		
Order Number	The unique number assigned to each order within a restaurant. This is usually but not always the number preprinted on the upper right hand corner of each check.	Char(8)	N
Restaurant Code	Links back to the restaurant and combines with Order Number to uniquely identify an Order.	Char(3)	N
Order Amount	The total amount of the order that the customer needs to pay for their meal. Does not include sales tax or gratuity.	Dec(6,2)	N
Gratuity Amount	The total amount of the tip that the customer leaves for the server or servers.	Dec(6,2)	Y
Sales Tax	The total amount of the sales tax that is added to the bill. Sales tax is based on a percent determined by the Region.	Dec(6,2)	Y
Check Date And Time	When the order was paid. Notice this is not the time when the customers sat down. It is only when we received payment. (Format: YYYYMMDDHHMM)	Char(12)	N
Item Code 1	Links back to the Item.	Char(5)	N
Quantity 1	How many of the item has been ordered.	Number	N
List Price 1	The price that is printed on the menu for each item.	Dec(6,2)	N
Total Amount 1	Calculated based on multiplying Quantity by List Price.	Dec(6,2)	N
Item Code 2	Links back to the Item.	Char(5)	N
Quantity 2	How many of the item has been ordered.	Number	N
List Price 2	The price that is printed on the menu for each item.	Dec(6,2)	N
Total Amount 2	Calculated based on multiplying Quantity by List Price.	Dec(6,2)	N
Item Code 3	Links back to the Item.	Char(5)	N
Quantity 3	How many of the item has been ordered.	Number	N
List Price 3	The price that is printed on the menu for each item.	Dec(6,2)	N
Total Amount 3	Calculated based on multiplying Quantity by List Price.	Dec(6,2)	N
	Dessert		
Dessert Code	The unique code assigned to each dessert. This value is independent of time, meaning the same dessert offered each October will have the same dessert code.	Number	N
Dessert Offered Date Range	A range of days that this dessert will be offered to the customers. Desserts are offered either continuously, on a seasonal basis, or as a special.	Char(21)	N
Dessert Name	The full name of the dessert that appears on the menu.	Char(30)	N

Logical data model

Starting with Chaos – Data Element Listing

Name	Definition	Format	Null?
Dessert (continued)			
Dessert Description	The text that appears under the name on the menu describing the dessert.	Char(200)	Y
Dessert Category Code	This includes all of the categories the dessert belongs to. It is in a list format separated by commas. For example, the dessert Banana Split might have this value: Indulgent,Frozen,Big	Char(200)	N
Dessert Price Amount	The price of this dessert. This is the list price from the menu, not including tax.	Dec(6,2)	N
Restaurant			
Restaurant Code	Unique identifier for a restaurant. Every manager knows their restaurant code.	Char(3)	N
Restaurant Region Code	The code within a region of the United States. EXAMPLE: NE = Northeast	Char(2)	N
Restaurant Region Name	The name of the region within the United States.	Char(30)	N
Region Sales Tax Rate	The percent charged on the total bill (not including gratuity) based on the specific region.	Number	N
Restaurant Owner 1 Name	The owner of the restaurant.	Char(30)	N
Restaurant Owner 1 Ownership Percent	A number from 1 to 100, describing the percent that the owner owns in the restaurant.	Decimal (5,2)	Y
Restaurant Owner 2 Name	The second owner, if applicable, for the restaurant.	Char(30)	Y
Restaurant Owner 2 Ownership Percent	A number from 1 to 100, describing the percent that the owner owns in the restaurant.	Decimal (5,2)	Y
Restaurant Owner 3 Name	The third owner, if applicable, for the restaurant.	Char(30)	Y
Restaurant Owner 3 Ownership Percent	A number from 1 to 100, describing the percent that the owner owns in the restaurant.	Decimal (5,2)	Y
Restaurant Maximum Capacity Number	The maximum number of people that can fit in the restaurant at any one time. This is determined by the regional health department. It includes both customers and employees.	Number	N

Logical data model

1. Build a subject area model

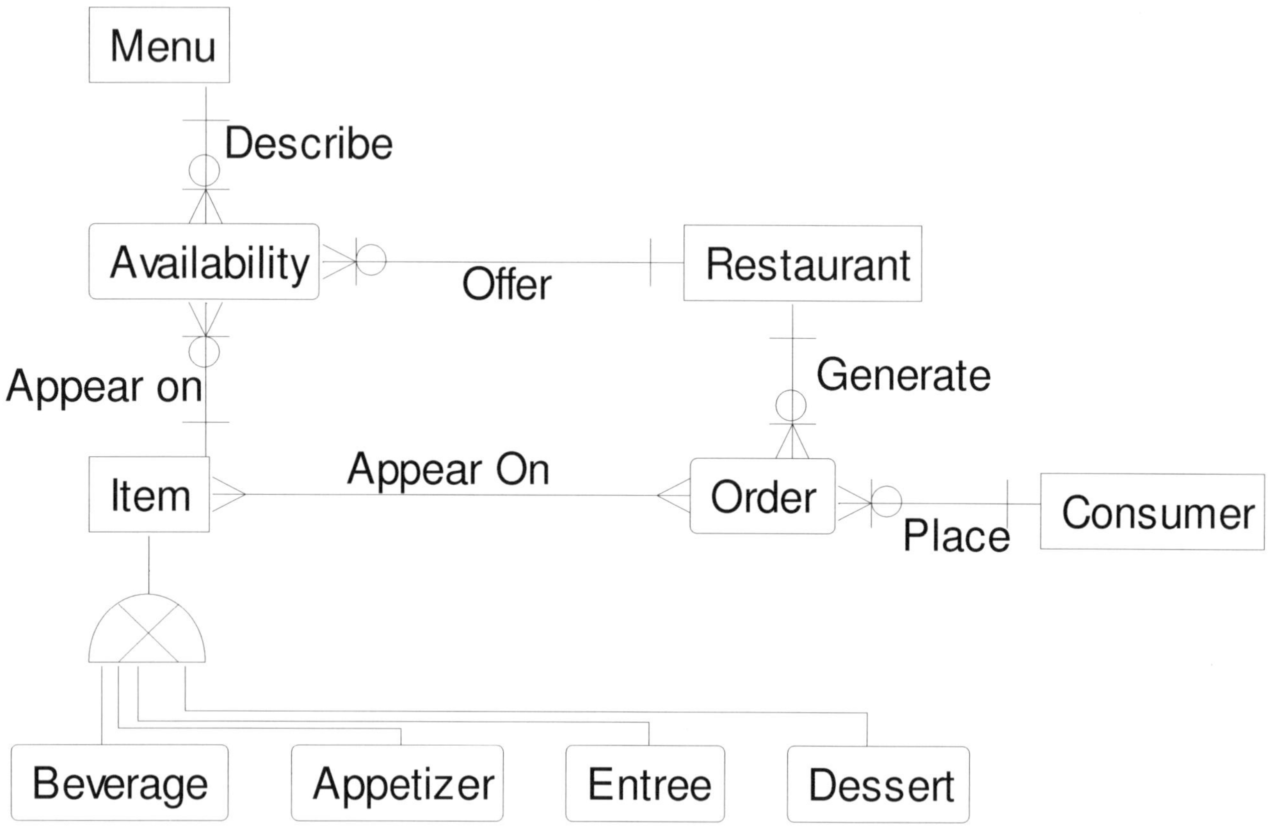

- Each Menu can describe many Items offered at many Restaurants.
- Each Restaurant may offer many Items on many Menus.
- Each Item may appear on many Menus in many Restaurants.
- Each Item may be a Beverage, Appetizer, Entrée, or Dessert.
- Each Restaurant may generate many Orders.
- Each Order must be generated by one Restaurant.
- Each Item must appear on many Orders.
- Each Order must contain many Items.
- Each Consumer may place many Orders.
- Each Order must be placed by one Consumer.

Logical data model

1. Build a subject area model

BACKGROUND

My first step is to build a subject area model. This can be either a BSAM or an ASAM, depending on whether we are normalizing for a business area or for an application. Note that the scope of this model might change (and most likely will) as we progress up the mountain. If we have an enterprise data model or an existing subject area model of this area, we need to use that instead of starting the subject area model from scratch.

MENU

A list of items available at a restaurant.

ITEM

An edible substance that is offered to consumers for a published price.

DESSERT

A course that typically comes at the end of a dinner, usually consisting of sweet food but sometimes of a strongly flavored one, such as some cheeses. Often, the dessert is seen as a separate meal or snack rather than a course, and may be eaten some time after the meal.

CONSUMER

An individual who dines in one of our restaurants.

ORDER

A request to purchase Items for an agreed price.

AVAILABILITY

Captures whether an Item is available for purchase from a given Menu in a given Restaurant.

RESTAURANT

An establishment for dining.

QUESTIONS AT THIS STEP

- What is within the scope of the project?
- What is outside the scope?
- What are the enterprise wide definitions and terms?
- Where will the data come from?

Logical data model

2. Sort data elements

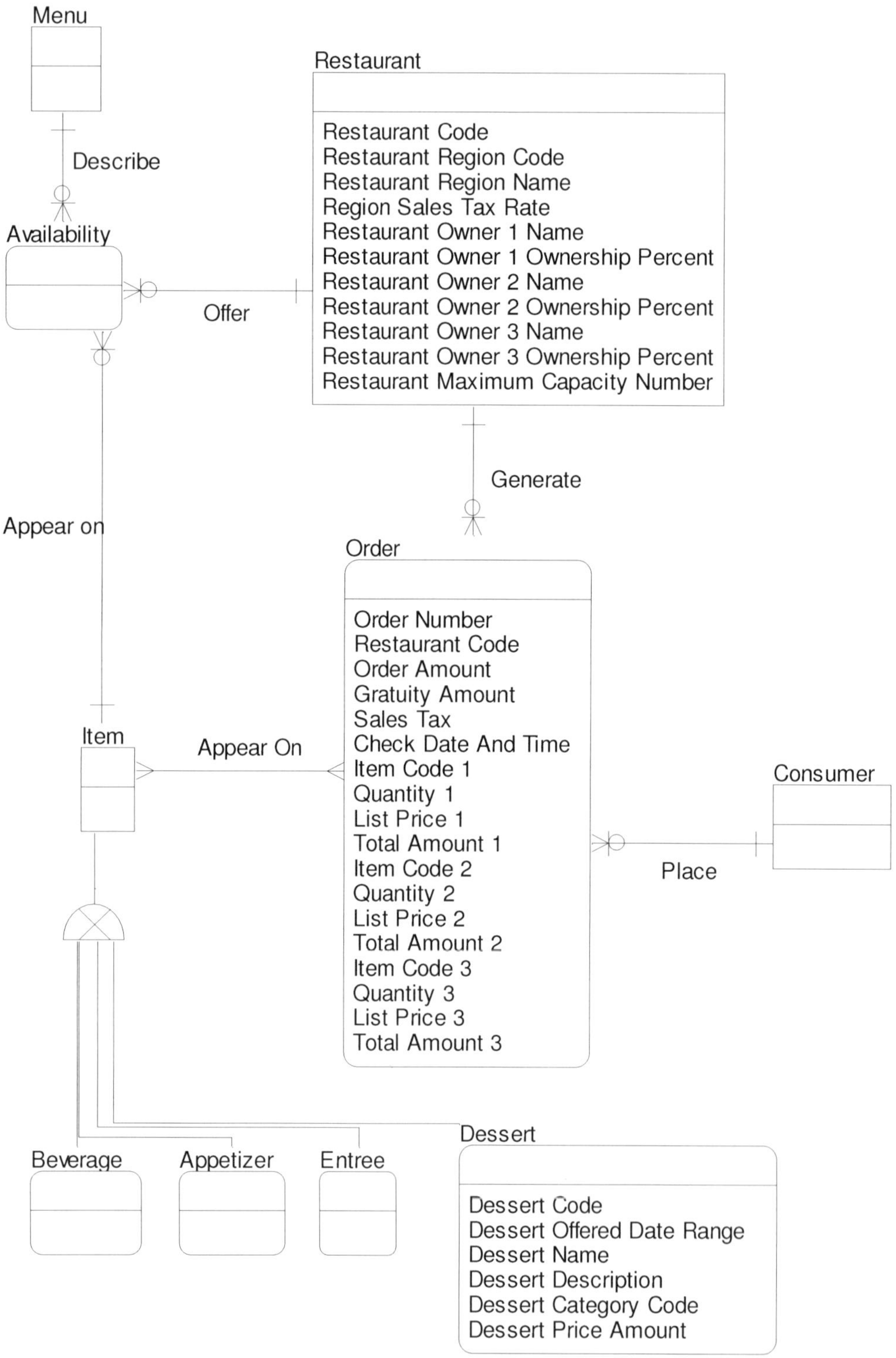

Logical data model

2. Sort data elements

BACKGROUND

This step involves assigning data elements to subject areas, much the same way that I first sorted the baseball cards by year. In deciding which bucket an entity belongs in, also read and most likely refine the definitions.

ACCURACY

You do not have to get this step 100% right. If I chose incorrectly, this will get fixed as part of the normalization steps we will go through on the following slides.

You can see from this model that we have some work ahead of us. Many of the data elements within the same subject area do not appear to be at the same level of detail, with the same participation and dependencies. So there will be some normalizing we will need to do. For example, in the restaurant entity, there is also information on the restaurant's region and owners. As we work our way up the Normalization Hike, we will be identifying these situations and correcting them.

TOP DOWN VS BOTTOM UP

This initial set of data elements can be captured one of two ways: top down or bottom up. Top down is driven from the business requirements, and therefore the data elements will be collected from meetings with business users and from requirements documentation. Bottom up is driven from existing applications, and therefore the data elements are collected from existing tables or source system extracts. Even though these approaches are very different, the results are the same: we have an initial set of data elements to play with.

Logical data model

3. Refine scope

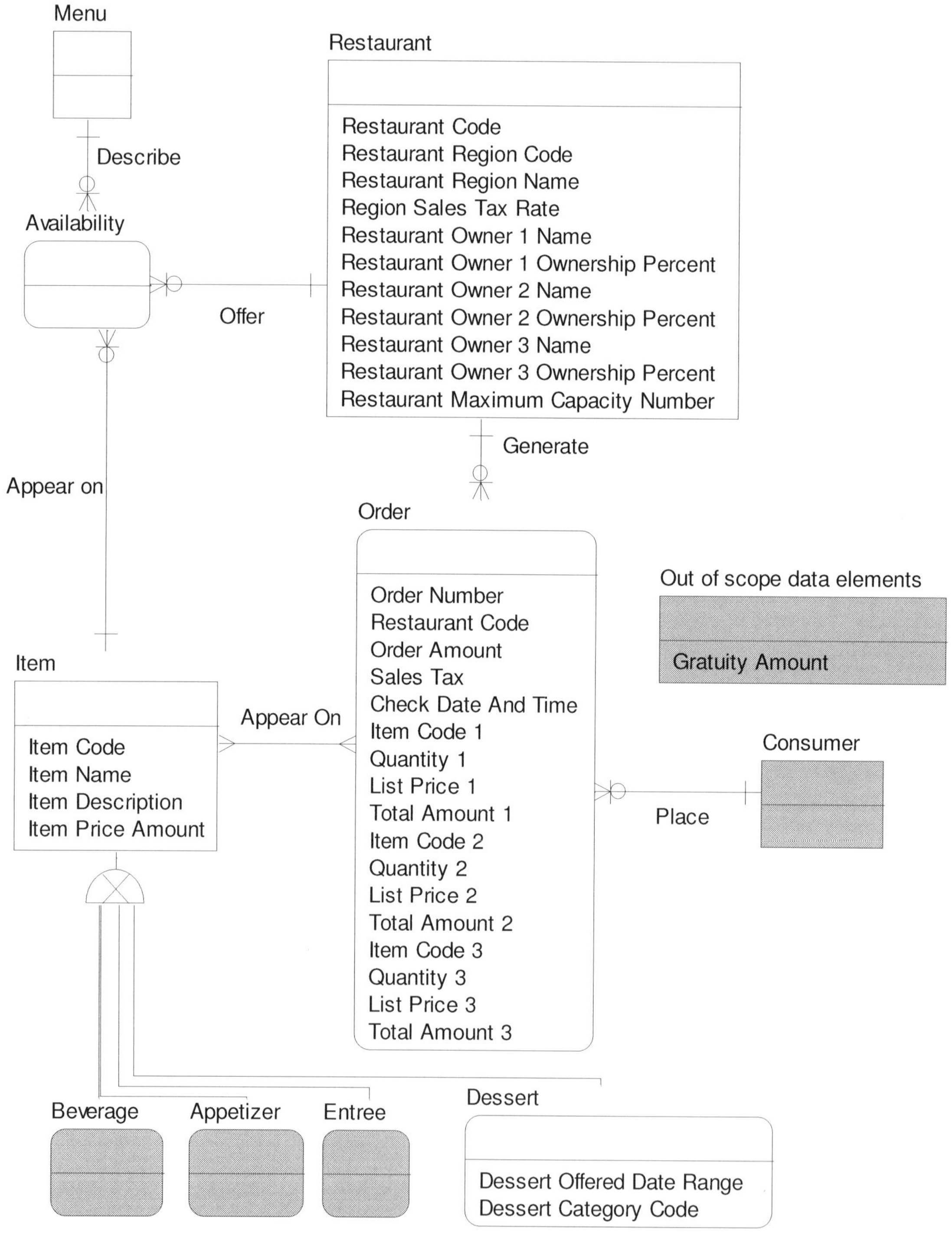

Logical data model

3. Refine scope

BACKGROUND

Correct scope is essential early in the normalization hike. You will find yourself asking questions around scope and possibly creating an out-of-scope bucket for subject areas and data elements. Scope is based primarily on the requirements, and secondarily (but sometimes equally if not more important) on the time available and money allocated for the project. Those entities shown in gray have been considered out-of-scope in this example.

Scope also involves deciding what is at a supertype level and what is at a subtype level. In this example, we learned that certain dessert data elements are really at the higher level of item. Note that most of the scope should already have been agreed to during the subject modeling.

QUESTIONS AT THIS STEP

- What is unique to desserts, and what is common across all items?
- Do we need to know anything about Menu and Consumer? Is any information available?
- Do we need to just focus on desserts, or are other types of items also relevant?
- What is in scope? What is out of scope?

Logical data model

4. Validate initial rules

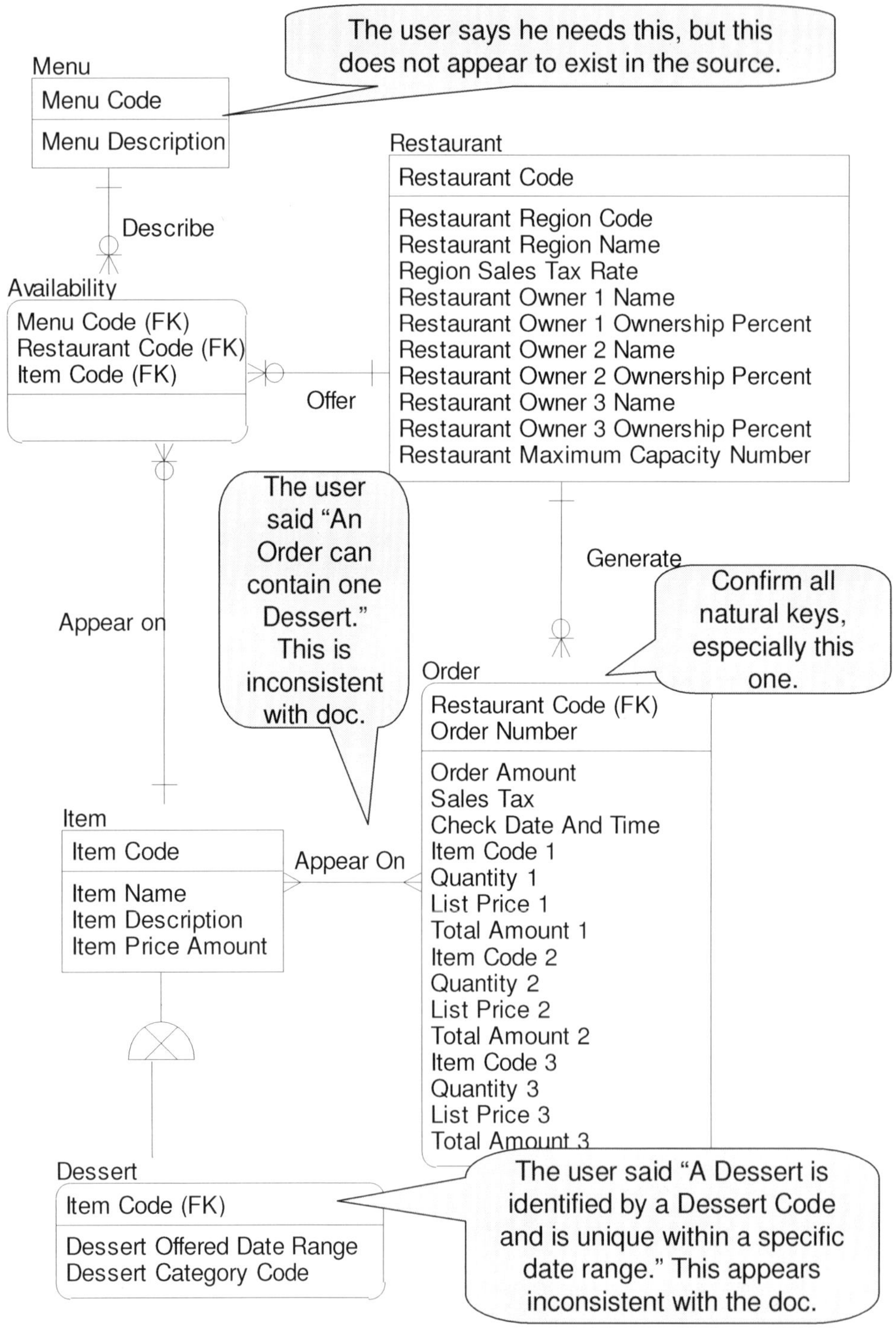

Logical data model

4. Validate initial rules

BACKGROUND

Business rules come from many places, such as from:

- Business users
- Source system experts
- ERP packages
- Requirements documents

This step is the trickiest of all ten, because rules are not always consistent across these areas. For example, assume that you meet a business user by the water cooler and had a short conversation about business rules. You then return to your desk and document these rules, and learn of several inconsistencies as documented on the facing page.

Guidelines in representing the right rules include:

- Business rules need to consistently represent either the way the world works today, or the way we are changing it to work in the future.
- Business rules need to be proven workable through the Normalization Hike, as there can easily be some inexactness in the English text. For example, can a check really contain just a single dessert?
- Business rules should never represent what people would like to be the business rules, unless this is an actual change to the business processes.

QUESTIONS AT THIS STEP

- What are the business keys to each entity, especially Order? Is the order number unique across restaurants?
- The user insists that a menu code and description are important to capture, yet they don't appear to exist in the source system.
- The user said and I quote, "A Dessert is identified by a Dessert Code and is unique within a specific date range." This appears to be inconsistent with our documentation.
- The user said and I quote, "An Order can contain one Dessert." This appears to be inconsistent with our documentation.

Logical data model

5. Separate multi-valued data elements

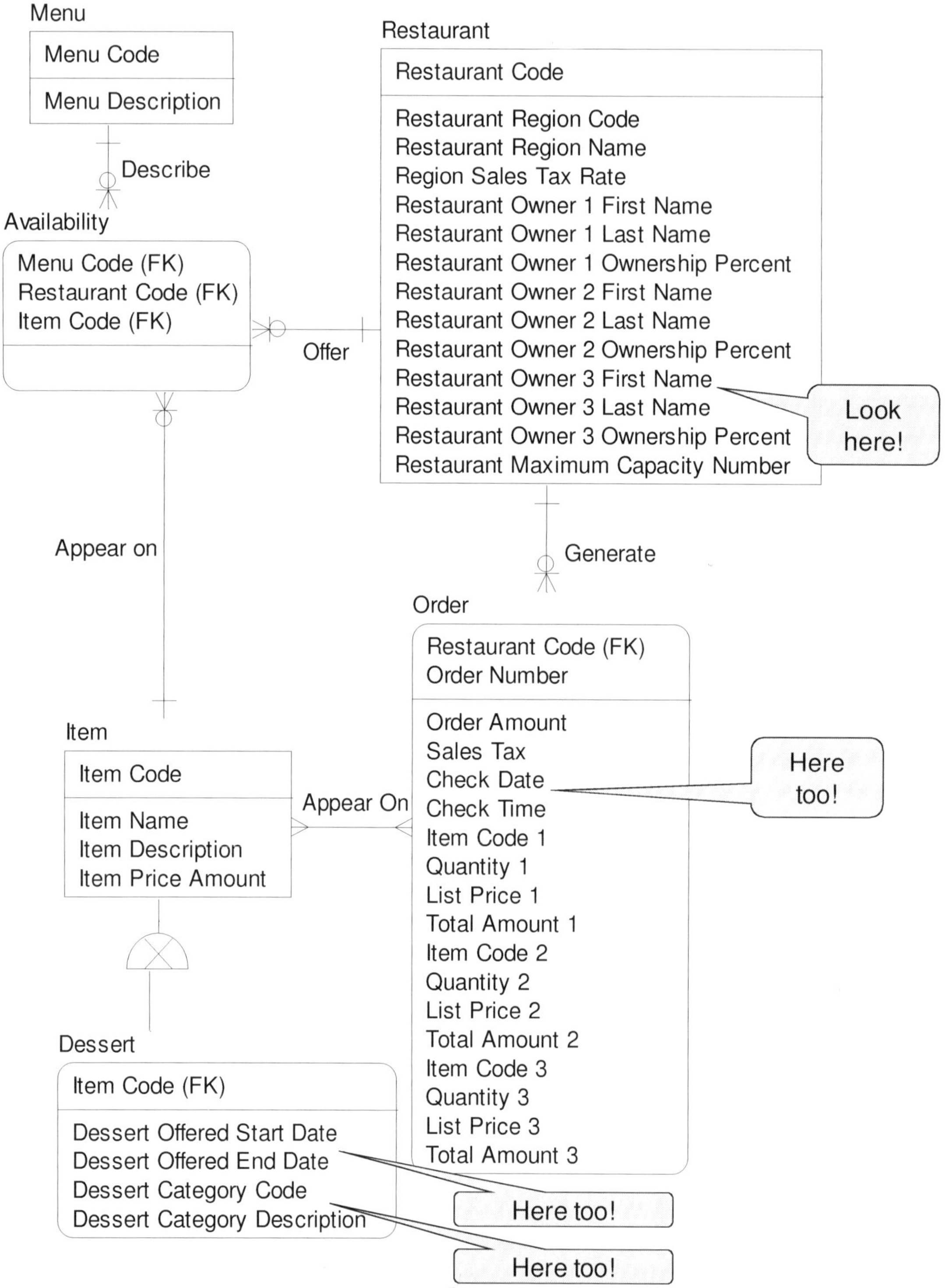

Logical data model

5. Separate multi-valued data elements

BACKGROUND

Multi-valued means that within the same data element we are storing at least two distinct values. In other words, we need to ensure that each data element is atomic and contains only one value. For example, *name* may contain both a first name and last name. *First name* and *last name* can be considered distinct data elements, and therefore "John Smith" stored within *name* is multi-valued, because it contains "John" and "Smith."

It is important to be practical when deciding whether a multi-valued data element. For example, Telephone Number might be a great candidate to parse for a telecommunications company, but may not be for a university. It can be easy to parse a data element on a data model, but very difficult and time consuming to do via code so be practical in your decisions.

TIPS

Enforce class words at this point. Class words are the high level domain of the data element, such as Name, Date, Identifier, and Code.

If a data element is larger than it should be, it might be being used for something it shouldn't be. Recently, we've identified a multi-valued data element within our sales organization subject area. This was a 7 character code in which only the last 4 characters were ever populated. Unfortunately, those first 3 characters became a great place to stash additional information for the users. Because it was not such an unusual length for a code, it went undetected for some time.

Even with the extra information the user was putting in, we did not break up this data element into 2 data elements because the user still considered it a single piece of business information.

QUESTIONS AT THIS STEP

- Is there business value to parsing Restaurant Owner Name?
- Is there business value to parsing Check Date And Time?
- Is there business value to parsing Dessert Offered Date Range?
- Is there business value to parsing Dessert Category Code?
- Is Order Number an intelligent key? How about Item Code? Restaurant Code? Menu Code?

Logical data model

6. Remove repeating data elements

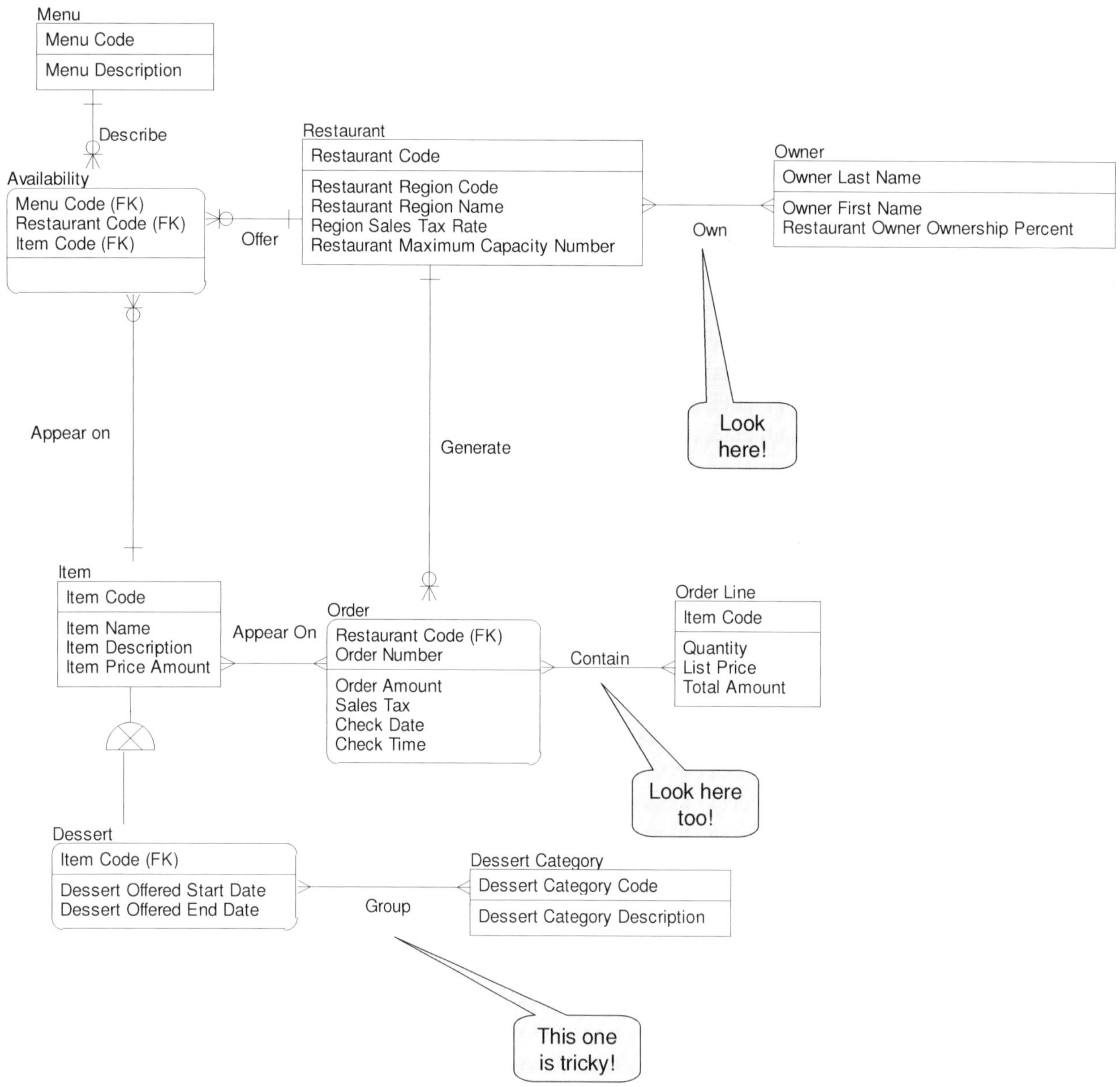

Logical data model

6. Remove repeating data elements

BACKGROUND

A repeating data element occurs when two or more of the same data element exists within the same entity. Repeating data elements is bad, because data elements fix the number of values an entity instance can have. If a data element is repeated three times in an entity, we can have at most three occurrences of this data element for a given entity instance. We cannot have four and we waste space if we have only one or two. Therefore, we need to move the data element that is repeating to a new entity.

In this example there are several opportunities to resolve repeating groups. Sometimes repeating groups can be hiding such as Dessert Category Code. One must read the definition to realize that this is a repeating group.

QUESTION AT THIS STEP

- Does a Restaurant Owner exist independently of its Restaurant?
- Is there any significance to 1, 2, and 3 in the Owner elements? In other words, does Restaurant Owner 1 indicate the primary owner, Restaurant Owner 2 the silent partner, etc?
- What is the unique identifier for an Owner?

Logical data model

7. Resolve many-to-many relationships

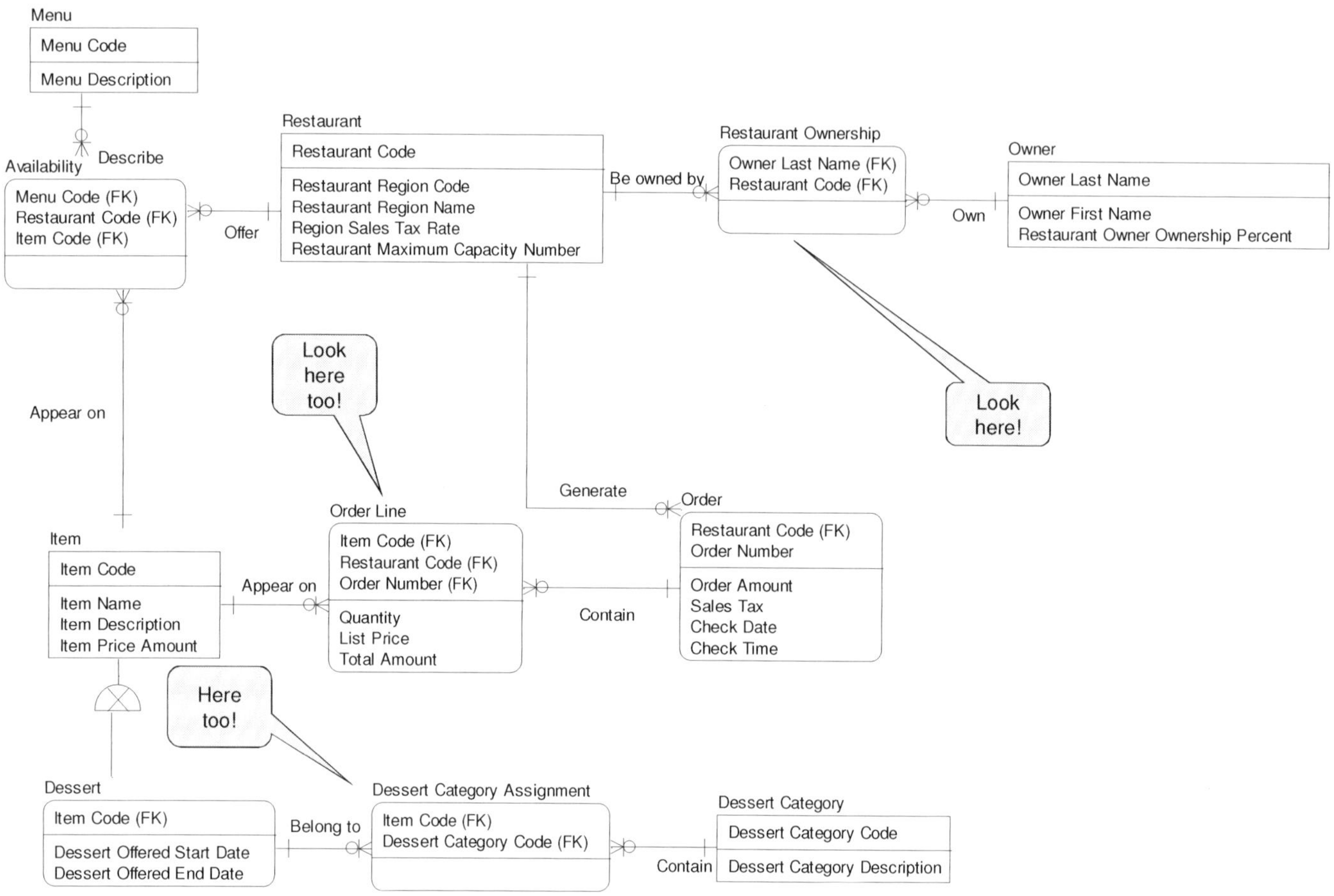

Logical data model

7. Resolve many-to-many relationships

BACKGROUND

Wherever there are many-to-many relationships on our model, we need to replace them with associative entities. Associative entities are entities that at a minimum contain the data element foreign keys from the two entities that made up the many-to-many relationship.

TIP

In coming up with a label for one side of an associative entity, pretend the associative entity does not exist and create a label as if you were reading from one kernel entity to the other.

QUESTION AT THIS STEP

Let's think more about Order Line? How is it really uniquely identified?

Logical data model

8. Remove data elements not dependent on whole primary key

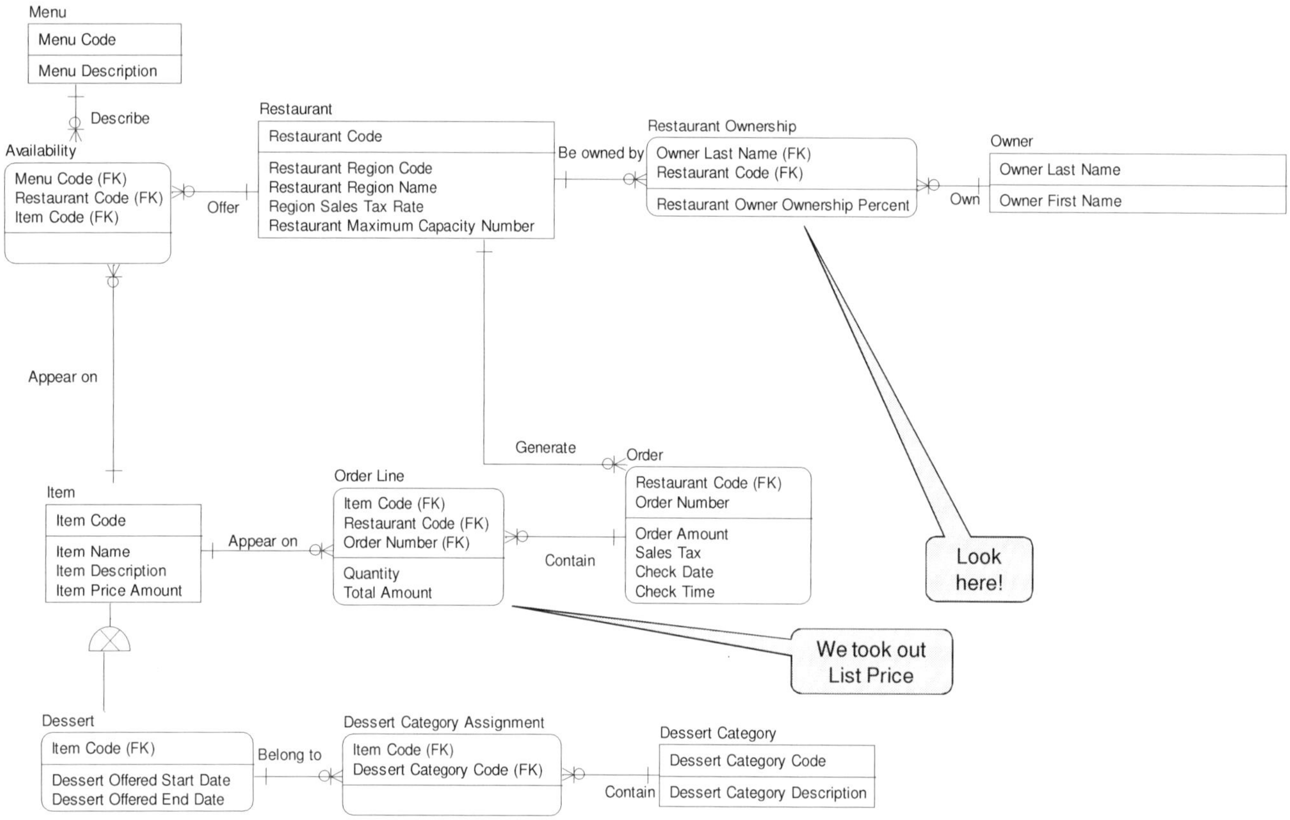

Logical data model

8. Remove data elements not dependent on whole primary key

BACKGROUND

We need to make sure that each entity contains the minimal primary key. Partial key dependencies must be resolved.

QUESTION AT THIS STEP

Is List Price in Order Line dependent only on Item Code? If yes, is it redundant with Item Price Amount?

Logical data model

9. Remove data elements not directly dependent on primary key

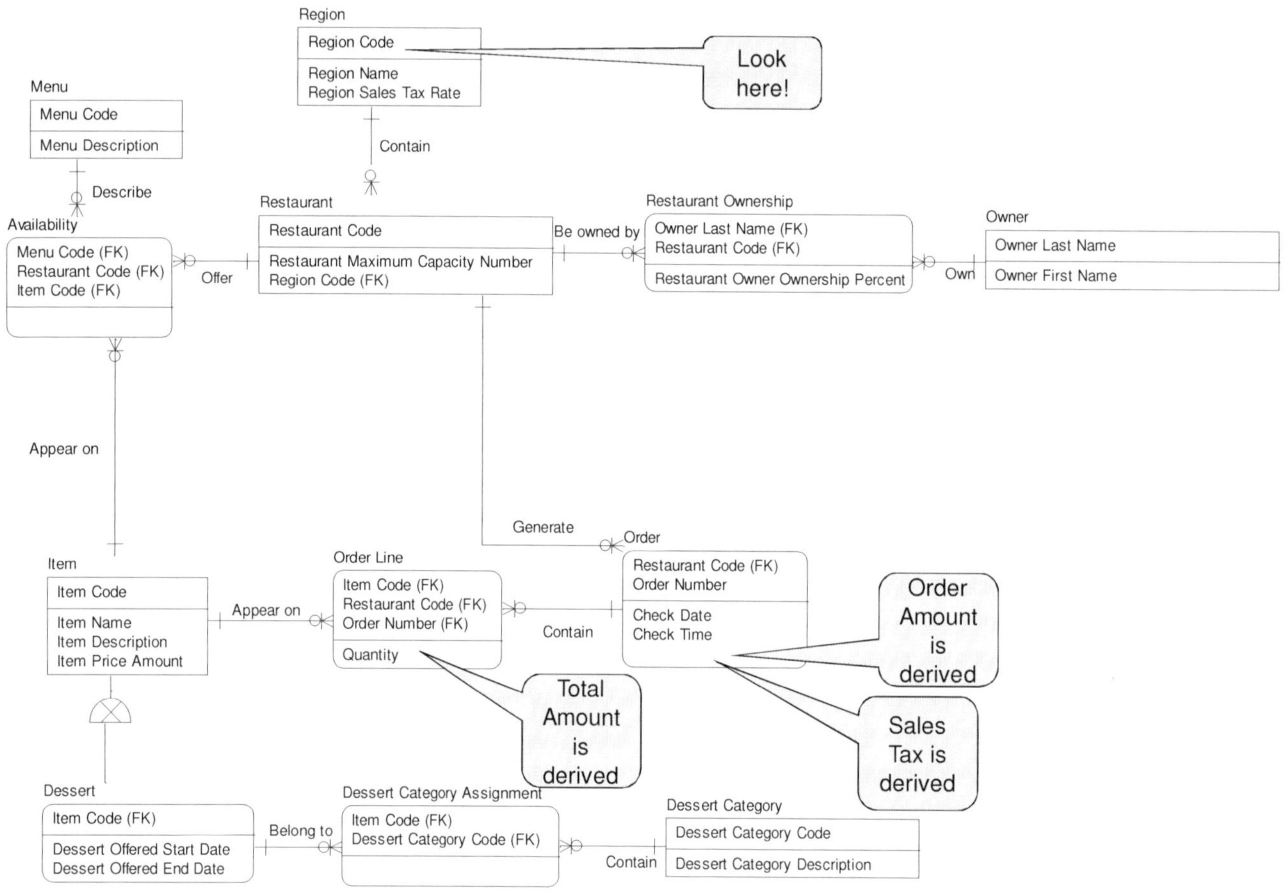

Logical data model

9. Remove data elements not directly dependent on primary key

BACKGROUND

Here we remove hidden dependencies. Each non-key data element must be directly dependent on the primary key, and not directly dependent on any other non-key data elements within the same entity.

Violations most commonly fall into the two categories illustrated in this example:

- derived data
- decodes embedded with codes in non-lookup entities

QUESTIONS AT THIS STEP

- Can a Region contain zero Restaurants?
- Sales Tax in Order is completely derived, correct?
- Total Amount in Order Line is derived, right?
- Is Order Amount in Order derived too?

Logical data model

Covering Boyce-Codd Normal Form (BCNF) in steps 8 & 9

Enrollment

Student Number
Course Number

Student Last Name (AK1.2)
Course Name (AK1.1)
Date Enrolled

Student #	Course #	Student Last Name	Course Name	Date Enrolled
123	789	Jones	Literature	9/1/11
58	789	Smith	Literature	9/15/11
58	567	Smith	Acting 101	2/25/11
123	567	Jones	Acting 101	3/5/11
123	90	Jones	Juggling	4/1/11

Logical data model

Covering Boyce-Codd Normal Form (BCNF) in steps 8 & 9

EXPLANATION OF BCNF

Raymond Boyce and Edgar Codd defined BCNF to be a model with no overlapping candidate keys. A candidate key is one or more data elements that uniquely identify a record. Therefore a candidate key can be either a primary or alternate key (and nothing else). To arrive at an overlapping situation, at least one of the candidate keys must be composite. Composite means that the key contains more than one data element.

WHY STEPS 8 AND 9 COVER BCNF

3NF applies the dependency rules to non-key data elements. BCNF applies the dependency rules to primary and alternate key data elements. If we simply ignore whether the data elements are key or not we can automatically apply 3NF and BCNF. Notice that in Steps 8 and 9 there is no reference to key or non-key. Therefore simply applying Steps 8 and 9 will cover 3NF and BCNF.

CAN'T CALL IT 3NF+!

BCNF was defined in 1974 as an improvement to 3NF. Rather than call this improved 3NF something like 3NF+, it is called the last names of the two inventors. Codd is the same Codd who defined the previous levels of normalization.

EXAMPLE

In the example on the facing page, Student Last Name is dependent on Student Number and Course Name is dependent on Course Number. Therefore, we need to split this up into three tables as shown.

Logical data model

Fun with Boyce-Codd Normal Form (BCNF)!

Account

Account Identifier
Account Code (AK1.1,AK2.1) Account Open Date Account Type Code (AK1.2) Account Type Description (AK2.2)

Account Id	Account Code	Account Open Date	Account Type Code	Account Type Description
123	M20081	3/5/2010	C	Checking
583	M20081	1/4/2011	S	Savings
584	M20081	3/10/2011	B	Brokerage
126	A20074	4/20/2010	S	Savings
127	A20074	3/18/2011	B	Brokerage

Logical data model

Fun with Boyce-Codd Normal Form (BCNF)!

EXERCISE Is this model in BCNF? If no, how do we fix it?

HINT What is the relationship between an Account and its Type (e.g. Brokerage, Savings, Checking)?

Your model:

Logical data model

10. Look for hidden business rules in the primary keys of entities with three or more identifying relationships

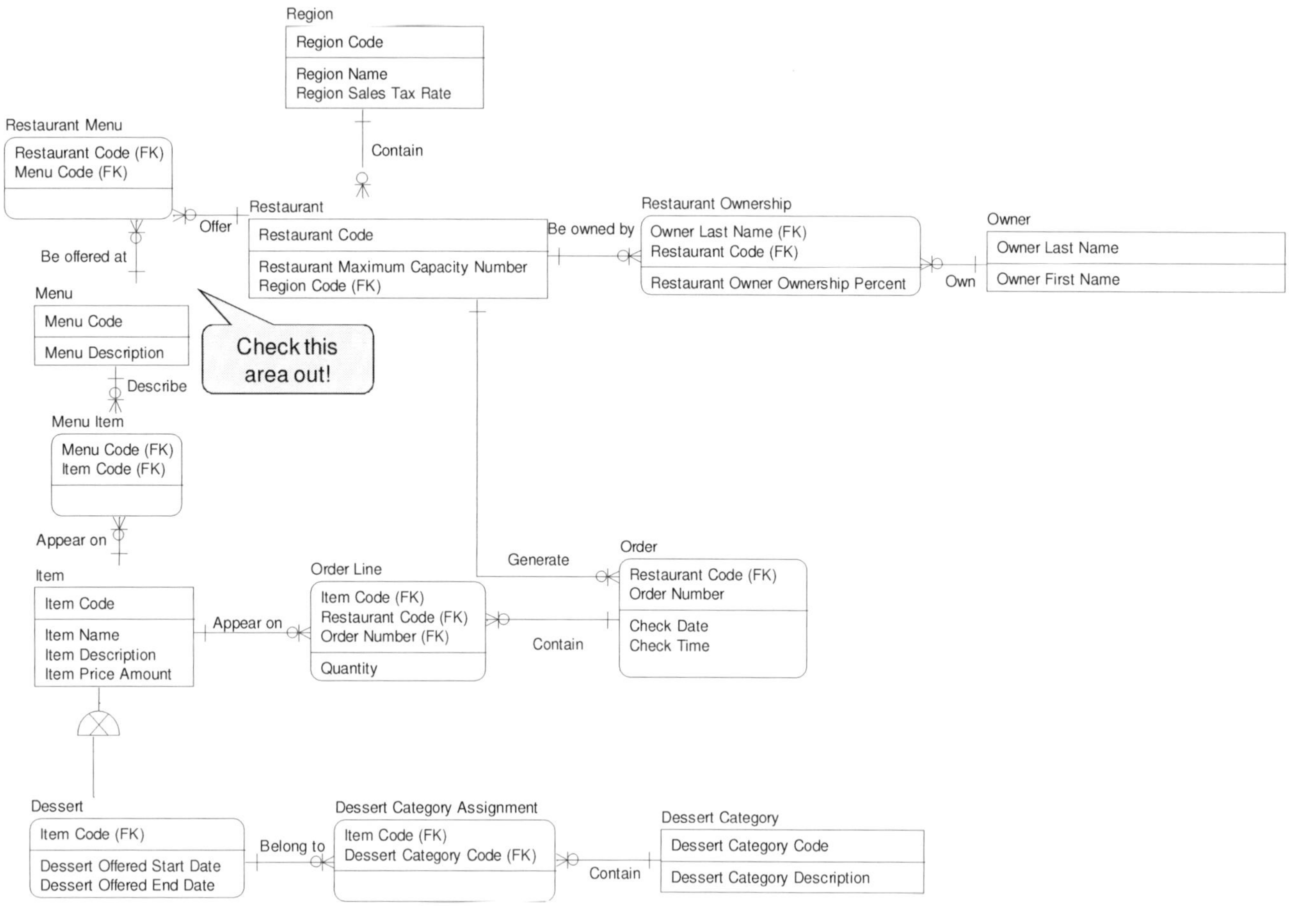

Logical data model

10. Look for hidden business rules in the primary keys of entities with three or more identifying relationships

BACKGROUND

Sometimes instead of a many-to-many relationship we might find ourselves with many-to-many-to-many relationships (and even more complex). In these situations ask yourself "Are business rules hiding in the primary key of these complex associative entities?" If the answer is "yes", show these rules. Showing these rules increases model integrity and removes redundancies from the model.

In the model on the facing page, there are rules between Menu and Restaurant and also between Menu and Item that we now show. Not all Restaurants offer all Menus and not all Menus contain all Items and these are the rules which are now enforced on the model.

ABOUT 4NF AND 5NF

Ronald Fagin redefined 4NF in 1977 and 5NF in 1979. Normalization has been around a long time! There is quite a bit of formal notation around both of these, which could explain why these levels of normalization are rarely understood and therefore practiced. What is even more complex is that informally there is no difference between the two levels! Informally, both 4NF and 5NF say "Show hidden rules!"

4NF states that all many-to-many-to-many relationships (and beyond) cannot be broken down into any smaller pieces. 5NF says that you should keep decomposing the model into more boxes and lines until you can't go any further. You reach the end in 5NF when putting the tables back together again no longer produces the original model. Just remember to show the hidden business rules and you complete both levels of normalization.

QUESTION AT THIS STEP

Are there any business rules hiding in Availability?

Logical data model

10. Look for hidden business rules in the primary keys of entities with three or more identifying relationships

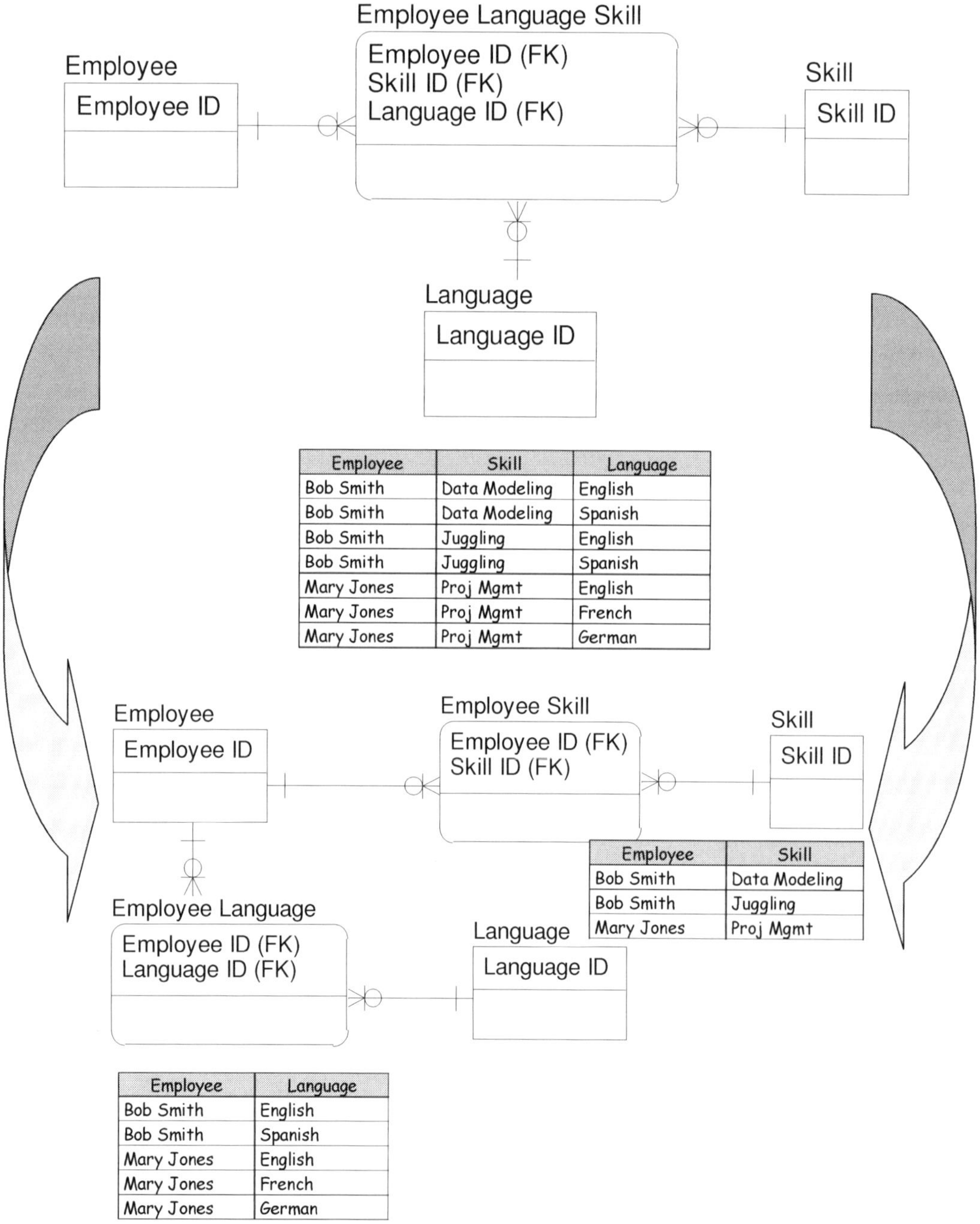

Employee	Skill	Language
Bob Smith	Data Modeling	English
Bob Smith	Data Modeling	Spanish
Bob Smith	Juggling	English
Bob Smith	Juggling	Spanish
Mary Jones	Proj Mgmt	English
Mary Jones	Proj Mgmt	French
Mary Jones	Proj Mgmt	German

Employee	Skill
Bob Smith	Data Modeling
Bob Smith	Juggling
Mary Jones	Proj Mgmt

Employee	Language
Bob Smith	English
Bob Smith	Spanish
Mary Jones	English
Mary Jones	French
Mary Jones	German

Logical data model

10. Look for hidden business rules in the primary keys of entities with three or more identifying relationships

EXAMPLE

By breaking apart Employee Language Skill we are able to remove data redundancies and enforce more business rules.

QUESTION AT THIS STEP

Are Language and Skills independent of each other?

Logical data model

10. Look for hidden business rules in the primary keys of entities with three or more identifying relationships

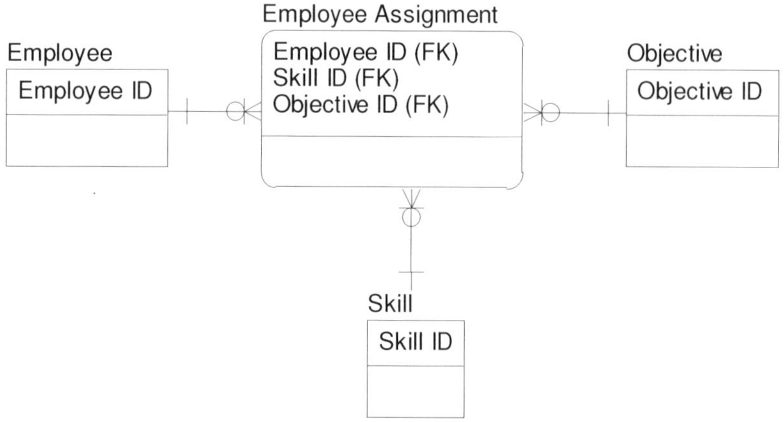

Employee	Skill	Objective
Bob Smith	Data Modeling	Design Sales Data Mart
Bob Smith	Facilitation	Analyze Sales Data Mart Reqs
Bob Smith	Juggling	Entertain at Company Picnic
Mary Jones	Juggling	Entertain at Company Picnic
Mary Jones	Proj Mgmt	Manage Sales Data Mart

Logical data model

10. Look for hidden business rules in the primary keys of entities with three or more identifying relationships

EXERCISE Is the model on the facing page in 5NF? If not, restructure it below.

Your model:

Logical data model

Is there life after 5NF?

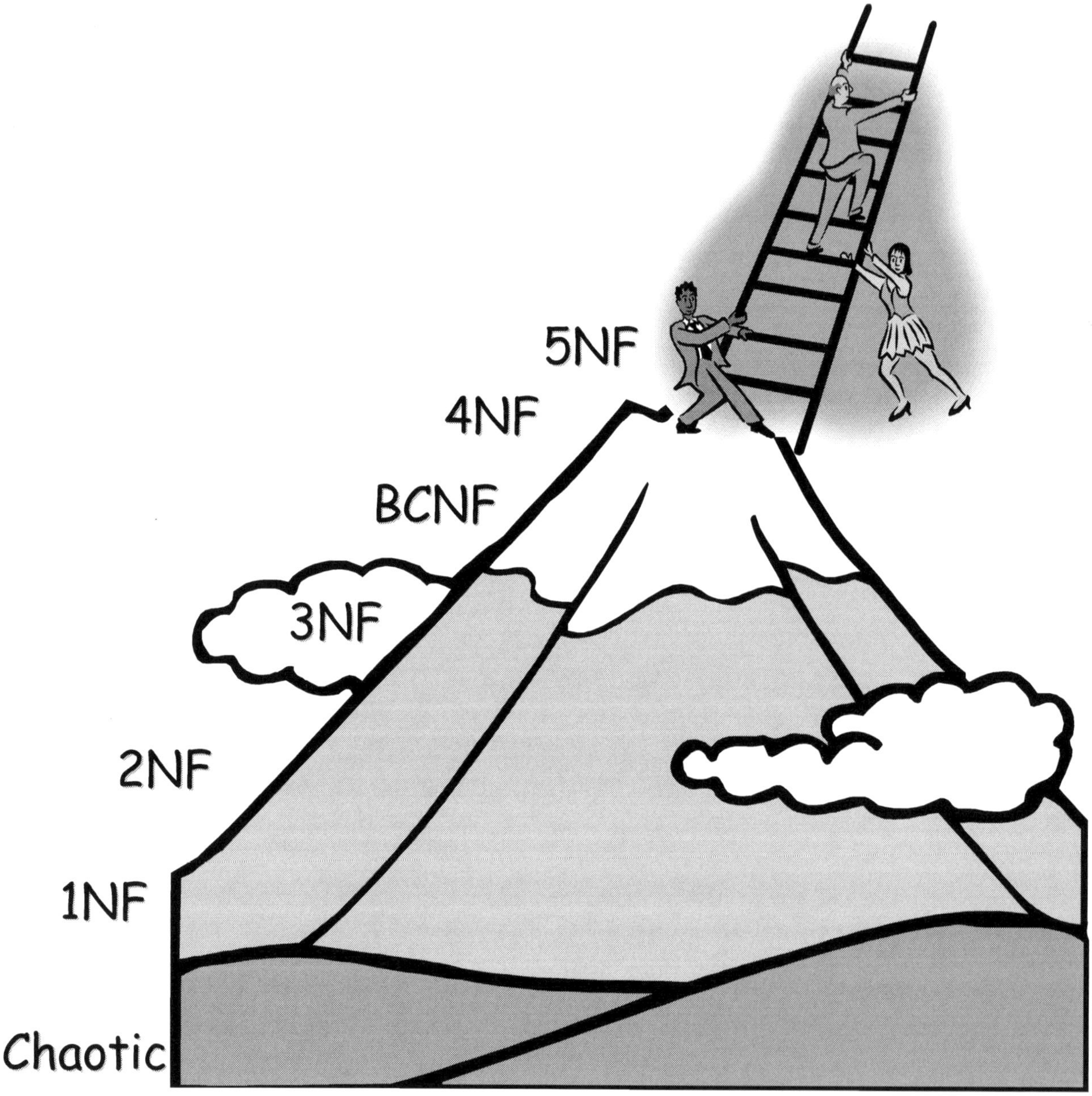

Make sure every data element is single-valued and depends completely and only on its primary key, and make sure there are no hidden business rules in any primary keys

Logical data model

Is there life after 5NF?

BACKGROUND

If you were going to summarize the different levels of normalization, you can cover up through 5NF with this statement: "Make sure every data element is single-valued and depends completely and only on its primary key, and make sure there are no hidden business rules in any primary keys."

There are higher levels of normalization defined. Domain Key Normal Form (DKNF) was clarified by Ronald Fagin in 1981 and Sixth Normal Form (6NF) was clarified by Date in 2002 to capture temporal data.

DKNF enforces that all constraints (primary key and domain) be correct and complete. This means for example, that if you have a data element called Gender Code, it is connected with an appropriate domain, such as {Male, Female}.

There isn't too much published on 6NF and what is out there appears contradictory. For instance, some say 6NF is the same as DKNF. Date published a book which includes a description of 6NF titled "Temporal Data and the Relational Model."

If I was to summarize DKNF and 6NF and anything else beyond (7NF?), it would be "If you didn't fix it up to this point, fix it now!" Make sure your model contains high integrity including the use of domains, which is something we usually don't leverage yet can offer much value in terms of higher data quality and greater model consistency.

Physical data model

The physical data model is the technical solution

History

Performance

User friendly

Network

Perception

Software

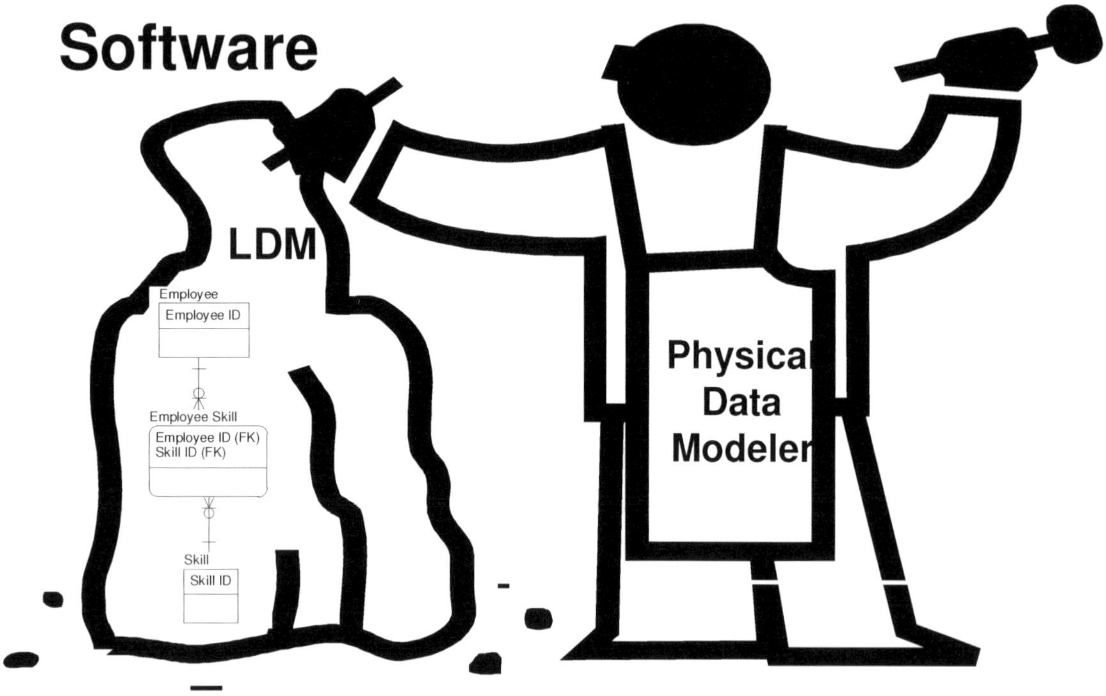

Security

Hardware

Space

Backup and recovery

Physical data model

The physical data model is the technical solution

BACKGROUND

The logical data model represents a business solution. The physical data model represents a technical solution. The technical solution needs to take into account all of the software and hardware and networking components of the application. Physical data models based upon the same logical data model will vary greatly if one is for an application to be run on FoxPro and another is for an application to be run on Teradata, for example. A physical data model designed for FoxPro will vary quite a bit from its logical data model to compensate for the lack of scalability and robustness present in FoxPro. Teradata, however, is a much more powerful platform. As a result, a physical data model designed for Teradata will more closely resemble the logical.

A way to summarize the physical data model is that it accounts for the realities which are not of concern on the logical. The logical is an ideal model; the physical model incorporates compromises to make things work efficiently.

Physical data model

Summary of physical data modeling techniques

	Rel	Dim
Denormalization	✓	"Flattening" = Star Schema
Indexing	✓	✓
Views	✓	✓
Partitioning	✓	"Snowflaking"

Physical data model

Summary of physical data modeling techniques

RELATIONAL AND DIMENSIONAL PHYSICAL DATA MODELS

As with subject area and logical data models, there are two types of physical data models: Relational and Dimensional.

Physical relational data models are used for operational systems, integration hubs such as a data warehouse or operational data store, and data marts focused on static reporting or non-metric facts.

Physical dimensional data models are built in general exclusively for reporting on metric facts such as quantities and amounts.

PHYSICAL DATA MODELING TECHNIQUES

Denormalization is a term that is applied exclusively to physical relational models, because you can't denormalize something unless it has already been normalized. However, the denormalization techniques can be applied to dimensional models as well, you just can't use the term 'denormalization'.

Physical data model

Denormalization overview

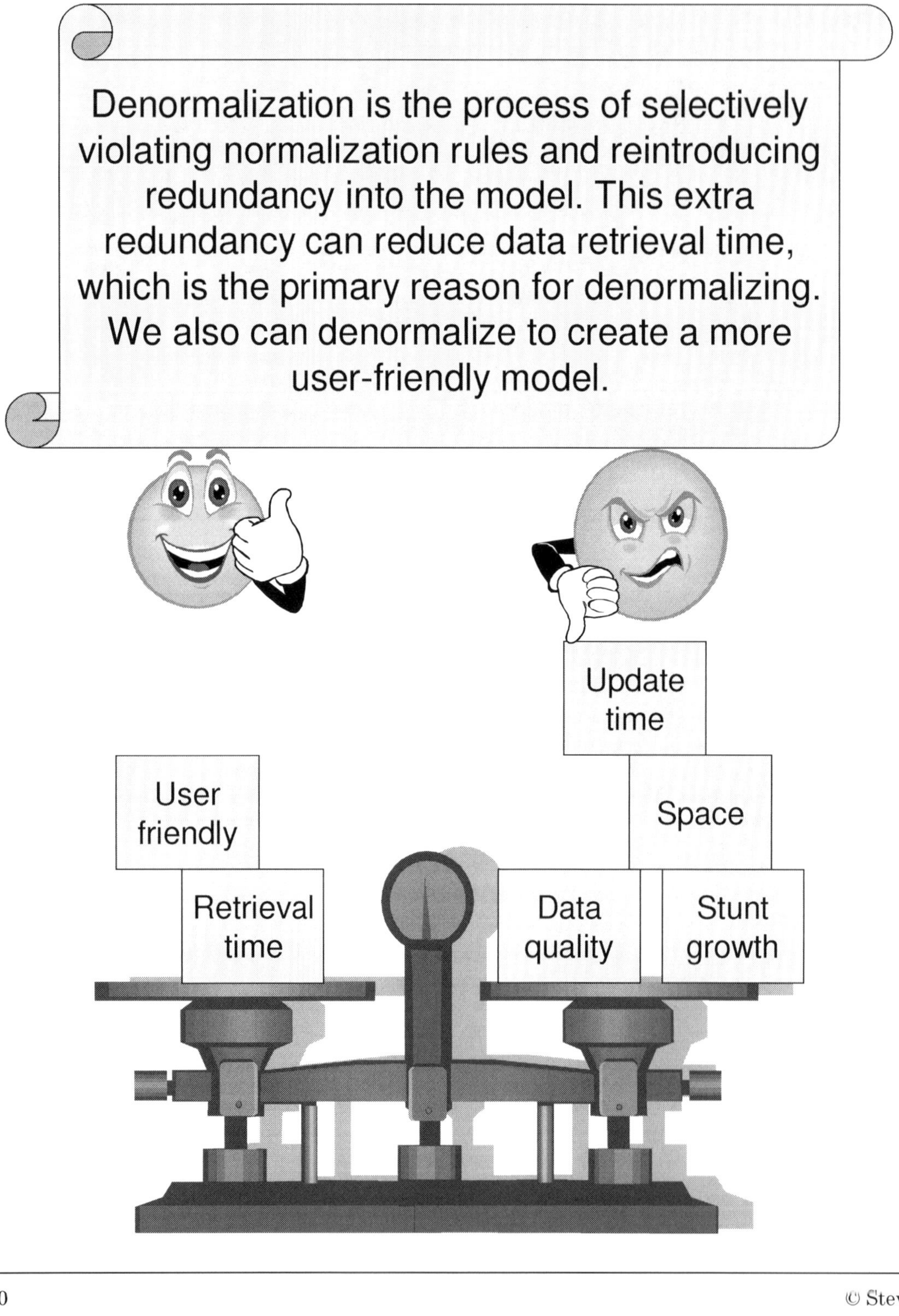

Physical data model

Denormalization overview

BACKGROUND

Denormalization is the process of selectively violating normalization rules and reintroducing redundancy into the model. This extra redundancy can reduce data retrieval time, which is the primary reason for denormalizing. We also can denormalize to create a more user-friendly model.

INCREASES UPDATE, DELETE, AND INSERT TIME

When we repeat the value of a data element, we can usually reduce retrieval time. However, if we have to change the value that we are repeating, we need to change it wherever it occurs. If we are repeating *company* information for each *employee*, for example, and a *company name* value is changed, we will need to make this update for each *employee* instance that works for this company.

TAKES UP MORE SPACE

In a table with a small number of records, extra storage space incurred by denormalization is usually not substantial. However, in tables with millions of rows, every character could require megabytes of additional space. You might be thinking that space is cheap. It is true that space is becoming cheaper every day. However, I recently had to purchase more storage space for one of my projects, and I was amazed at the amount of time required to go through the budgeting process and red tape to actually receive the storage space. Space was cheap, but time was not.

INTRODUCES DATA QUALITY PROBLEMS

By having the same value appear multiple times, we substantially increase opportunities for data quality issues when those values change. Imagine, for example, if we failed to update all *employee* instances of a company name change if company information is denormalized into *employee*. Also, denormalizing reduces the number of relationships and therefore reduces the amount of referential integrity on our model. Denormalizing company information into *employee* means we can no longer enforce the rule that each *employee* must work for a valid company.

STUNTS GROWTH OF THE APPLICATION

When we denormalize, it can become harder to enhance structures to meet new requirements, because before we add data elements or relationships we need to understand all the hidden rules on the physical data model that were shown on the logical data model. If *year* and *month* are denormalized into *day*, we can quickly retrieve year and month information when viewing a particular day. However, it would be very challenging to expand this denormalized time structure to add *week*, for example. We would have to sort through all the redundant data and then add new redundant data for *week*.

Physical data model

Denormalization Survival Guide

The view is awesome!

But descending can be dangerous!

Physical data model

Denormalization Survival Guide

BACKGROUND

Denormalization is the most dangerous of all of the physical data modeling techniques. Denormalization brings back negative design qualities that the process of normalization removed. Therefore be very selective when you are denormalizing.

The Normalization Hike brought us up to the top of the mountain. After admiring the world from the top of the mountain for some time, reality sets in. We eventually have to leave this beautiful, well understood view, and work our way back down the trail. Going down the mountain is usually more dangerous than going up. There are certain rules in hiking downhill, such as walking heel to toe and maintaining a consistent momentum and pace. Following these rules will lead to safely finding a spot on the descent to camp for the night. After reaching fifth normal form, we too have to succumb to reality and realize that our design is probably going to require some changes in order for it to be efficient using current technology. There are therefore also certain rules you must follow for your own safety when descending this fifth normal form lookup point, and modifying your physical data model for your current environment. The Denormalization Survival Guide is a set of factors to ensure you make the right denormalization decisions.

SOME QUOTES

In the reality in which we design very large databases, selective denormalization is often required – but it is important to initiate the design from a clean (normalized) starting point and use an engineering approach for choosing denormalization.
Stephen Brobst, Chief Technology Officer, Teradata

Normalize the data to at least the third normal form. At the same time, do not compromise on query performance (demoralization is allowed to increase performance).
Straight from the Database Guidelines document of a large Biotech company

Physical data model

Denormalization Survival Guide factors

	Operational	Integration hub	Reporting
Usage			
Data Volatility			
Structure volatility			
Space			

Physical data model

Denormalization Survival Guide factors

BACKGROUND

It is important to have an objective reason for denormalizing. There are several factors to consider within the context of the type of application being developed.

USAGE

Usage refers to the frequency the same data elements are accessed. When data elements are retrieved frequently across normalized structures, performance issues and user-friendly issues can arise. Performance issues are due to the time it takes to join foreign key to primary key across tables. User-friendly issues are due to complexity with the sheer quantity of tables and relationships. Usage is a very important factor in data mart design, but not usually relevant in operational systems. Usage becomes important factor for an integration hub when users access the integration hub directly.

DATA VOLATILITY

Data volatility refers to the frequency data element values are changed. When data element values change frequently, we need to carefully consider update performance and data quality when folding a set of data elements into a single table. Special consideration needs to be given when data element values change at different rates across denormalization candidates. Operational systems with usually high rates of change have data volatility as a very important factor.

STRUCTURE VOLATILITY

Structure volatility refers to the frequency data element structure is changed. It is always easier to reroute relationships and add new tables, than to figure out the implied relationships in a denormalized structure. This question is critical for applications needing a long life, such as most operational systems and all integration hubs.

SPACE

Redundancy refers to the quantity of extra space needed for the denormalized structure. We need to consider the participation ratio between the entities and the total length of characters in those data elements that will be repeated in the denormalized structure. The participation ratio is the rough estimate of how many children exist for given parent, and total length of characters is the sum of the length of all of those data elements usually in the parent entity. Redundancy is of concern to all types of applications, especially those with large amounts of history such as integration hubs. Space leads not just towards using extra megabytes (after all "space is cheap"), but also to performance issues in loading and retrieving this extra space.

Physical data model

Denormalization Survival Guide Example for Relational Data Mart

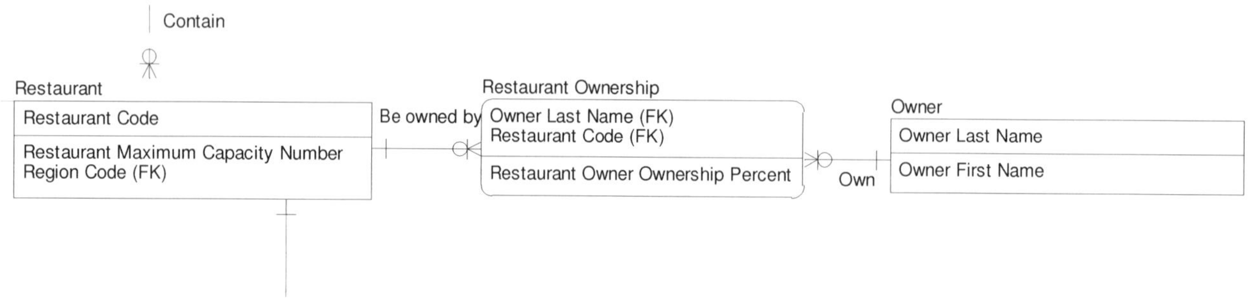

How often will these concepts be used together in queries and reports?

☐ Very often (30)

☐ Seldom or not at all (-30)

What is the participation ratio?

☐ Low (20)

☐ High (-20)

What is the length of each row that would be repeated?

☐ Short (20)

☐ Long (-20)

Physical data model

Denormalization Survival Guide Example for Relational Data Mart

WHY NOT MAKE IT A GAME?

The example on the facing page shows two entities from a relational data mart. The question is, "Should this structure be denormalized?" Looking at the important factors for a data mart from the previous page we need to consider are Usage and Space.

TURNING FACTORS INTO A QUESTION AND ANSWER SET OF GUIDELINES

Each of these factors can be turned into a set of questions with answers along with point values. For example, imagine asking the following questions for each of these two factors and assigning point values where the higher the final score, the greater the chance for denormalization. If the score is low, keep the model normalized!

USAGE

- How often will these concepts be used together in queries and reports?

REDUNDANCY

For space there are two considerations: number of rows and length of each row. Therefore there are two questions:

- What is the participation ratio?
- What is the length of each row that would be repeated?

Physical data model

Denormalizing techniques

Standard
FUBES
Repeating data elements
Summarization
Aggregation

Normalized model with sample data

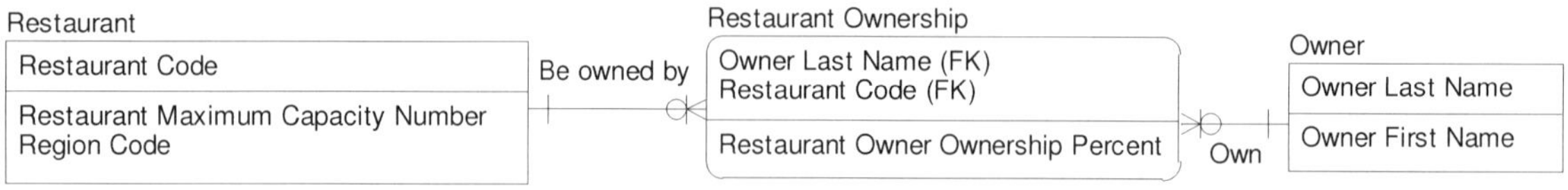

Restaurant Code	Max	Region
AB	150	NE
RE	225	SW
DE	75	SE

Last Name	Restaurant Code	Owner Percent
Winkler	AB	50
Murphy	AB	50
Martin	RE	100
Martin	DE	50
Murphy	DE	50

Last Name	First Name
Winkler	Henry
Martin	Steve
Murphy	Eddie

Physical data model

Denormalizing techniques

BACKGROUND

Once you decide you need to denormalize, there are 5 different techniques that can be used.

STANDARD

The standard method is the most common of the five denormalization techniques. The parent entity in the relationship disappears, and all the parent's data elements and relationships are moved to the child entity. Recall the child entity is on the many side of the relationship and contains the foreign key back to the parent entity, which appears on the one side of the relationship.

FUBES

FUBES (fold up but easily separate) is an acronym I made up for a technique that combines the standard method of denormalizing with also allowing access to just the parent data elements. There is an additional data element that contains a level code and additional instances for each of the parents.

REPEATING DATA ELEMENTS

In the repeating data elements technique, the same data element or group of data elements is repeated two or more times in the same entity. Also known as an *array*, a repeating group requires fixing the number of times something can occur.

SUMMARIZATION

Summarization is used when there is a need to report on higher levels of granularity than what is captured on the logical data model.

AGGREGATION

Aggregation is when you are combining two or more entities into one where a one-to-one relationship exists between the entities. You do not incur the redundancy from the Standard technique.

Physical data model

Denormalization technique: Standard

Option 1: Get rid of Restaurant

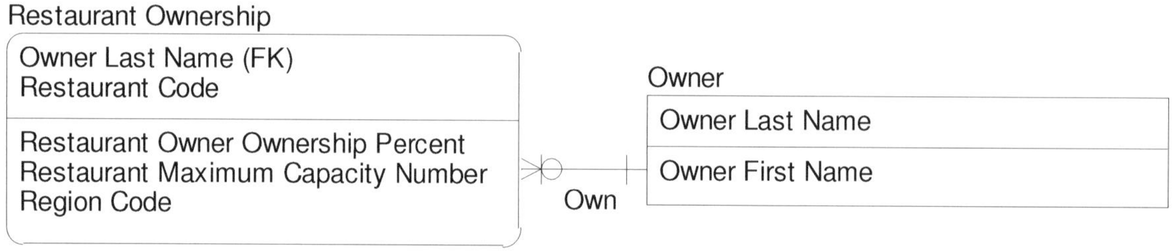

Last Name	Restaurant Code	Owner Percent	Max	Region
Winkler	AB	50	150	NE
Murphy	AB	50	150	NE
Martin	RE	100	225	SW
Martin	DE	50	75	SE
Murphy	DE	50	75	SE

Last Name	First Name
Winkler	Henry
Martin	Steve
Murphy	Eddie

Option 2: Get rid of Owner

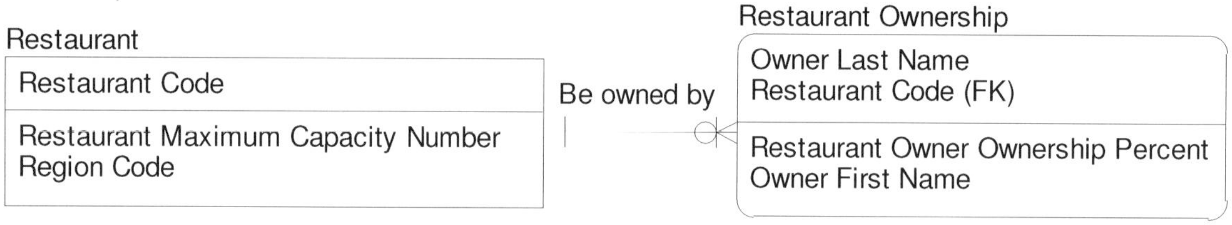

Restaurant Code	Max	Region
AB	150	NE
RE	225	SW
DE	75	SE

Last Name	Restaurant Code	Owner Percent	First Name
Winkler	AB	50	Henry
Murphy	AB	50	Eddie
Martin	RE	100	Steve
Martin	DE	50	Steve
Murphy	DE	50	Eddie

Physical data model

Denormalization technique: Standard

BACKGROUND

Standard denormalization is the traditional way of denormalizing. The parent data elements and relationships get folded up into the child entity.

WHEN TO USE

The standard way of denormalizing is ideal for the following situations:

- When you need to maintain the flexibility that existed on the normalized model. We still could support the many-to-many between Restaurant and Owner.
- When a majority of the time the retrieval required is only at the lowest level.
- When a user-friendly structure is required. At least one relationship has been removed making it less complicated for users to navigate (assuming users have access to the underlying structures which is a large assumption).

EXAMPLE

There are three options, two on the facing page and one below.

Option 3: Get rid of both Restaurant and Owner

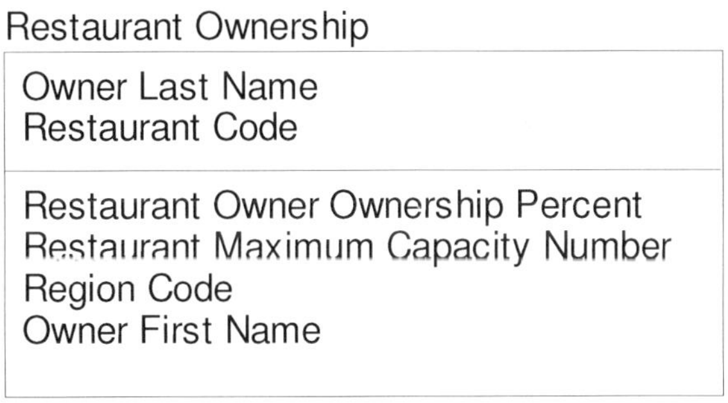

Last Name	Restaurant Code	Owner Percent	Max	Region	First Name
Winkler	AB	50	150	NE	Henry
Murphy	AB	50	150	NE	Eddie
Martin	RE	100	225	SW	Steve
Martin	DE	50	75	SE	Steve
Murphy	DE	50	75	SE	Eddie

Physical data model

Denormalization technique: FUBES

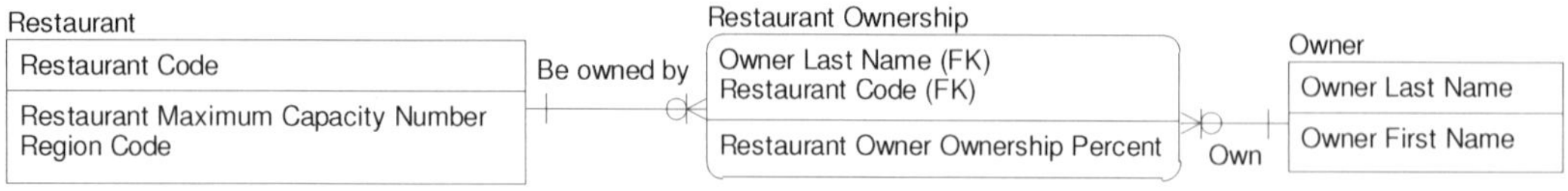

Restaurant Code	Max	Region
AB	150	NE
RE	225	SW
DE	75	SE

Last Name	Restaurant Code	Owner Percent
Winkler	AB	50
Murphy	AB	50
Martin	RE	100
Martin	DE	50
Murphy	DE	50

Last Name	First Name
Winkler	Henry
Martin	Steve
Murphy	Eddie

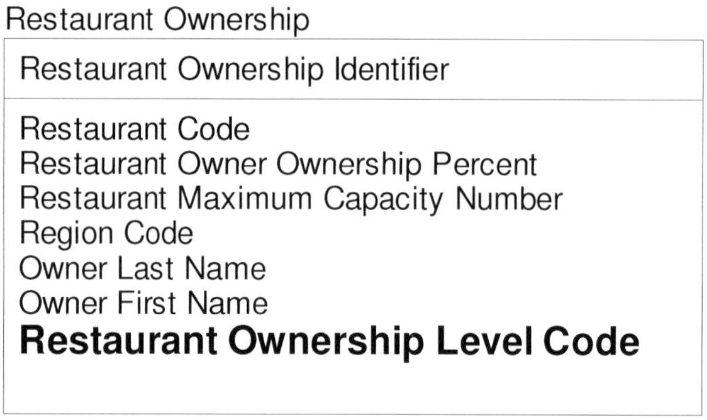

Restaurant Code	Owner Percent	Max	Region	Last Name	First Name	Level Code
AB	50	150	NE	Winkler	Henry	Ownership
AB	50	150	NE	Murphy	Eddie	Ownership
RE	100	225	SW	Martin	Steve	Ownership
DE	50	75	SE	Martin	Steve	Ownership
DE	50	75	SE	Murphy	Eddie	Ownership
AB		150	NE			Rest
RE		225	SW			Rest
DE		75	SE			Rest
				Winkler	Henry	Owner
				Murphy	Eddie	Owner
				Martin	Steve	Owner

Physical data model

Denormalization technique: FUBES

BACKGROUND

Fold Up But Easily Separate (FUBES) is when you denormalize two or more tables together, yet still have the ability to access individual instances from each of the entities. You can use FUBES when you would like everything from the Standard option, but also want to be able to access all entities instances that have been denormalized.

FUBES requires that a level or type code be added to the entity so that each of the entity instances can be retrieved.

WHEN TO USE

FUBES is the most flexible denormalization option, and also takes up the most space. Its primary use is for hierarchies, an example being shown on the following page.

The drawback for FUBES is that you need to include the level code in all the queries on the table. So for example, to access month information, we would need to select on the primary key plus where *time level code = month.* This requires slightly more complexity in queries and can lead to errors if this data element is accidentally omitted from queries. This complexity however, can be masked in the reporting tool.

Physical data model

Denormalization technique: FUBES

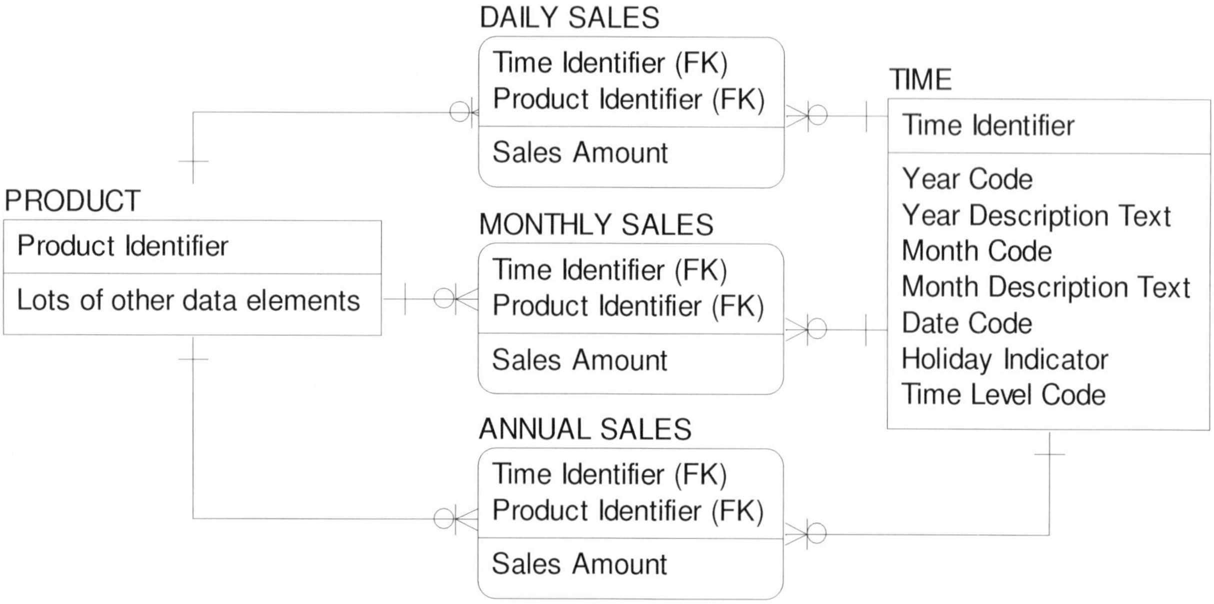

Several instances of *time*

Time Identifier	Year Code	Month Code	Date Code	Time Level Code
1	2011			Year
2	2011	Jan		Month
3	2011	June		Month
4	2011	June	6/1/2011	Date
5	2011	June	6/2/2011	Date

Physical data model

Denormalization technique: FUBES

EXAMPLE

FUBES should be chosen when there is value in denormalizing yet there is a still a need to access parent instances. Having an instance for each parent allows us to achieve better report performance as we can directly tie to parent levels without having to roll up from the child. We can store sales at a year level for example and save the query time of summarizing daily level sales up into a year level.

Although I did not show all the time data elements, you can see that for each child we are repeating the parent level data elements, just like the standard method. In addition, the *time level code* lets us immediately access parent instances which we could not do with the standard method.

Physical data model

Denormalization technique: Repeating data elements

Option 1:

Owner

Owner Last Name

Owner First Name
Restaurant Code 1
Restaurant Maximum Capacity Number 1
Region Code 1
Restaurant Owner Ownership Percent 1
Restaurant Code 2
Restaurant Maximum Capacity Number 2
Region Code 2
Restaurant Owner Ownership Percent 2
Restaurant Code 3
Restaurant Maximum Capacity Number 3
Region Code 3
Restaurant Owner Ownership Percent 3

Last Name	First Name	Code 1	Max 1	Reg 1	% 1	Code 2	Max 2	Reg 2	% 2
Winkler	Henry	AB	150	NE	50				
Murphy	Eddie	AB	150	NE	50	DE	75	SE	50
Martin	Steve	RE	225	SW	100	DE	75	SE	50

Option 2:

Restaurant

Restaurant Code

Restaurant Maximum Capacity Number
Region Code
Restaurant Owner Ownership Percent 1
Owner Last Name 1
Owner First Name 1
Restaurant Owner Ownership Percent 2
Owner Last Name 2
Owner First Name 2
Restaurant Owner Ownership Percent 3
Owner Last Name 3
Owner First Name 3

Code	Max	Region	% 1	Last Name 1	First Name 1	% 2	Last Name 2	First Name 2
AB	150	NE	50	Winkler	Henry	50	Murphy	Eddie
RE	225	SW	100	Martin	Steve			
DE	75	SE	50	Martin	Steve	50	Murphy	Eddie

Physical data model

Denormalization technique: Repeating data elements

BACKGROUND

The repeating data elements technique is when you copy one or more data elements from one entity into one or more other entities. It is done primarily for performance because by repeating data elements across entities we can reduce the number of joins needed to return results. If we repeat *customer last name* in *order* for example, we avoid navigating back to *customer* whenever just *customer last name* is needed for display with order information.

It can also be used to repeat sets of data elements to create an array or simulate a spreadsheet.

WHEN TO USE

The repeating-group technique is useful in the following situations:

- **When it makes more sense to keep the parent entity instead of the child entity.** It can make more sense when the parent entity is going to be used more frequently than the child or if there are rules and data elements useful to preserve in the parent entity format.
- When an entity instance will never exceed the fixed number of data elements added.
- **When you need a spreadsheet.** We would repeat the one or more data elements that appear in the spreadsheet column headers. This can lead to producing the report in less time than by stringing together a large number of entity instances.
- When the repeated data element or elements are accessed often and experience little or no changes over time.
- **When the standard denormalization option is preferred but space is an issue.** Possibly there would be too huge an impact on storage space if the entire parent entity was folded up into the child and repeated for each child value. Therefore only repeat those data elements that provide the greatest benefits.

Physical data model

Denormalization technique: Repeating data elements

SALES SUMMARY REPORT

SALES SUMMARY REPORT
Product Identifier Month Code Year Code
Current Month - 1 Total Sales Amount Current Month - 2 Total Sales Amount Current Month - 3 Total Sales Amount Current Month - 4 Total Sales Amount Current Month - 5 Total Sales Amount Current Month - 6 Total Sales Amount Current Month - 7 Total Sales Amount Current Month - 8 Total Sales Amount Current Month - 9 Total Sales Amount Current Month - 10 Total Sales Amount Current Month - 11 Total Sales Amount Current Month - 12 Total Sales Amount Lots of other sales report data elements

Physical data model

Denormalization technique: Repeating data elements

EXAMPLE

At the end of a given month, the oldest value is removed and a new value is added. This is called a rolling 12 months. Faster performance and a more user-friendly structure lead us to adding repeating groups in this example and purposely violating 1NF.

DIMENSIONAL TECHNIQUE

In dimensional modeling terms, this is called a pivoted fact table. A set of metrics become a single row instead of multiple rows. Very similar to a spreadsheet.

Physical data model

Denormalization technique: Summarization

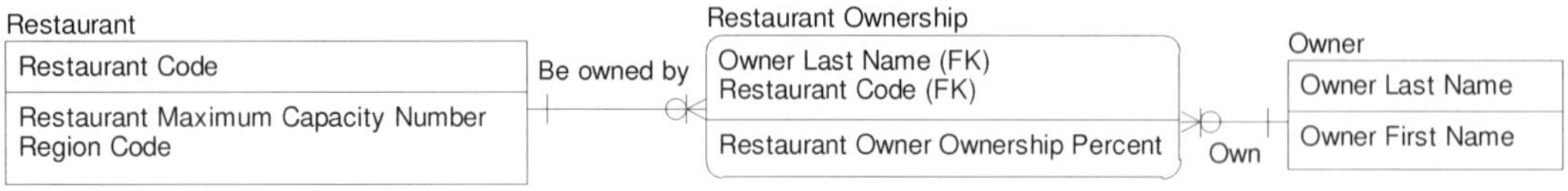

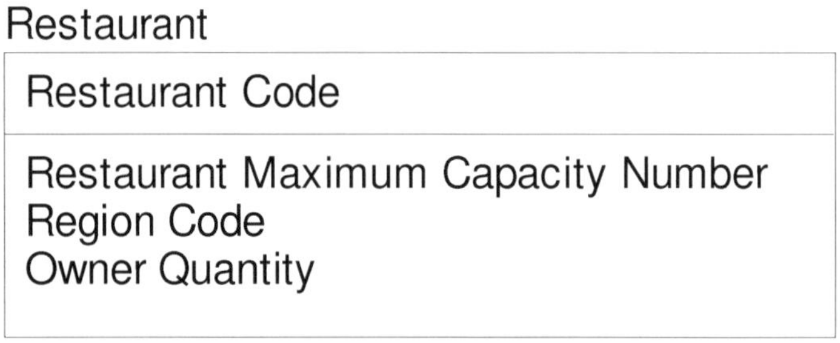

Restaurant Code	Maximum	Region	Owner Quantity
AB	150	NE	2
RE	225	SW	1
DE	75	SE	2

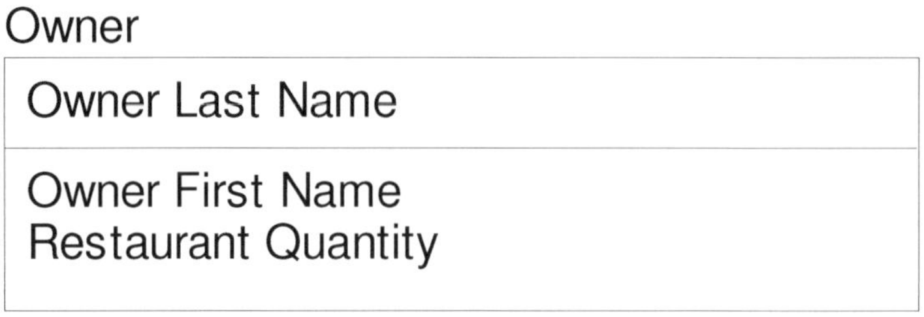

Last Name	First Name	Restaurant Quantity
Winkler	Henry	1
Martin	Steve	2
Murphy	Eddie	2

Physical data model

Denormalization technique: Summarization

BACKGROUND

A summary table contains information at a higher level of granularity than exists in the business. In our restaurant and owner example, we are storing quantities instead of the actual values.

WHEN TO USE

Extra redundancy from the summary tables not only takes up more space but leads to extra development effort. It takes a greater time of the batch processing window to populate summary tables, so make sure the value is greater than the cost. Summary structures are more common with transaction data.

Physical data model

Denormalization technique: Summarization

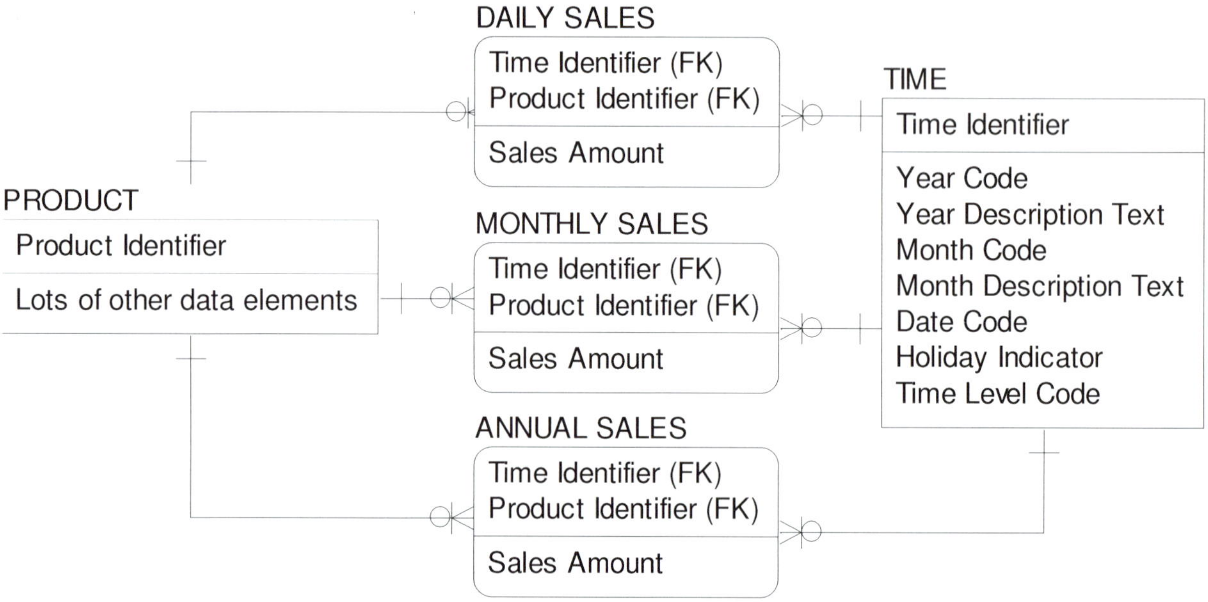

You can also summarize by ignoring one or more dimensions

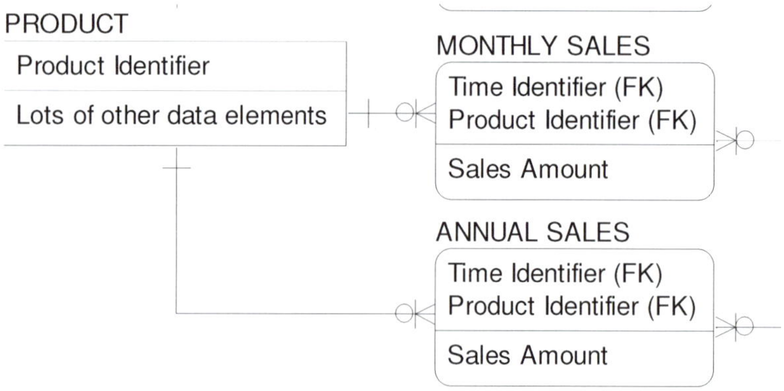

What is our total sales amount of Product XYZ?

Physical data model

Denormalization technique: Summarization

EXAMPLE

The summary table in this example allows the user to answer high-level questions without spending time figuring out how to do it with very low-level tables. The response time is also much quicker because of the highly summarized nature of the data.

The only difference between a summary fact table and a base fact table is the level of grain. A base fact table contains the lowest level within a data mart, and a summary table contains a higher level of grain.

HIGHEST LEVEL OF SUMMARIZATION

The highest level of summarization is to ignore one or more dimensions altogether. In the example on the facing page, if the user ignores the time dimension and just queries on the sales of products, this would be an example of a very high level of summarization.

To summarize, or not to summarize

What factors are important when deciding whether to summarize?

1.

2.

3.

4.

5.

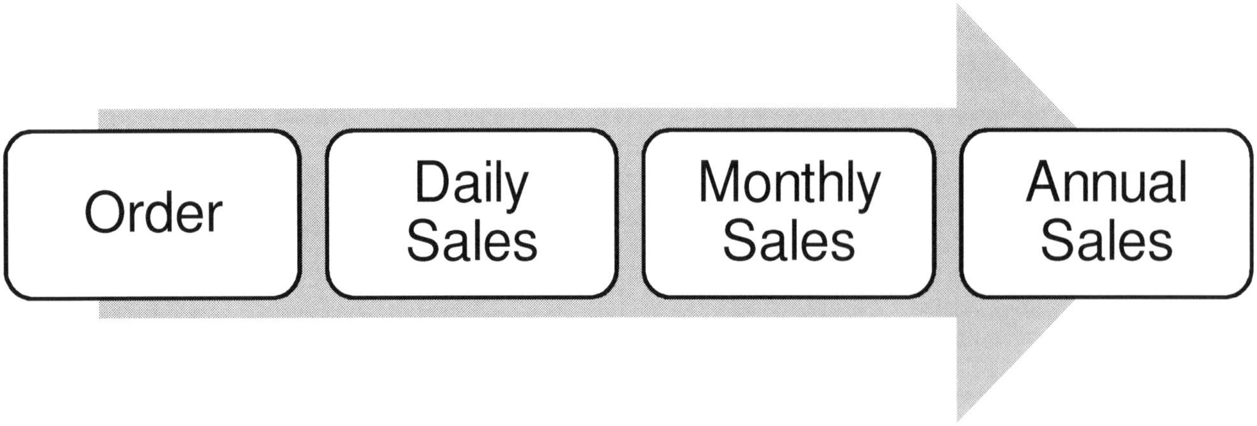

To summarize, or not to summarize

BACKGROUND

As a data modeling expert in your company, you are frequently being asked modeling advice. On your way to the coffee machine one day, a project team manager stops you and explains: "Our team is working hard to document business rules, yet we feel we are lacking a number of IT rules. For example, what are the rules around when we should build a summary table?"

CHALLENGE

How would you respond? List the factors you would consider important in deciding whether to build a summary table.

PURPOSE

Develop guidelines to consistently apply the construction of summary structures.

TIPS

There are definitely situations where it does NOT make sense to build a summary table.

Physical data model

Denormalization technique: Aggregation

Relational example:

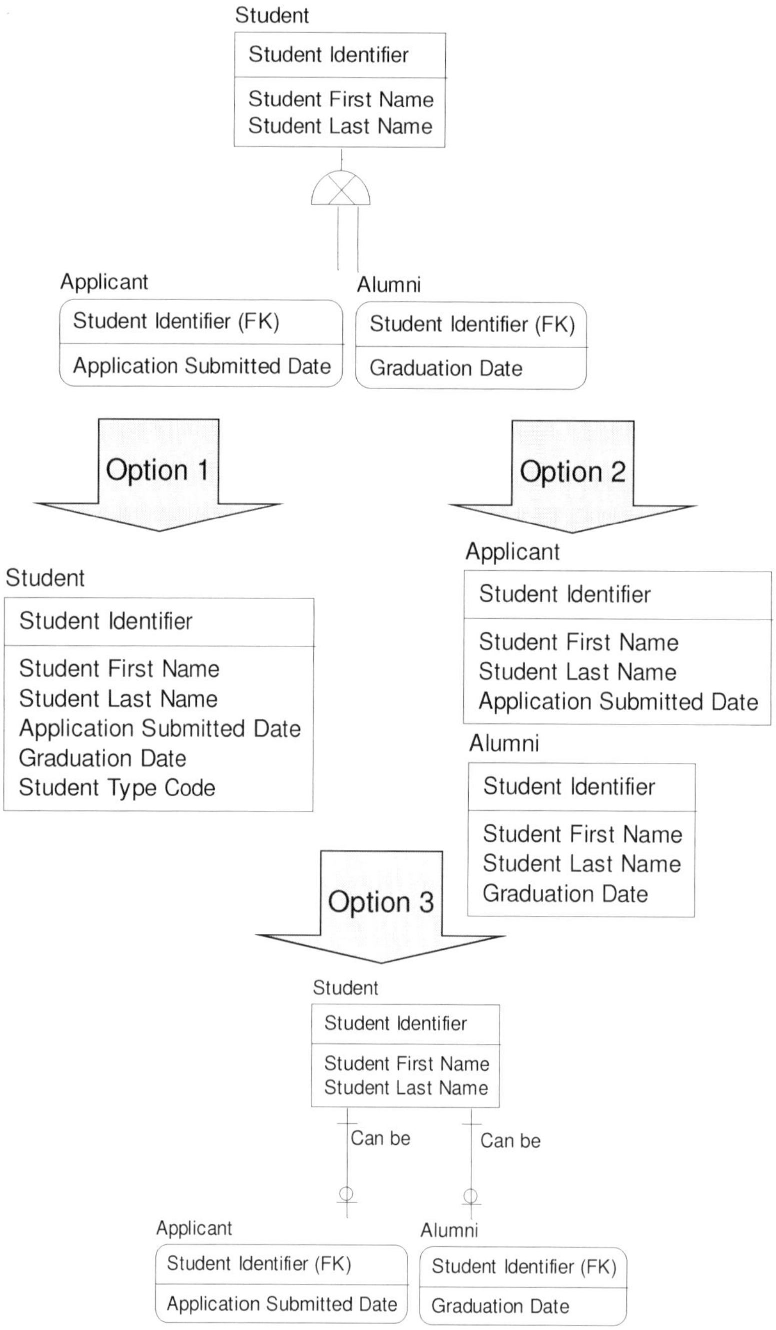

Physical data model

Denormalization technique: Aggregation

BACKGROUND

Aggregation is when you combine two or more tables together that have a one-to-one relationship. Option 1 is called rolling up, Option 2 is rolling down, and Option 3 which is identity (not a aggregation technique but shown here for completeness), is when the subtype symbol is replaced with one-to-one relationships.

DIMENSIONAL TECHNIQUE

A merged fact is when fact tables from different marts are combined into a single structure (see below for example). Fact tables with the same grain are combined to reduce database overhead and allow users to answer even more business questions. If fact tables do not have the same grain, or are sparsely populated, zeros (or worse nulls) can appear as measurement values which can cause confusion on the reporting side. "Why are there zero shipments on Tuesday, April 1st, 2011?"

WHEN TO USE

Rolling up is ideal when extra flexibility is required or when the subtypes are representing a lifecycle where subtypes can move through the different stages in the lifecycle. Rolling down is usually ideal for reporting situations where the supertype can be too generic. It is also used in situations where there are very little common properties across the subtypes. Identity preserves the most rules however performance can suffer.

Dimensional example:

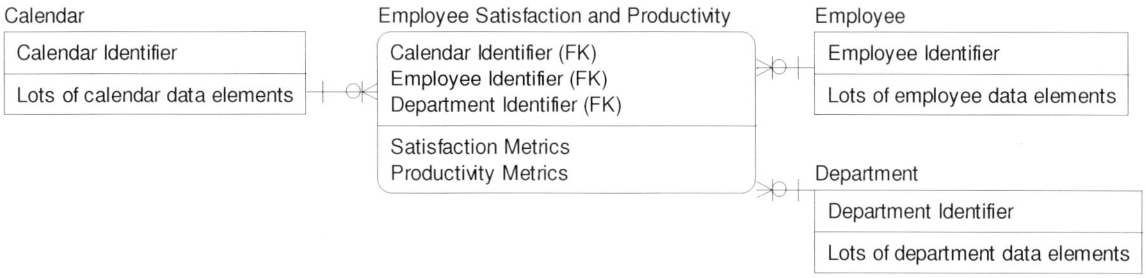

Physical data model

Indexing explanation

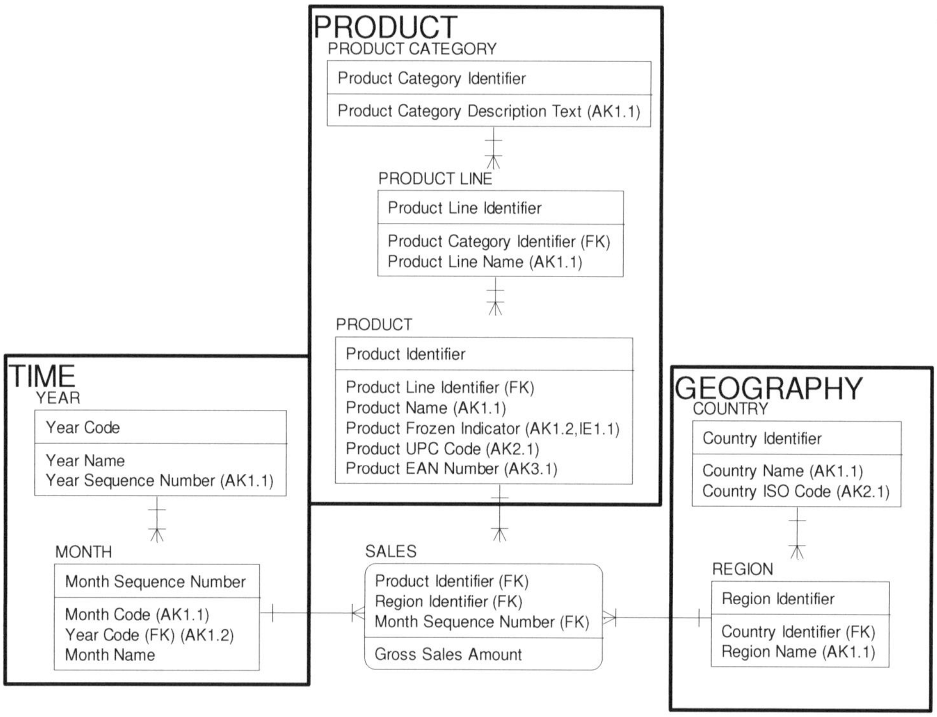

Some of the factors to consider in choosing indexes

- The space the index requires
- The number of rows in the table
- The columns most frequently used to access rows in the table
- The number of distinct column values
- The maximum rows per value
- Whether the rows are accessed by values or through a join
- The projected number of INSERTS, UPDATES and DELETES

Physical data model

Indexing explanation

EXPLANATION

An index is a value and a pointer to instances of that value in a table. There are many factors to consider to choosing indexes, some shown on the facing page, and the pros and cons are shown below.

EXAMPLE

In the example on the facing page, the primary, alternate and foreign keys were indexed. Note that if a key contains more than 1 data element, they are indexed by the order in which the keys appear. A composite index is an index on at least two data elements. The order the data elements appear is the order in most cases on how they are indexed. In the Product table for example, there is a composite index on the alternate key Product Name and Product Frozen Indicator.

Here are some questions that can be asked against this structure:

- What was our Gross Sales Amount for all Frozen products from the Northeast in January 2007?
- What 3 products generated the most sales from Canada in 2008? Show their UPC.
- What was the Gross Sales Amount for our Dark Chocolate line in 2007?

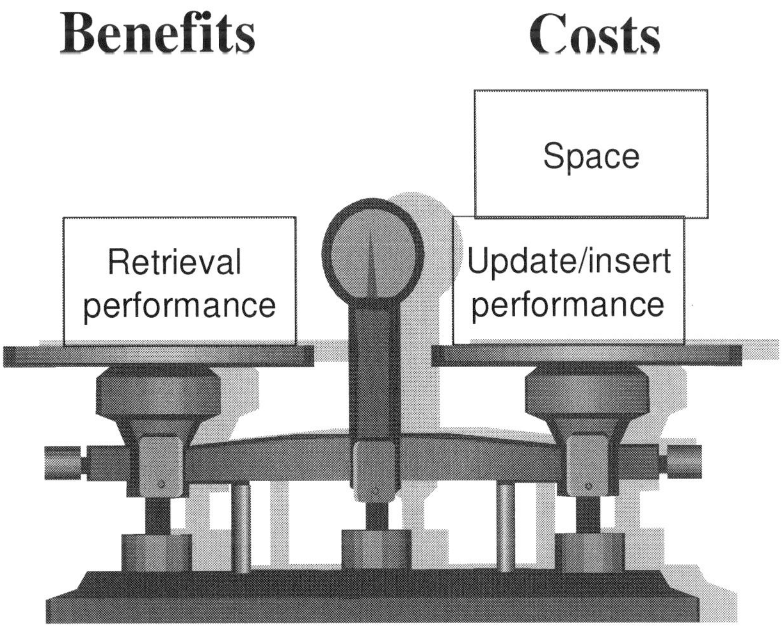

Physical data model

Views explanation

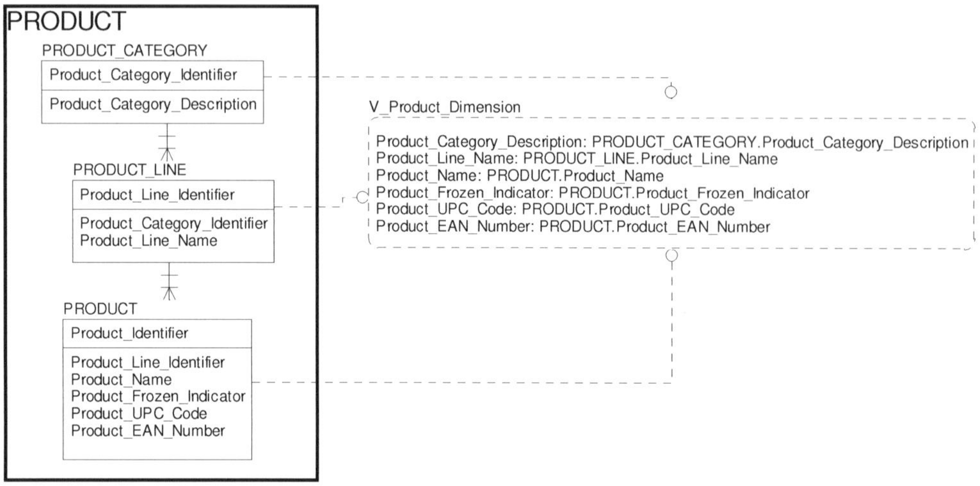


```
CREATE VIEW V_Product_Dimension AS
        SELECT PRODUCT_CATEGORY.Product_Category_Description,
PRODUCT_LINE.Product_Line_Name, PRODUCT.Product_Name,
PRODUCT.Product_Frozen_Indicator, PRODUCT.Product_UPC_Code,
PRODUCT.Product_EAN_Number
        FROM PRODUCT_CATEGORY, PRODUCT_LINE, PRODUCT
        WHERE PRODUCT_CATEGORY.Product_Category_Identifier =
PRODUCT_LINE.Product_Category_Identifier AND
PRODUCT_LINE.Product_Line_Identifier = PRODUCT.Product_Line_Identifier
```

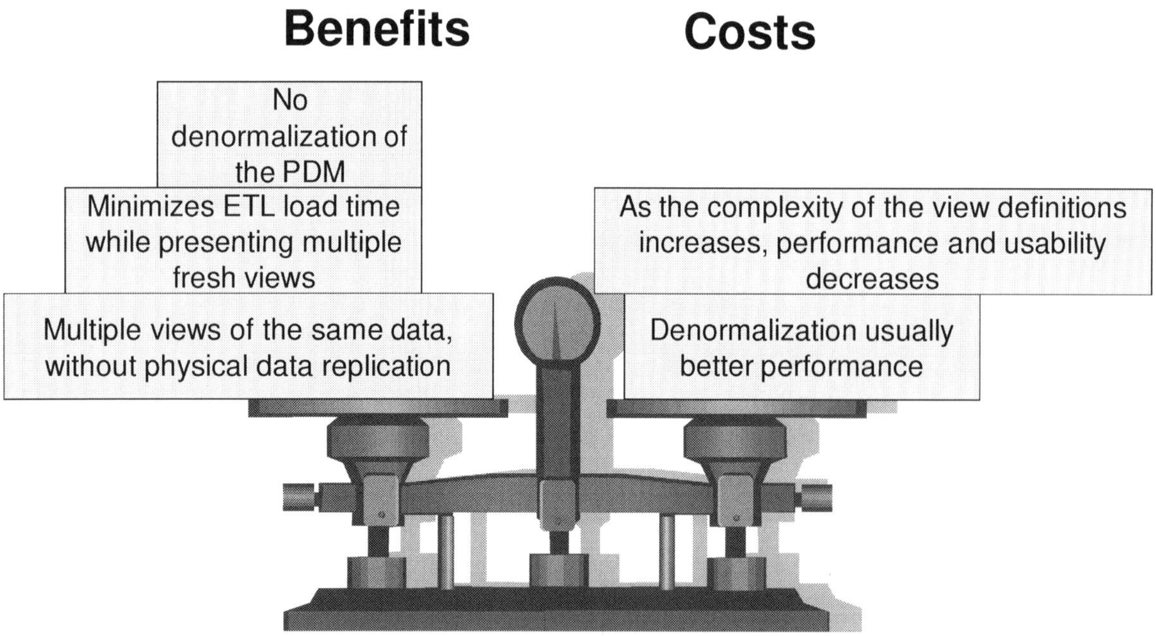

Physical data model

Views explanation

BACKGROUND

A view is a virtual table. It is a "view" into one or many tables or other views that contain or reference the actual data elements. We can use views in almost all situations where we are considering denormalization. Views can offer the same benefits as denormalization *without the drawbacks associated with data redundancy and loss of referential integrity.* A view can provide user-friendly structures over a normalized structure, thereby preserving flexibility and referential integrity. A view will keep the underlying normalized model intact and at the same time present a denormalized or summarized view of the world to the business.

STANDARD VIEW

The standard view runs the SQL to retrieve data at the point when a data element in the view is requested. It can take quite a bit of time to retrieve data depending on the complexity of the SQL and the data volume.

MATERIALIZED VIEW

Materialized views or snapshots can match and even sometimes beat retrieval speed from actual tables because they are generated at some predetermined time and stored in system cache.

Every database package has a different name for this type of view. For example,

- Oracle: Materialized view
- DB/2: Materialized query table
- SQL server: Indexed views
- Teradata: Join index (or aggregate join index)

EXAMPLE

A view is shown on the model as a rectangle with rounded corners and outlined by a dotted line. There is SQL query language behind the view.

Physical data model

Partitioning explanation

Partitioning is when a database table is split up into two or more tables. Vertical partitioning is when data elements are split up, and horizontal is when rows are split up.

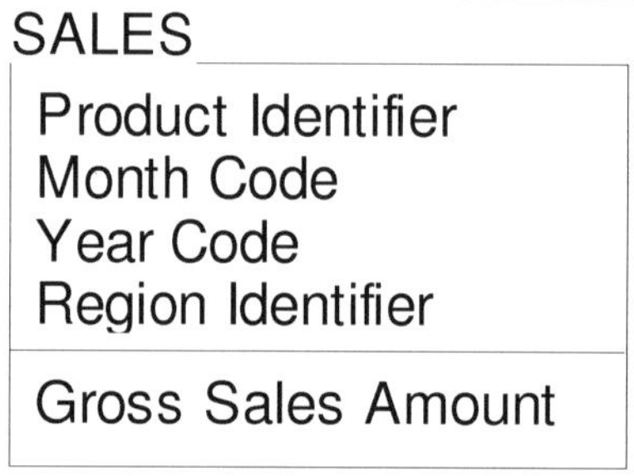

Could horizontally partition by Year

Could vertically partition by moving volatile data elements into their own table

.

Physical data model

Physical data model technique: Partitioning

BACKGROUND

Partitioning is when a database table is split up into two or more tables. Vertical partitioning is when data elements are split up and horizontal is when rows are split up. It is common for both horizontal and vertical to be used together. That is, when splitting rows apart we in many cases learn that certain data elements only belong with one set of rows.

Partitioning can be used as a reactive technique, meaning that even after an application goes live, the designer might choose to add partitioning after monitoring performance and space and determining that an improvement is needed.

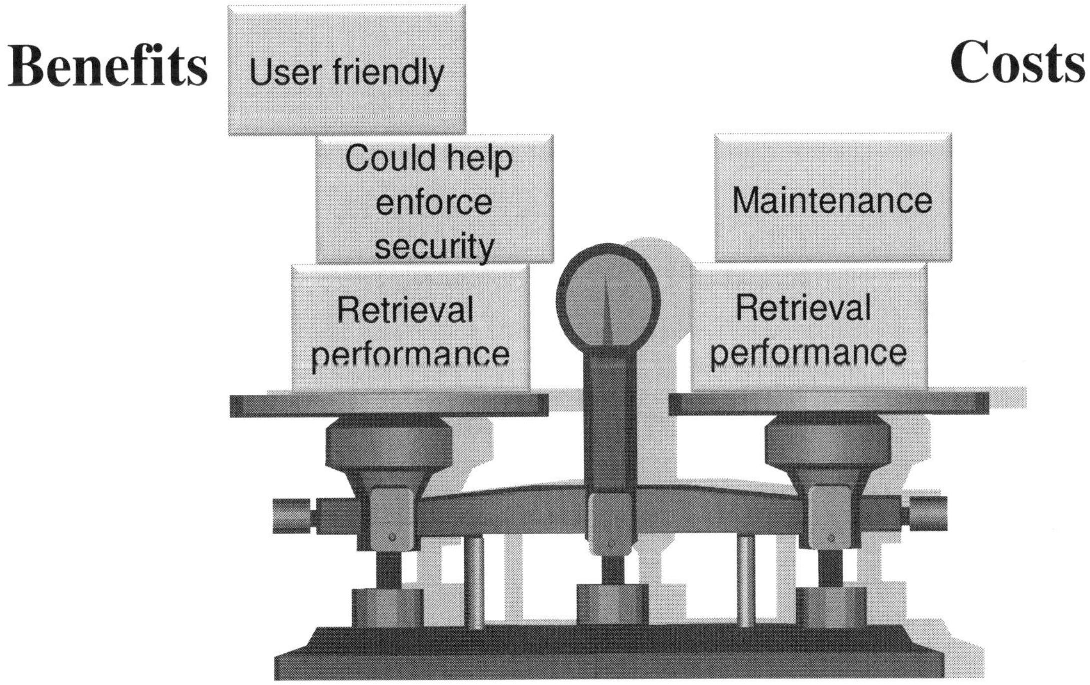

Physical data model

Star schema vs. Snowflake

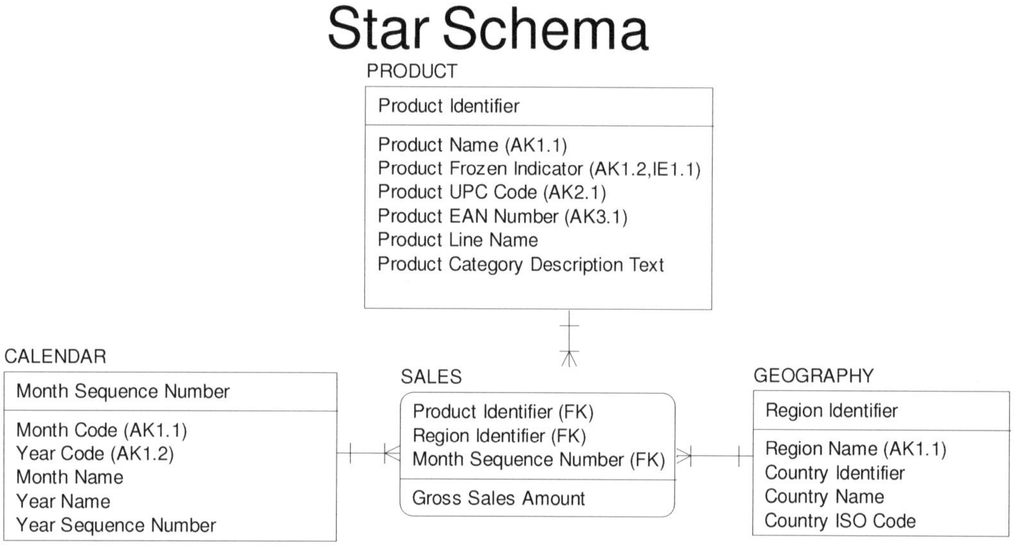

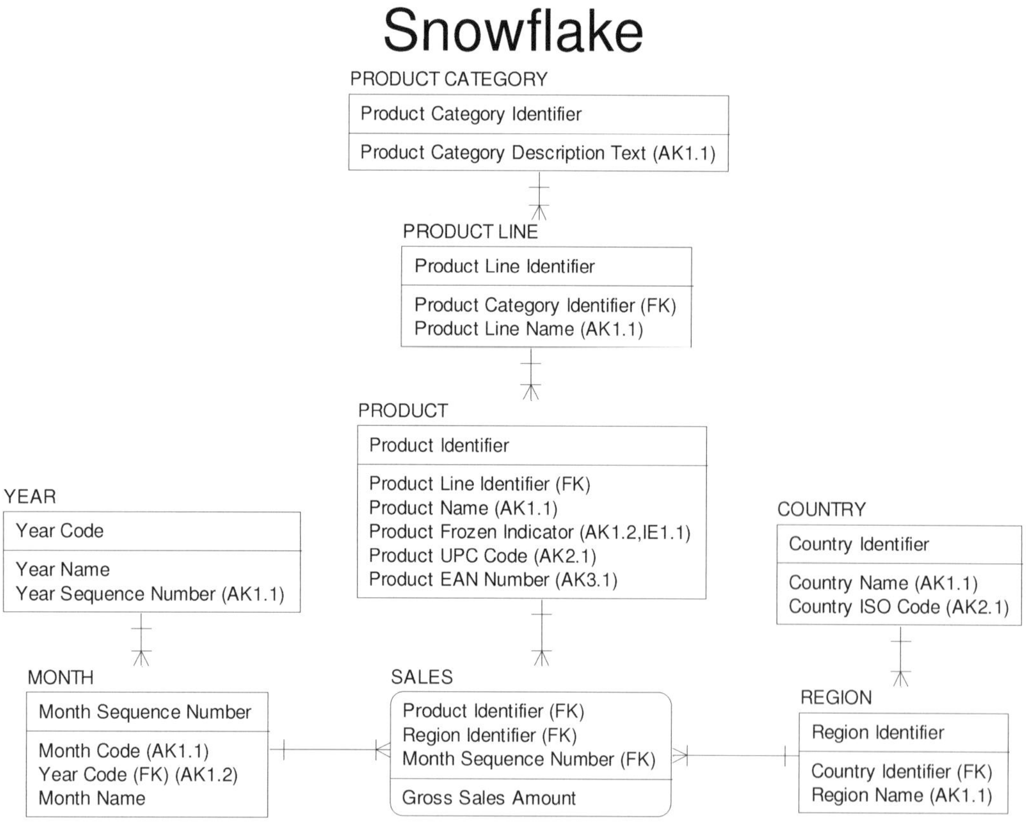

Physical data model

Star schema vs. Snowflake

STAR SCHEMA

A star schema is when each set of tables that make up a dimension is flattened into a single table. Notice I used the phrase "flattened" instead of "denormalized" because a dimensional model is never normalized to begin with, but instead separated into different tables by hierarchy level. The meter is in the center of the model and each of the dimensions relate to the meter at the lowest level of detail. A star schema is relatively easy to create and implement, and visually appears elegant and simplistic to both IT and the business.

SNOWFLAKE

We "snowflake" due to a number of factors including if having one flattened table takes up too much space, if the ETL effort is too great, or if the usage patterns dictate. I read in a recent data modeling article the following quote: "A snowflake schema is a star schema with fully normalized dimensions...A snowflake schema can be produced from a star schema by normalizing each dimension table." This is not usually a true statement. Snowflaking is a physical design practice where tables are broken out from dimension structures due to space and performance issues. Sometimes the tables (called outriggers) are broken out following the rules of normalization but more than likely they are broken out by different levels or rates of change. An advantage of the snowflake representation is that it explicitly shows the hierarchy structure of each dimension, which can help show how the data can be sensibly analyzed. Sometimes the snowflaked model can even contain more tables then the original logical dimensional model.

CHOICES, CHOICES, CHOICES

There are a number of factors to consider in deciding whether to go the star schema or snowflake route. Consider how the data will be most frequently accessed, and consider performance and space implications carefully (not just for today but also for 5-10 years in the future). Most dimensional models are star schemas, and are usually snowflaked due to data volatility or summarization requirements.

Dimension tables are traditionally wide (lots of columns) and fact tables are traditionally deep (lots of rows). Avoid structures that are both deep and wide.

Physical data model

Additional physical dimensional modeling terminology

Degenerate dimension

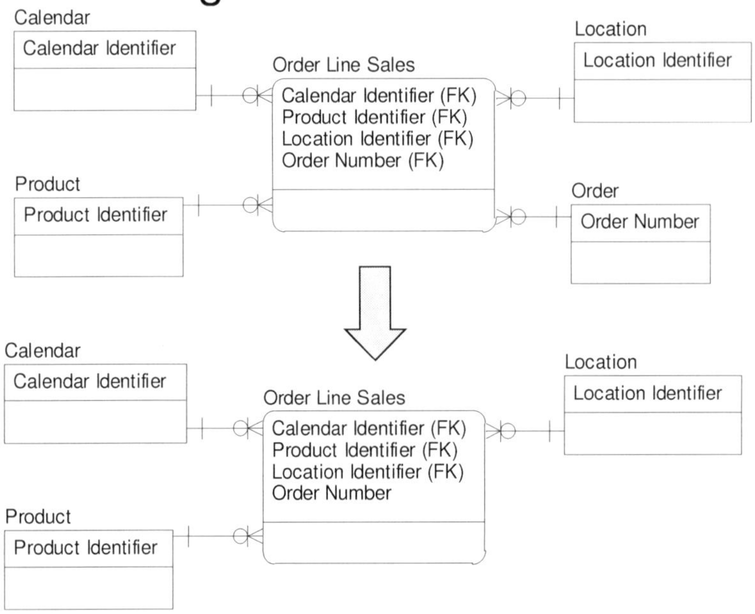

Junk dimension

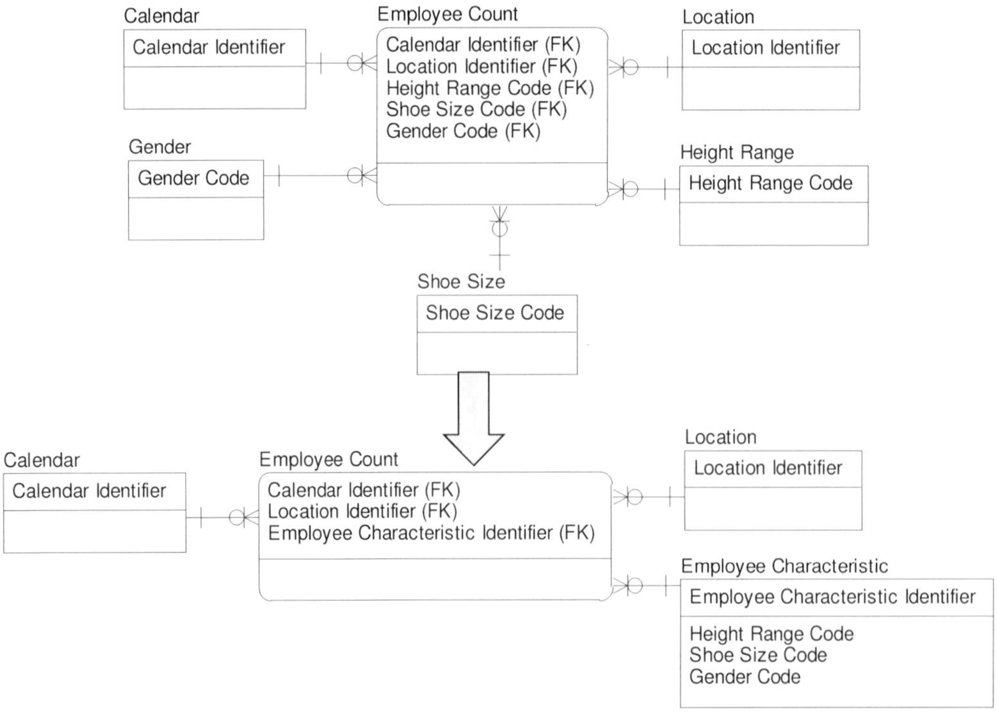

Physical data model

Additional physical dimensional modeling terminology

DEGENERATE DIMENSION

A degenerate dimension is a dimension whose data element(s) have been moved to the fact table. A degenerate dimension is most common when the original dimension contained only a single data element such as a transaction identifier. The modeler needs to carefully consider filter and storage space implications.

JUNK DIMENSION

A dimension containing all the possible combinations of a small and somewhat related set of indicators and codes. Factors to consider in creating junk dimensions are:

- **Usage**. Make sure the dimensions folded into a single table are often queried together by the business. This is the most important factor.
- **Number of dimensions in the fact table**. If you have more than 25 dimensions, there is a good chance the design might be more efficient with a junk dimension.
- **Size of junk dimension**. If an outer join produces more than 100,000 rows, you might consider restructuring or not using the junk dimension.

Junk dimensions can either be populated with all possible combinations during initial load, or can be populated as values come in during normal load times. The decision depends on the stability and volume of the data.

Slowly changing dimensions

Explanation

- An SCD is every reference subject area in the data warehouse
- It is not limited just to dimensions
- It reminds us that we need to decide how to handle data changes

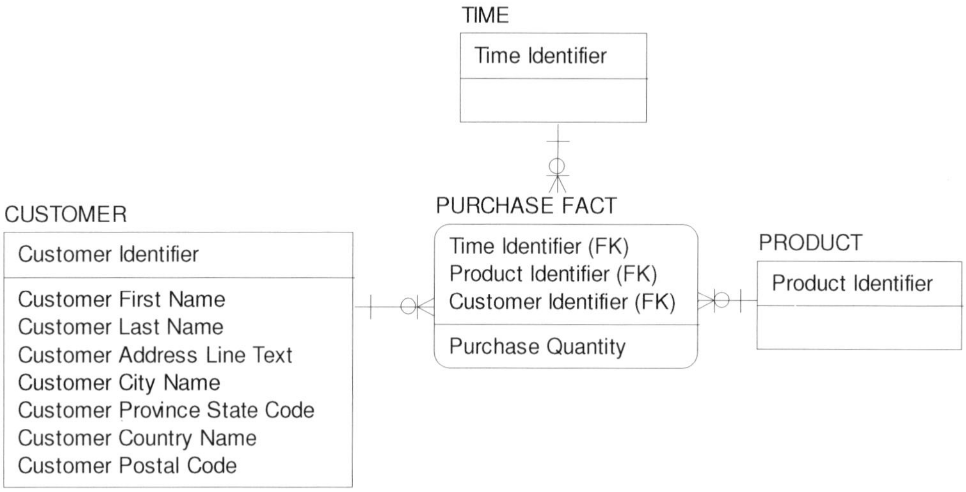

Slowly changing dimensions

Explanation

BACKGROUND

In the physical dimensional model, we need to incorporate history. Transaction data and reference data behave very differently from each other in terms of value updates. Transaction data occurs very frequently and usually once they occur they are not updated (e.g. once an order has been delivered you can no longer change its properties such as Order Quantity). Reference data on the other hand, is much less volumous but values can change more often (e.g. people move to different addresses, product names change, and sales departments have reorganizations). In the data warehouse environment, every reference subject area becomes a slowly changing dimension (SCD). This term has been coined by Ralph Kimball, and an SCD is any subject area (both relational and dimensional) whose values can change over time. There are three ways to handle these data changes: Type 1 stores no history, Type 2 stores all history, and Type 3 stores some history.

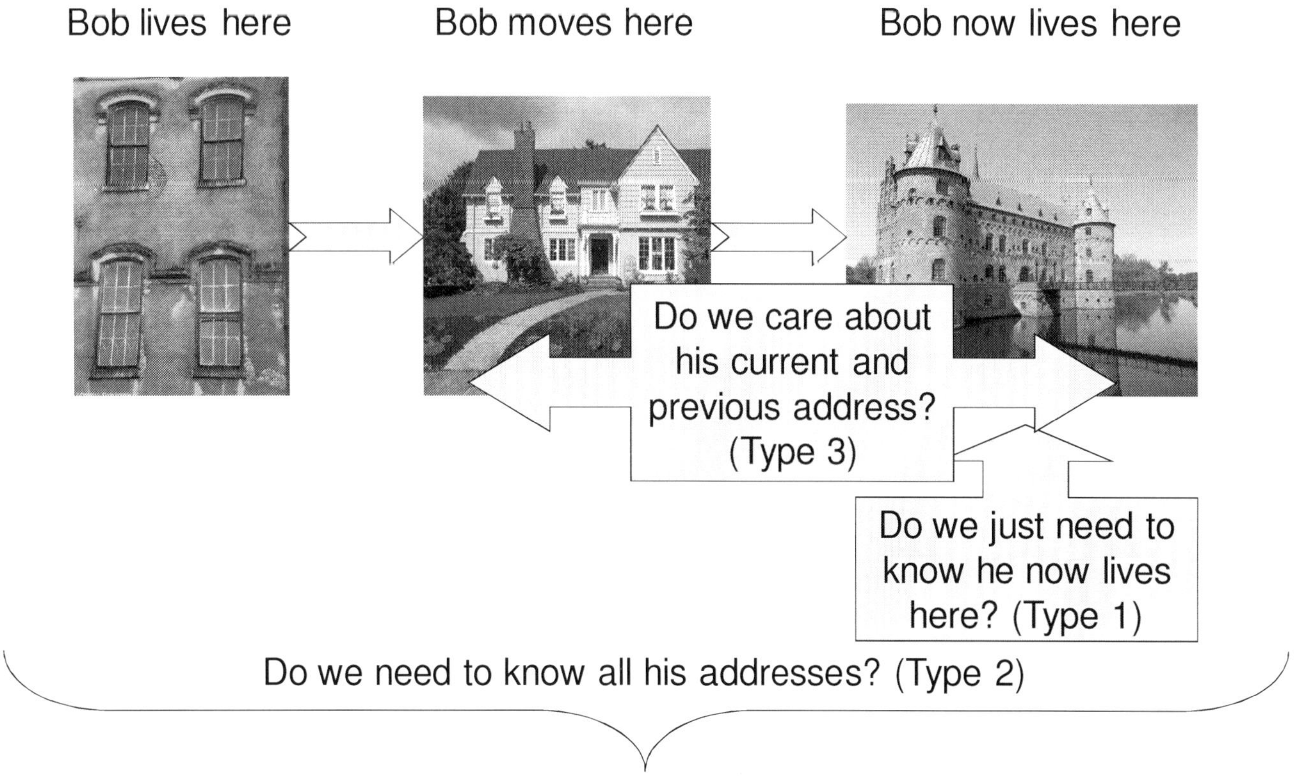

Slowly changing dimensions

Type 1

- No history
- Update else Insert
- Useful to correct errors
- Easiest to implement
- Least expensive for CPU and storage
- Ideal if no history required

EXAMPLE:

- Bob moves 5 times. We only store the 5th time, where he currently lives
- How much did we sell to Bob over the last 3 years?

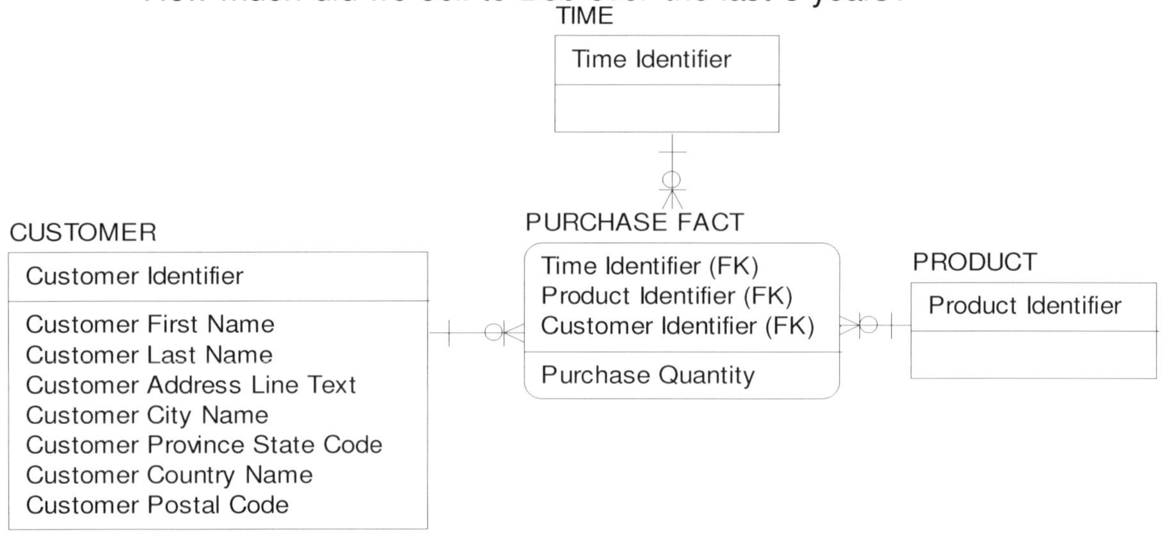

CUSTOMER

ID	FIRST	LAST	ADDRESS
123	Steve	Smith	10 Main
456	Bob	Jones	~~15 Park~~ 25 Elm

PURCHASE FACT

CUST	TIME	PROD	QTY
123	789	122	500
456	987	675	1000
456	356	278	750

Slowly changing dimensions

Type 1

EXPLANATION

Many times when history of reference data is not mentioned in a functional requirements document, Type 1 SCD is used. In many cases the user might want history on reference data, but has never used it before! They probably don't know to ask for it. Maybe they haven't given it much thought on what to do with it. Don't except omission as Type 1. Once Type 1 is invoked, it's very hard to change to something else in the data warehouse because of the large volumes in the fact tables. It would be equivalent to redoing a large portion of the warehouse.

Slowly changing dimensions

Type 2

- All history
- Update and Insert
- Most expensive for CPU and storage
- Most complex
- Requires creativity
- New surrogate key or append date to key

EXAMPLE:

- Bob moves 5 times. We store all 5 times as separate rows, along with when he moved and why for each move.
- How much did we sell to Bob when he lived at 14 Main Street?
- Which of Bob's addresses had the most sales?

- New surrogate key -

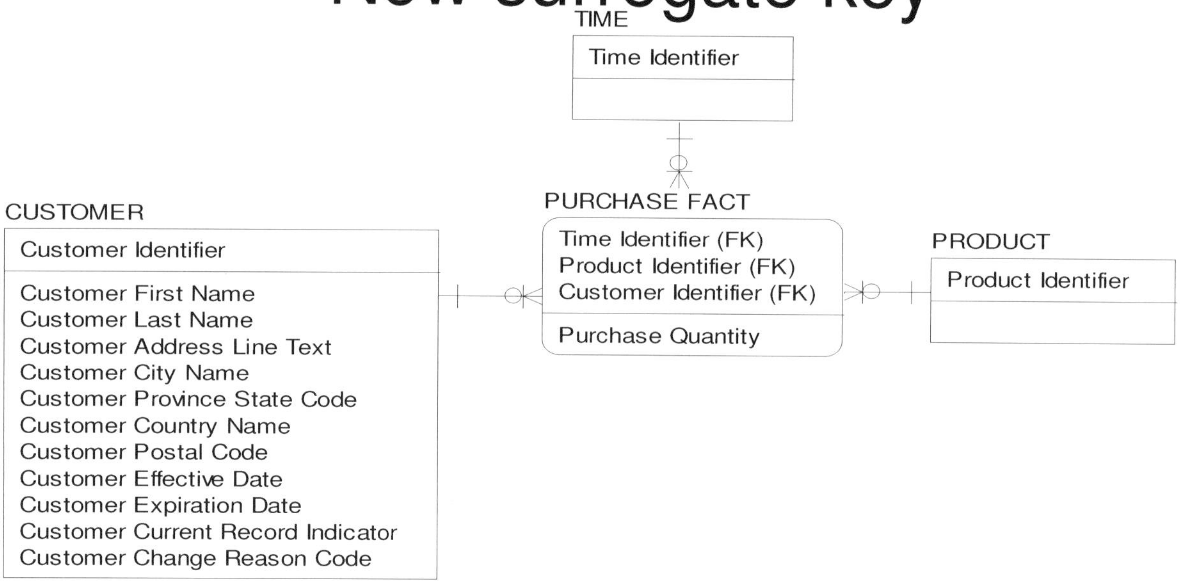

Slowly changing dimensions

Type 2

EXPLANATION

Type 2 allows you to represent the entire environment at a point in time (aka Chronology or Audit). The dimension foreign key is no longer a reference data instance, but a reference data instance at a particular point in time. It becomes a snapshot. Having a date in the primary key of Type 2 gives us the flexibility to use Type 1 or Type 2 in the same dimension. If we want to use Type 1 we just join on the original surrogate key. If we want to use Type 2 we use both the original surrogate key and the date.

- Original surrogate key & date -

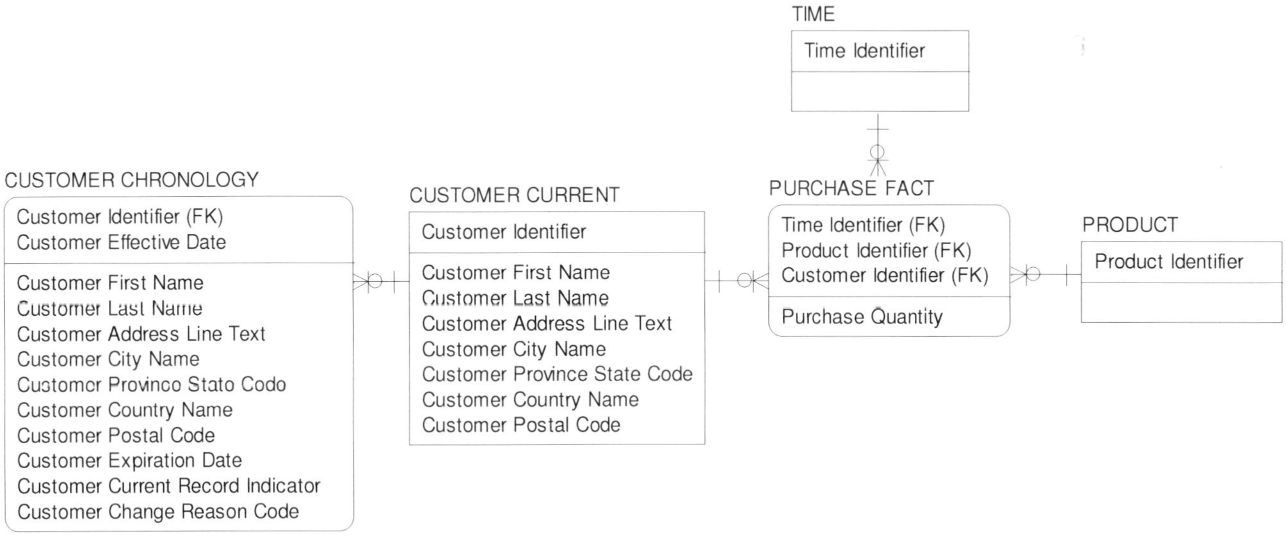

Slowly changing dimensions

Type 3

- Store some changes on some columns
- History is usually original or previous
- Columns instead of rows
- Least used

EXAMPLE:

- Bob moves 5 times. We store the address details from his original address and his most current.
- How much did we sell to Bob when he lived at his original address?

PURCHASE FACT

CUST	TIME	PROD	QTY
123	789	122	500
456	987	675	1000
456	356	278	750

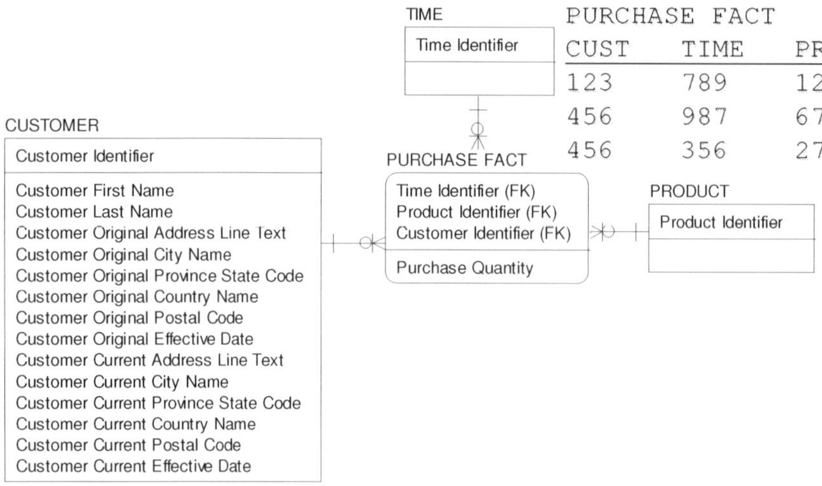

CUSTOMER

ID	FIRST	LAST	ORIG	EFF	CURR	EFF
123	Steve	Smith	10 Main	4/1/2006	10 Main	4/1/2006
456	Bob	Jones	15 Park	6/15/2000	25 Elm	7/13/2010

Slowly changing dimensions

Type 3

EXPLANATION

Type 3 is very useful when there are only a couple of data elements that need date tracking. Sometimes though, this is all you need. History is stored in columns instead of rows, similar to an array or repeating groups structure. Type 3 is frequently chosen for purely technology reasons such as to simplify development, save storage space, or increase query performance.

Applying the Data Model Scorecard®

Capturing interactions

There is a requirement to build a business application that reports trends on consumer interactions. An interaction is a contact between an employee and a consumer for a specific product. An interaction can take place through a variety of medium such as through phone, email, and mail. Interactions fit into one of three categories: complaints, compliments and questions. Here are examples of some of the interactions:

"I love your product." (compliment)
"I hate your product." (complaint)
"I found a strange object in your product." (complaint)
"Where can I buy your product?" (question)
"I found your product difficult to assemble." (complaint)

A consumer can have many interactions on many products. For example, Bob can call Monday because he didn't like Product XYZ, he can call Tuesday and say that he now liked Product XYZ, and can call Wednesday and say that he loves Product ABC. Consumer Interaction in this example would contain three records, and at a high level look something like this:

Consumer	Product	Employee	Interaction	Date received
Bob	XYZ	Mary	Didn't like product	Monday 4/1/2011
Bob	XYZ	Jane	Liked product	Tuesday 4/2/2011
Bob	ABC	Mary	Loved product	Wednesday 4/3/2011

The requirement is to produce a report for each product that shows for the previous 12 months, the number of complaints, compliments and questions for each product. This report has to allow the users to "drill down" to get to the interaction level of detail and see the actual interaction such as "Loved product". See bar chart on facing page.

How good is the data model on the facing page?

Applying the Data Model Scorecard®

Capturing interactions

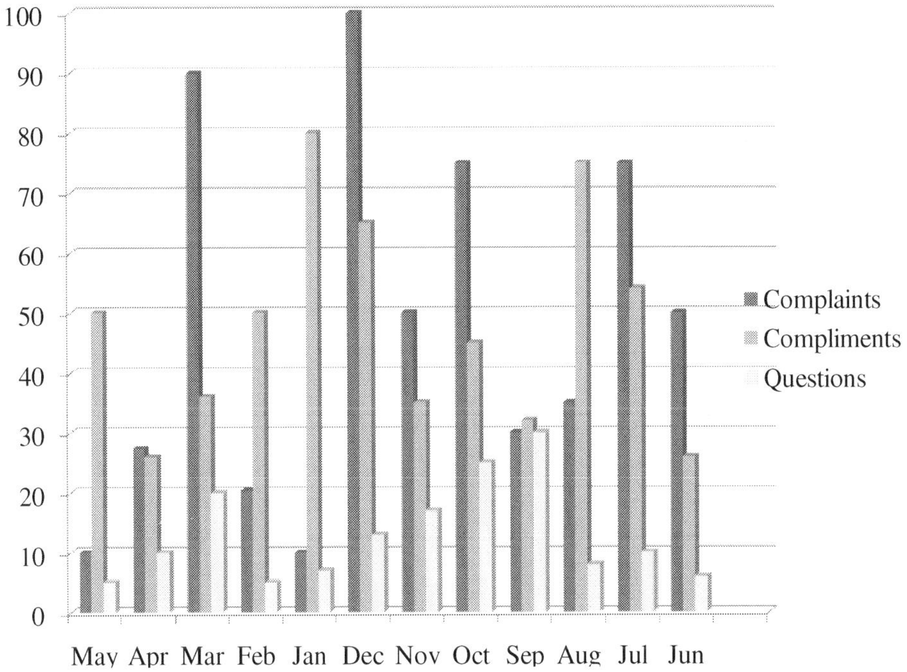

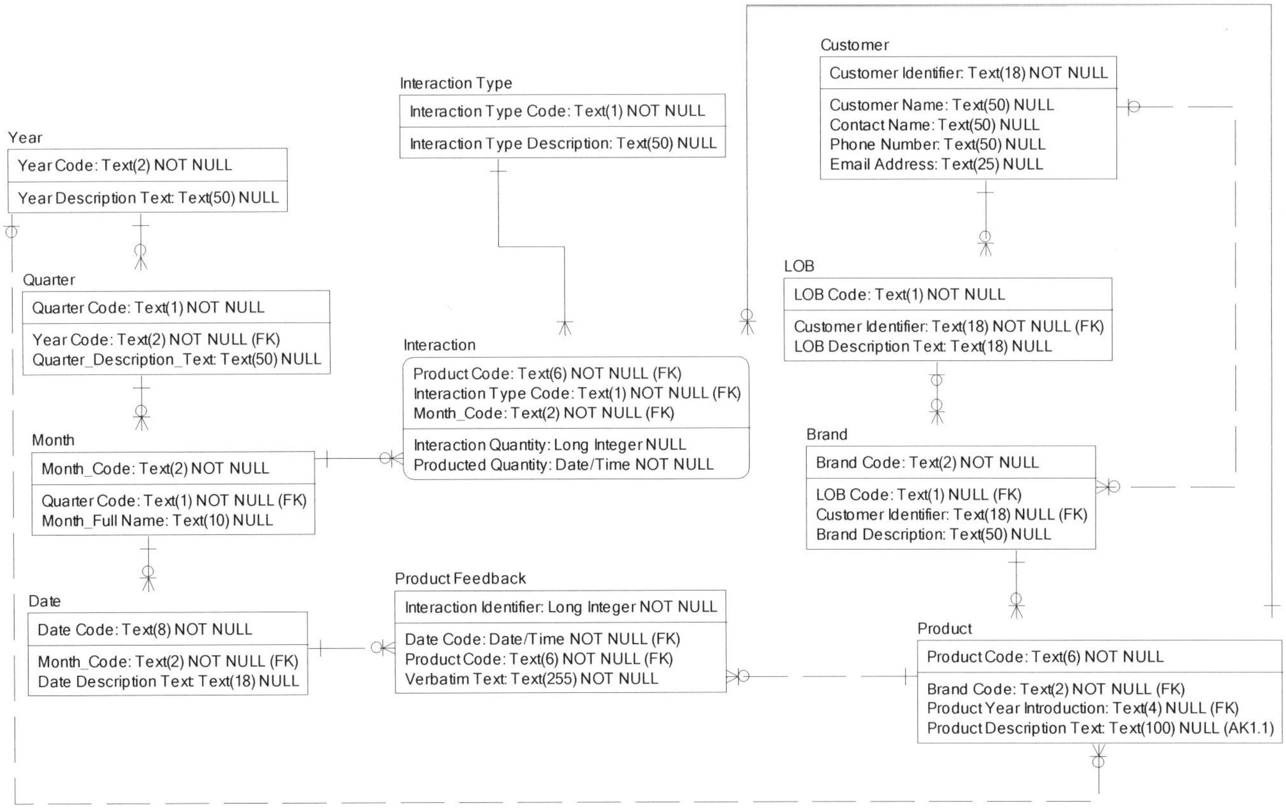

Applying the Data Model Scorecard®

Interaction Report for Product BB40 from May 2011

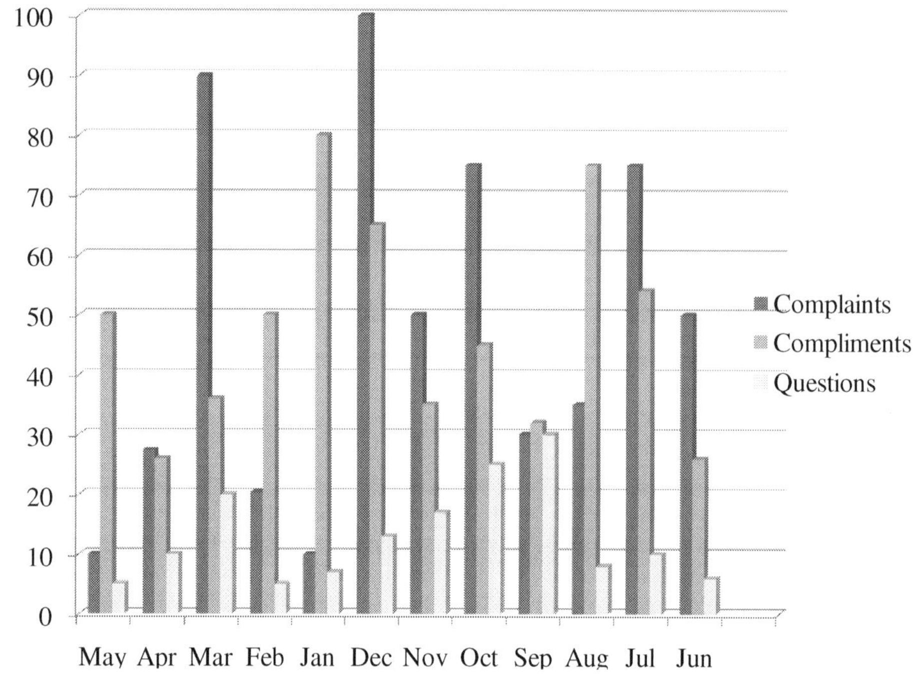

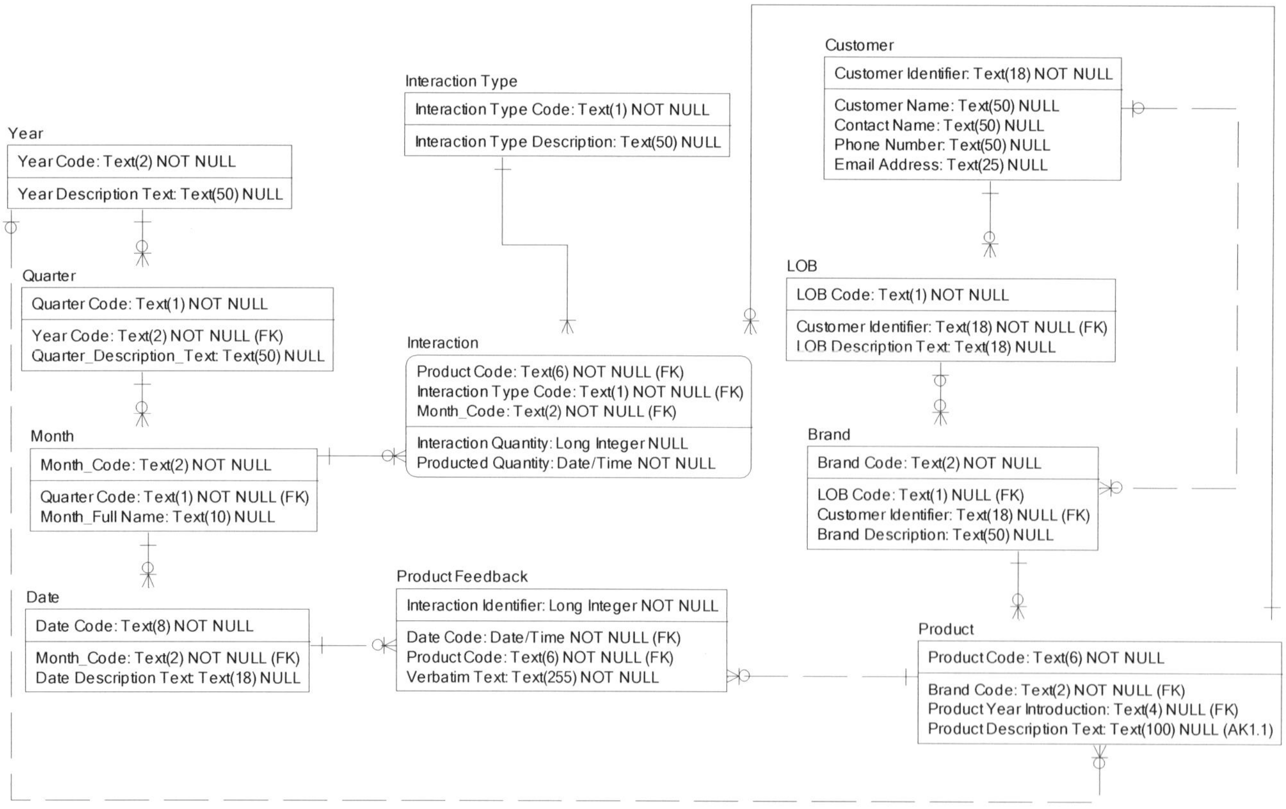

Applying the Data Model Scorecard®

1. How well do the characteristics of the model support the type of model?

EXPLANATION

This question ensures that the model type (subject area, logical, or physical – and then either relational or dimensional) of the model satisfies the criteria for this level of detail.

ANTHING YOU WOULD CATCH IN THE MODEL ON THE FACING PAGE FOR THIS CATEGORY?

1.

2.

3.

4.

5.

6.

7.

8.

9.

10.

#	Category	Total score	Model score	%
1	How well do the characteristics of the model support the type of model?	10		
2	How well does the model capture the requirements?	15		
3	How complete is the model?	15		
4	How structurally sound is the model?	15		
5	How well does the model leverage generic structures?	10		
6	How well does the model follow naming standards?	5		
7	How well has the model been arranged for readability?	5		
8	How good are the definitions?	10		
9	How consistent is the model with the enterprise?	5		
10	How well does the metadata match the data?	10		
	TOTAL SCORE	100		

Modules 2 and 3

Data Model Scorecard® Category #2: Correctness

Category Question: How well does the model capture the requirements?

This module is your guide to: Ensuring the model captures the requirements

Data Model Scorecard® Category #3: Completeness

Category Question: How complete is the model?

This module is your guide to: Validating model scope

Category overview

How well does the model capture the requirements?

CORRECTNESS

Confirms the model meets the requirements

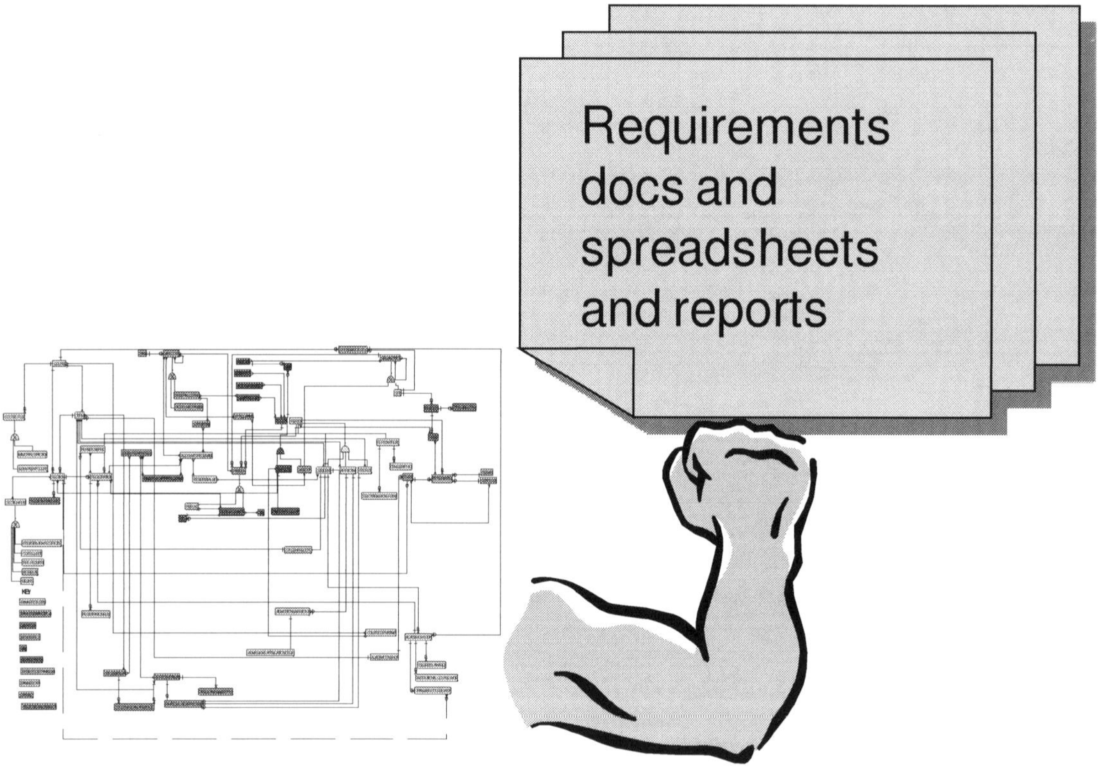

Not easy to validate!

- Need to understand content!
- Sketchy requirements
- Conflicting requirements
- Changing requirements
- Often can't use a model!

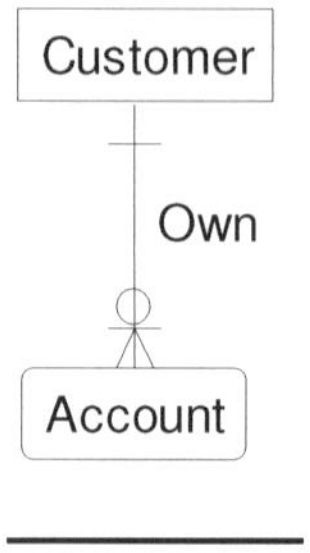

1. *Each Customer can own many Accounts.*
2. *Each Account must be owned by one and only one Customer. This means you can't have joint accounts. Is this true Sally the Steward?*

Category overview

How well does the model capture the requirements?

EXPLANATION

This is the "correctness" category. This category confirms that the model meets the requirements. All of the functionality detailed in a requirements document should be supported in the model. All reports required of a data mart should be producible from the data model. If there are no written requirements (or inadequate written requirements), there needs to be a business user or sponsor who can confirm that the model meets the requirements. In fact, even with great written requirements, having a business person "sign off" on the model is crucial. It can be challenging for a modeler to get "sign off" when the business person may not comprehend data modeling constructs. The modeler in these frequently occurring situations needs to come up creative ways to validate the model without showing the model, such as converting the model into sentences that can then be validated individually, or build prototypes or report mockups.

PURPOSE

We need to ensure our model represents the data requirements, as the costs can be devastating if there is even a slight difference between what was required and what was delivered. Besides not delivering what was expected is the potential that the IT/business relationship will suffer. The model needs to meet business expectations.

CHALLENGE

This can be the most difficult of all 10 categories to grade, the reason being that we really need to understand how the business works and what the business wants from their application. If we are modeling a sales data mart, for example, we need to understand both how the invoicing process works in our company, as well as what reports and queries will be needed to answer key sales questions from the business.

What makes this category even more challenging is the possibility that perhaps the business requirements are not well-defined, or differ from verbal requirements, or keep changing usually with the scope expanding instead of contracting.

To quote Will Rodgers:
It ain't what we don't know that gets us in trouble, it's what we know that ain't so.

Category overview

How complete is the model?

Confirms all requirements are in the model, and nothing extra

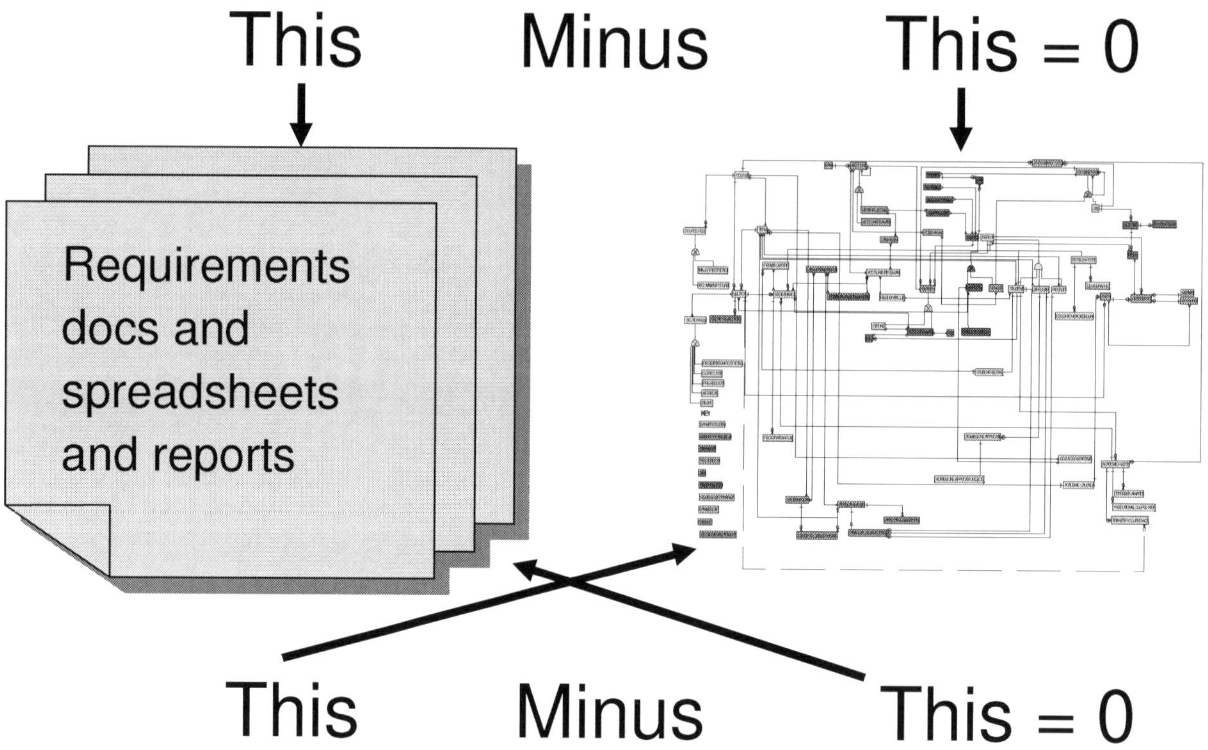

Data model – requirements = something (Scope creep)
Requirements – data model = something (Phase II)
Includes metadata (e.g. definitions, stewardship, AKs)

Category overview

How complete is the model?

EXPLANATION

This category checks for data model components that are not in the requirements or requirements that are not represented on the model. If the scope of the model is greater than the requirements, we have a situation known as "scope creep." This means that we are planning on delivering more than what was originally required. This may not necessarily be a bad thing, as long as this additional scope has been factored into the project plan. If the model scope is less than the requirements, we will be leaving information out of the resulting application, usually leading to an enhancement or "Phase 2" shortly after the application is in production. For completeness, we need to make sure the scope of the project and model match, as well as ensuring all the necessary metadata on the model is populated.

Regarding metadata, there are certain types that tend to get overlooked when modeling, such as definitions and alternate keys. These types of metadata along with ones that are mandatory parts of our model such as data element name and format information need to be checked for completeness in this category.

The completeness category ensures the scope of the model matches the scope of the requirements. You can validate the correctness category and this category in parallel, as the red flags and proactive measures are very similar.

PURPOSE

To meet the scope of the requirements. In a dimensional model for example, the grain of the fact table must answer all of the relevant questions.

CHALLENGE

It can be difficult to grade this category without written signed off requirements and without a metadata checklist which contains the types of metadata that are required and those that are optional.

Metadata Bingo

Overview

A tool for identifying stakeholder metadata priorities.

Definition

Name

Source

Transformation Logic

Stewardship

Nullability

Metadata Bingo

Overview

BACKGROUND

Metadata Bingo is a game where the people on your project team complete "cards" identifying which types of metadata are most important to capture at different levels of detail. We then consolidate these cards, and tally the scores to see which types of metadata "win" and will be captured. By knowing up front as a team which types of metadata we will capture, we will meet expectations in this area during our data modeling. There should be no surprises with the types of information we capture, and nothing should fall through the cracks. For example, if the entity name is important to your project, then this is a type of metadata that will be identified while using this tool.

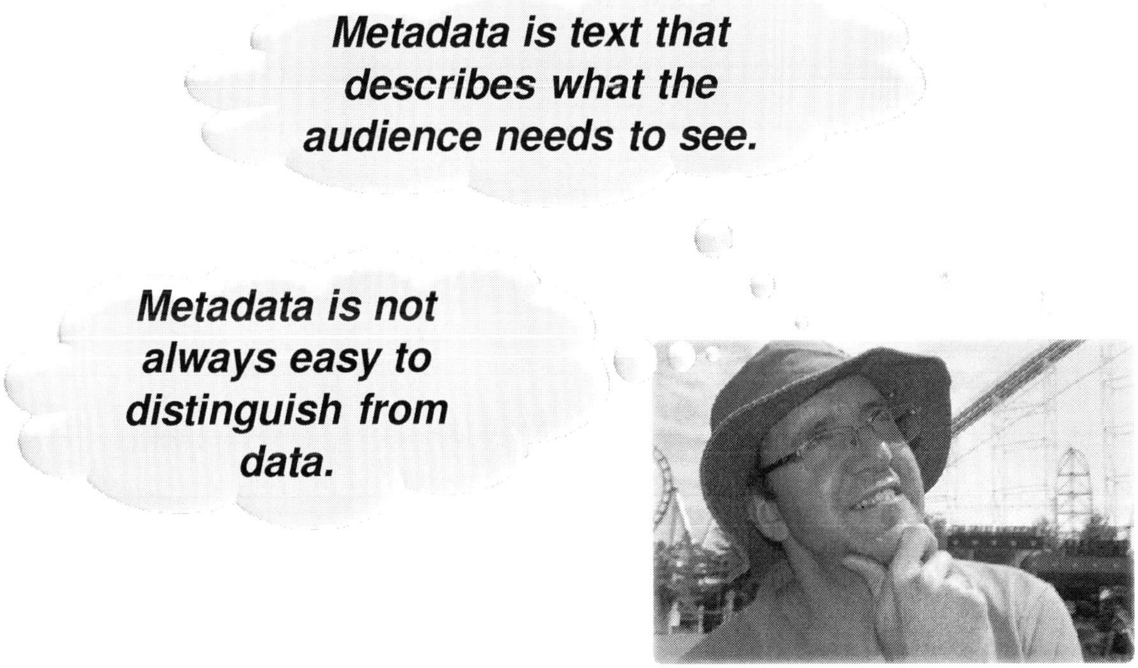

Metadata Bingo

Data Model Bingo Card

		SAM			LDM			PDM			
Code	**Descriptive information**	**L**	**M**	**H**	**L**	**M**	**H**	**L**	**M**	**H**	**Questions & Issues**
A	File name			x			x			x	
B	Business name										
C	Description										
D	Version control										
E	Primary modeler										
F	All modelers										
G	Modeling tool										
H	Scorecard score										
I	Purpose										

Metadata Bingo

Data Model Bingo Card

BACKGROUND

This card is completed by putting a check in the appropriate column, depending on whether the type of metadata is of high, medium, or low interest in capturing. In this bingo card you can't have a data model without a name. Therefore the name row is already populated with X's for high priority. You might need to explain on this card a couple of the abbreviations. SAM = Subject Area Model, LDM = Logical Data Model, PDM = Physical Data Model, L = Low priority, M = Medium priority, H = High priority.

METADATA DESCRIPTIONS

- **File Name**. This is the name that the data model is saved under on your computer or network server. It is usually a short name such as the project acronym, along with a file extension.
- **Business Name**. This is the full unabbreviated name of the data model. This usually includes at a minimum the full name of the project or application.
- **Description**. The description for a data model might include a number of important pieces of information, including an overview to the subject areas included in the model or the type of design (operational or BI).
- **Version Control**. Is it important to keep track of any changes made to the data models over time? Do you need a record of whenever a new entity is added, or any other change is made to the model?
- **Primary Modeler**. This is the main person who is recognized as the primary author of the model. This is not the person necessarily who is responsible for the model today.
- **All Modelers**. A record of any modeler who has touched the model.
- **Modeling Tool**. The software tool that was used to build the model.
- **Scorecard Score**. The most recent Data Model Scorecard® score of the model.
- **Purpose**. The reason why the model is being built. Can also include the audience.

Metadata Bingo

Entity Bingo Card

Code	Descriptive information	HIGH	MEDIUM	LOW	Questions & Issues
A	Standard enterprise name				
B	Alias				
C	Definition	X			
D	Steward name and department				
E	History requirements				
F	Source				

Metadata Bingo

Entity Bingo Card

BACKGROUND

Notice on this Entity Bingo Card that the entity definition is already checked off as high, and therefore this is a type of metadata that must be captured.

METADATA DESCRIPTIONS

- **Standard Enterprise Name**. This is the name given to an entity that is consistent with the rest of the organization. Standardizing the name means that people from outside the department can easily recognize and understand this concept.
- **Alias**. With so many different names for the same concepts, there is a strong need for aliases. An alias is another name or reference for something. A department has their own terminology and in many cases in order to fit their information in with the business, the department needs to give up their terminology and use the standard names. An alias provides a place to keep the original department name so that those familiar with the department concept can recognize the enterprise concept.
- **Definition**. A critical piece of metadata. Describes what the concept is, including if necessary examples, derivations, and comparisons.
- **Steward Name And Department**. The steward name is the name of the person or department who is responsible for the actual data within an entity.
- **History Requirements**. The entity level is the optimal level to capture how much history is requested from the users. Capturing this information at this level and as early as possible in the analysis process, can prevent being in the situation where there is a difference between the amount of history your source system has and the amount your user requests.
- **Source**. Basic source information is very useful to capture at the entity level. By capturing the source application for each entity, you can make sure you can meet the user's expectations based on the source.

Metadata Bingo

Data Element Bingo Card

		Numeric			Code			Date			Id			Text			
Code	**Descriptive information**	**H**	**M**	**L**	**H**	**M**	**L**	**H**	**M**	**L**	**H**	**M**	**L**	**H**	**M**	**L**	**Questions & Issues**
A	Standard name																
B	Alias																
C	Definition	X			X			X			X			X			
D	Business purpose	X															
E	Sample values				X												
F	Default value																
G	Mapping																
H	Format	X			X			X			X			X			
I	Nullability	X			X			X			X			X			
J	Keys and indexes										X						

Metadata Bingo

Data Element Bingo Card

BACKGROUND

To keep this card simple, each data element is assigned to one of 5 buckets:

- **Numeric.** Numerics include all of the measurements in our application, such as quantities, weights, volumes, and amounts.
- **Code.** Codes include any shortened phrase for something else.
- **Date.** Dates include time and date information in any format.
- **Identifier.** Identifiers (Ids) include all identifiers for our large tables such as Customer and Item.
- **Text.** Text includes name, definition, and other types of text based fields.

METADATA DESCRIPTIONS

- **Standard Enterprise Name**. This includes both the logical and physical corporate wide standard name. Logical is the full business name, whereas physical is the abbreviated database name.
- **Alias**. Aliases have several different uses when it comes to data elements. They can provide mappings back to business user understanding terminology, legacy applications, or report labels.
- **Definition**. It's ironic that the definition, the most important type of metadata, is also the most corrupted.
- **Business Purpose**. A business purpose is the reason why we have this concept. So, for example, Gross Sales Amount might be defined as the total amount received in a particular time period, by multiplying list price times quantity purchased.
- **Sample Values**. Showing some actual values is extremely useful for codes, where a definition might only go so far.
- **Default Value**. Having a default value means if the data element is left blank what value will be stored in it? Will it stay blank or will it default to a "Yes", a "No", or "Blue", or some other value.
- **Mapping**. Lineage of data elements, including the formulas or equations that are applied to a target data element. For example, the list price and total quantity data elements are multiplied together to arrive at a gross sales amount.
- **Format**. Examples include Character(16), Integer, Decimal(15,2), Varchar(256), etc.
- **Nullability**. Nullability is an indicator which determines whether the data element can be left empty.
- **Keys And Indexes**. For keys, this includes primary, foreign, and alternate keys. Indexes are any data elements which are accessed for retrieval purposes often enough to warrant a quick reference to speed retrieval up.

Avoiding the Super Star

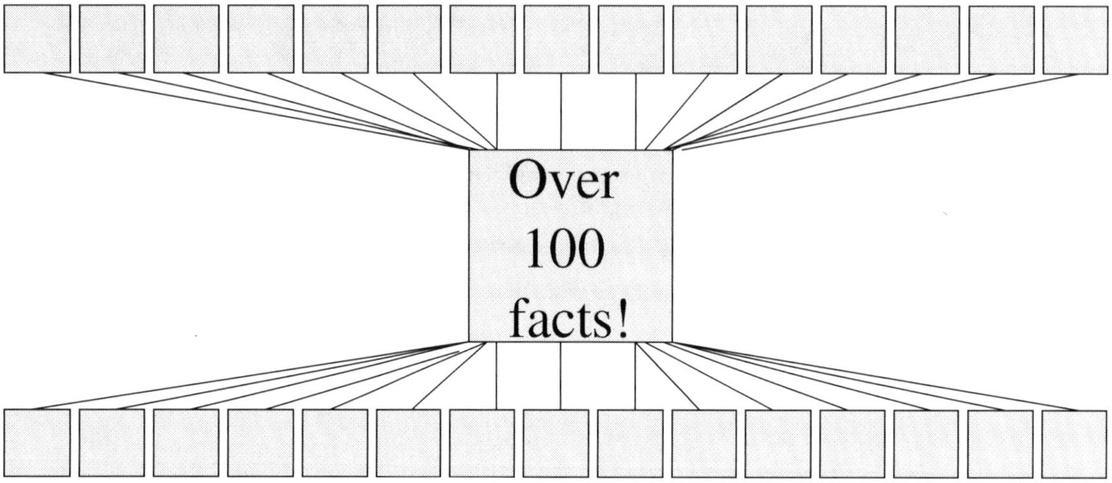

Here is my advice on this Super Star:

Avoiding the Super Star

BACKGROUND

A star schema is designed to efficiently answer metric business questions, such as those questions that return amounts, quantities, and counts. For example, "What are our total sales by customer and product over the last six months?" Stars are generally small in scope with a handful of dimensions surrounding a single fact table. But a colleague one day stops by your desk with a printout of a star schema that makes you jump right out of your seat. It is a Sales super star! Over 1000 data elements from the Sales area are on this model. You learn that this star was produced by placing every metric data element from Sales in the fact table and every non-metric data element in a dimension. The fact table contains over 100 different metrics and there are over 30 dimensions!

CHALLENGE

You are even more shocked to learn that this star schema is in production! It is experiencing some performance and space issues, and your colleague would like advice on how best to restructure this model. What is your response?

PURPOSE

Dimensional modeling is not always as easy as it looks. If we build a dimensional model following an approach of assigning measures to meters and everything else to dimensions without regard to business requirements, we wind up with a dimensional model that is not user friendly nor efficient and also difficult to maintain.

TIPS

Scope applies to all types of models. What happens when one doesn't elicit requirements?

Requirements lifecycle

How the pieces fit together

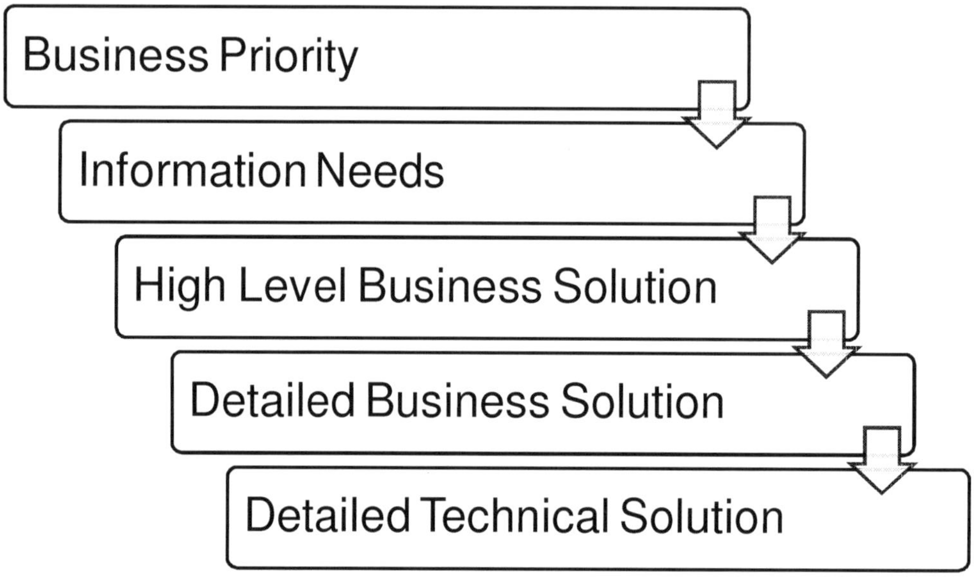

Program and Project

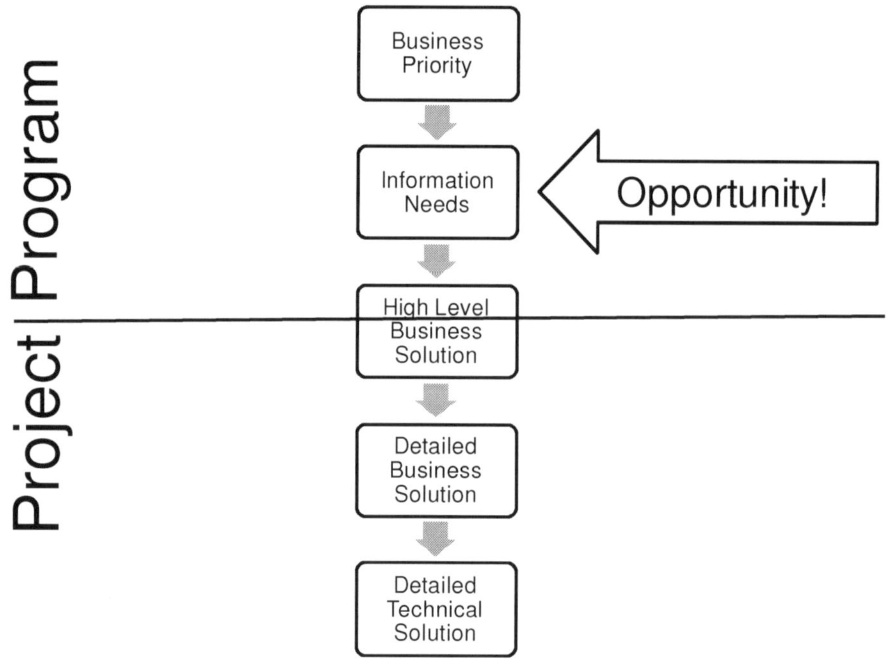

Requirements lifecycle

How the pieces fit together

EXPLANATION

Results from requirements elicitation techniques are captured in software development deliverables. For example, the interface analysis work is typically captured in a source/target mapping document. There are many complexities involved with producing deliverables, including not all deliverables are relevant for all situations and there are dependencies between deliverables. This is where a framework is needed.

A framework is a logical structure for classifying and organizing information. There are a number of different frameworks such as the Zachman Framework and TOGAF. Common themes across frameworks are acknowledging levels of detail and separation of data from process. The framework I use is shown on the facing page.

There are different levels of detail starting with business priorities. A business priority can be based upon goals, strategies, drivers, or directions the business would like to take. It is a great idea to connect projects with a business priority to ensure each small piece contributes to some larger whole (also good for job security ☺).

Business priorities require knowing information, like how well we've done, what we are planning on doing next, and how we stack up against the competition. This information is made precise through templates such as the Interview Template and Grain Matrix.

The high level business solution captures how to meet the information needs on one piece of paper. I have found it valuable over the years to have both enterprise and project high level subject area models (SAMs).

The detailed business solution equates to the logical data model (LDM) and captures all of the data elements and business rules independent of technology. The detailed technical solution adds the technology and is frequently called the physical data model (PDM).

PROGRAM VS PROJECT

A program is a large cross-department and often enterprise effort for the purpose of accomplishing something big such as enterprise analytics, cross-platform integration, Customer Relationship Management (CRM), etc. It has a begin date and if lucky no end date. A program contains multiple projects. A project is a tactical timeboxed effort for the purpose of delivering part of its corresponding program.

Techniques for eliciting requirements

On eliciting requirements

> ***Elicitation is:***
> ***•To draw forth or bring out (something latent or potential)***
> ***•To call forth or draw out (as information or a response)***
>
> Merriam-Webster Online Dictionary

- More work than simply *gathering* requirements
- Emphasis is on actively engaging stakeholders
- Demonstrate through Book Sales App

Techniques for eliciting requirements

On eliciting requirements

FROM MERRIAM-WEBSTER ONLINE DICTIONARY

The definition of elicitation is:
to draw forth or bring out (something latent or potential)
to call forth or draw out (as information or a response).

ELICITATION TECHNIQUES FROM BABOK 2.0

There are a number of different techniques that can be used, depending on the resources available and level of detail required from the outcome. The main techniques are:

- Interviews
- Document and Interface Analysis
- Observation (aka Job Shadowing)
- Requirements Workshops (aka JAD)
- Brainstorming
- Prototyping (aka Storyboarding)

Note that much of the information in the next few pages that go into each of these techniques are based upon BABOK 2.0 supplemented with my own experiences.

BOOK SALES

To illustrate the process of eliciting requirements as well as documenting and scoping requirements, we will use a Book Sales example.

Techniques for eliciting requirements

Interviewing

Preparation

- Define the interview's focus or goal
- Identify potential interviewees
- Design the interview

Session

- Opening: State purpose of interview
- During: Maintain focus on interview goals
- Closing: Summarize session – also anything overlooked?

Wrap up

- Interviewer organizes the information and sends the notes to the interviewee for review

Designing the interview requires crafting questions considering:

- Interview time limitations (and whether it is a one-shot interview)
- Personality of the interviewee
- Interviewee hidden agendas (and open agendas)
- Interviewee technical expertise (e.g. Can they read a data model?)
- Interviewee enthusiasm for the project

Techniques for eliciting requirements

Interviewing

EXPLANATION

An interview is a systematic approach designed to elicit information from a person or group of people in an informal or formal setting by talking to an interviewee, asking relevant questions and documenting the responses. For the purpose of eliciting requirements, interviews are of two basic types:

- **Structured Interview** where the interviewer has a pre-defined set of questions and is looking for answers.
- **Unstructured Interview** where, without any pre-defined questions, the interviewer and the interviewee discuss topics of interest in an open-ended way.

Successful interviewing depends on several factors including:

- Level of understanding of the domain by the interviewer.
- Experience and preparation of the interviewer in conducting interviews.
- Readiness of interviewee to provide the relevant information.
- Rapport of the interviewer with the interviewee.

APPROACH

Preparation:

- Define the interview's focus or goal before proceeding
- Identify potential interviewees
- Design the interview. Includes determining type of questions to be asked close-ended vs open-ended. Also includes organization of the questions. Examples of organization would be general questions to specific questions, start to finish, detail to summary, etc.

Session:

- **Opening the interview.** The interviewer states the purpose of the interview, addresses any initial concerns raised by the interviewee, and explains that notes will be taken and shared with the interviewee after the interview.
- **During the interview.** The interviewer maintains focus on the established goals and pre-defined questions.
- **Closing the interview.** The interviewer asks the interviewee for areas that may have been overlooked in the session. Lastly, the interviewer summarizes the session, reminds the interviewee of the upcoming review process and thanks the interviewee for their time.

Wrap up:

- After the interview is complete, the interviewer organizes the information and sends the notes to the interviewee for review.

Techniques for eliciting requirements

Questions are the heart of the interview

Closed questions	Open questions
• Simple, information gathering questions • Response to a closed question is a "yes" or "no" or a very brief answer	• Stimulating, with longer, more complex answers • Used to draw out a wide range of responses on a broad topic • Ask for opinions, thoughts or feelings

Top 10 interview tips

- **"Pretend you're being questioned by a six-year old"**
- **Five Why's will make you Wise**
- **Listen, listen, listen**
- **Play back**
- **Forget what you think you know about the business**
- **Don't try to impress**
- **Timebox**
- **"Measure" and "Dimension" are ok terms to use**
- **"Sit on desks for 30 minutes a day"**
- **Have a standard interview template**

Techniques for eliciting requirements

Questions are the heart of the interview

EXPLANATION

Tony Alessandra, in The Art of Asking Questions, has some great pointers on when to ask open vs closed questions. Below is his advice on when to ask each type of question. In addition, on the facing page, are some of the tips I live by when interviewing.

WHEN TO ASK CLOSED QUESTIONS

They allow specific facts to be gathered:
Do you need to see Gross Sales Amount by Day or by Month?
Who is the business expert on sales?
Who else will use the system?

They are easy to answer and seldom intimidating:
Will you be available to check out my screen mockup today at 4?
Can I see some sample reports?
The lowest calendar level you need for reporting is Month, correct?

They are useful to check the accuracy of the communication:
Have I captured the key metric formula correctly?
Is this definition for Title correct?
Is it true that a Title can exist in the source system, yet have no orders against it?

WHEN TO ASK OPEN QUESTIONS

They do not lead the answer:
Define what you mean by a book sales application?
Why do you need full history on Title?
Why do you need these two separate reports?

They draw out ideas and feelings:
What do you expect this project to accomplish for you?
What do you do?
What do you want to do?

They encourage elaboration on objectives and problems:
What types of questions do you spend lots of time answering in Excel?
What do you want to change about the existing reporting system?
How do you calculate Gross Sales Amount?

Techniques for eliciting requirements

Interviewing: Write the opening question

Bob has worked 15 years on the support for the order entry operational system which is the major source of data for book sales. He always makes time for a good conversation.

Your opening interview question:

Mary is the key business user. She thinks she knows exactly what she wants from the Book Sales application.

Your opening interview question:

Jim works in IT in producing reports from the order entry operational system for the business. He will no longer provide this function after the Book Sales application is in production. He can be confrontational at times.

Your opening interview question:

Joan was the key business user for the Royalty Reporting application. This project was a dismal failure and Joan stopped talking to the IT department as a result.

Your opening interview question:

Techniques for eliciting requirements

Interviewing: Write the opening question

INSTRUCTIONS

You have the opportunity to interview several people for the Book Sales application. Write the opening question you would ask for each of these individuals.

Techniques for eliciting requirements

Prototyping

How do you establish a new restaurant in your chain?

Restaurant		
Restaurant Code	Max Number	Region Code
AB	150	NE

Ownership		
Last Name	Restaurant Code	Ownership Percent

Owner	
Last Name	First Name

ACTION
New restaurant is created

New Rows
Updated Rows
Delete Rows
Unchanged

Restaurant		
Restaurant Code	Max Number	Region Code
AB	150	NE

Ownership		
Last Name	Restaurant Code	Ownership Percent

Owner	
Last Name	First Name
Winkler	Henry
Martin	Steve
Murphy	Eddie

ACTION
Several new owners are created

Restaurant		
Restaurant Code	Max Number	Region Code
AB	150	NE

Ownership		
Last Name	Restaurant Code	Ownership Percent
Winkler	AB	50
Murphy	AB	50

Owner	
Last Name	First Name
Winkler	Henry
Martin	Steve
Murphy	Eddie

ACTION
Henry Winkler and Eddie Murphy each own 50% of the AB restaurant

Or

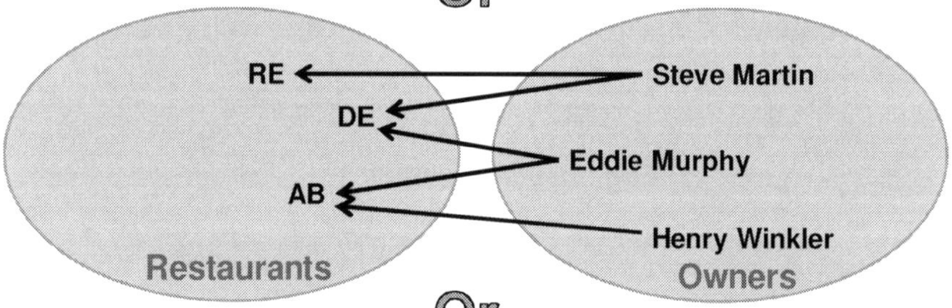

Or

		Restaurant		
		AB	RE	DE
Owner	Henry Winkler	50%		
	Eddie Murphy	50%		50%
	Steve Martin		100%	50%

"I think I got it"

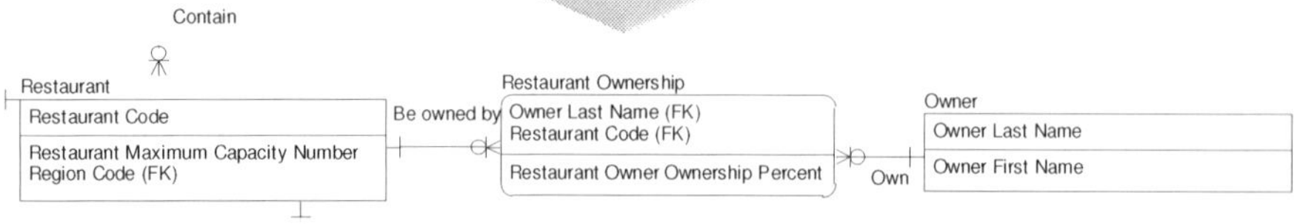

Techniques for eliciting requirements

Prototyping

EXPLANATION

Prototyping is a concrete means of identifying, describing and validating relational and dimensional requirements. A horizontal prototype models a shallow and possibly wide view of the system's functionality. It typically does not have any business logic running behind the visualization. A vertical prototype models a deep and usually narrow slice of the entire system's functionality.

TIPS

- Manage expectations. The prototype is not a production system!
- For detailed prototypes, verify that what appears in the prototype actually maps back to data elements in the source.
- Validate that the prototype represents the user's needs. Scenarios are useful to 'test' the interfaces.

EXAMPLES

The facing page contains three simple prototyping techniques to validate relational requirements. The technique below uses a spreadsheet to create a rough screen mock-up showing the dimensional levels and measure for a proposed business application. You do not need to know how to program to build a prototype, you just need to know your audience!

MINUTES TO BIRTH AFTER LABOR INDUCEMENT

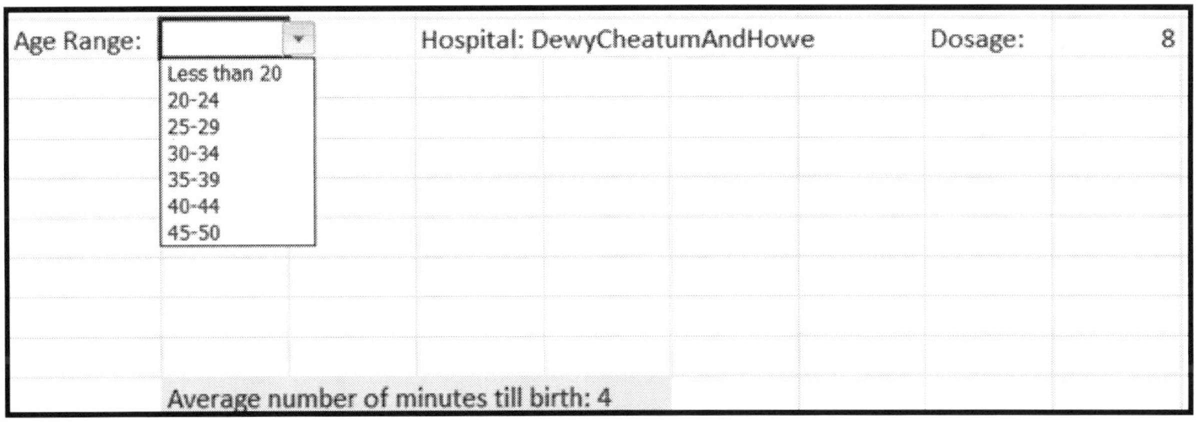

Scoping and validating requirements

Interview template

Interview summary

- Consumer Contact Data Mart -

Date: May 10th, 2011

Duration: 1 hour

Interviewer: Mary Smith

Interviewee information

Name: Henry Winkler

Phone: 718-555-1212

Email: HWinkler@widgets.com

Title: Manager of Consumer Contact Data Entry Team

Interest: Henry will be one of the key business users for the Consumer Contact Data Mart. In addition, he has extensive experience with using the data entry application to run operational reports.

Purpose of interview

Validate the business requirements document (v 1.0) and fill in any gaps in my understanding and in the requirements.

Takeaways

Henry needs a very important metric which can not be delivered today without much manual effort. This metric, called Complaints Per Million, is also not mentioned in the requirements document. It is calculated by dividing…

Next steps

Need to discuss data mart due date with project manager – hopefully can extend by 2 weeks to accommodate new measure.

Sit with Steve Martin who works for Henry the next time he manually calculates this measure.

Interview Steve next.

Scoping and validating requirements

Interview template

BACKGROUND

Interviews with business experts, business users, and source system experts are the primary ways of understanding requirements, filling in gaps, and building rapport. The time dedicated to interviews is usually very limited and therefore this time must be well spent. To make the most of this time, create a standard interview template such as what appears on the facing page. Store the interview findings in a common place and make the collection of interview write-ups part of the overall documentation deliverable. Customize the template to make it work with your organization and project team.

INTERVIEWEE INFORMATION

Store their phone number, email, and other contact information. Also, their interest and involvement with the project.

PURPOSE OF INTERVIEW

It is very important to capture the purpose of the interview, as it will help keep the interview focused. Make it as specific as possible so that it could be accomplished within the interview time (usually about 1 hour).

TAKEAWAYS

This is a summary of the interview. It can start off as a sketch pad during the interview and then get written up more formally after the interview. Depending on how much information is collected, you might want to have several subsections such as Reporting Requirements, Business Rules, and System Information.

NEXT STEPS

Capture what you would like to accomplish the next time you meet with this person, writing the names of other people that now need to be interviewed, and any other follow ups from this interview including tracking down documentation and questions and possible issues.

YOU CAN USE THIS TOOL...

to ensure requirements are documented. So many requirements happen verbally, and this template ensures these requirements don't get lost. In addition, in writing the purpose of the interview before the interview, you will be better prepared for the interview and the interview will be more focused because you will know exactly what you want to get out of it.

Scoping and validating requirements

Family Tree explanation

A Simple Example

Source		Data element in our data model		
Data element	Table	Transformation	Data element	Table
LIST_PRICE	PRICE	Price * Qty	TOTAL_AMOUNT	SALES_FACT
ORDER_ QUANTITY	ORD			

You can use the Family Tree to

- Document lineage for each data element
- Get reality check
- Capture how to calculate derived measures
- Capture data requirements when working in complex project teams

Scoping and validating requirements

Family Tree explanation

BACKGROUND

The Family Tree contains the complete list of data elements (including derived data elements) for the application, and the sources and transformations for each, along with several other key pieces of data element metadata, including definition and format.

YOU CAN USE THIS TOOL TO...

document the lineage for each data element in the data model, including derived measures for business usage in a reporting application. It serves as a great reality check against the requirements identified in the Grain Matrix (discussed next). It also is helpful when working on complex project teams as it lets you "divide and conquer".

EXAMPLE

The example on the facing page illustrates a simple mapping from the source to a data element in our model. TOTAL_AMOUNT is derived by multiplying LIST_PRICE by ORDER_QUANTITY.

TOOLS

The most common tool for creating and maintaining a mapping document is Excel. The advantage is its widespread use and everyone understands a spreadsheet. The disadvantage is they are difficult to centralize and control. More recently, organizations are storing this mapping in Extract, Transform, and Load (ETL) tools and therefore the mapping can be centralized and automatically ported over to the reporting tool for use by the business (e.g. accessing definitions).

Scoping and validating requirements

Grain Matrix explanation

The Grain Matrix captures the levels of reporting for each measure. It can be built from business questions or reports, top down or bottom up. It is a powerful technique to validate and scope reporting requirements.

Scoping and validating requirements

Grain Matrix explanation

BACKGROUND

Did you see the movie "The Last Starfighter"? The neatest gadget in this movie was a device which would let you interpret any other language. The Grain Matrix lets you do the same thing, except instead of interpreting a language, it is used to interpret reporting levels within a data mart. The Grain Matrix is a spreadsheet, which captures the levels of reporting for each fact or measurement. It is the spreadsheet view of an initial design, which could result in one or more star schemas. Both business users and the project team can understand and validate the reporting requirements through this spreadsheet. Business users might "speak" the language of reports, whereas technical people might "speak" the language of data models or star schema designs. Note that this is only for reporting applications, such as for data marts.

PURPOSE

- **To agree on the levels of reporting without showing a model.** I recently validated with the business all of the reporting requirements for a financial data mart, without showing a single data model! No one got scared away!
- **To uncover sourcing issues early.** For example, if on the Grain Matrix the user has requested Gross Sales Value at a day level, yet the source application only stores it at a month level, this is an issue. Either the Grain Matrix will need to be updated to store this fact at the month level, or an allocation algorithm will be needed.
- **To uncover new dimensions.** If you notice several facts that appear very similar except for a slight variation, such as a unit of measure or currency code, you might want to propose a new dimension.
- **To capture data requirements when working in complex project teams.** When it's difficult to meet with the rest of the project team, and multiple people are working on the requirements portion, the Grain Matrix is a good tool to use because you can assign portions to each person.

Scoping and validating requirements

Before we can complete the Grain Matrix, we need precise and complete business questions

	Precise?	Complete?	Rewritten (include assumptions)
How is my company doing?			
What is our top sales channel?			
What is our average cost per book?			
How many copies of **Data Modeling Made Simple with CA ERwin Data Modeler** should we print?			
Will ebook sales cannibalize print book sales?			

Scoping and validating requirements

Before we can complete the Grain Matrix, we need precise and complete business questions

MANY WAYS TO ACHIEVE GOAL OF PRECISE AND COMPLETE BUSINESS QUESTIONS

The end result of the elicitation techniques is a set of precise and complete business questions. Precision means it is obvious and clear in the business question what the user needs to see. Completeness means it is obvious and clear what the user needs to see it by. There are many sources of valuable business questions, including, your own experience, organization drivers and goals, business processes, measures, key terms, and existing reporting. Beware that some of these questions though, can lead to privacy or security issues.

IMPORTANCE OF CLEAR AND COMPLETE DEFINITIONS

Also, clear and consistent definitions of key terms in business questions are essential for getting a refined set of questions (e.g. removing duplicates). For example, what does Net Sales Amount mean? What does a Customer mean? Clear definitions remove all ambiguity and confusion.

ON THE FACING PAGE

Would you consider the business questions on the facing page to be precise and complete? If yes, put a check mark in the appropriate Precise and/or Complete columns. If no, make assumptions and fix them!

USE BUSINESS QUESTION PRIORITY MATRIX TO...

categorize the business questions. Those questions in the upper left quadrant are the ones that normally should be delivered first. Those questions in the lower right quadrant hopefully will never get implemented!

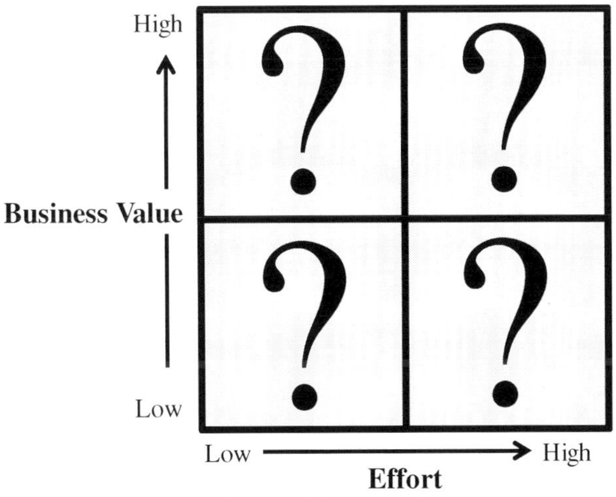

Scoping and validating requirements

Book Sales Grain Matrix

1. How is my company doing? What is our percent change in gross revenue, net revenue, and books sold by title over the last three years?
2. What is our top sales channel for the last six months in terms of books sold?
3. What is our worst sales channel for the last six months in terms of books sold?
4. What season this past year did we experience the greatest percent increase in net revenue by title? Greatest percent decrease?
5. Compare net sales last quarter between Amazon and Barnes & Noble.
6. Which region did we sell more books last quarter, North America or Europe?
7. I want to see the total number of books we sold by title and sales channel.
8. I want our total net revenue by title and sales channel.
9. How many copies of **Data Modeling Made Simple** did we sell in the Asia/Pacific region last year?
10. Will ebook sales cannibalize print book sales? Compare ebook and print sales measured in gross revenue, net revenue, and books sold for two of our titles, **fruITion** and **recrEAtion**, over the last two years.

Assumptions:

Scoping and validating requirements

Book Sales Grain Matrix

INSTRUCTIONS

Fill in the grain matrix below based upon the business questions on the facing page. Write the measurements in columns, levels of detail in the rows, and reference the questions within each cell. Keep track of any assumptions you make.

Scoping and validating requirements

Converting Grain Matrix to Logical Dimensional Data Model

	Gross Revenue Change Percent	Gross Revenue Amount	Net Revenue Change Percent	Net Revenue Amount	Books Sold Change Percent	Books Sold Quantity
Title	1	1,10	1,4	1,4,8,10	1	1,7,9,10
Year	1	1,10	1	1,10	1	1,9,10
Quarter				5		6
Season			4	4		
Month						2,3
Sales Channel				5,8		2,3,7
Region						6,9
Medium		10		10		10

One Business Solution

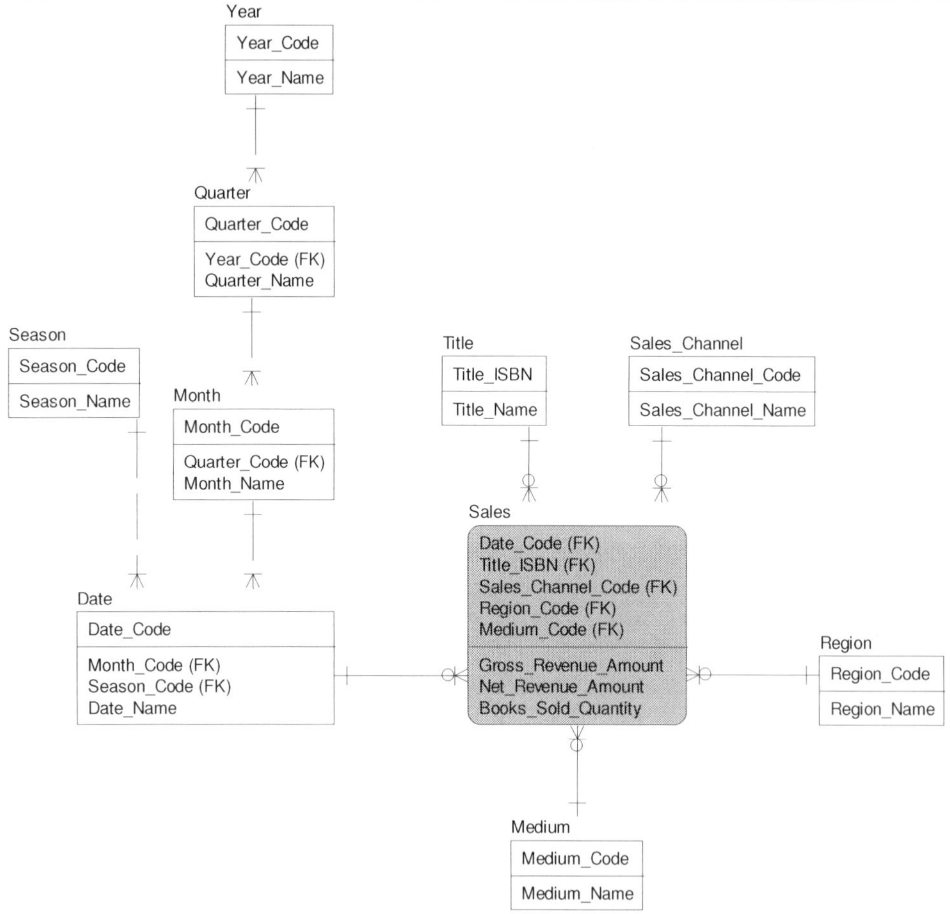

Scoping and validating requirements

Converting Grain Matrix to Logical Dimensional Data Model

EXPLANATION The grain matrix can be scoped into one or many business applications. In this example, you see two logical dimensional models that can be built from the complete grain matrix for Book Sales.

Another Business Solution

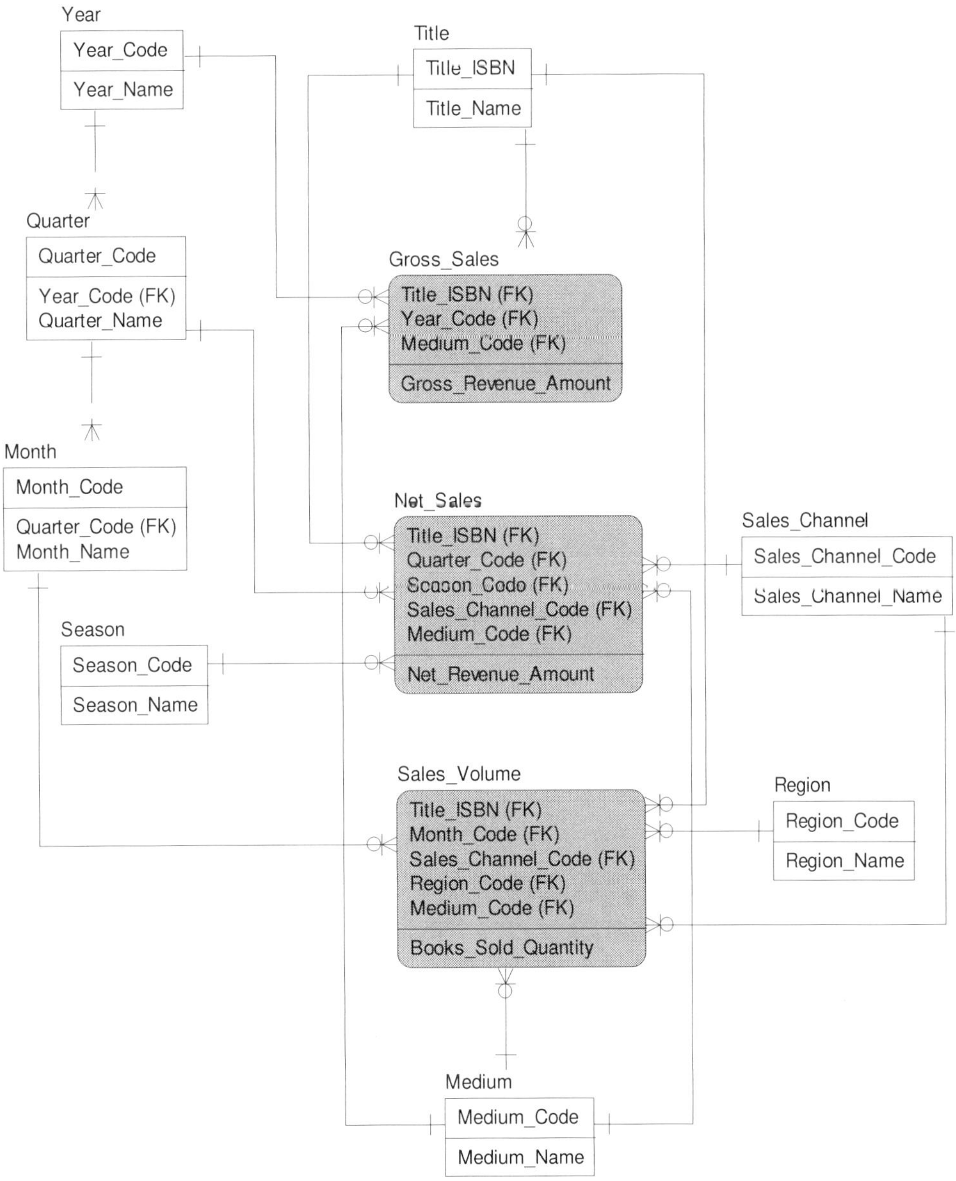

Applying the Data Model Scorecard®

Interaction Report for Product BB40 from May 2011

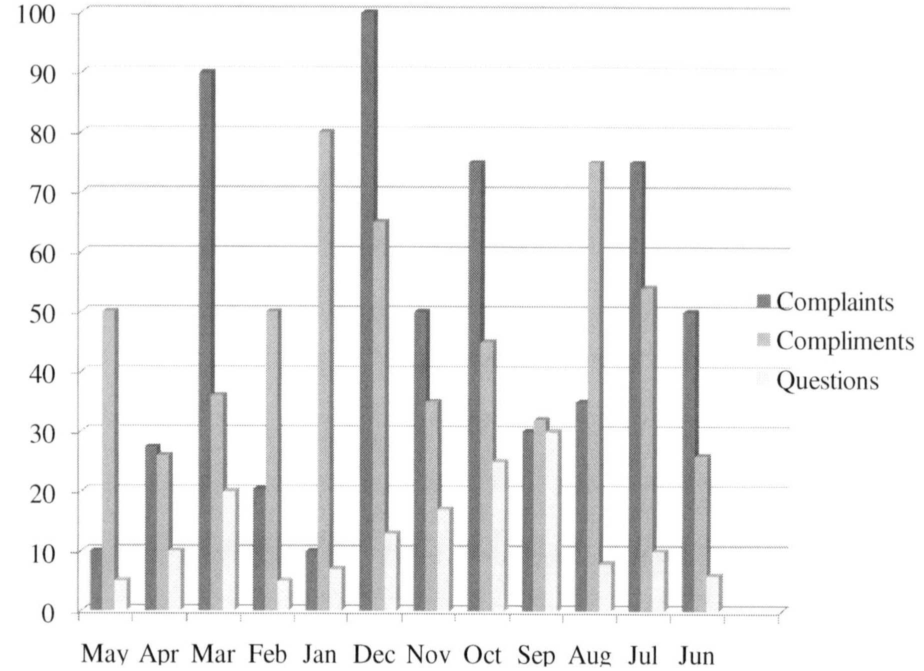

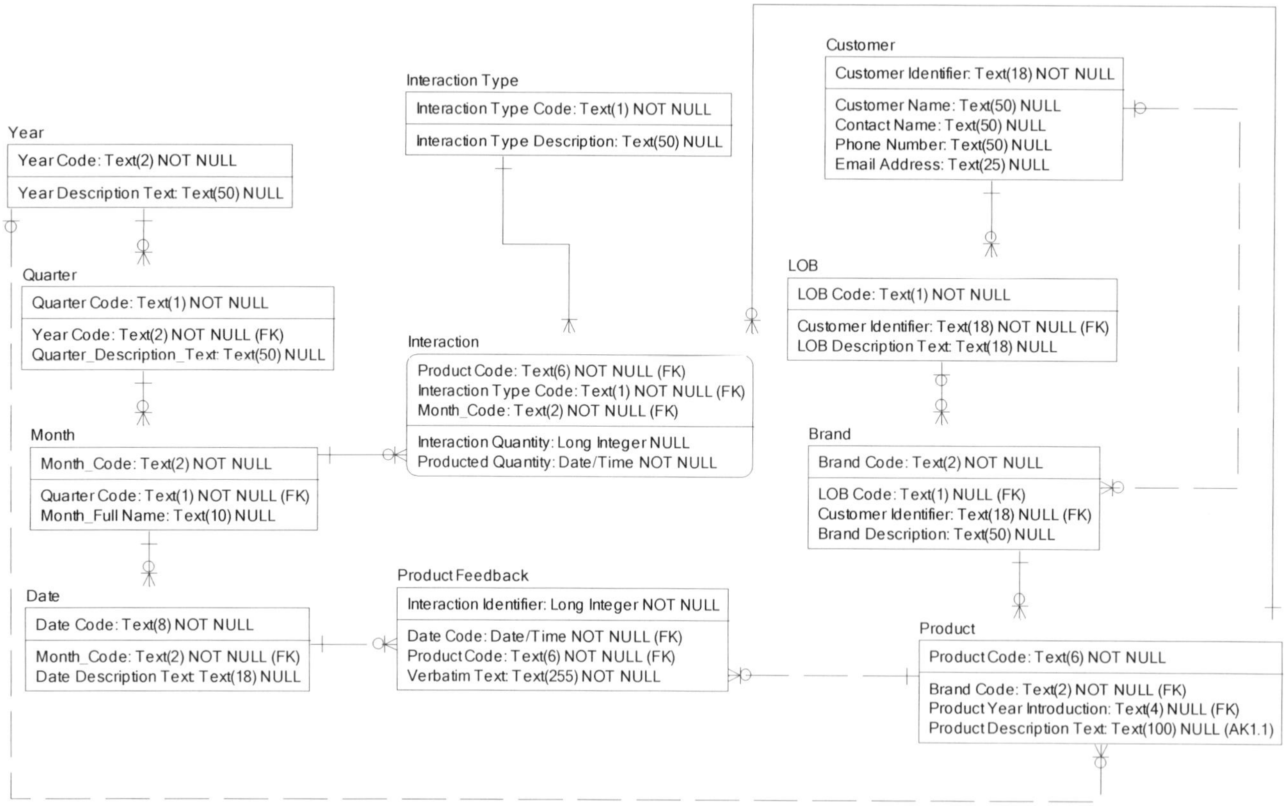

Applying the Data Model Scorecard®

2. How well does the model capture the requirements?

EXPLANATION

This is the "correctness" category. This category confirms that the model meets the requirements. All of the functionality detailed in a requirements document should be supported in the model.

ANTHING YOU WOULD CATCH IN THE MODEL ON THE FACING PAGE FOR THIS CATEGORY?

1.
2.
3.
4.
5.
6.
7.
8.
9.
10.

#	Category	Total score	Model score	%
1	How well do the characteristics of the model support the type of model?	10		
2	How well does the model capture the requirements?	15		
3	How complete is the model?	15		
4	How structurally sound is the model?	15		
5	How well does the model leverage generic structures?	10		
6	How well does the model follow naming standards?	5		
7	How well has the model been arranged for readability?	5		
8	How good are the definitions?	10		
9	How consistent is the model with the enterprise?	5		
10	How well does the metadata match the data?	10		
	TOTAL SCORE	100		

Applying the Data Model Scorecard®

Interaction Report for Product BB40 from May 2011

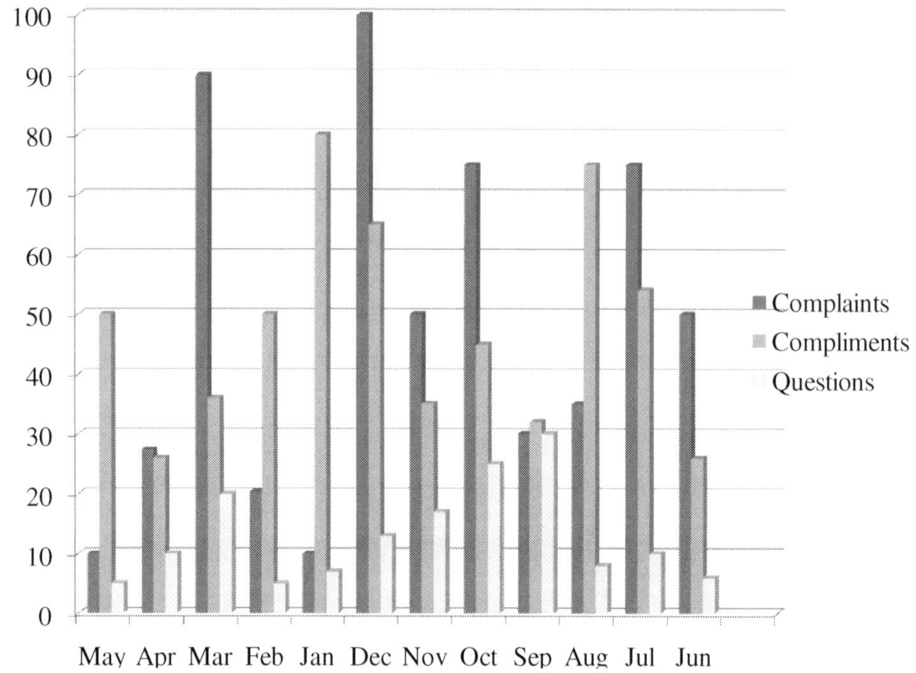

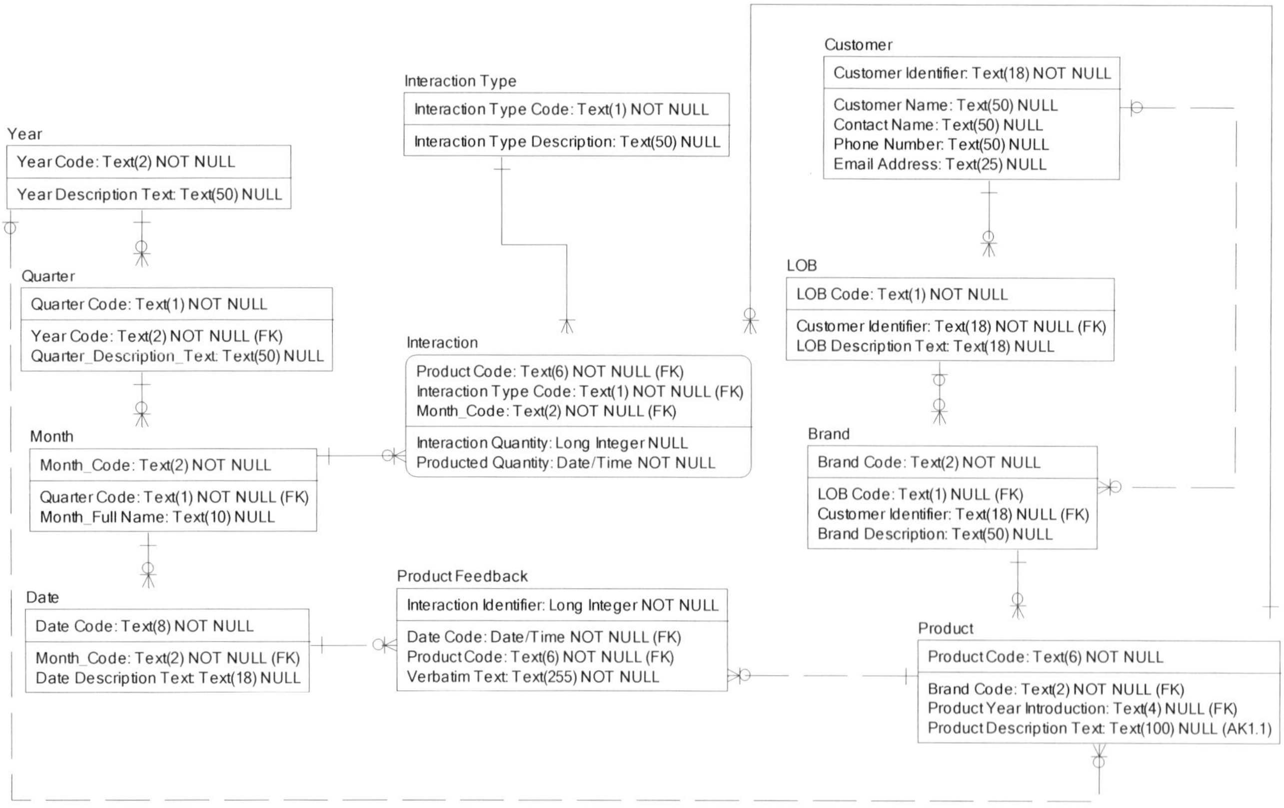

Applying the Data Model Scorecard®

3. How complete is the model?

EXPLANATION

This category checks for data model components that are not in the requirements or requirements that are not represented on the model. For completeness, we need to make sure the scope of the project and model match, as well as ensuring the model contains all of the required metadata.

ANTHING YOU WOULD CATCH IN THE MODEL ON THE FACING PAGE FOR THIS CATEGORY?

1.
2.
3.
4.
5.
6.
7.
8.
9.
10.

#	Category	Total score	Model score	%
1	How well do the characteristics of the model support the type of model?	10		
2	How well does the model capture the requirements?	15		
3	How complete is the model?	15		
4	How structurally sound is the model?	15		
5	How well does the model leverage generic structures?	10		
6	How well does the model follow naming standards?	5		
7	How well has the model been arranged for readability?	5		
8	How good are the definitions?	10		
9	How consistent is the model with the enterprise?	5		
10	How well does the metadata match the data?	10		
	TOTAL SCORE	100		

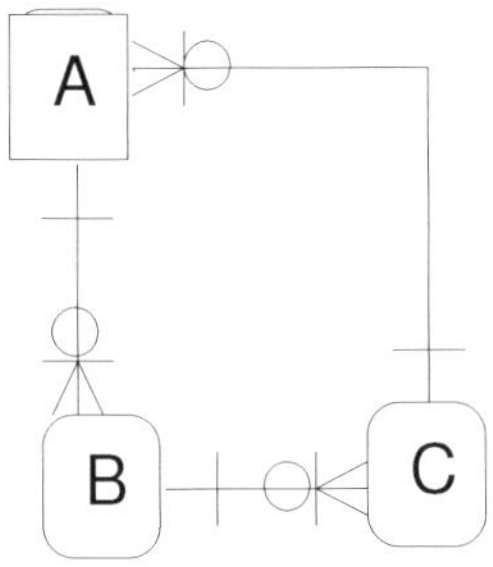

Module 4

Data Model Scorecard® Category #4: Structure

Category Question: How structurally sound is the model?

This module is your guide to: Applying acceptable modeling principles

Category overview

How structurally sound is the model?

Confirms the model follows good design principles

Many violations flagged by our modeling and database tools, such as CA ERwin Data Modeler:

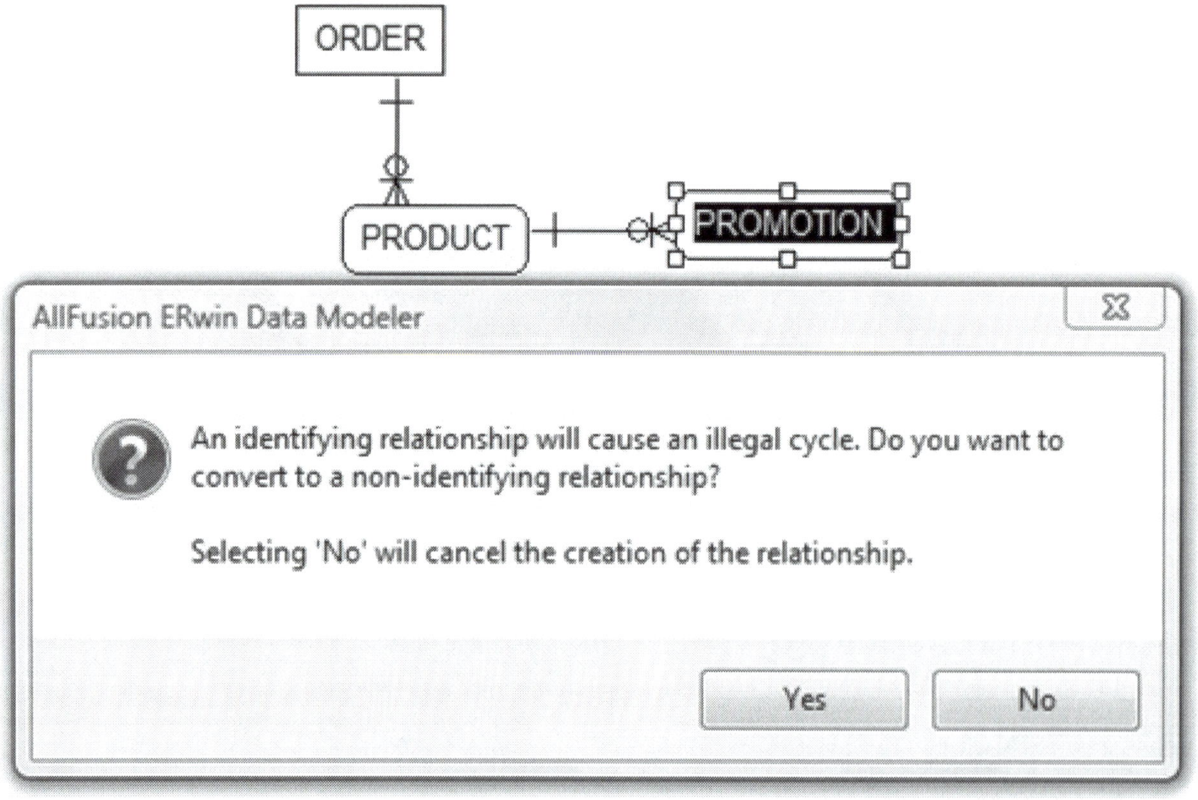

Category overview

How structurally sound is the model?

EXPLANATION

The structure category focuses on data modeling and database best practices. It validates the design practices employed to build the model. Unlike the Model Type category, the Structure category does not distinguish subject area from logical from physical, or relational from dimensional. Unlike the Correctness and Completeness categories, the Structure category allows us to completely overlook the actual subject matter being modeled. Having null primary and alternate keys, circular relationships, entities containing no data elements, the same data element defined differently across entities – these are all examples of structure violations. Many of the potential problems from this category are quickly and automatically flagged by our modeling and database tools.

PURPOSE

To minimize relational database issues.

CHALLENGE

There could be structural soundness issues that escape the human eye, or are very tedious to check for. For example, ensuring that if the same data element appears more than once on the same model, it has the same format across the model.

Category overview

Structural violation examples

1. Null candidate keys
2. An entity without any data elements (on LDM or PDM)
3. An entity without any relationships
4. Circular relationships
5. No length specified
6. Same data element with different format
7. Default format
8. Partial key relationship
9. Relationship missing an end
10. Two entities with the same name

Category overview

Structural violation examples

NULL CANDIDATE KEYS	An alternate or primary key that can be empty. Even though some databases permit null alternate keys, this is not a best practice.
AN ENTITY WITHOUT ANY DATA ELEMENTS	On a logical or physical data model, an entity should have at least one data element.
NO RELATIONSHIPS	With few exceptions, an entity should have at least one relationship. One exception would be a common code table.
CIRCULAR RELATIONSHIPS	A "Catch-22" situation, where no entity instances can be created because of mandatory relationships which start and end at the same entity.
NO LENGTH	For example, varchar2( ).
SAME DATA ELEMENT WITH DIFFERENT FORMAT	For example, on the same model if Last Name is 30 characters long in the Customer Entity and Last Name is 20 characters long in the Prospect entity.
DEFAULT FORMAT	Many modeling tools use default formats, such as char(18) and varchar(10).
PARTIAL KEY RELATIONSHIP	A relationship between two entities where the entire primary key from the parent entity is not migrated to the child entity.
RELATIONSHIP MISSING AN END	A dangling relationship that ends in space, and is not connected on both sides.
TWO ENTITIES WITH THE SAME NAME	For example, having the Customer entity twice in the same model.

Category overview

Explaining structural soundness through structural unsoundness

How many structural soundness violations can you find?

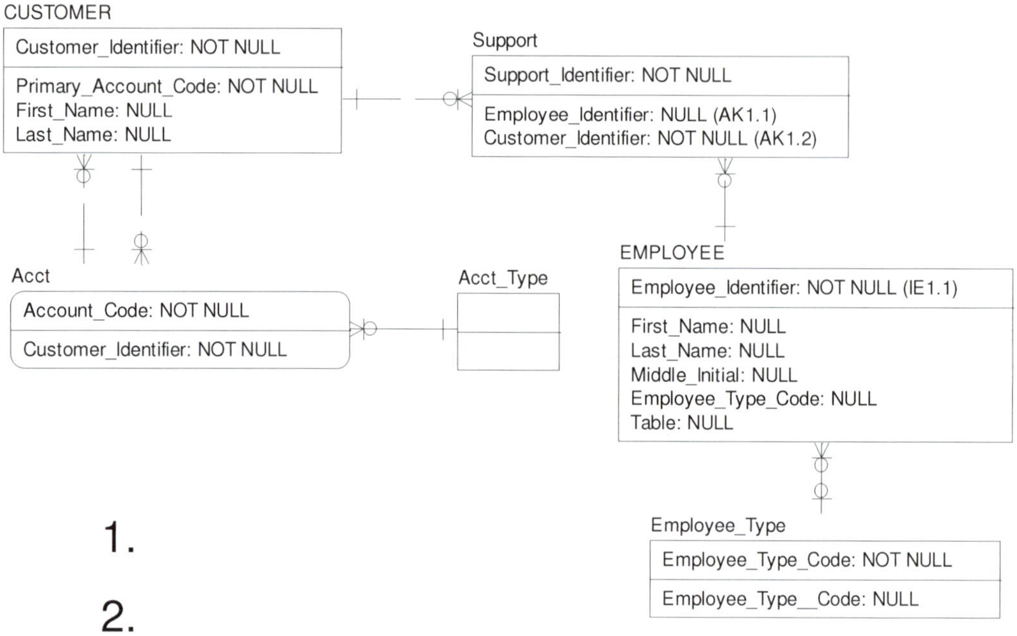

1.
2.
3.
4.
5.
6.
7.
8.
9.
10.

Category overview

Explaining structural soundness through structural unsoundness

SOME FUN

Sometimes it's easier to explain something by looking at the something's opposite. The model on the facing page is definitely structurally unsound. How many structural soundness violations can you find?

Category overview

Something strange?

CHALLENGE You are participating in a data model review and part of the model is shown below. Would you sign off on this model or is there something structurally wrong with the model?

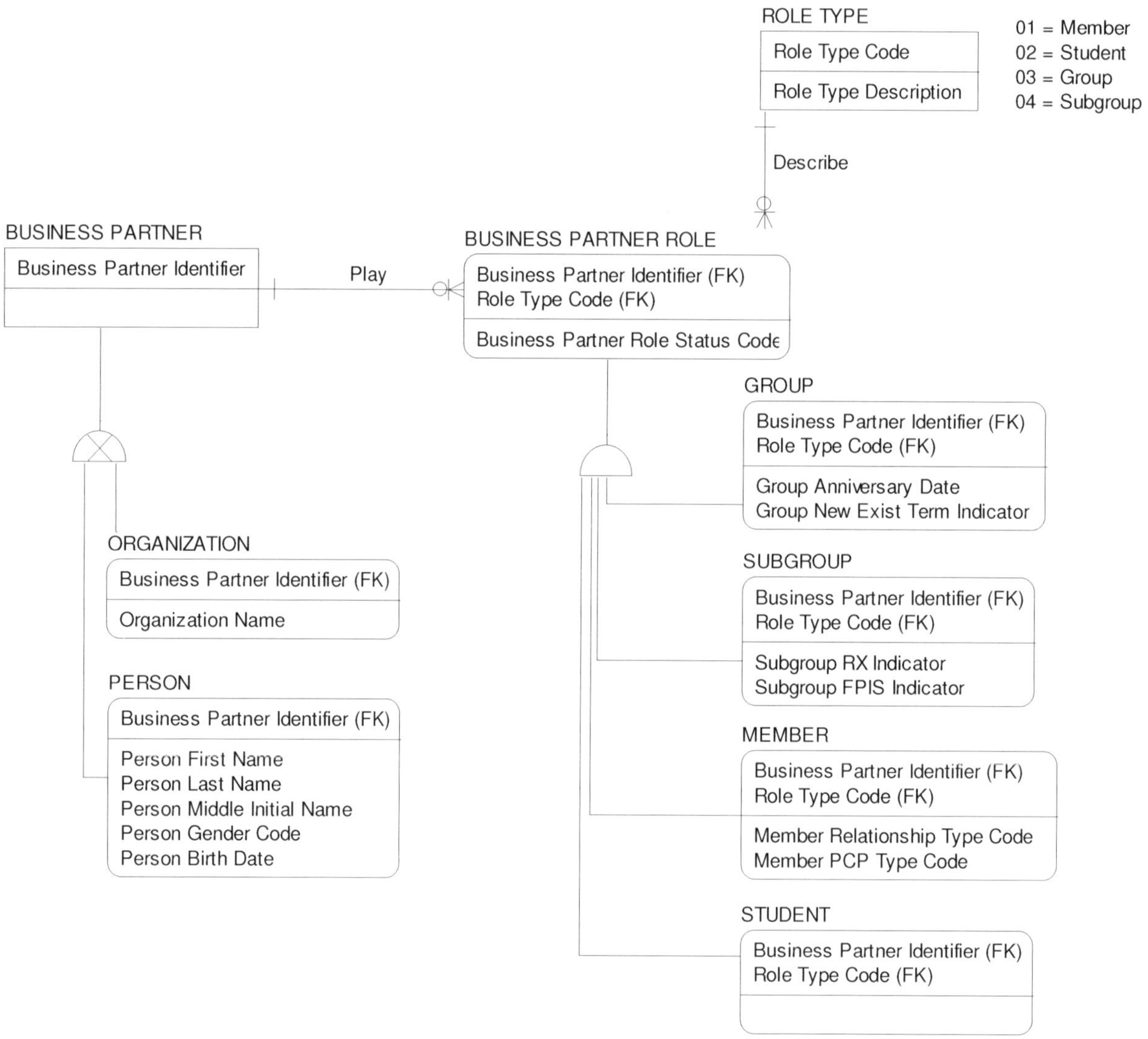

Category overview

Null AK?

CHALLENGE Can an alternate key be null? If yes, when? If no, why not?

Order

Order_Identifier: NOT NULL
Order_Number: NULL (AK1.1) Order_Quantity: NULL Order_Date: NULL

Applying the Data Model Scorecard®

Interaction Report for Product BB40 from May 2011

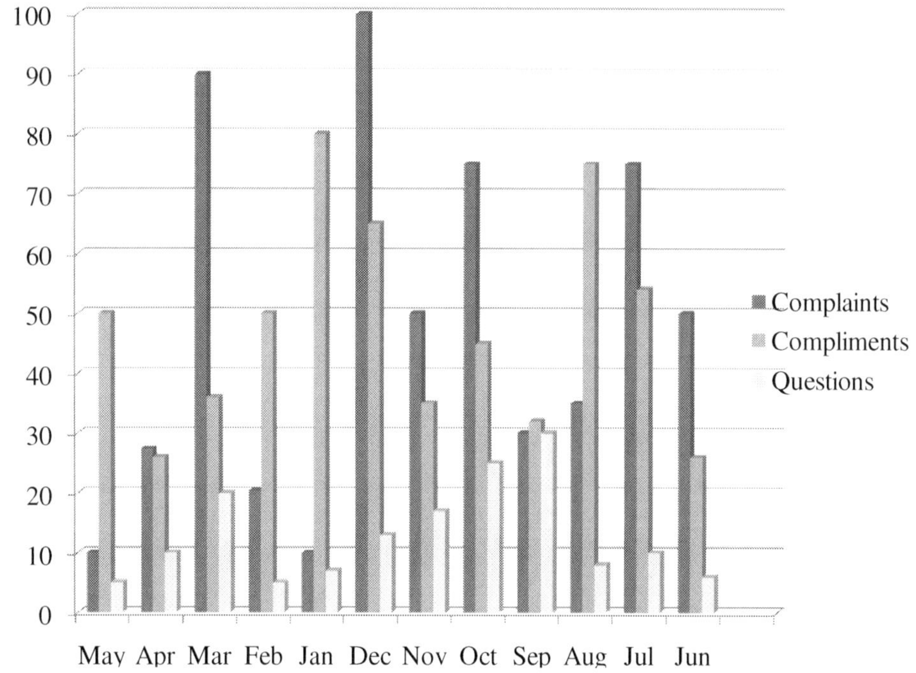

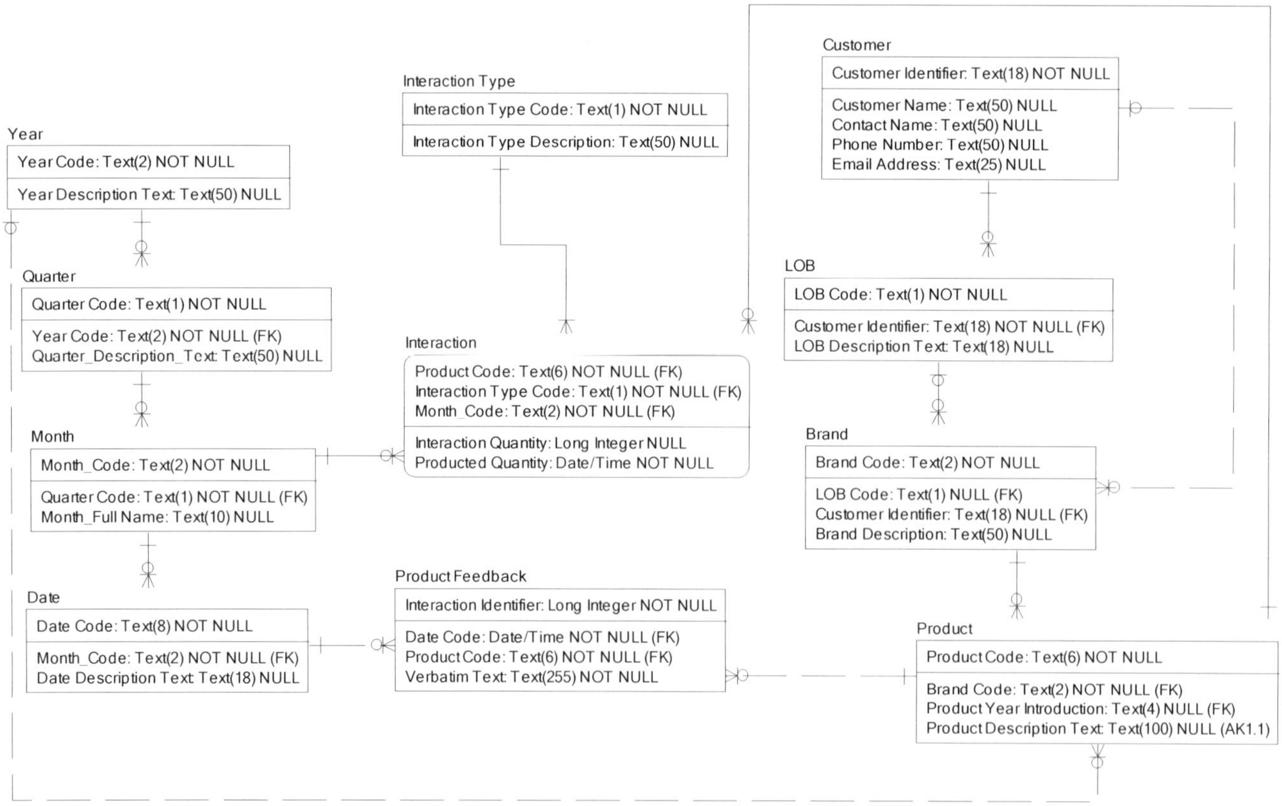

Applying the Data Model Scorecard®

4. How structurally sound is the model?

EXPLANATION

The structure category focuses on data modeling and database best practices. It validates the design practices employed to build the model.

ANTHING YOU WOULD CATCH IN THE MODEL ON THE FACING PAGE FOR THIS CATEGORY?

1.
2.
3.
4.
5.
6.
7.
8.
9.
10.

#	Category	Total score	Model score	%
1	How well do the characteristics of the model support the type of model?	10		
2	How well does the model capture the requirements?	15		
3	How complete is the model?	15		
4	How structurally sound is the model?	15		
5	How well does the model leverage generic structures?	10		
6	How well does the model follow naming standards?	5		
7	How well has the model been arranged for readability?	5		
8	How good are the definitions?	10		
9	How consistent is the model with the enterprise?	5		
10	How well does the metadata match the data?	10		
	TOTAL SCORE	100		

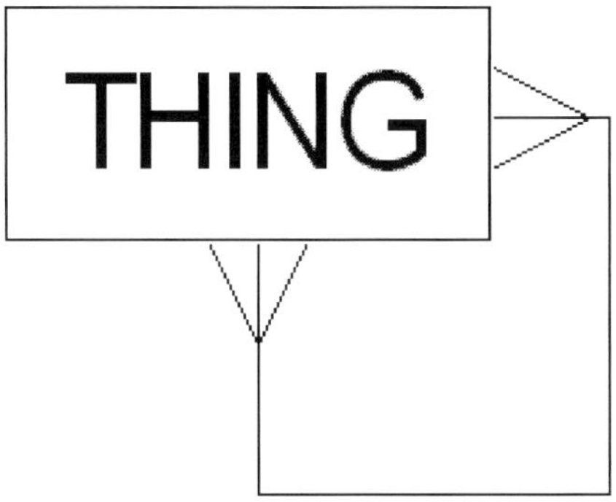

Module 5

Data Model Scorecard® Category #5: Abstraction

Category Question: How well does the model leverage generic structures?

This module is your guide to: Determining the optimal use of generic concepts

Category overview

How well does the model leverage generic structures?

ABSTRACTION

Confirms an appropriate use of abstraction on the model

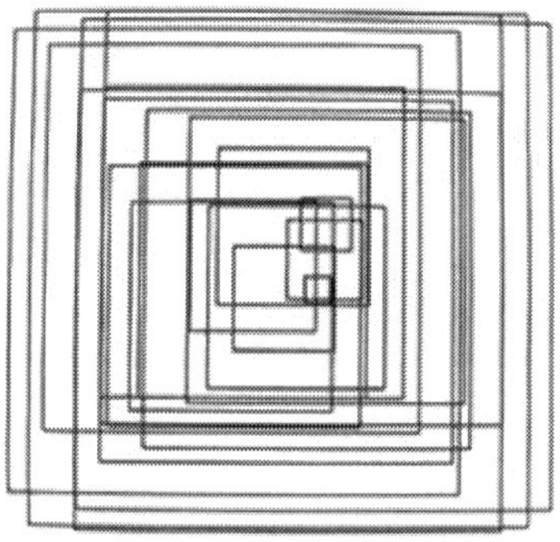

Customer is now Party/Role ("Who?")

Finished Good is now Product ("What?")

Month is now Time ("When?")

Mailing Address is now Location ("Where?")

Order is now Event ("Why?")

Invoice Receipt is now Document ("How?")

Justify why are you abstracting and then we can decide if it is worth the effort.

Category overview

How well does the model leverage generic structures?

EXPLANATION

This category confirms an appropriate use of abstraction on the model. One of the most powerful tools a data modeler has at their disposal is abstraction, the ability to increase the types of information a design can accommodate using generic concepts. Going from Customer Location to a more generic Location for example, allows the design to more easily handle other types of locations, such as warehouses and distribution centers. Abstraction can be properly applied (or abused!) at the entity, relationship, and data element levels.

PURPOSE

To have the right level of flexibility.

CHALLENGE

You need to know how to phrase "what if" scenarios, and find people in the business who can answer these questions. For example, if you are considering the "Who" concept, and currently you only have Customer on your model, someone needs to confirm that in the not so distant future you will have other types of party roles, such as Employee and Supplier.

Also, you (or your management) will need to know how to weigh the potential value of abstraction with the effort required implementing an abstract structure. As a modeler I thought abstraction was the most amazing concept – then, I volunteered to take over a development project and my first assignment was to implement an abstract structure I designed! It was very painful and I learned that flexibility always comes with a price!

Power of abstraction

Abstraction explanation

A logical data modeling process where we redefine data elements, relationships, and/or entities into more generic structures

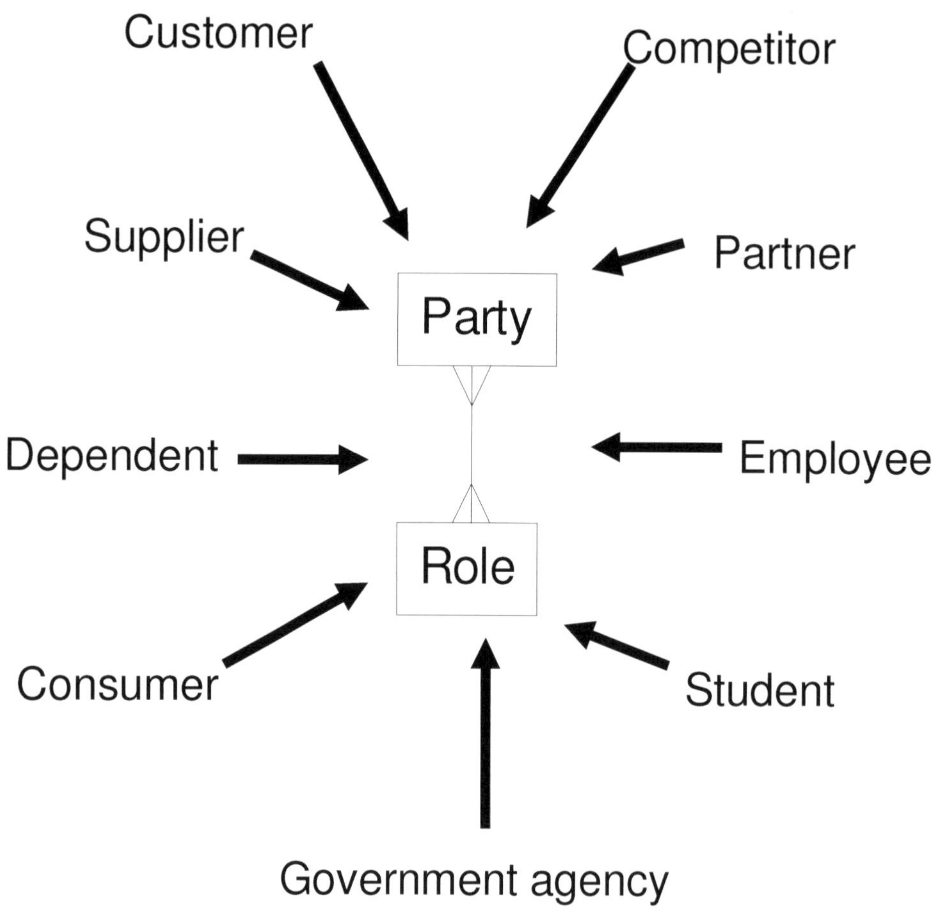

Power of abstraction

Abstraction explanation

BACKGROUND

For artists, abstraction is a tool. It lets them efficiently capture and represent complex topics. We data modelers are artists, and abstraction is an efficient tool at our disposal also.

The data modeler is responsible not only for correctly representing the requirements of an application, but also for having the foresight to design flexible structures in areas where requirements may change in the near future.

Abstraction is part of the logical data modeling process and is usually performed after normalizing. Abstraction brings flexibility to your logical data models by redefining and combining some of the data elements, entities, and relationships within the model into more generic terms. Abstraction is the removal of details in such a way as to broaden applicability to a wide class of situations while preserving the important properties and essential nature from concepts or subjects. By removing these details, we remove differences and therefore change the way we view these concepts or subjects, including seeing similarities that were not apparent or even existent before.

For example, instead of having separate *customer* and *employee* entities, there may be situations in which it would be valuable to have the generic *person* entity. *Person* can include concepts that may need to be added to an application in the near future. If *contractor* is required by an application that is built upon a model that already uses *person*, many (or even all) of the data elements and relationships assigned to *person* might also be applicable for *contractor*, and therefore the model and application will experience few or no changes.

Power of abstraction

Abstraction example

Customer	Supplier	Associate
First name	Company name	First name
Last name	Contact first name	Last name
Phone number	Contact last name	Phone number
Fax number	Phone number	Mobile number
Tax id	Fax number	Social Security #
First order date	Credit Rating	Email address
DUNS #	First PO Date	Hire date
	DUNS #	Clock #

- ☑ An Associate can be assigned to many Customers
- ☑ A Customer can contact many Associates
- ☑ An Associate manages the relationship with many Suppliers
- ☑ A Supplier can contact many Associates

Power of abstraction

Abstraction example

BACKGROUND

Create an abstract data model using these entities, data elements, and business rules. For this example we are keeping the relationships simple. But in real life there could be many more details. For example, the relationship between Associate and Customer can be an Account Manager relationship, a Customer Service relationship, a Call Upon relationship, or many other types of business relationships.

Power of abstraction

Where abstraction fits

1. Normalize
2. Apply the <u>Abstraction Safety Guide</u> in this order:
    a. Data Elements
    b. Entities
    c. Relationships
3. Document in detail

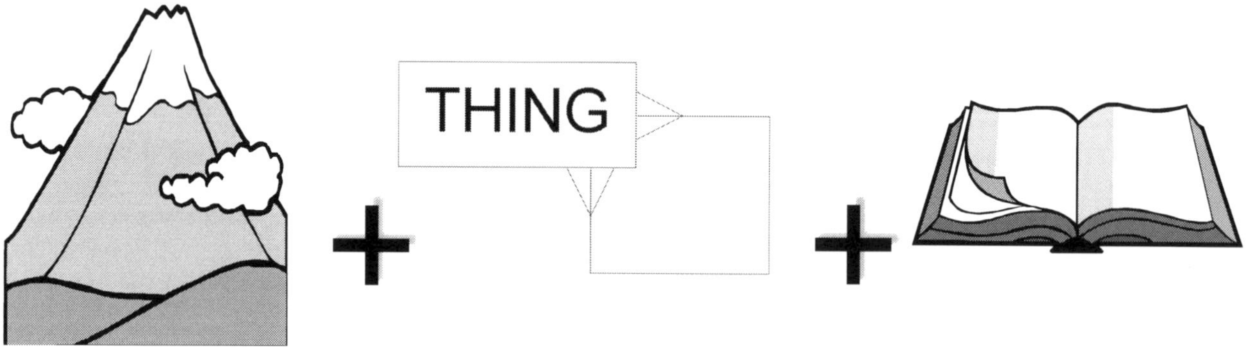

Power of abstraction

Where abstraction fits

SEQUENCE

I recommend starting with data elements. I usually start with data elements because abstracting data elements creates other opportunities for abstracting entities and relationships. Once we start with data elements and abstract where appropriate, we can more easily see what is common across entities.

After data elements, let's abstract entities and relationships. Entities next because they can open the door to abstract more data elements, entities, or relationships. Then relationships. Note that after abstracting each of these, there might still be some opportunities for abstracting at any of these three levels that were not apparent or did not exist in the first iteration. This is because when we abstract we sometimes open up new opportunities we did not think of before.

Here is our model after Step 1 (normalization) is applied:

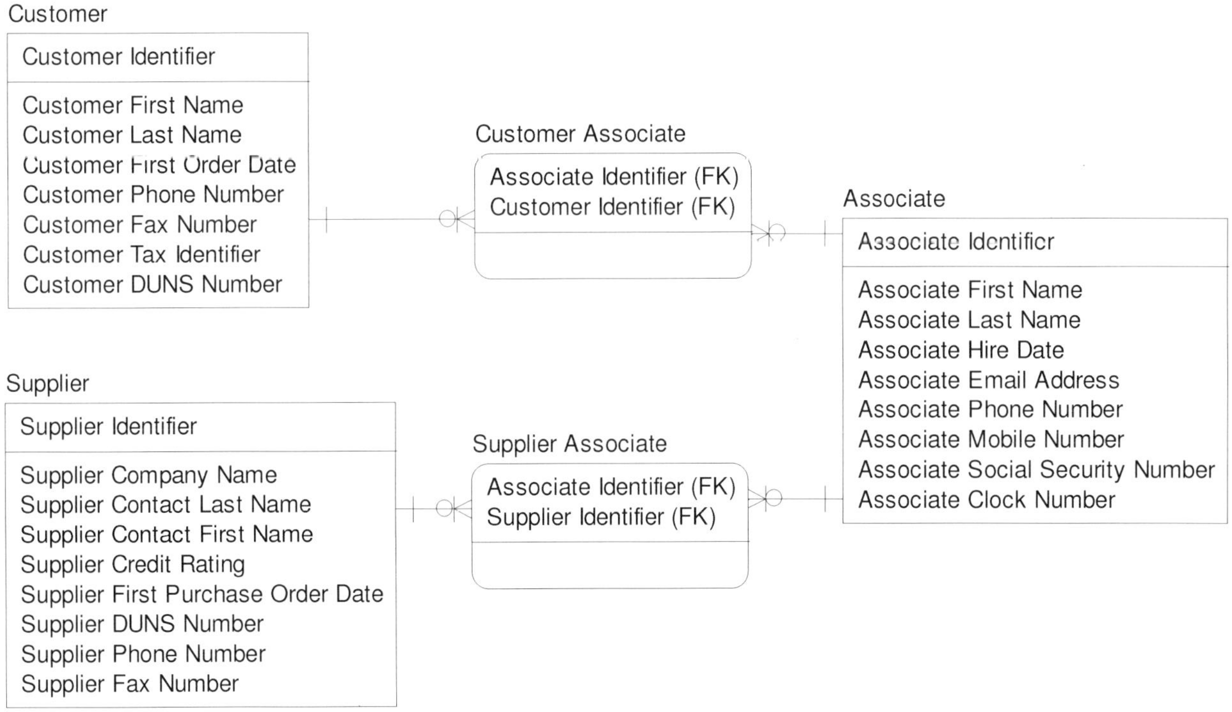

Power of abstraction

Abstraction Safety Guide (ASG)

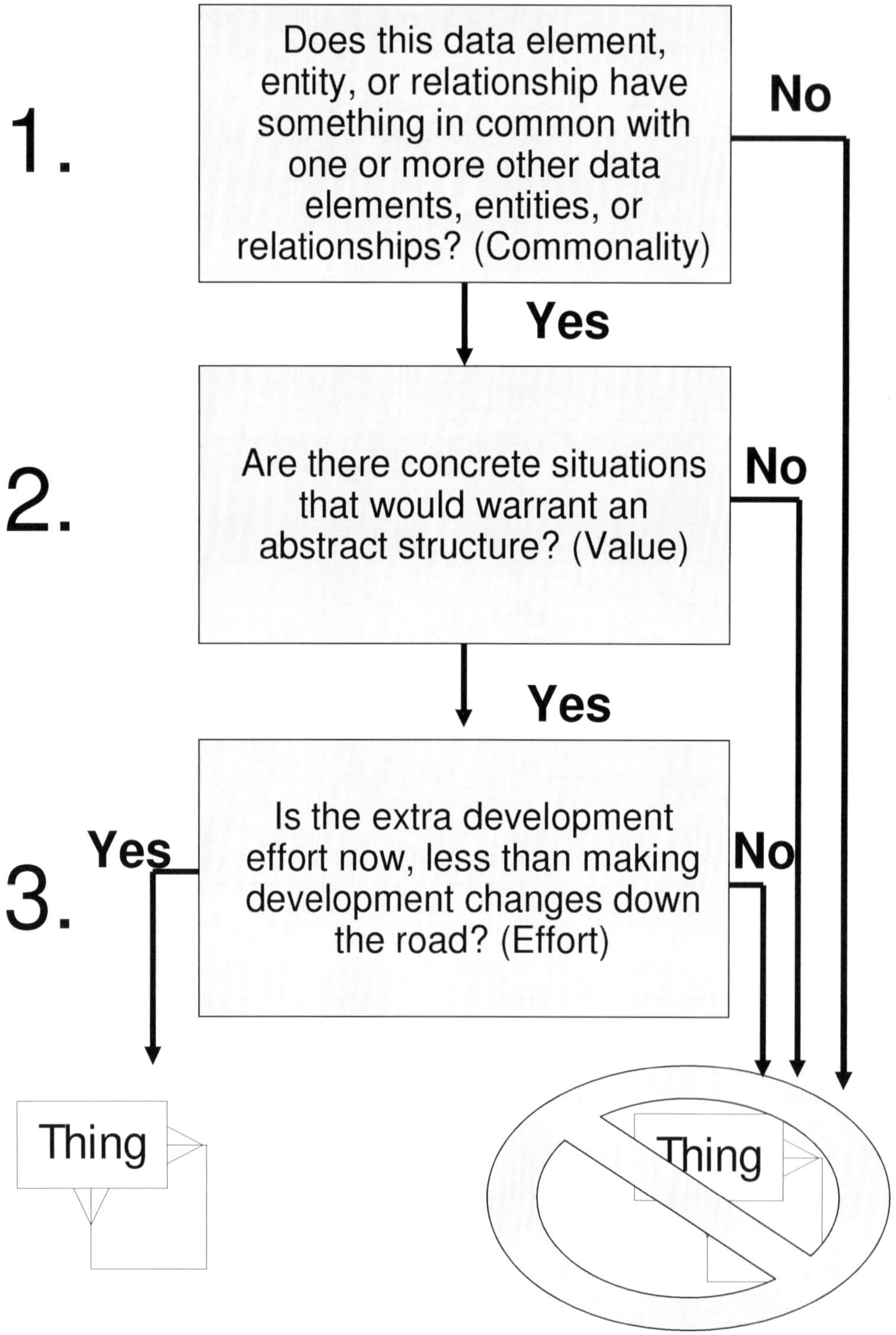

Power of abstraction

Abstraction Safety Guide (ASG)

BACKGROUND

The Abstraction Safety Guide contains three questions to decide where to abstract:
Does this data element, entity, or relationship have something in common with one or more other data elements, entities, or relationships? If yes, are there concrete situations that would warrant an abstract structure? If yes, is the extra development effort now, less than making development changes down the road?
If the answer to all 3 is "Yes!", abstract!

COMMONALITY

The first of these three questions asks, "Do we have a match anywhere on our model?" Did we find two or more entities, relationships, or data elements that appear to share a common trait? This is the detective work when we scan our model in search of anything that might appear to match something else. Remember playing the card game Concentration when you were a child? You would put a deck of picture cards face down on a table and then turn over two to see if they match. It is the same concept on the data model. If we don't find a match, we move on.

VALUE

Now that we have found several potential candidates for abstraction, we need to ask for each of these, "Are there concrete situations that would warrant an abstract structure?" In other words, is there value in abstracting? Many times when we abuse abstraction and over-abstract, we avoid asking this question. In determining the value of abstraction, ask the business experts questions like "Would your application need additional types of....?", and fill in the end of this question with what you are considering to abstract. For example, "Would your application need additional types of order lifecycle dates?"

EFFORT

The final question is around the effort involved in implementing the abstract structure. After determining that there is value in having such an abstract structure, we now need to answer the question, "Is the extra development effort now, substantially less than the development effort down the road?" This is a very tricky question, because it depends on who you ask. If you ask the data modeler (probably yourself) or anyone from the data administration team, the answer will probably be a resounding "Yes, it is worth the effort now." That is because we are looking ahead for the next requirement that can take advantage of these abstract structures. We are looking beyond just the current application. But who really needs to answer the question is the individual or department that pays the bills for the current application.

Power of abstraction

Abstracting the data elements

Before After

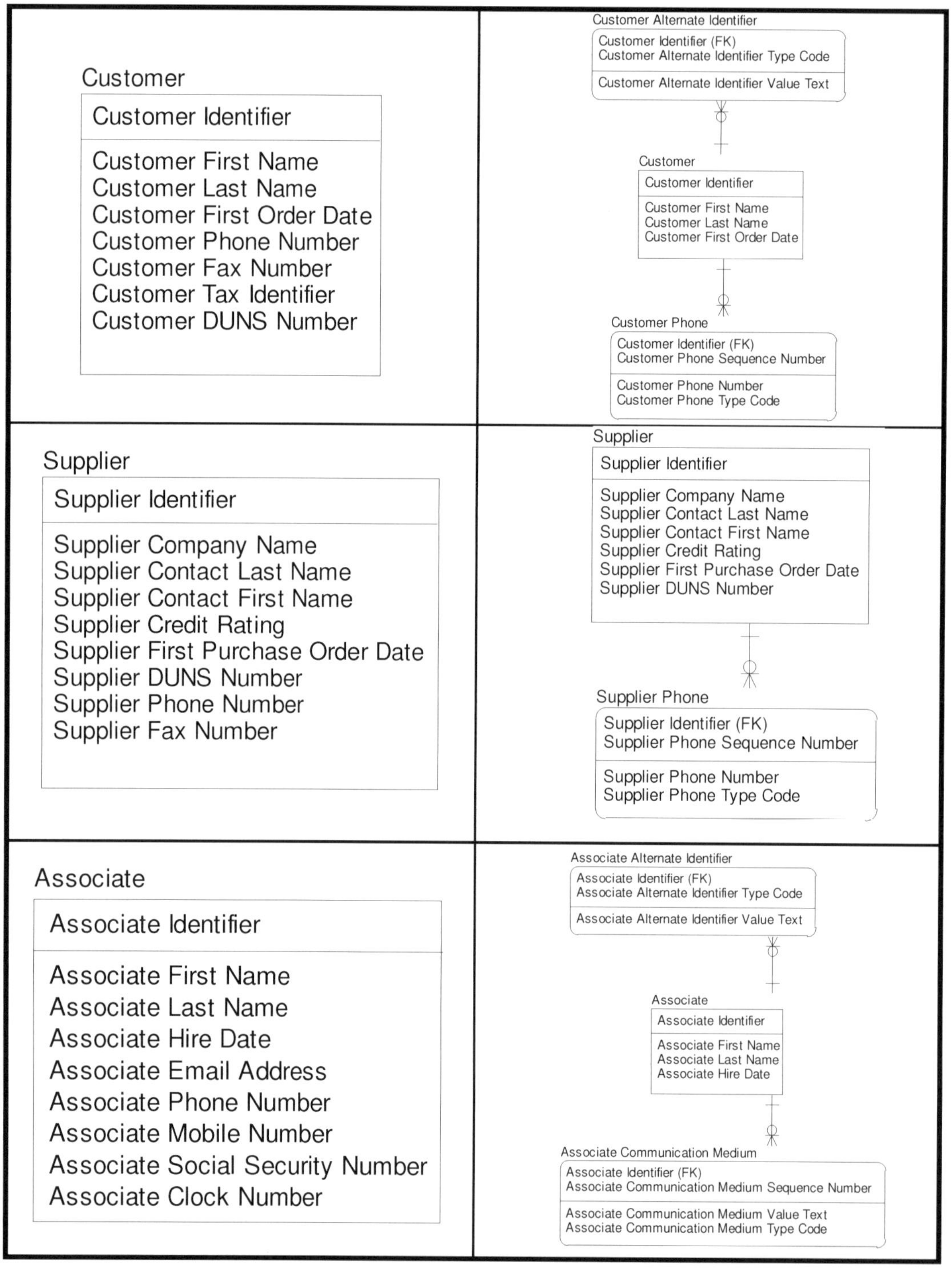

Power of abstraction

Abstracting the data elements

CUSTOMER

Phone and Fax number have become abstracted into Customer Phone where the Customer Phone Type is "Phone" or "Fax", and Customer Phone Number is the actual phone number. The same idea is applied to the Tax id and DUNS# in Customer Alternate Identifier.

SUPPLIER

Here Phone and Fax are abstracted into Supplier Phone using the same idea we saw with Customer. Notice that there is only a single alternate identifier for Supplier, DUNS #, therefore there was no need to create the Alternate Identifier abstract structure.

ASSOCIATE

Associate mimics the Customer structure with Associate Phone containing Phone Number and Pager Number, and Associate Alternate Identifier containing Social Security Number and Clock Number. As an additional abstraction step, we can include email address with the phone concept to create Communication Medium. We are taking "baby steps" and so we first abstracted the phone information and then realized that email address and phone numbers are really just different ways of communicating with someone.

Here is the model after abstracting the data elements:

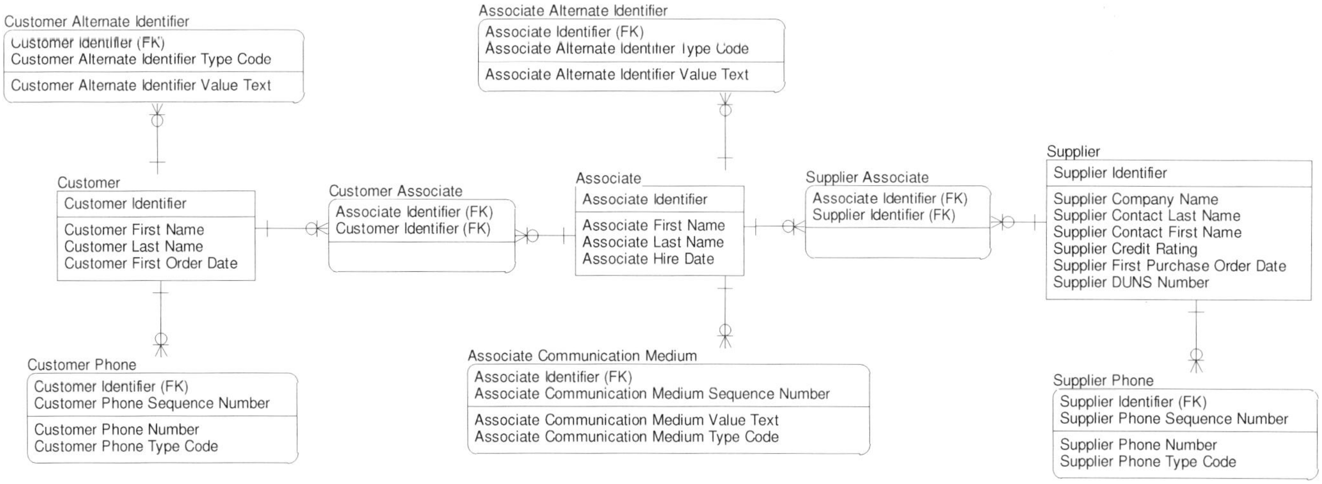

Power of abstraction

Parties and roles

Party is a person or organization of interest to the enterprise. It is similar to the concept of "Who?". That is, who is important to the business?

Roles are necessary to achieve the holistic picture

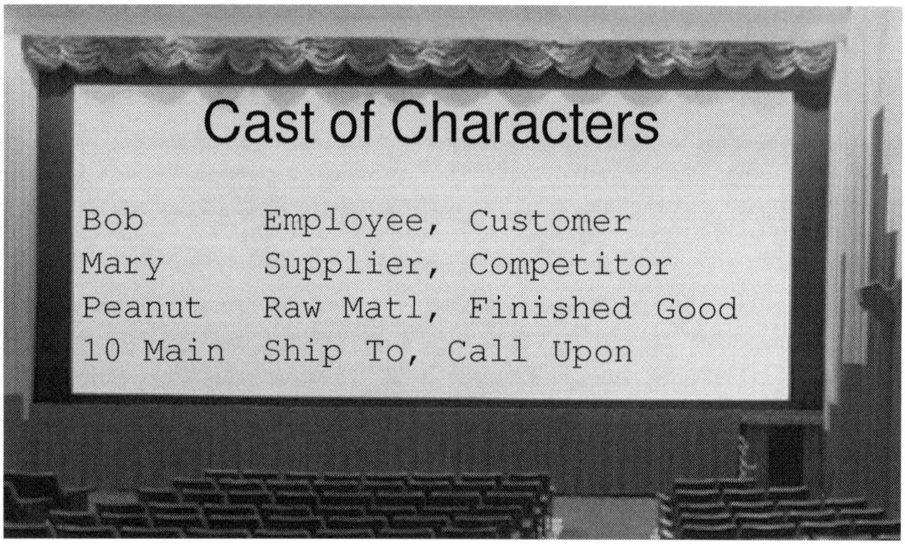

Two types of roles

- Event-independent roles
  - Member
  - Provider
- Event-dependent roles
  - A Claim turns the Provider into the Primary Care Physician
  - A Claim turns the Member into the Claimant

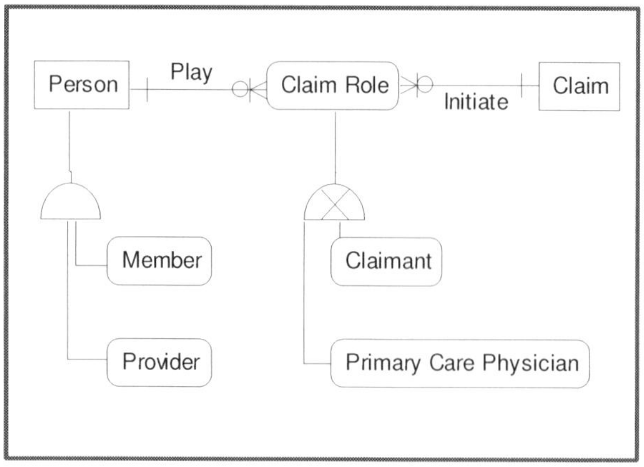

Power of abstraction

Parties and roles

INTRODUCING PARTY

Party is a person or organization of interest to the enterprise. It is similar to the concept of "Who?". That is, who is important to the business? Party is a very popular abstract entity in many organizations. All companies have people and organizations that can play different roles and Party is a very good way to encompass all of their common properties. Do you use Party in your organization? It can be called a more serious term such as Business Partner, Involved Party, and even Ephemeral Being!

LOVE/HATE RELATIONSHIP WITH PARTY

People have a love/hate relationship with Party. Those that love it admire its flexibility. Those that hate it despise its vagueness. In the example on the facing page, Party was not admired and therefore we used Person with an overlapping subtype to encompass the role concept.

ABOUT ROLES FROM WILLIAM KENT

"At the beginning of a mystery, we need to think of the murderer and the butler as two distinct entities, collecting information about each of them separately. After we discover that 'the butler did it', have we established that they are the same entity? Shall we require the modeling system to collapse their two representatives into one?"

EVENT-INDEPENDENT VS. EVENT-DEPENDENT ROLES

Event independent roles are parts a party, product, or location can play regardless of what daily business events occur (e.g. Customer, Provider, Member). Event dependent roles on the other hand, are directly impacted by daily business events. Bob the Provider for example, can become Bob the Primary Care Physician when the 'Claim Received' business event occurs.

Power of abstraction

Adding Party and Role and documenting

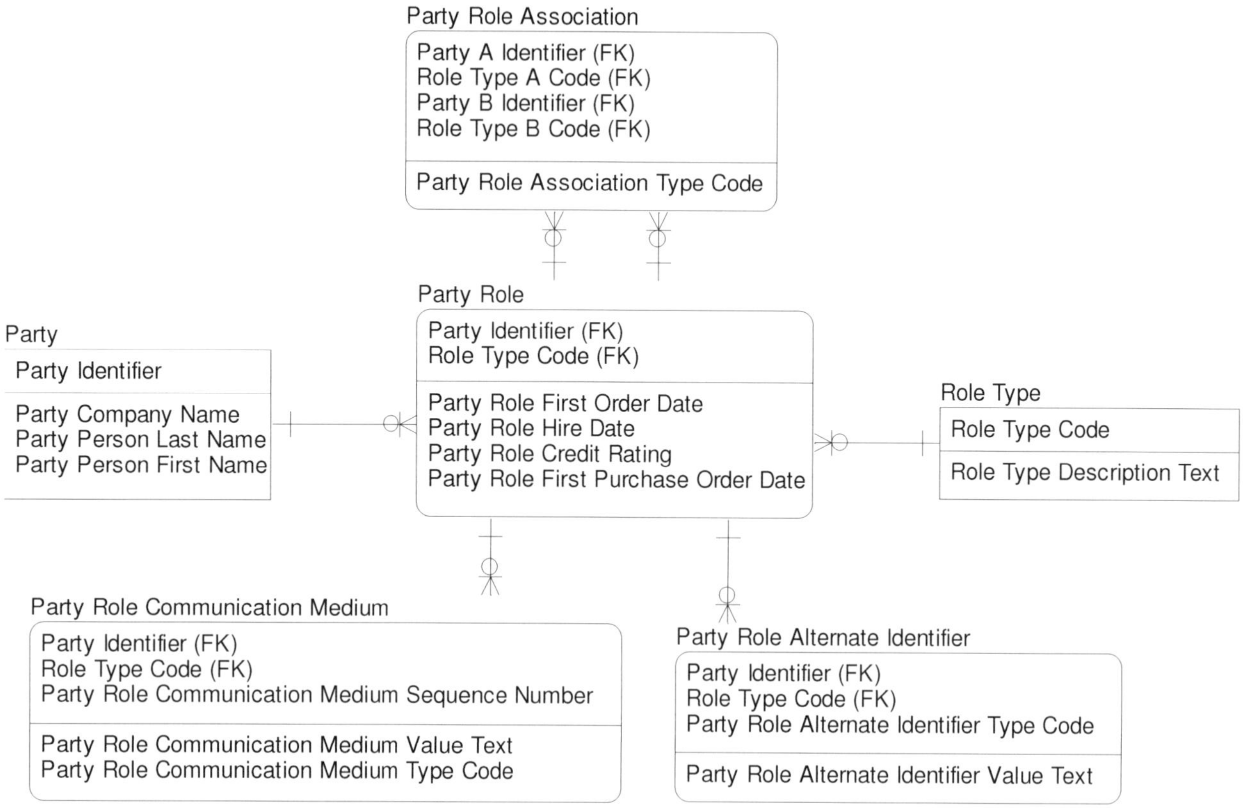

Power of abstraction

Adding Party and Role and documenting

EXAMPLE

Note that in many cases entities and relationships are abstracted at the same time. This is because once we abstract an entity we can move all of the common data elements and relationships up to the more abstract level. So in this example the relationship from Associate to Supplier and from Associate to Customer got abstracted to the Party Association level when we introduced the Party concept.

IMPORTANCE OF DOCUMENTATION

What's a Communication Medium Type Code anyway?

When you abstract, the rows tell the meaning instead of the columns. It becomes very important to document well. Note that to enforce the capture of metadata, additional tables can be used. These tables are code and description tables (aka lookups, code tables) that would provide definitions for each value. Having it stored this way can also make it easier for the report user to access the metadata. I call these types of tables Metadata Entities.

Power of abstraction

Abstraction vs. Normalization

- Both abstraction and normalization strive to add flexibility to the design, but
  - Normalization makes sure existing business requirements have minimal redundancy and maximum flexibility
  - Abstraction does this for future requirements
- Normalization applies to the values, abstraction applies to the types

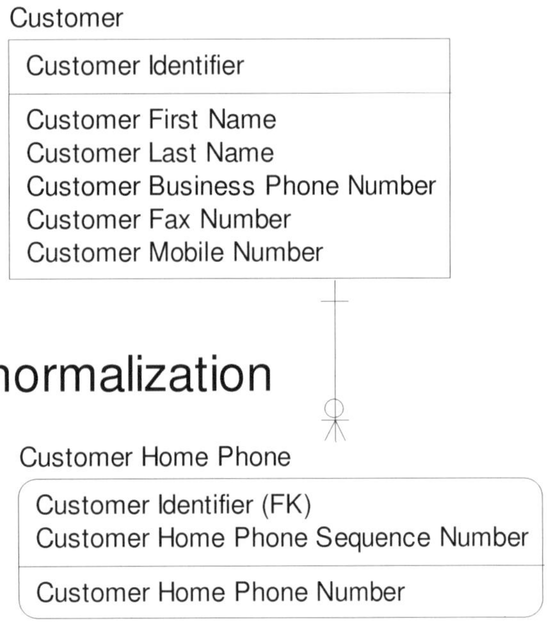

normalization

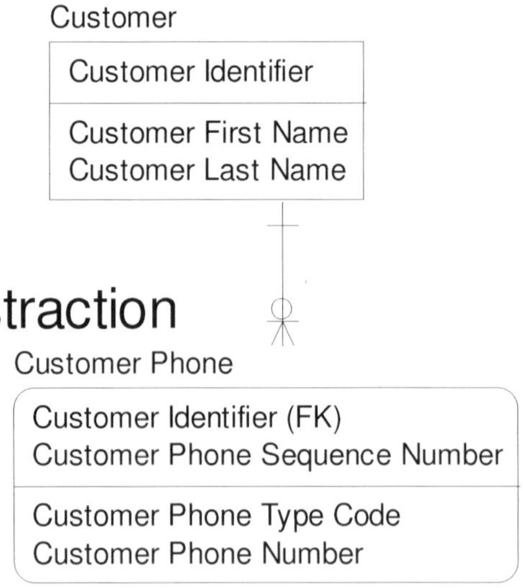

abstraction

Power of abstraction

Abstraction vs. Normalization

BACKGROUND

An abstract model can still be normalized. We are simply redefining our structures to mean more generic concepts, without violating any normalization rules. It is important to be aware of the distinction between normalization and abstraction. When we normalize, we assign the business data elements to their most appropriate entities to remove redundancy and increase flexibility of *existing* concepts. When we abstract, we redefine business concepts to increase flexibility of introducing *new* concepts.

EXAMPLE

For example, if a Customer can have two or more home phone numbers, we will normalize home phone number into its own entity and define a one-to-many relationship between the entities Customer and Customer Home Phone. This reduces the redundancy of having Customer Home Phone 1 Number, Customer Home Phone 2 Number, and so on, in the Customer entity. Normalizing home phone number lets us represent any number of home phone numbers for a customer without any design or development changes. However, if we abstract Customer Home Phone Number into Customer Phone Number, we can now handle multiple additional types of phone numbers that we could not previously, such as fax, cell, and pager phone numbers. Redefining concepts to handle new types of information is abstraction, which is different from normalization where we are building flexibility into existing concepts.

Power of abstraction

Why abstraction is great

Abstraction is awesome!

- ☐ Increases application stability
- ☐ Facilitates integration
- ☐ Reduces design time
- ☐ Forces greater understanding of entities
- ☐ Creates new business opportunities
- ☐ Absolves the modeler from capturing business rules

"A tactician knows what to do when something needs doing. A strategist knows what to do when nothing needs doing."

Savielly Tartakover

Power of abstraction

Why abstraction is great

INCREASES APPLICATION STABILITY

A new association type was required in our Sales Organization structure. Due to using an abstract association concept, there were no database changes needed. We just added a new row.

FACILITATES INTEGRATION

You can bring disparate source systems or subject areas together, such as storing customer locations and warehouses in the abstract Location structure. Abstraction automatically provides *structure* integration, and could assist business teams with providing truc *data* integration.

REDUCES DESIGN TIME

We were able to create a global integration model in less than a week. Instead of listing every possible location in our business, we were able to abstract to a concept called "Location". We drew our relationships to Location, that otherwise would have been associated to a number of Location's subtypes, which would have taken a much longer time to analyze.

FORCES GREATER UNDERSTANDING OF ENTITIES

Before grouping separate entities together, we need to understand each entity and what it has in common with other entities, hence increasing our understanding.

CREATES NEW BUSINESS OPPORTUNITIES

I know of a global furniture company that was able to identify new sales opportunities after viewing their customers and employees and vendors as roles and parties.

ABSOLVES THE MODELER FROM CAPTURING SOME BUSINESS RULES

Sometimes this is a good thing, especially if the data modeler does not know all of the rules, or if rules can change over time. This can also be a bad thing, causing frustrating data quality problems. The end result is that the data modeler is pushing the work to a different team member – usually the developer.

Power of abstraction

Why abstraction is pure evil

Abstraction is pure evil!

- ☐ Model becomes vague and imprecise
- ☐ Fewer rules in the database
- ☐ Increased development
- ☐ Performance issues
- ☐ Difficult to justify long term benefits to a project-focused team
- ☐ Reporting tools can have difficulty with abstraction
- ☐ Last but not least – users hate navigating abstract structures!

Power of abstraction

Why abstraction is pure evil

MODEL BECOMES VAGUE AND IMPRECISE

You need more explanation and documentation. I was once on an airplane reviewing an abstract model for a meeting, when a young girl sitting next to me asked me what I was doing. I was so happy she took an interest in my diagram, that I explained to her the data modeling basics along with the purpose of this particular model. Her next question was "What's a Business Party?" Good question!

FEWER RULES IN THE DATABASE

If a customer has to have a phone number, the only way to enforce this business rule in our current abstract Communication Medium Type structure is through code. The responsibility falls more on the developer than on the data modeler.

GREATER DEVELOPMENT EFFORT

If the source or target of an abstraction structure is not abstract, it is usually a time consuming and complex development effort to populate or extract data from an abstract structure.

PERFORMANCE ISSUES

It can take the software tools longer to find the data if they are first looking for row values to find other row values.

DIFFICULT TO JUSTIFY LONG TERM BENEFITS TO A PROJECT-FOCUSED TEAM

If you are working with a project that has been pulling extra hours to deliver on time, the last thing that the project manager wants to hear is that the database structure's flexibility will require several additional weeks of work, yet the company may benefit from this flexibility over the next 3-5 years.

REPORTING TOOLS CAN HAVE DIFFICULTY WITH ABSTRACTION

Many reporting tools need columns to tie to (and not rows) and therefore they don't work well with abstraction. Some tools let you build views to hide abstraction and present columns for the reporting tool.

USERS HATE NAVIGATING ABSTRACT STRUCTURES!

Imagine giving a non-technical user Party and Role and explaining how to extract the employee profile. Not an easy activity.

We're all connected

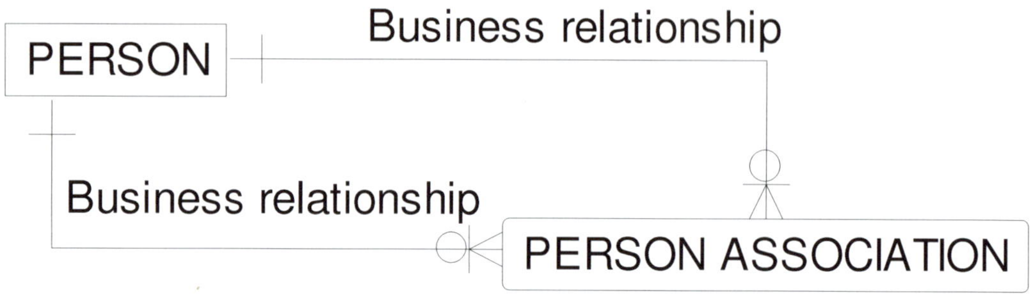

1. What are the pros and cons with using this LDM to represent this business rule?

Pros	Cons

2. If this was our PDM, which types of applications would it work best?

3. If this was our PDM, which types of applications would it work worst?

We're all connected

BACKGROUND

Assume there is a rule in your company that an employee must work for one and only one manager. A modeler in your group is modeling the human resource area and has created the logical data model on the facing page to capture this rule.

CHALLENGE

Answer the following questions:

- What are the pros and cons with using this LDM to represent this business rule?
- If this was our PDM, which types of applications would it work best?
- If this was our PDM, which types of applications would it work worst?

PURPOSE

Know both the good and evil side to abstraction.

TIPS

Abstraction works best where there is a need for application longevity yet future requirements cannot be predicted.

Subtyping

Explanation

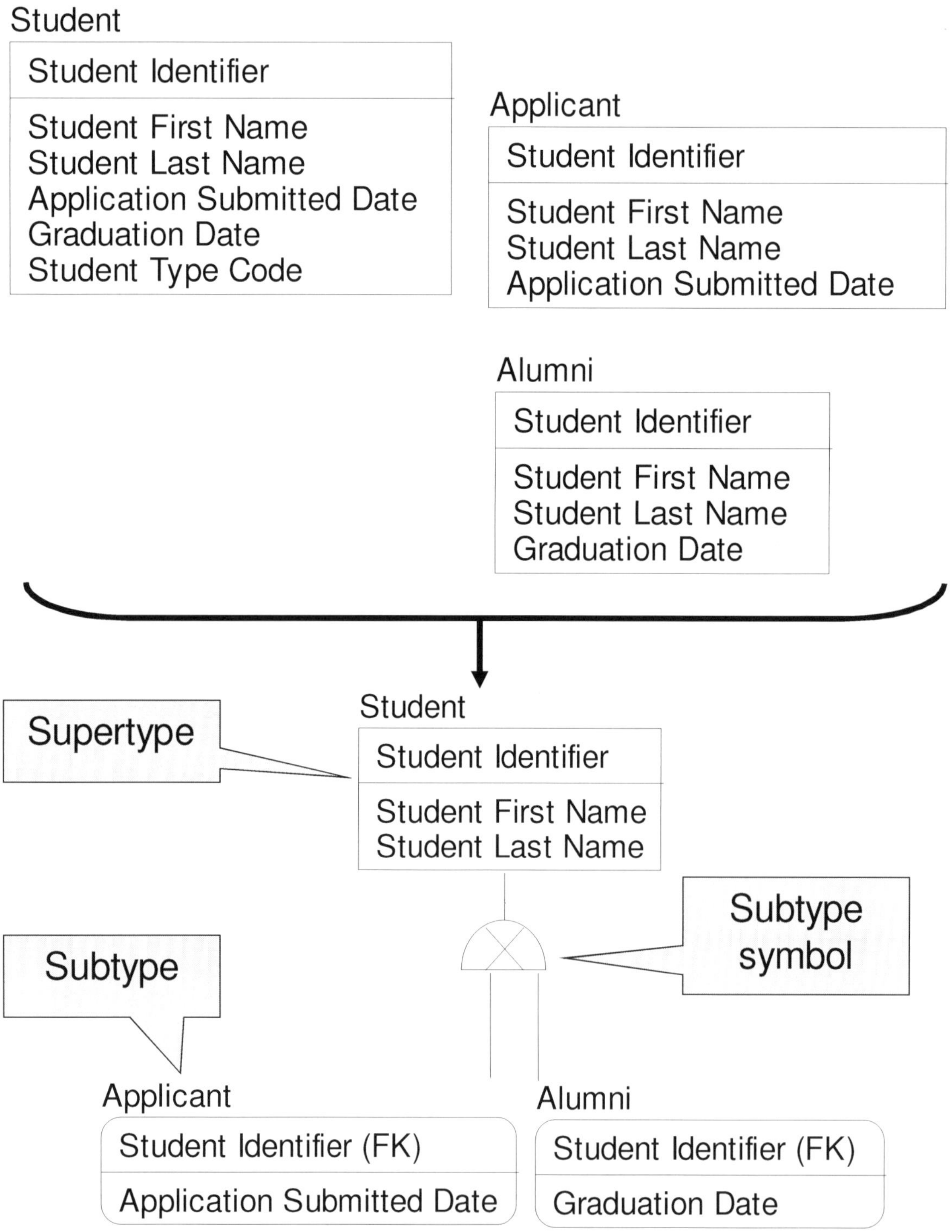

Subtyping

Explanation

BACKGROUND

Subtyping is grouping together the common properties of entities while retaining what is unique within each entity. The subtyping relationship exists between the supertype and each of its subtypes. There is no relationship implied by the subtyping symbol between the subtypes, except insofar as these subtypes share the same set of properties.

SYMBOLS

A subtype relationship connects an entity that defines the category and two or more additional entities that define each of the elements of the category. The parent entity of the category is considered the supertype and each child entity is considered a subtype.

There is a relationship defined between the supertype and subtypes that groups these subtypes together under the supertype. The subtype entities inherit all of the properties from the supertype entity, meaning any data elements or relationships at the supertype level also belong to the subtype entity.

A SUBTYPING SYMBOL CANNOT EXIST IN A RELATIONAL DB

It is important to note that the subtyping symbol cannot exist in a relational database. It is purely a logical construct. There are a number of options we will discuss when converting subtyping to a physical relational database design. However, an object oriented design could have subtyping both in the logical and physical models.

Subtyping

Different notations

Information Modeling

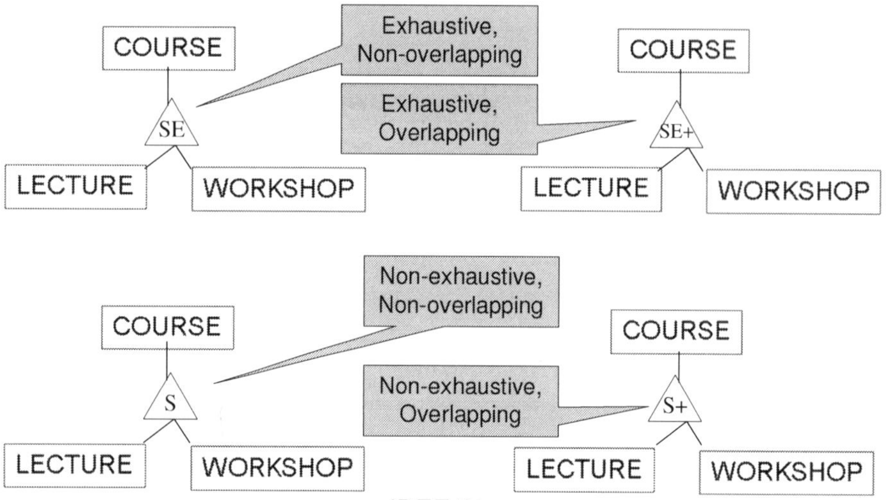

IDEF1X

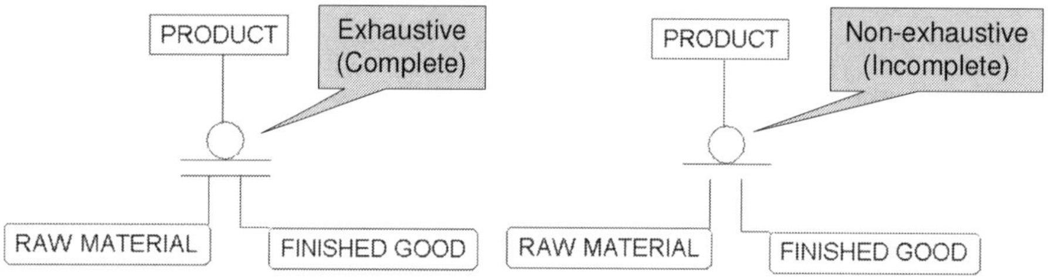

IE

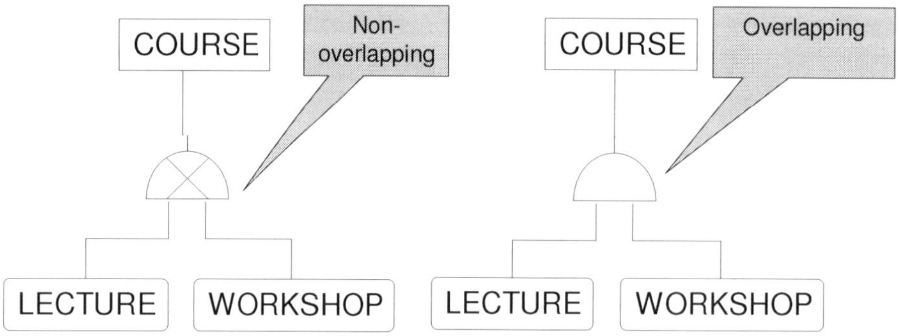

Box in Box

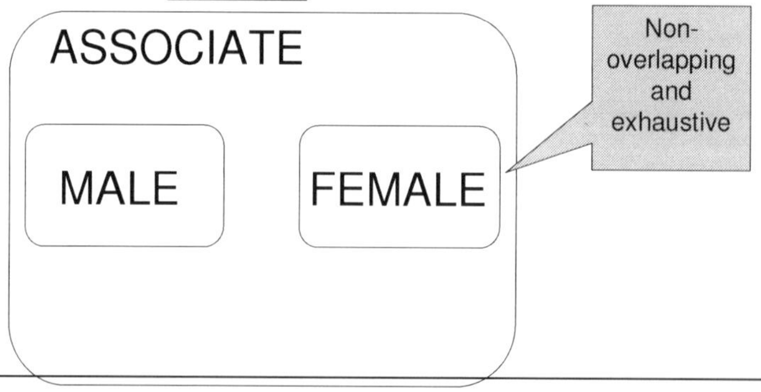

Subtyping

Different notations

INFORMATION MODELING

Bell Communications Research (Bellcore) was a pioneer in Information Modeling in the early 1990s during my time in their data modeling team. It is a notation that is the most comprehensive of the ones we will study, because it can represent all 4 possible types of subtypes. These 4 types represent different combinations of Exhaustive and Overlapping.

Exhaustive means that one of the shown relationships must exist for a given supertype instance. Non-exhaustive means that there could be more subtypes that are not shown. Reasons for not showing them include not knowing them yet or they are out of scope. Think of exhaustive as complete, and non-exhaustive as incomplete. Overlapping means that the same supertype instance can have properties from two or more of the subtypes. Non-overlapping means that a supertype instance can have at most one of the subtype's properties.

- SE (Exhaustive, Non-overlapping). There are no other options for course besides lecture or workshop. And a course can either be a lecture or workshop, not both.
- SE+ (Exhaustive, Overlapping). There are no other options for course besides lecture or workshop. And a course can be a lecture or workshop or have properties of both.
- S (Non-exhaustive, Non-overlapping). There can be other options for course besides lecture or workshop, such as a tutorial or boot camp. And a course can either be a lecture or workshop or something else.
- S+ (Non-exhaustive, Overlapping). There can be other options for course besides lecture or workshop, such as a tutorial or boot camp. And a course can either be a lecture or workshop or something else, or have properties of more than one of these.

IDEF1X

Integration DEFinition for Information Modeling (IDEF1X) shows subtyping as only Exhaustive or Non-exhaustive, it does not represent the overlapping concept.

IE

Information Engineering (IE) shows subtyping as only Non-overlapping or Overlapping, it does not represent the exhaustive concept.

BOX IN BOX

This is very popular in a number of the older Computer Aided Software Engineering (CASE) tools, including IEF. This notation is easy to visualize. However, if there are lots of subtypes (especially nested subtypes) with relationships and lots of data elements, it can be difficult to understand and read. This subtyping only supports non-overlapping and exhaustive.

Subtyping

Examples

An example with relationships

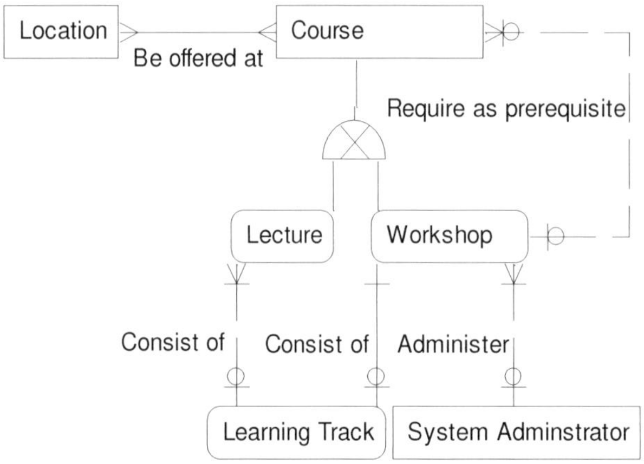

Our Party Example

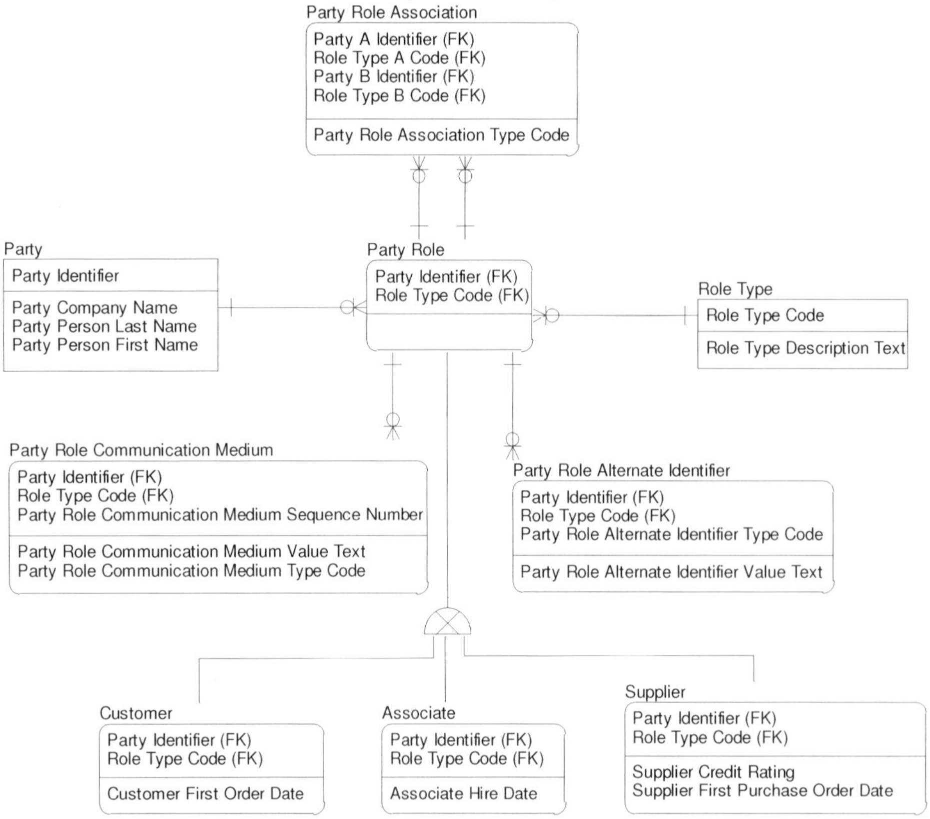

Subtyping

Examples

AN EXAMPLE WITH RELATIONSHIPS

This example shows several important types of relationships that can exist when supertypes and subtypes appear on a design.

In some cases the subtype can have business relationships to the supertype. Here a Course can be a Lecture or a Workshop. In addition, a Workshop usually requires prerequisites before taking it. Prerequisites can be both lectures and other workshops. In this example Lectures do not require prerequisites.

The supertype is related to the Location entity, inferring that both Lectures and Workshop can be offered at many Locations, and a Location can host many Lectures and Workshops.

Also note that a Learning Track must contain many Lectures but only a single Workshop, probably as the final course in the track.

A System Administrator can support many Workshops, and a Workshop can be supported by one System Administrator.

OUR PARTY EXAMPLE

Here we added subtypes to our abstract model to capture some of the information that was lost when we first abstracted. Note that the data elements specific to a particular entity are now shown in that entity. For example, Customer First Order Date is now shown in the Customer entity.

CREATIVITY

How else could we have modeled our Party example using subtypes?

Subtyping

Pros and cons of subtyping

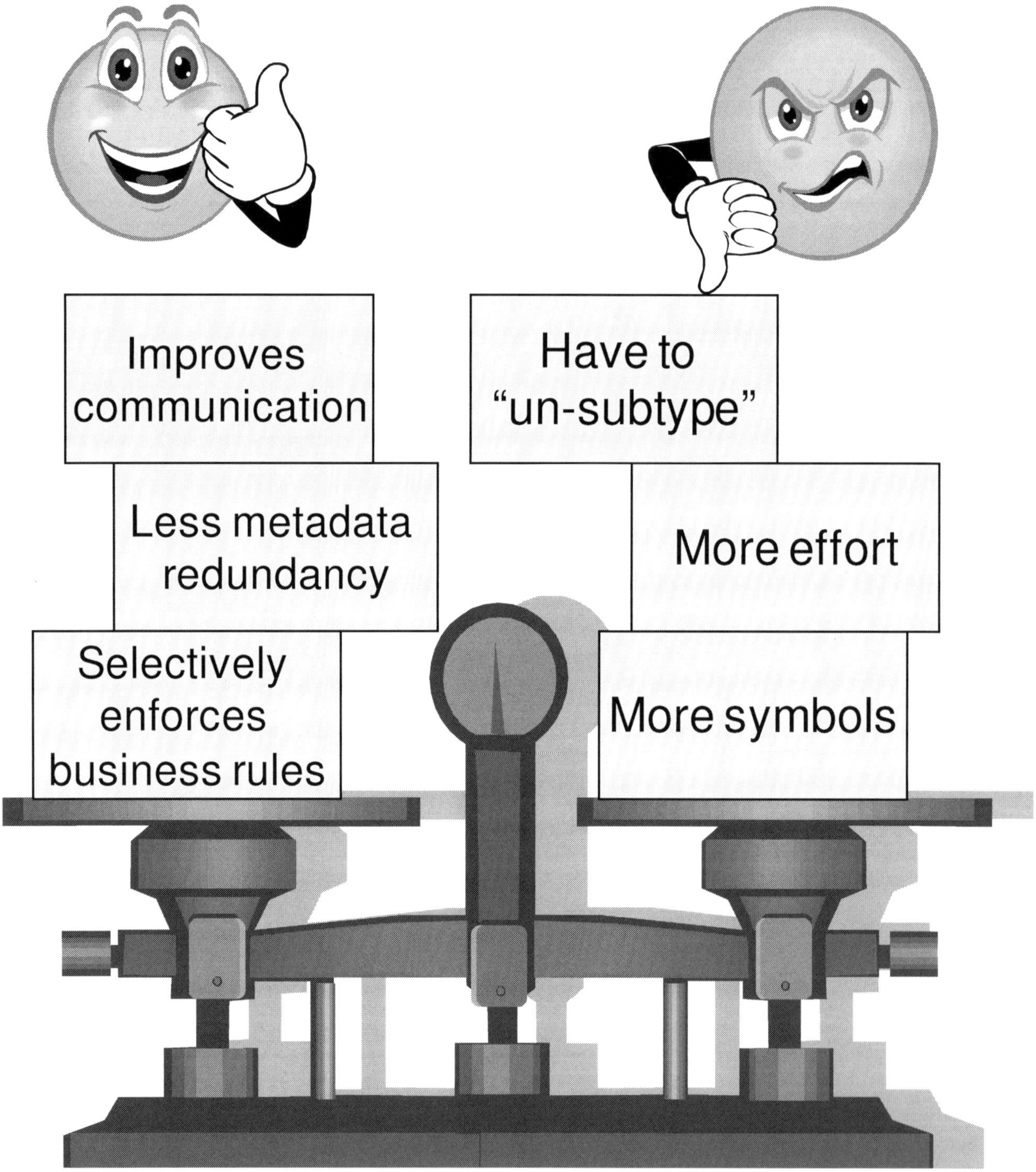

Subtyping

Pros of subtyping

PROS

- **Selectively enforce business rules.** When we abstract, we lose relationships and therefore can lose the rules behind those relationships. Subtyping lets us selectively represent business rules. If there is a relationship to enforce for only a particular subtype, we can do it and leave the relationship off the supertype.
- **Less metadata redundancy.** When we subtype, we move those data elements and relationships that are common across entities to a single supertype. This reduces redundancy, because we are not repeating those common properties. However, it does not automatically reduce data redundancy. This means that without an effort to clean up redundant data, there will still be redundant information.
- **Improves communication.** You can show or hide supertypes and subtypes depending on the business expertise of the audience. For instance, you would show the business user manager only the higher level supertype Contract, whereas the functional analyst might see all the different subtypes of Contracts. Also subtyping helps you play the politician. When groups have different terms for the same general concept, you can allow each term (at least initially) to exist on the model underneath a common supertype. One group might call it Off Invoice, the other might call it Bill Back but they are all promotion allowances.

CONS

- **More entities and relationships on the model than pure abstraction.** Although you reduce redundancy when you subtype, more boxes and lines are on the model. When showing all supertypes and subtypes on the design, it can make the model cluttered and therefore more overwhelming to the audience. However, if you properly arrange the model, it will be less overwhelming.
- **More effort to create the design.** You will need to not only determine the common ground between subtypes, but also determine which data elements and relationships should still exist at the subtype level. Therefore, this is even more work than just applying the three abstraction questions of commonality, value, and effort.
- **Have to "un-subtype" anyway when you get to the physical.** This is true but I believe your resulting physical design will be a better design if you first realized it was important to subtype on the logical. You would have already reduced redundancy and possibly optimize certain relationships if you subtype first on the logical.

Getting physical with subtypes

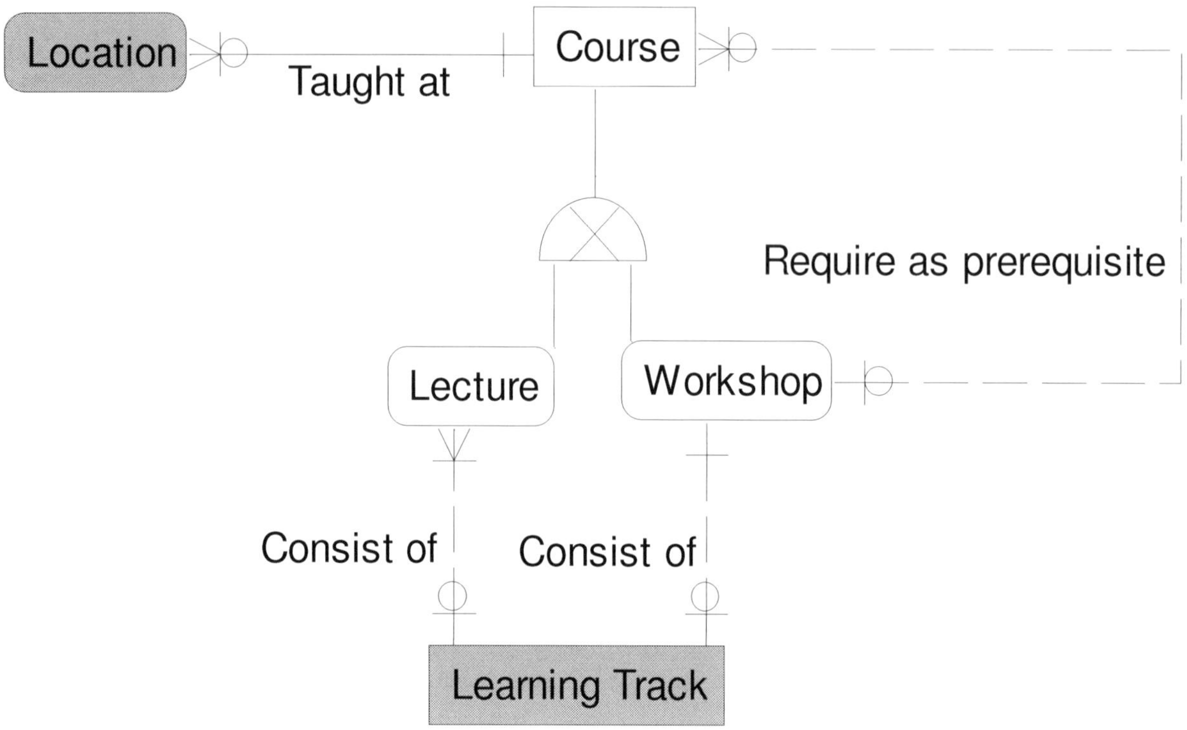

Rolling Down

Getting physical with subtypes

CHALLENGE

Rolling down: Remove the supertype entity and copy all of the data elements and relationships from the supertype to each of the subtypes.

Rolling up: Remove the subtypes and copy all of the data elements and relationships from each subtype to the supertype. Also add a type code to distinguish the subtypes.

Identity: Convert the subtype symbol into a series of one-to-one relationships, connecting the supertype to each of the subtypes.

For this Challenge, create these three physical data models.

Rolling Up

Identity

Metadata entities

Explanation with example

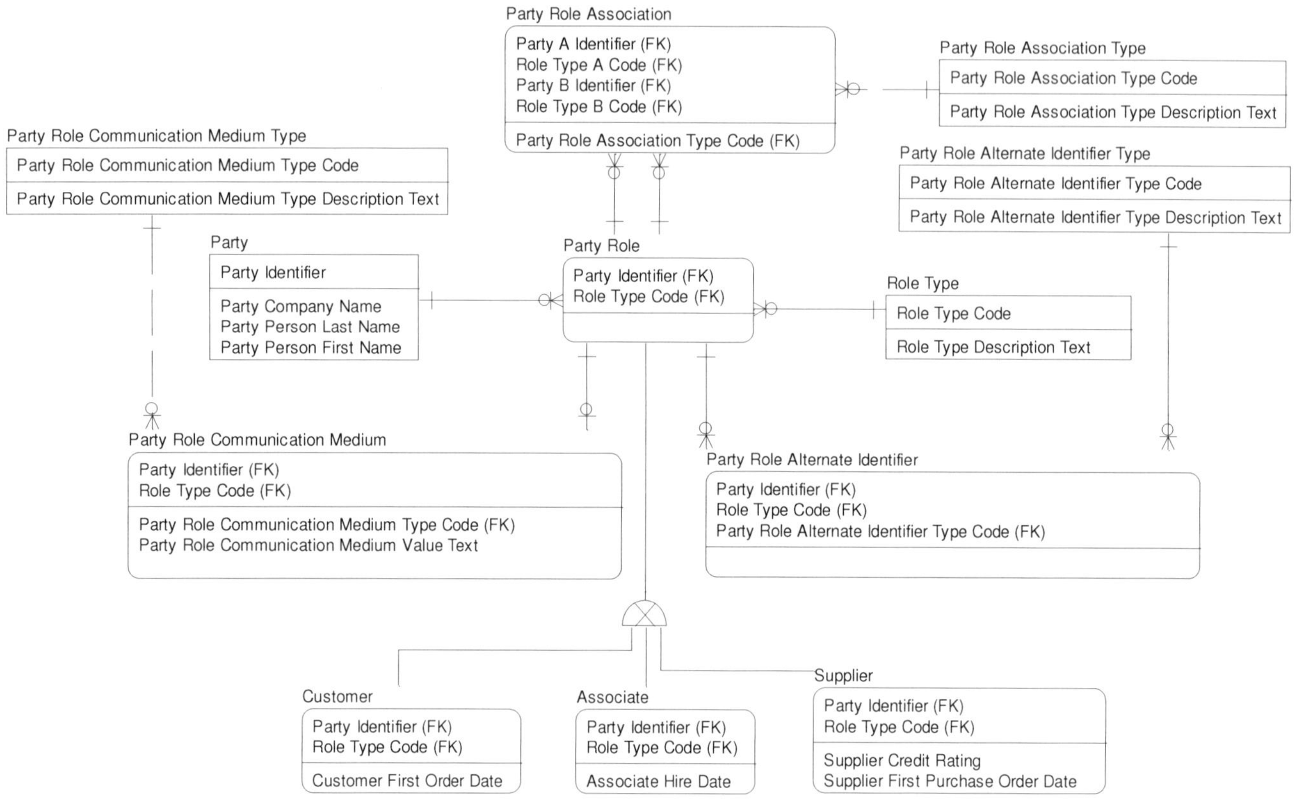

Metadata entities

Explanation with example

BACKGROUND

Metadata entities are entities on our model that contain as values metadata for business entities on our design. They do not contain business values like the other entities we deal with (Customer, Employee, etc.). Metadata entities become extremely important when we abstract because they allow us to put back the domain integrity we lost by abstracting back into our design.

Examples of metadata entities in this example are Party Role Alternate Identifier Type, Party Role Association Type, and Party Role Communication Medium Type. Party Role Alternate Identifier Type might contain the values Clock Number and Social Security Number. Party Role Communication Medium Type might contain the values Phone Number and Mobile Number and Email Address. They help to enforce the possible values (e.g. we can only have Phone Number and Mobile Number and Email Address and cannot have a new type until it has been entered into the metadata entity). They also help with having business descriptions somewhere in the database, even though it is not a column it is still stored as a value.

PARTY ROLE COMMUNICATION MEDIUM TYPE

Code	Description
01	Phone
02	Fax
03	Mobile
04	Email

PARTY ROLE ALTERNATE IDENTIFIER TYPE

Code	Description
01	Tax Identifier
02	DUNS
03	Social Security Number
04	Clock Number

PARTY ROLE ASSOCIATION TYPE

Code	Description
01	Customer Associate
02	Supplier Associate

Metadata entities

Pros and Cons

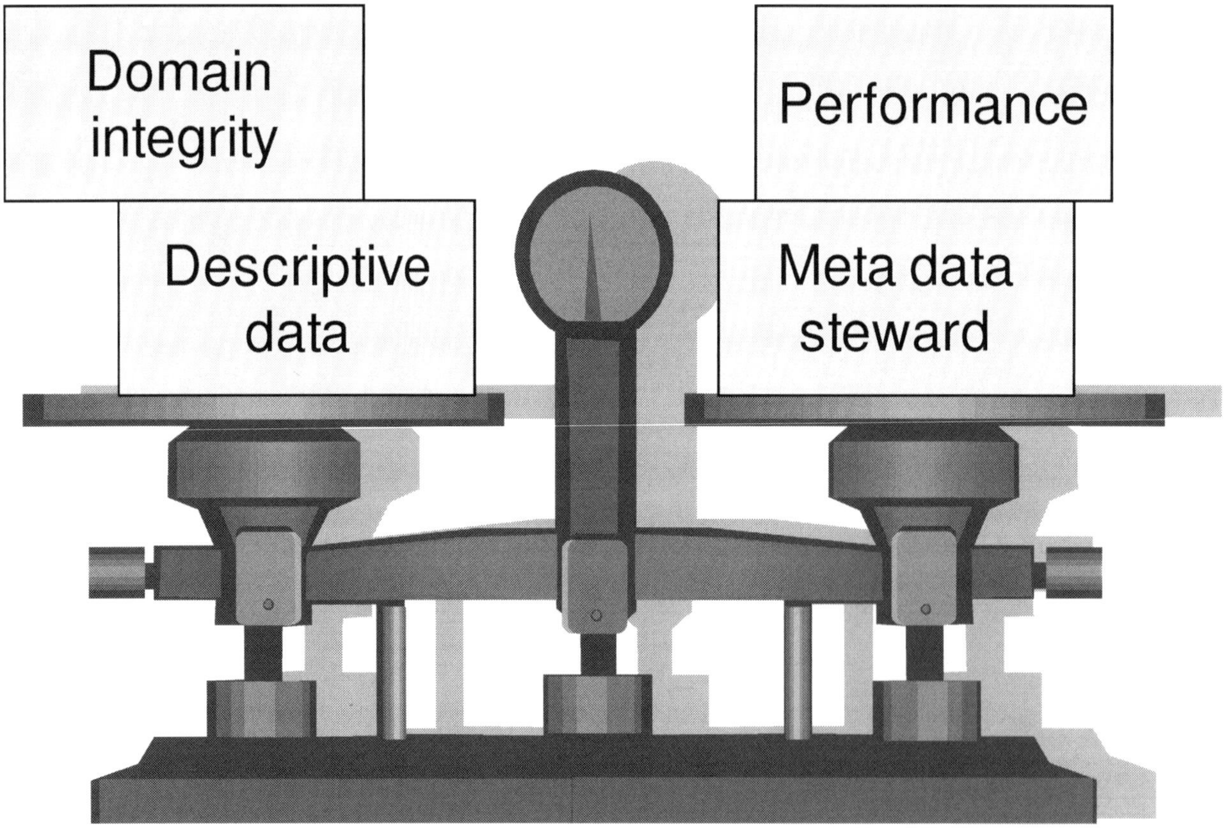

Metadata entities

Pros and Cons

PROS

- **Gain back the domain integrity that we lost by abstracting.** These entities enforce relationships between the abstract tables, relationships that might have been there on the original model but have been lost as a result of making things more generic.
- **Descriptive data is available to technical team, SQL queries, users and reporting tools.** This data is very valuable because it is really the only place in the design such reliable metadata can exist, and it can save people the added time and frustration of going to other places to determine what the code "01" means.

CONS

- **Need a metadata steward**. The biggest disadvantage to using these tables however, is that someone needs to maintain them. Who do you think that would be? More than likely, it will be the person who designed them, namely the data modeler. That puts the data modeler into an interesting situation, as they are now responsible not just for the design, but also for maintaining some of the data. Optionally, the development team can put a process in place for the users to maintain the tables themselves. This frees the data modeler up from maintaining these tables and puts them out of the critical path of holding up the business from completing their business processes. However, having the users maintain the data means there is probably a bigger risk that the users might use these metadata tables for more than originally intended.
- **Performance problems loading data.** Whenever there are additional relationships enforced on a design, we have the opportunity of having loading performance problems because the database is validating the data upon loading it and this slows the load time down. It is not uncommon as a solution to this problem to remove the RI (referential integrity) prior to loading the data.

Reusable abstraction components

Explanation

Abstract modeling patterns that can replace application-specific sections on the model

Patterns are awesome!

All the benefits of abstraction plus

- ☐ Designs created faster
- ☐ Development time reduced
- ☐ Improved consistency across models

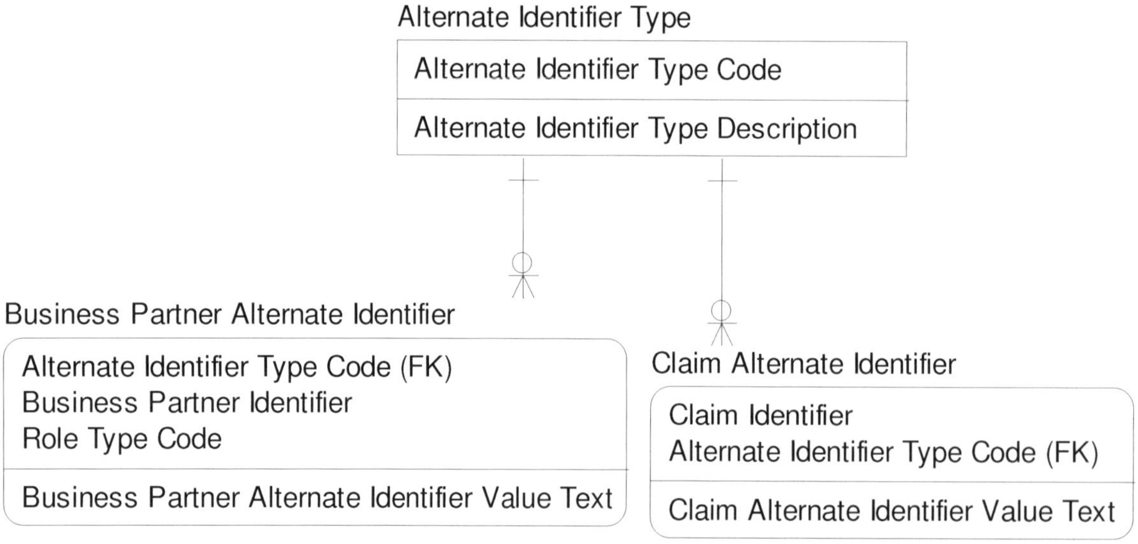

Reusable abstraction components

Explanation

BACKGROUND

The more we abstract, the more we realize that the same rather tiny abstraction building blocks or components keep appearing in our designs, with very slight variations. You need to first understand your application before you can successfully apply these components.

GOALS

- **Creates designs faster.** By knowing that these abstraction components exist and when to use them, you can simply 'plug them in' to your model. For example, there is an abstraction component concept for alternate identifiers. As soon as you apply the 3 questions and identify several alternate identifiers in your logical data model, you can use the alternate identifier abstract structure in your design. This can drastically decrease modeling time because you don't have to create new abstract structures. Note you also can reuse definitions and other types of metadata from these components. For example, once you define the Alternate Identifier entity, you should be able to reuse the definition of this entity wherever Alternate Identifier is reused.
- **Saves development time.** If you continually reuse the same designs, there is a very good chance you will be able to reuse other parts of the software lifecycle as well. You will be able to reuse potentially some of the code and reporting and mapping and population logic. For example, if you have programming code to populate the alternate identifier structures for customer, you can probably reuse a large portion of this code to populate the alternate identifier structures for supplier.
- **Improves consistency across data models.** By using the same abstraction components over and over again you increase the consistency across your models. This leads to greater understanding and integration between your applications. For example, if the alternate identifier abstract concept is structured the same in three different models, someone very familiar with only one of the models would be able to understand this concept in all three models. This helps reduce the loss of business meaning that abstraction can introduce. After someone is explained the alternate identifier concept once, they will understand alternate identifier everywhere it appears.

Actual implementations

Data warehouse and Reference database

Data Warehouse

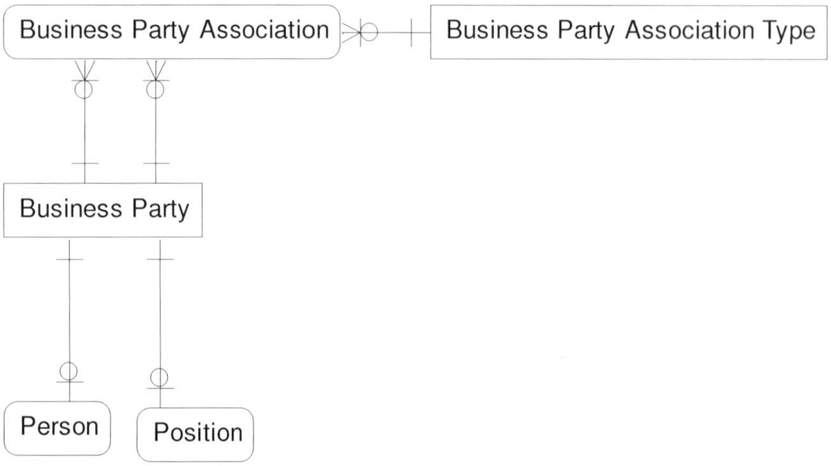

Reference Database

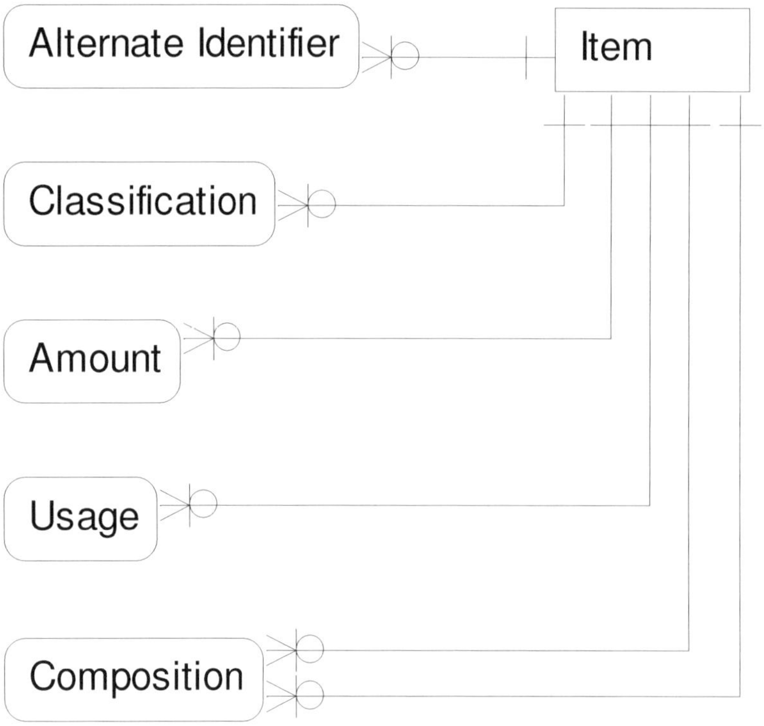

Actual implementations

Data warehouse and Reference database

DATA WAREHOUSE

This is how the Sales Organization subject area was designed. We've abstracted the common data elements into the Business Party entity. We've increased the flexibility of abstraction by also abstracting the relationships between the subtypes of Position, Person, and Organization. This means that the business rules between Position and Person exist in the Business Party Association concept instead of as relationships between the subtypes.

Notice that we can enforce the business rules that only a Position and Person can have a relationship. We do this through the relationships from Business Party Association Type to Business Party Association. Values for Business Party Association Type include "Person to Position".

REFERENCE DATABASE

This is how an Item reference database was designed. Notice how abstraction is applied to data elements and relationships. There is an Alternate Identifier table very similar to our earlier example, which contains other ways to uniquely identify an Item (e.g. UPC). There is also a Classification table to capture the groupings or categories an item can belong to and the hierarchy between these groupings or categories. The Amount table abstracts standard amounts associated with an item, such as list price and weight.

Product Availability

An organization sells products in many countries. There are about 100 data elements in the Product entity, only a few being shown on this model.

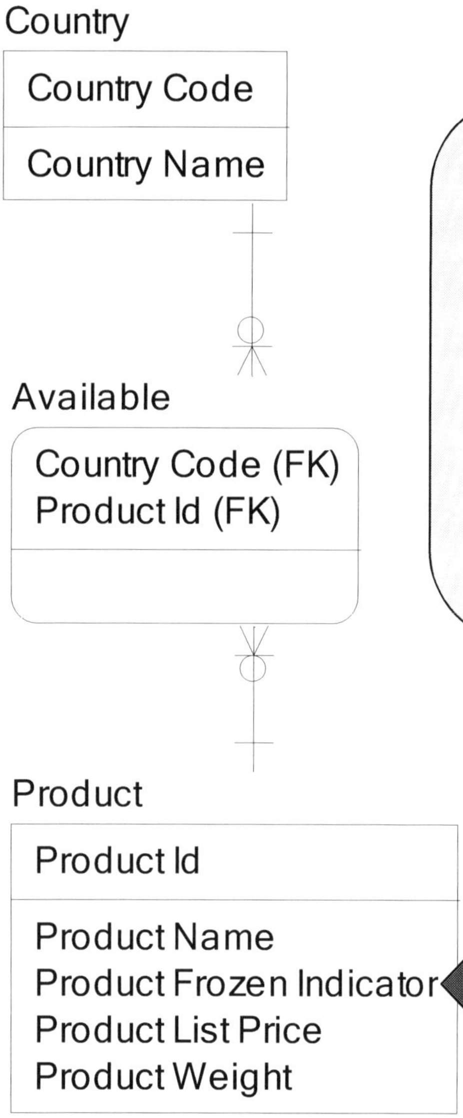

How would you capture the business rule that certain product data elements are only relevant and required for certain countries?

Required for Mexico but not for Canada

Product Availability

BACKGROUND

An organization sells products in many countries. The logical data model on the facing page captures which product is available in which country. There are about 100 data elements in the Product entity, only a few being shown in this model.

Although certain data elements such as Product Name must be populated for all countries, there are other data elements such as Product Frozen Indicator that are only relevant for certain countries. Product Frozen Indicator for example, might be a required data element for Mexico but should never be considered for Canada.

CHALLENGE

How would you capture the business rule that certain product data elements are only relevant and required for certain countries?

Applying the Data Model Scorecard®

Interaction Report for Product BB40 from May 2011

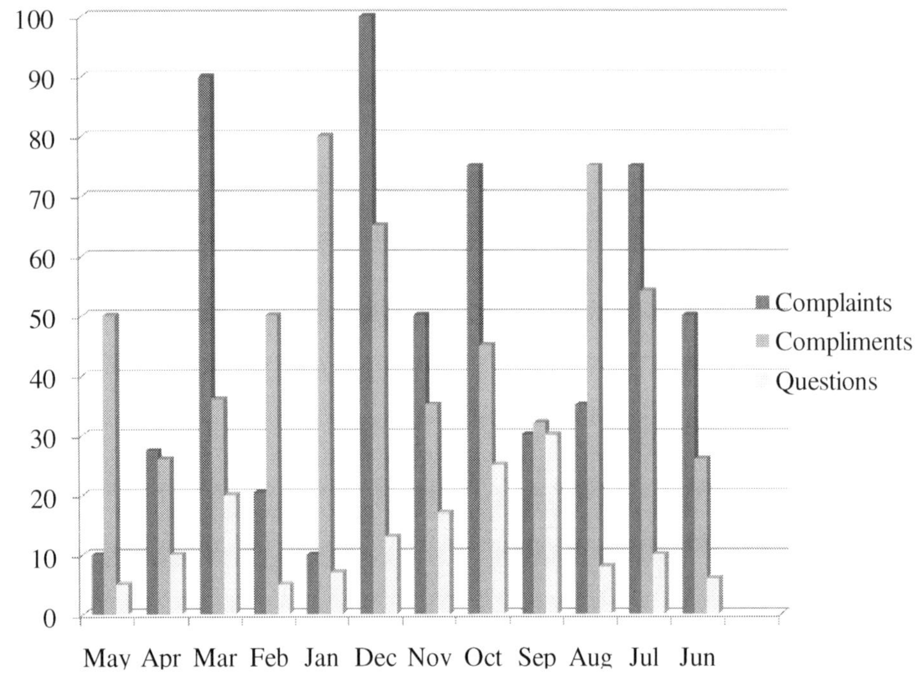

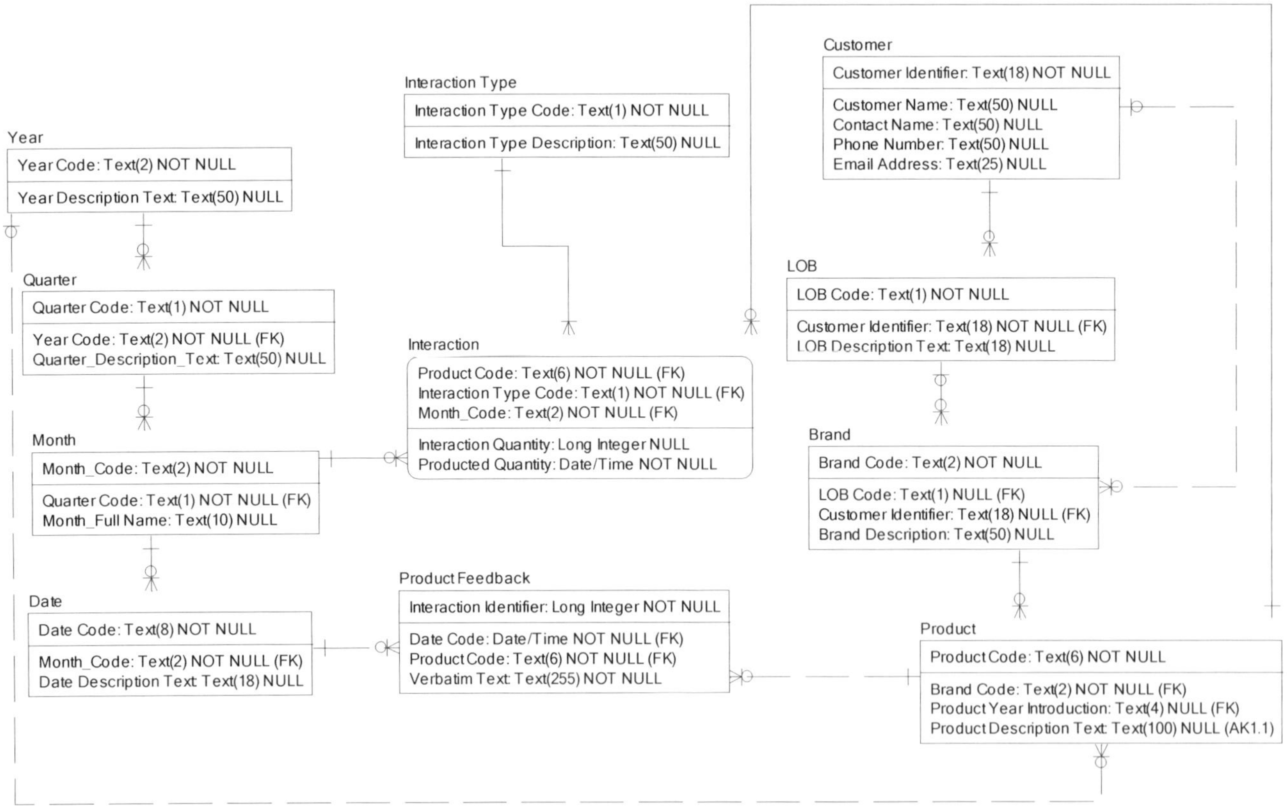

Applying the Data Model Scorecard®

5. How well does the model leverage generic structures?

EXPLANATION

This category confirms an appropriate use of abstraction on the model. One of the most powerful tools a data modeler has at their disposal is abstraction, the ability to increase the types of information a design can accommodate using generic concepts.

ANTHING YOU WOULD CATCH IN THE MODEL ON THE FACING PAGE FOR THIS CATEGORY?

1.
2.
3.
4.
5.
6.
7.
8.
9.
10.

#	Category	Total score	Model score	%
1	How well do the characteristics of the model support the type of model?	10		
2	How well does the model capture the requirements?	15		
3	How complete is the model?	15		
4	How structurally sound is the model?	15		
5	How well does the model leverage generic structures?	10		
6	How well does the model follow naming standards?	5		
7	How well has the model been arranged for readability?	5		
8	How good are the definitions?	10		
9	How consistent is the model with the enterprise?	5		
10	How well does the metadata match the data?	10		
	TOTAL SCORE	100		

Module 6

Data Model Scorecard® Category #6: Standards

Category Question: How well does the model follow naming standards?

This module is your guide to: Using consistent naming standards

Category Overview

How well does the model follow naming standards?

Naming standards

- Ensure structure integration
- Increase team understanding across areas

3 categories

4. Structure
5. Term
6. Syntax
    - Plural or singular
    - Hyphens, spaces, or Camelback
    - Upper case, initial upper case, or lower case

Category Overview

How well does the model follow naming standards?

EXPLANATION

Correct and consistent naming standards are extremely helpful for knowledge transfer and integration. New team members who are familiar with similar naming conventions on other projects will avoid the time to learn a new set of naming standards. This category focuses on naming standard structure, abbreviations, and syntax.

STRUCTURE

Structure is the types of components of a name. A popular standard for data element structure is one Subject Area, zero, one, or many Modifiers, and one Class Word. A subject area is a concept that is basic and critical to the business. A modifier qualifies this subject area and a class word is the high-level domain for a data element. Examples of class words are Quantity, Amount, Code, and Date.

TERM

Term includes proper spelling and abbreviation. An abbreviations list can be used to name each logical and physical term. Organizations should have a process in place for efficiently creating new abbreviations if a term cannot be found on a list. The process should be carefully managed to prevent different abbreviations being created for the same or similar term, and for creating the same abbreviation for completely different terms.

SYNTAX

Syntax includes whether the term should be plural or singular, whether hyphens, spaces, or Camelback (i.e. initial upper case such as CustomerLastName) should be used, and case (i.e. upper case, initial upper case, or lower case).

PURPOSE

Ensures structure integration. Efforts to bring together information from multiple systems will be less painful if the data elements are named consistently across projects. Besides this integration benefit, it can also increase team understanding across areas and reduce the amount of time it takes for new members to come up to speed.

CHALLENGE

Weighing consistency vs. correctness. Write and enforce grandfathering rules on earlier standards.

Applying naming standards

Naming standards can create a conflict of interest

What's good for the company is not necessarily good for a specific project

Good for the company

Increases consistency within the organization

Facilitates integration

Facilitates reuse of data

Helps new team members come up to speed quicker

Enables better data quality

Can put a strain on the project

Stifles creativity

Takes time to learn

Standard may not be intuitive

"You can't tell me what to do!"

Design is completely or partially based on a design that didn't originally follow standards, or followed out of date standards (So why start now?)

In the pursuit of consistency and purity, don't lose sight of one of the fundamental objectives of modeling: communication. Sometimes we must sacrifice rigid adherence to standards for familiarity and better quality feedback from non-technical participants in the modeling process. Graeme Simsion, Data Modeling Essentials

A naming standards document should be easily accessible and no more than 3 pages.

Applying naming standards

Naming standards can create a conflict of interest

BACKGROUND

Naming standards are great for the organization, but they can cause extra pressure on each project. When project deadlines are creeping near, complying with naming standards might take time away from completing the project deliverables.

GOOD FOR COMPANY

- **Increases consistency within the organization.** Different departments can communicate with each other because they use the same set of standards.
- **Facilitates integration**. If you were responsible for integrating Order and Customer into a single design, and Order and Customer both used the same data element name for the unique Customer Id (say CUST_ID), it would make this integration activity easier and less prone to error.
- **Facilitates reuse of data.** If we know what the abbreviations mean there is a greater chance we can use the same data elements.
- **Helps new team members come up to speed quicker.** Learning only one set of naming standards allows someone to interpret designs without first spending time trying to learn a new set of standards for each project.
- **Enables better data quality.** For example, by ending each data element with a valid class word we are in a better position to only have a single piece of business information within each data element thereby improving data quality.

COULD PUT A STRAIN ON THE PROJECT

- **Stifles creativity.** Designers might feel constrained if the names need to fit a certain structure.
- **Takes time to learn.** There could be a learning curve when applying a naming standard.
- **Standard may not be intuitive.** It may not make common sense at first why certain abbreviations and name components exist as they do.
- **"You can't tell me what to do!"** Sometimes it can be hard to convince people to follow standards.
- **Design is completely or partially based on a design that didn't originally follow standards, or followed out of date standards.** If the original application called it CST_NAM and it really should be called CUST_NAM, which should we use? Should we be right and inconsistent and call it CUST_NAM or wrong yet consistent and call it CST_NAM?

Applying naming standards

Applying naming structure

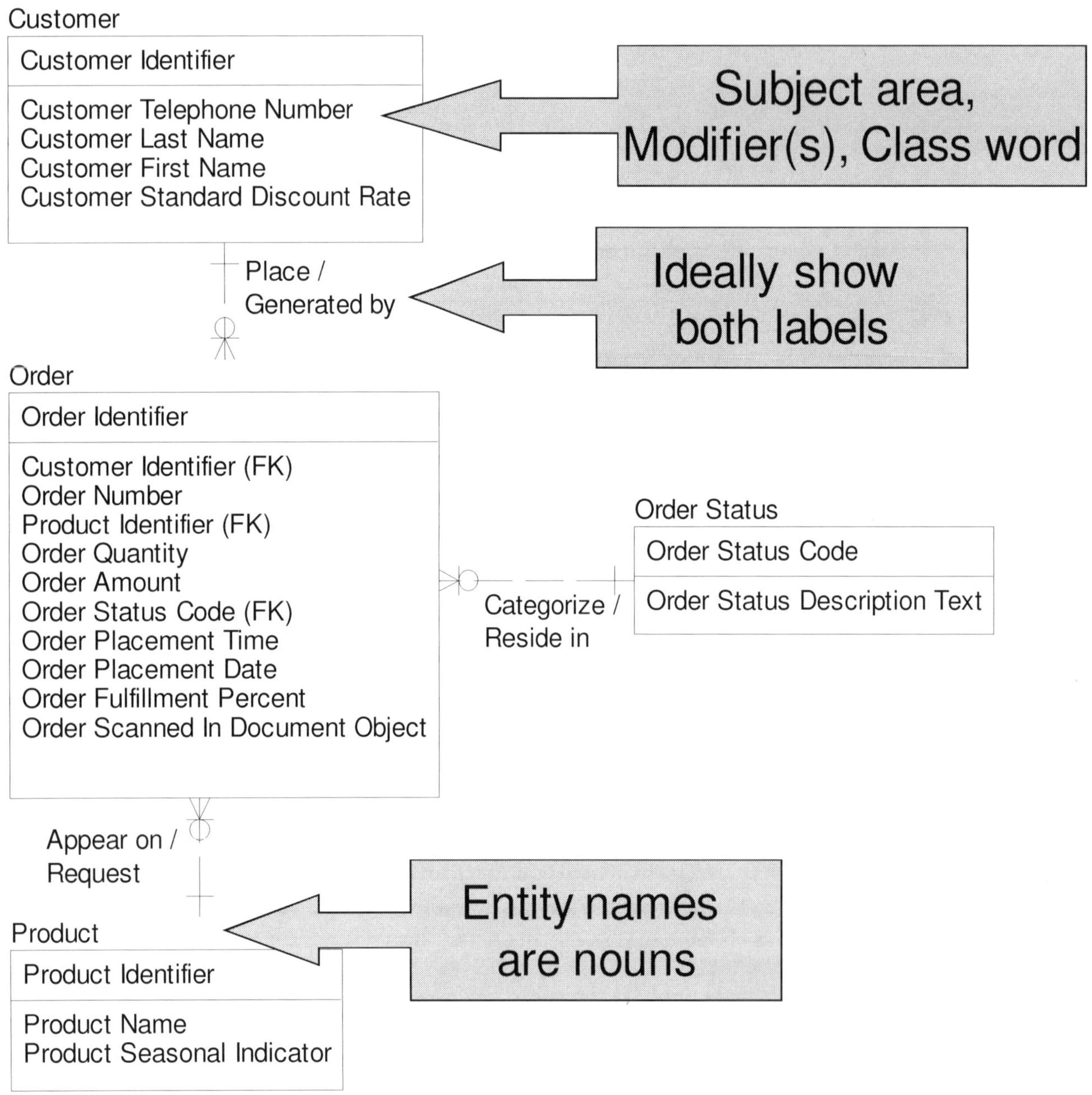

Applying naming standards

Applying naming structure

BACKGROUND

Naming structure refers to the types of terms that make up an entity, data element, or relationship name. For structure, the key word is 'type', as we are not referring to terms such as 'Customer' but instead types such as nouns, verbs, and modifiers.

ENTITY

An entity name is a noun. It is not a property of the noun (i.e. a data element), but the noun itself. Customer is an entity name, but Customer Last Name is not.

DATA ELEMENT

A popular standard for data element structure is one Subject Area, zero, one, or many Modifiers (aka Descriptors), and one Class Word. A subject area is a concept that is basic and critical to the business. A modifier qualifies this subject area and a class word is the high-level domain for a data element. Examples of class words are Quantity, Amount, Code, and Date.

Many naming standards state using the logical entity name as the first part of the data element name. For example, the entity Month would contain Month Code and Month Description Text. However, if within an architecture, the same data element can exist within different entities, you would have to rename the data element each time. Month Code in a Month entity within the data warehouse for example, would need to be renamed to Time Month Code in a Time dimension within a data mart. I find it is a better practice to keep the name the same and instead of using a logical entity name as the first part of a data element name, use the subject area. So if Month is a subject area, this is what it would be called in both the data warehouse and mart.

RELATIONSHIP

The relationships should be named with clear concise labels which are meaningful to the business user of the information. The relationship labels should be active verbs that describe the relationship. Think about the business interaction between the entities; it should provide a clue for devising a good name. When models become large, I hide one or both labels from the visual to improve readability. Also, there is more than one best practice on relationship names. I prefer not to preface labels with "be", "can", "may", and "is". These are implied by the relationship.

Applying naming standards

Class word overview

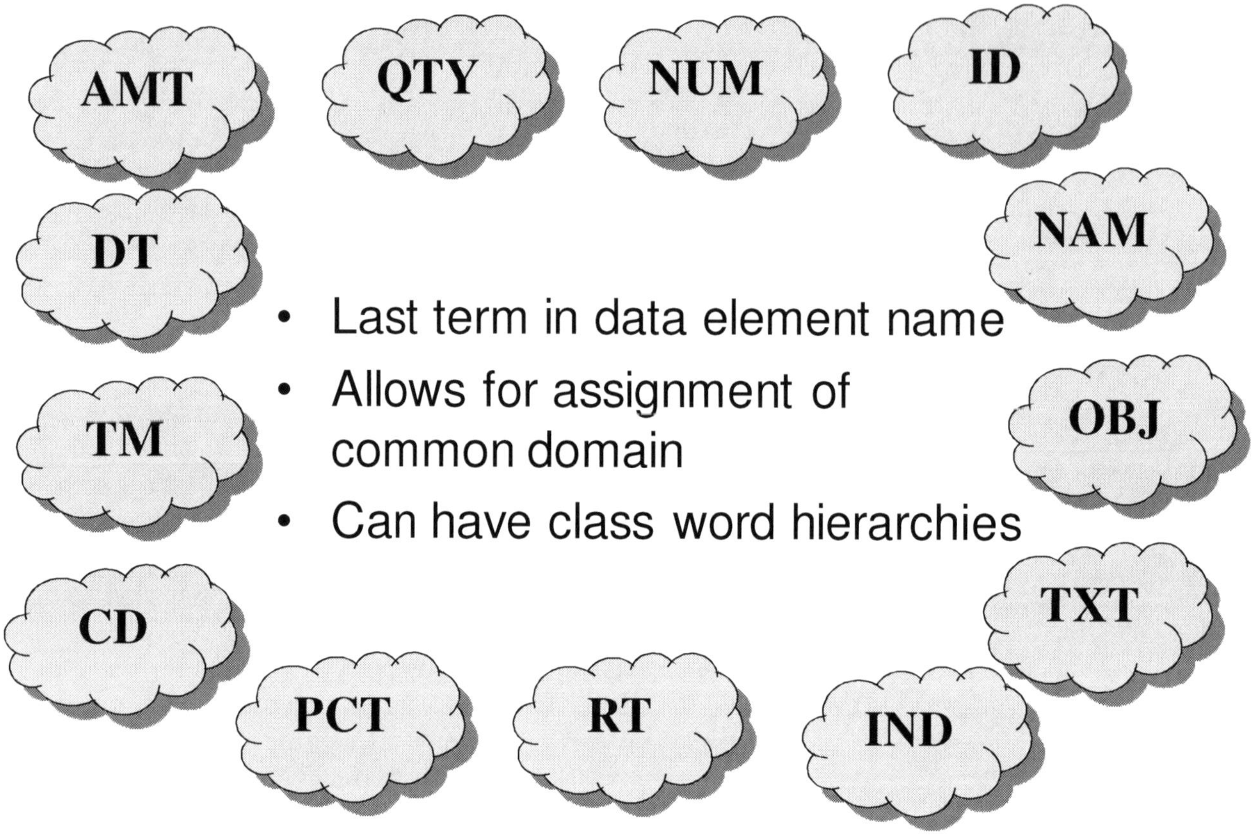

- Last term in data element name
- Allows for assignment of common domain
- Can have class word hierarchies

Applying naming standards

Class word overview

BACKGROUND

A class word is the last part of a data element name that represents the high level domain in which the data element belongs. A common list of class words appears on the facing page. If an industry tends to put a lot of importance on a specific domain, it can become its own class word. For example, while consulting at an aluminum rolling plan in the Midwest, I noticed a number of data elements ending in the class word *Temper*. While reviewing models of a utility company, they had a class word called *Wattage*. Some would argue that *Temper* and *Wattage* are really just *Quantities*, but they were important enough to their respective companies to be separate class words.

COMMON CLASS WORDS

Amount (AMT). Numeric value expressing a quantity of monetary currency; when denominated in other than U.S. Dollars, an *Amount* field must be accompanied by a *Code* class element which identifies the currency.

Code (CD). Symbols used to represent one other attribute, the decode.

Date (DT). Alphanumeric value representing a month, day, and year.

Identifier (ID). A data element used to completely or partially identify a table.

Indicator (IND). A flag used by the business to show which of two conditions apply. Where there are more than two possible conditions, or where a third *(not sure or unknown)* condition may exist the *Code* class word should be used.

Name (NAM). Word or phrase that designates a person, place, or thing.

Number (NUM). An Alphanumeric value that cannot be mathematically manipulated. Often NUM is used for business identifiers, such as employee number, serial number, part number, and telephone number.

Percent (PCT). The numeric ratio of two numbers, multiplied by 100.

Object (OBJ). Image, document, multimedia, BLOB (Binary Large OBject).

Quantity (QTY). A non-monetary accumulation (either positive or negative) of some unit. Includes the count of a number of things, such as number of customers.

Rate (RT). Numeric value representing the quotient of two numbers. PCT is multiplied by 100, RT is not.

Text (TXT). Information, primarily in the form of words, stored as a unit.

Time (TM). Alphanumeric value representing the time of day; hour, minutes, and seconds.

Applying naming standards

Applying naming term

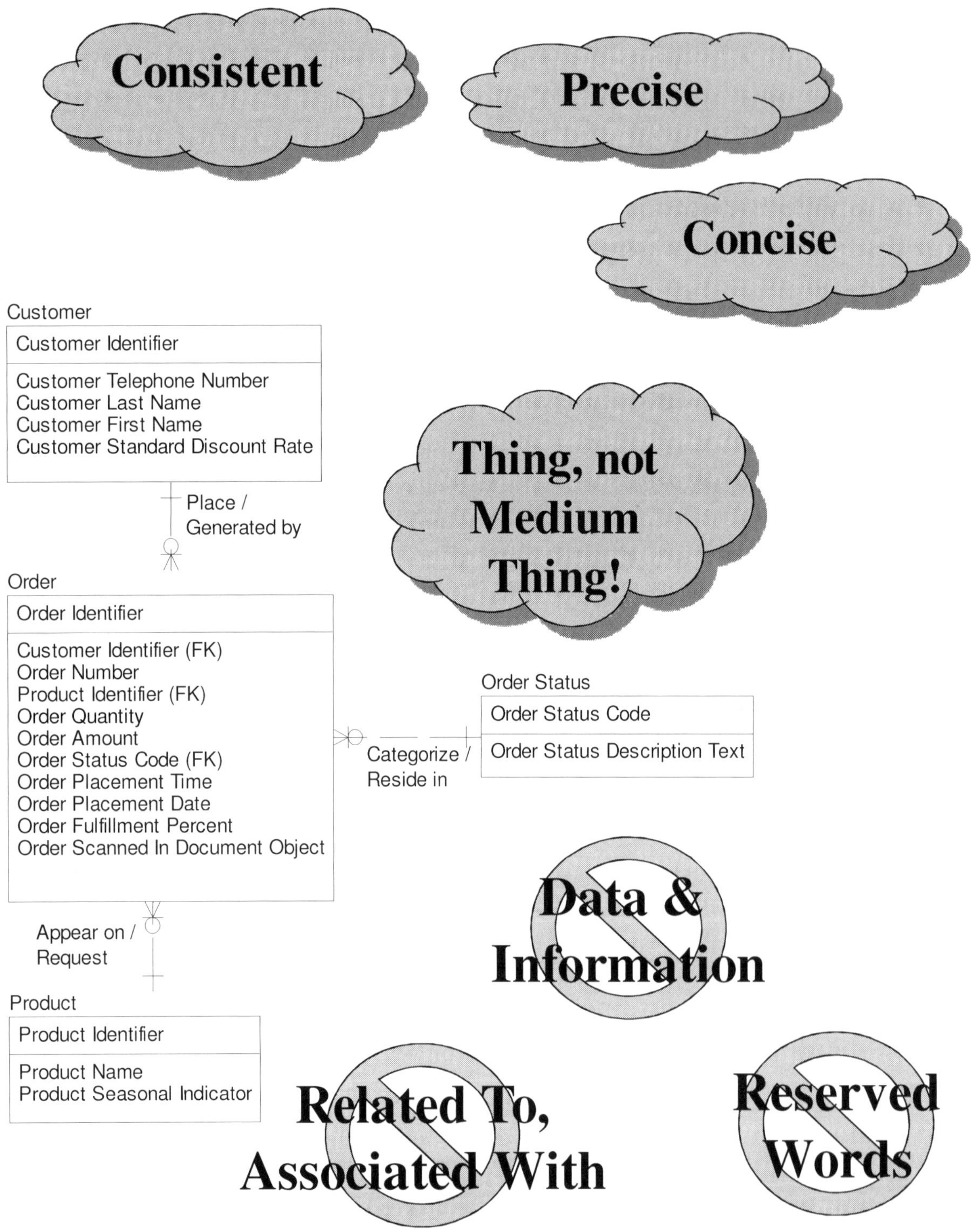

Applying naming standards

Applying naming term

BACKGROUND

Term refers to proper spelling and abbreviation. Traditionally logical names are spelled out completely and physical names contain some form of abbreviation. An abbreviations list can be used to name each physical term.

GENERAL TO ENTITIES, DATA ELEMENTS, AND RELATIONSHIPS

- **The name must be consistent across all models**. For example, if the entity term 'Customer' is used on a specific model, the term must be consistent on other models.
- **Create names as discretely and precisely as possible**. For example, if the system scope addresses a specific type of student, such as only foreign students, use Foreign Student, rather than just Student.
- **Limit physical data model terms to the database with the lowest common denominator**. For example, if your company uses a database platform that allows up to an 18-character length data element name, and another database platform that allows up to 32 characters, limit your data element name to 18 characters.
- Never use phrases like *data* or *information* in an entity name; they do not adequately describe what a given entity represents.
- **Stay away from database reserved words, such as *DATA*, *TABLE*, and *VARCHAR***. A good list of reserved words appears in this article: http://www.dbazine.com/db2/db2-disarticles/gulutzan5

SPECIFIC TO ENTITIES

Reflect the thing the entity represents, rather than any medium on which it is handled. For example, when naming an entity to describe the event oriented data associated with the receipt of a complaint from a student, use something like Student Complaint, rather than Student Complaint Letter.

SPECIFIC TO RELATIONSHIPS

Use meaningful names. Names like "related to" or "associated with" do not add enough meaning to the name to be useful when communicating the relationship to others.

Applying naming standards

Applying naming syntax

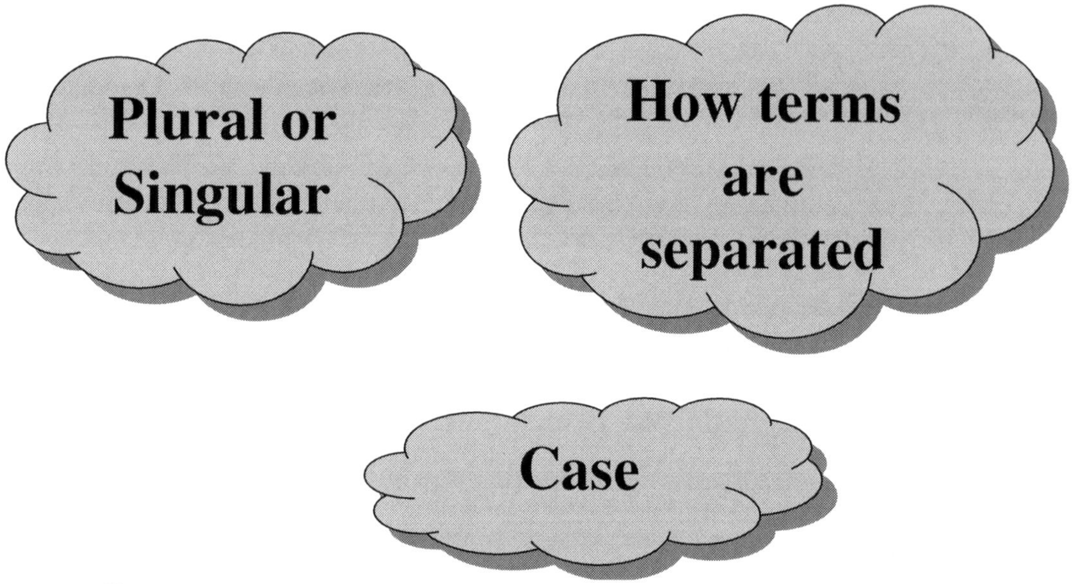

Customer

Customer Identifier

Customer Last Name
CustomerLastName
customer_last_name
CUSTOMER_LAST_NAME
Cust_Last_Name
customer last name
Customer First Name
Customer Telephone Number
Customer Standard Discount Rate

Applying naming standards

Applying naming syntax

BACKGROUND

Syntax refers to whether the term should be plural or singular, whether hyphens, spaces, or Camelback (i.e. initial upper case with no spaces such as customerLastName) should be used, and case (i.e. upper case, initial upper case, or lower case).

GENERAL TO ENTITIES, DATA ELEMENTS, AND RELATIONSHIPS

Use alphabetic characters only; avoid using special characters like "/?!@#$%^&*()+-=',."

SPECIFIC TO ENTITIES

Use singular nouns to name data entities. If occurrences of an entity represent employees, name the entity *Employee*, rather than the plural *Employees*; *Student*, rather than *Students*. This minimizes vagueness about what a single entity occurrence represents.

Applying naming standards

Naming standards resources

Saves 🕐 & $

Quicker learning curve

Facilitates integration

EXAMPLES

- ☐ ISO 11179
- ☐ Columbia University
- ☐ Data Modeling Handbook
- ☐ ERP vendors
- ☐ Search online!

Applying naming standards

Naming standards resources

BACKGROUND

There are a number of useful naming standards resources available for free (or almost free) on the Web. ISO 11179 is the most well-known. It is also fairly voluminous and can be challenging to find relevant sections to your business. Advantages to using someone else's standards (and preferably an industry standard) is that someone else has already done a lot of work on them and you don't have to reinvent the wheel. Also, someone else maintains them, so time and money are saved on an ongoing basis as well. In addition, when people first join a company, it can be a quicker learning curve if they are already familiar with the naming standards. Also, with mergers and acquisitions, using similar naming standards can facilitate integration.

ISO 11179

International Standard ISO 11179, *Information Technology Specification and Standardization of Data Elements* describes a set of rules for developing naming conventions together with standards for data classification, attribution, definition and registration. Here is a link to a good summary of this standard: http://www.gils.net/naming.html. And here is a link to a site which lists all of the ISO 11179 documents: http://isotc.iso.org/livelink/livelink/fetch/2000/2489/Ittf_Home/PubliclyAvailableStandards.htm.

COLUMBIA UNIVERSITY

Columbia University also has robust naming standard guidelines published along with a 30 plus page dictionary of abbreviations at https://dwr.ais.columbia.edu/info/Data%20Naming%20Standards.html.

DATA MODELING HANDBOOK

The Data Modeling Handbook, by Reingruber and Gregory, includes many pages on standards that are very useful.

ERP VENDORS

If you are using an ERP package, chances are that sooner or later you will need to expand it with additional data elements and tables. ERP vendors are very explicit about how to name these new objects, to distinguish them from those that come with the package. For example, SAP/R3 recommends adding a 'Z_' in front of customized tables.

Applying naming standards

5 Questions on Naming Standards

1. Would you allow more than one abbreviation for the same term? If yes, when? If no, why not?

2. Five new tables need to be added to an existing system which follows a different naming standard. Should these new tables follow the naming standard used in this app or the current naming standard? Explain your answer.

3. How about five new data elements which need to be added to an existing table in a system which follows a different naming standard?

4. At what point (if any) would you postpone the deployment of a new system for not following naming standards?

5. Who in your organization is responsible for ***enforcing*** naming standards?

Applying naming standards

5 Questions on Naming Standards

BACKGROUND

Answer the five questions on the facing page. Naming standards are not always so straightforward to apply and especially enforce!

Applying the Data Model Scorecard®

Interaction Report for Product BB40 from May 2011

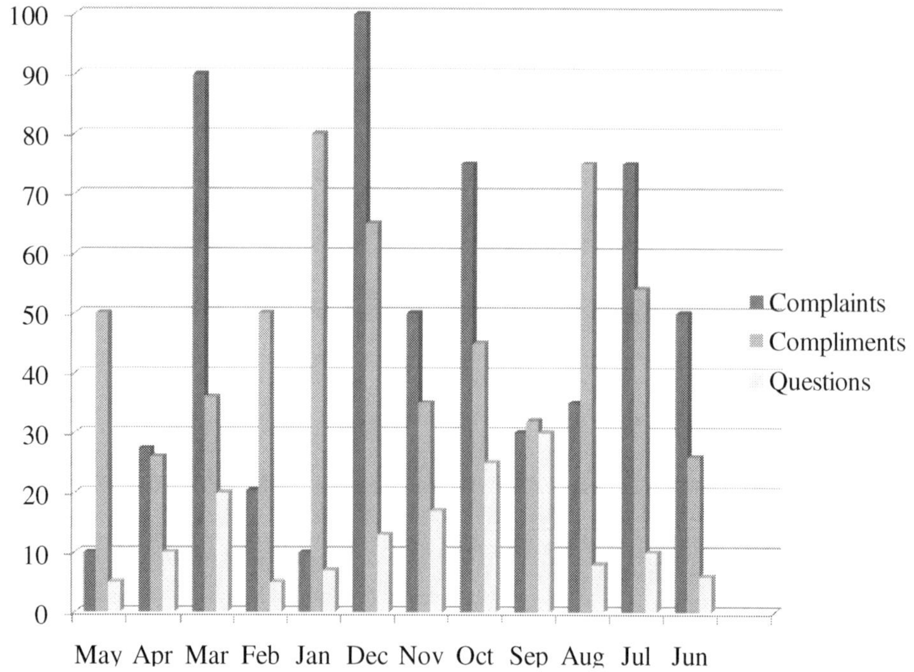

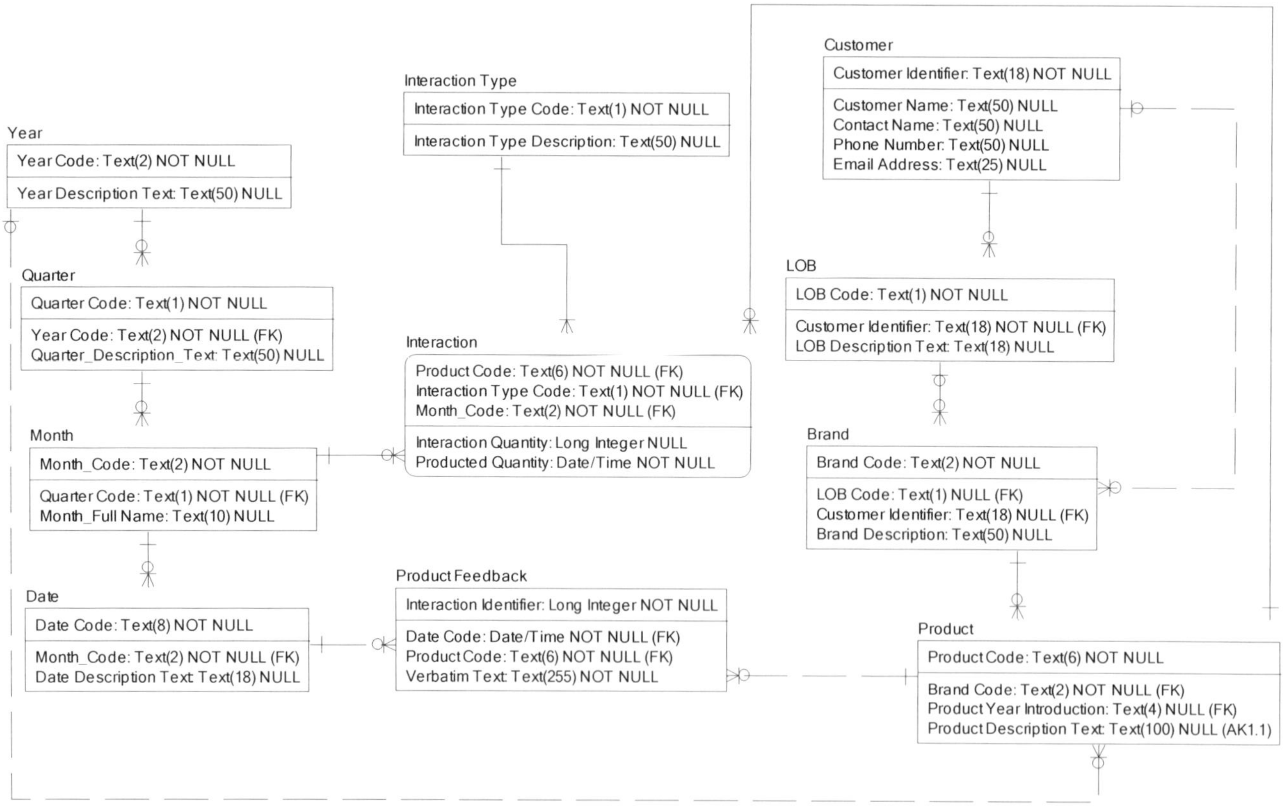

Applying the Data Model Scorecard®

6. How well does the model follow naming standards?

EXPLANATION

This category focuses on naming standard structure, abbreviations, and syntax.

ANTHING YOU WOULD CATCH IN THE MODEL ON THE FACING PAGE FOR THIS CATEGORY?

1.
2.
3.
4.
5.
6.
7.
8.
9.
10.

#	Category	Total score	Model score	%
1	How well do the characteristics of the model support the type of model?	10		
2	How well does the model capture the requirements?	15		
3	How complete is the model?	15		
4	How structurally sound is the model?	15		
5	How well does the model leverage generic structures?	10		
6	How well does the model follow naming standards?	5		
7	How well has the model been arranged for readability?	5		
8	How good are the definitions?	10		
9	How consistent is the model with the enterprise?	5		
10	How well does the metadata match the data?	10		
	TOTAL SCORE	100		

Module 7

Data Model Scorecard® Category #7: Readability

Category Question: How well has the model been arranged for readability?

This module is your guide to: Arranging the model for maximum understanding

Category overview

How well has the model been arranged for readability?

READABILITY

Confirms the model is visually easy to follow so that the other scorecard categories can be accurately measured

Treat white space like air

Minimize relationship line length and direction turns

Reference DEs by chronology. Transaction DEs by class word.

Child entities below parent entities

A diagram is a sentence in a graphical language. The purpose of any language is to communicate. A "good" diagram is therefore one which communicates effectively.
Daniel Moody

Category overview

How well has the model been arranged for readability?

EXPLANATION

A data model is a communication tool and therefore needs to be easy to read. Readability needs to be considered at a model, entity, data element, and relationship level. At a model level, I like to see a large model broken into smaller logical pieces. I also search for the "heart" of the model.

At an entity level, I like to see child entities below parent entities. Child entities being on the many side of the relationship, and parent entities on the one side of the relationship. So if an *order* contains many *order lines*, *order line* should appear below *order*.

At a data element level, I like to see some logic applied regarding the placement of data elements within an entity. For example, on reference entities such as *customer* and *employee*, it is more readable to have the data elements listed in an order that makes sense for someone starting at the beginning of the entity and working down sequentially. For example, *city name*, then *state name*, then *postal code*. For transaction entities such as *order* and *claim*, I have found it more readable to group the data elements into class words, such as all amount data elements grouped together.

At a relationship level, I try to minimize relationship line length, and the number of direction changes a relationship line makes. I also look for missing or incomplete relationship labels, if labels are appropriate on the model. The larger the model, the less useful it is to display labels as the extra verbiage can make the model harder to read.

PURPOSE

Ensures your model is easy to read so that the other scorecard categories can be accurately measured.

Layout techniques

Characteristics of a beautiful model

- ❑ Look for the heart
- ❑ Aim for a frame
- ❑ Empty space
- ❑ Proper use of font and color
- ❑ Reasonable number of entities on page
- ❑ Avoid UPPERCASE
- ❑ Background

Layout techniques

Characteristics of a beautiful model

GENERAL GUIDELINE

Put yourself in your audiences' shoes.

LOOK FOR THE HEART

That is, upon looking at a data model, which part of the model are your eyes naturally attracted toward? This tends to be an entity or entities with many relationships to other entities, similar to the hub on a bicycle tire with many spokes to the outside rim of the tire. This "heart" needs to be carefully positioned so that the reader can identify it early on and use this as a starting point to walk through the rest of the model.

AIM FOR A FRAME

The model should form a box, with entities and relationships making up the frame. Another way of saying this is that the model should not be a leaning tower. It should be 'squared off'. It is easier on the brain this way and helps with easily identifying what is and is not within the diagram. The modeler can optionally add a border around the model to emphasize this frame.

EMPTY SPACE

Are the entities all clustered together on a certain part of the model? We need to space out the modeling constructs to make them as readable as possible.

PROPER USE OF FONT AND COLOR

Color is a very a good technique to highlight certain areas of the model. For example, areas that are issues or to differentiate subject areas or applications. Different formats, such as larger font or bold can be used to highlight as well. 11 point font is ideal.

REASONABLE NUMBER OF ENTITIES ON PAGE

Between 15 and 30 entities are usually a good number to have on one page. Too much more than this and the model becomes overwhelming. A subject area model can be used to present the "big picture"

AVOID UPPERCASE

Uppercase text is difficult to read. Use initial caps instead.

BACKGROUND

It is a good idea to have the background be a different color than the entities, such as a gray background with white entities.

Layout techniques

Entity layout best practices

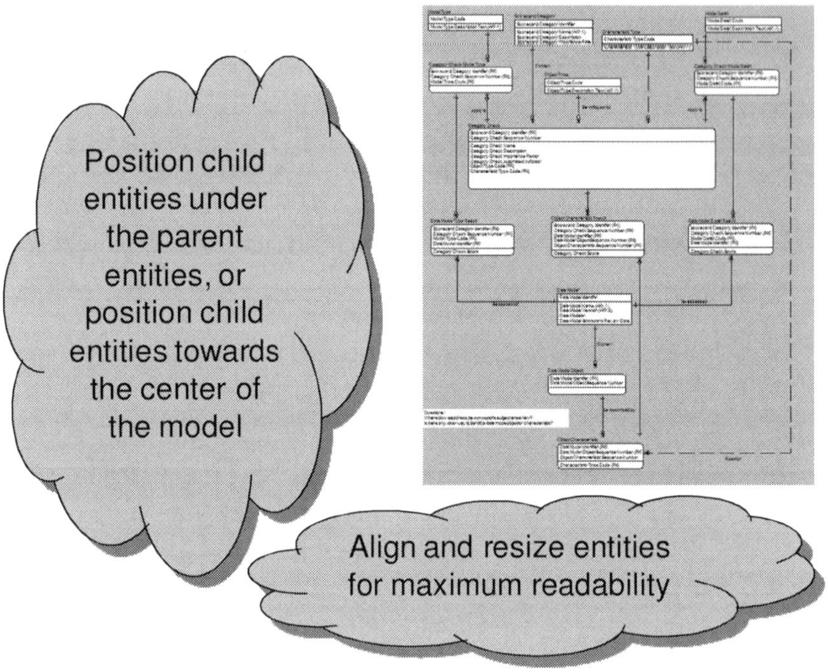

- Colors can differentiate
  - Subject areas
  - Customized versus package
  - Phase I versus Phase II
  - Ownership
  - Hot areas (i.e. open issues)
  - Entity type
    - Dependent vs. independent
    - Fact vs. dimension
    - Who, what, when, where why, and how
  - Schema
  - To distinguish background from model

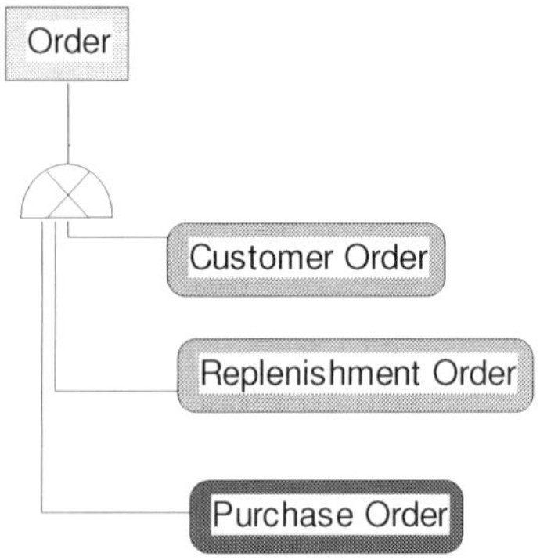

Minimal new reporting structures are in the DW

Moderate new reporting structures are in the DW

Extensive new reporting structures are in the DW

Layout techniques

Entity layout best practices

BACKGROUND

The main benefits to laying out the entities appropriately are:

- **Easier readability on the model.** By laying out the entities in their most appropriate places, we make it easier to walkthrough and review the models. It is simpler to tell the story within the data model and clearly read the relationships from parent entity to child entity.
- **Quicker detection of errors and issues.** Just like we saw with properly laying out the data elements, laying out the entities properly can lead to more quickly finding errors and issues. You might more rapidly notice circular relationships, for example.

POSITION

Position child entities under the parent entities, or position child entities towards the center of the model. This simple statement will improve the layout of the entities on the model dramatically. So if a Customer can place many Orders, Customer is the parent entity and Order is the child entity.

COLOR

If you have easy access to a color printer, or you are reviewing the data model through your computer or a projector, color might be the best option. When everything else on the model is black and white, a red or a yellow object really stands out. If you need to show multiple types of information, color works very well. In this example, red draws to our attention those areas which a new data mart requires, but which do not yet currently exist in the data warehouse. Color can also be used to indicate the following:

- Issues
- Entity type
- Dependent vs. independent
- Fact vs. dimension
- Who, what, when, where why, and how
- Schema on a physical data model
- To distinguish background from model (e.g. white entities on gray background or gray entities on white background)

Layout techniques

Data element sequence

Sequence

1. PK
2. AK
3. FK
4. Concept
5. SYS

Reference by Chronology

Student

Student_Identifier
Student_First_Name Student_Middle_Name Student_Last_Name Address_Line_1_Text City_Name State_Name Postal_Code

Transaction by Classword

Order

Order_identifier
Order_Number (AK1.1) Customer_Identifier Original_Delivery_Date Revised_Delivery_Date Actual_Ship_Date Actual_Delivery_Date Order_Comments_Text Order_Quantity Extract_File_Batch_Number

Layout techniques

Data element sequence

BACKGROUND

This sequencing is done to improve the readability and understanding of the data elements within each entity. For example, positioning Customer First Name directly before Customer Last Name would be easier to review and understand than positioning Customer First Name somewhere in the middle of all of the customer data elements, and Customer Last Name towards the end of the customer data elements.

LOGICAL SEQUENCE

1. Primary key. Always list the primary key first within each entity. This usually happens by default because most modeling tools will always put the primary key as the first data element or elements in the entity. If there is a composite primary key, list the data elements within the key in their order of importance or usage.

2. Alternate key(s). These alternate keys, because of their importance, should be listed next directly under the primary key. A majority of the time, these alternate keys are data elements that have business significance to the users. If there is a composite alternate key, list the data elements within the key in their order of importance or usage. If there is more than one alternate key, list the keys in their order of importance or usage.

3. Foreign key(s). Next list the foreign keys. List them in order of their importance or usage to the business users and functional analysts.

4. Remaining data elements grouped within concepts. By Class Word for transaction entities, and by Chronology for reference entities. So for example, for the fact table, Monthly Order Summary, I would group by class word. All of the amount data elements would be grouped together, as well as all of the quantity data elements. For Customer however, I would group by chronology, meaning according to how the data elements are traditionally presented to the business. Customer Last Name before Customer First Name, Customer Address Line Text before Customer Postal Code, Telephone Country Code before Telephone Number.

5. System data elements. These are the internally system-generated data elements (create date, user ids, batch dates, etc.) created by applications and are of no value to a business user. These data elements are not used in any kind of data entry or analysis, and therefore should always go at the end of each of the entities. I don't list these in order of importance, but I make sure I list them consistently in each of the entities (e.g. Create Date always precedes Update Date).

Layout techniques

Relationship layout best practices

Before

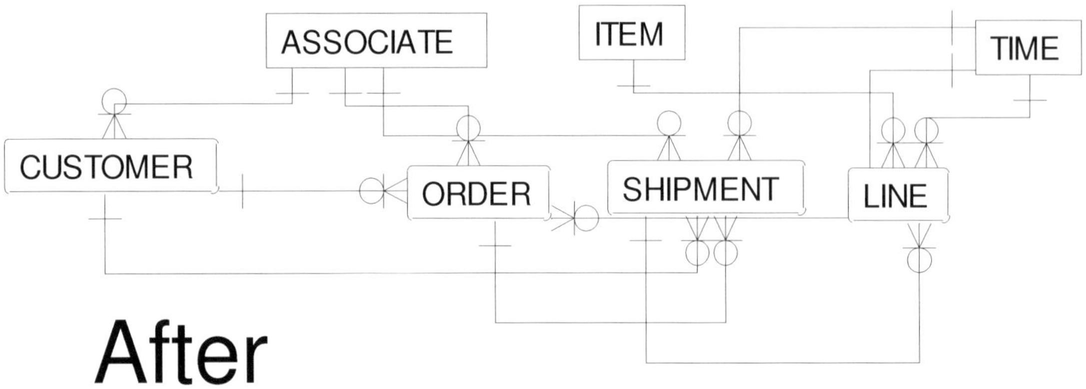

After

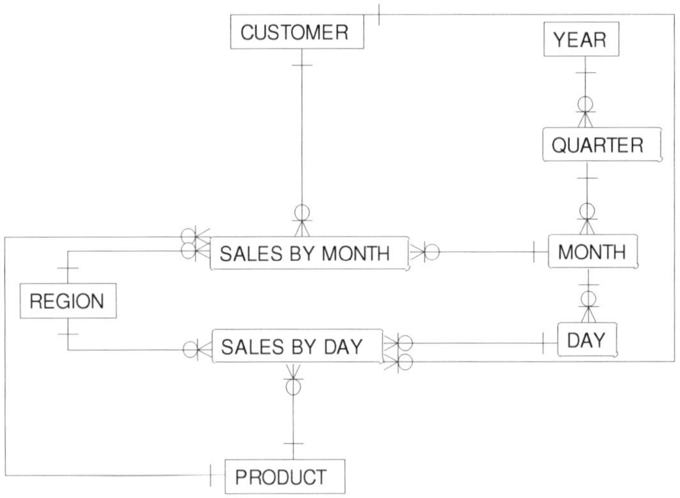

Before

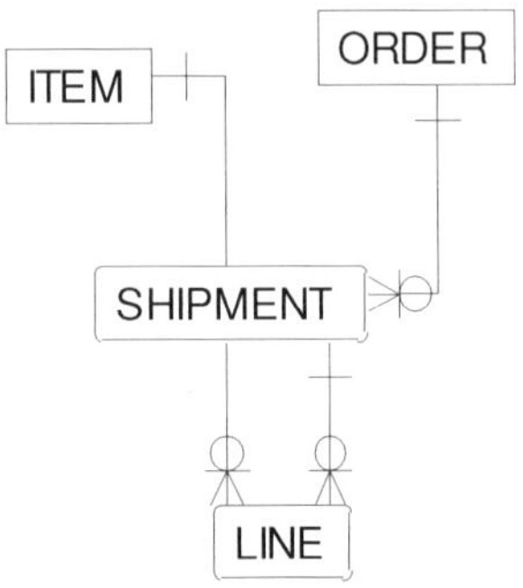

After

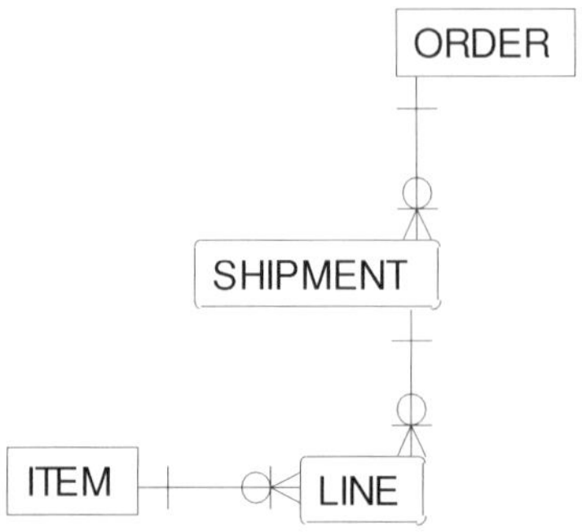

Layout techniques

Relationship layout best practices

BACKGROUND

The benefits of paying attention to the layout of relationship lines include:

- **Easier readability on the model.** By laying out the relationships to minimize crossing lines and eliminating relationships passing through entities that are not part of the relationship, we make the model easier to read and more straightforward to tell the story within the structures.
- **Quicker detection of errors and issues.** Just like we saw with properly laying out the data elements and entities, laying out the relationships can more quickly find errors and issues. You might more rapidly notice entities that should be related but are not, for example. You might also notice entities that are related but should not be.

GENERAL BEST PRACTICES

There are two tips that I encourage you to follow for relationships:

- **Minimize line length and direction changes.** It can be confusing to have long relationship lines that keep bending different directions.
- **Never let lines pass through entities.** This means that you have an entity that just happened to be placed on a relationship line, but does not participate in that relationship. Entities on either side of this entity participate in this relationship. This gives the false appearance that this entity is somehow attached to and therefore participates in this relationship.
- **Straight or curved lines better than zigzag.** Although some data modeling tools may not support straight or curved diagonal lines, they are preferred over zigzag lines.

Applying the Data Model Scorecard®

Interaction Report for Product BB40 from May 2011

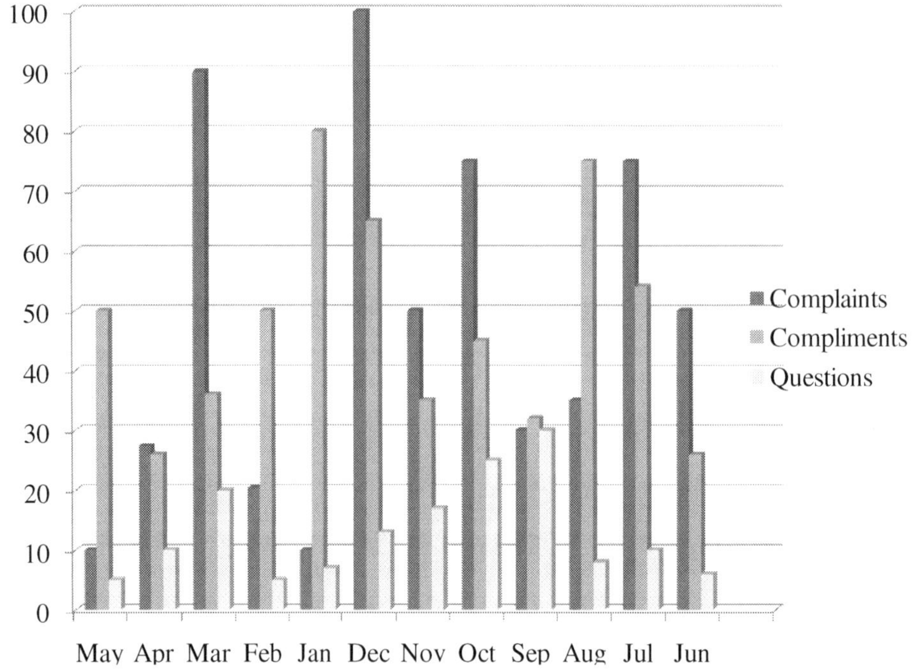

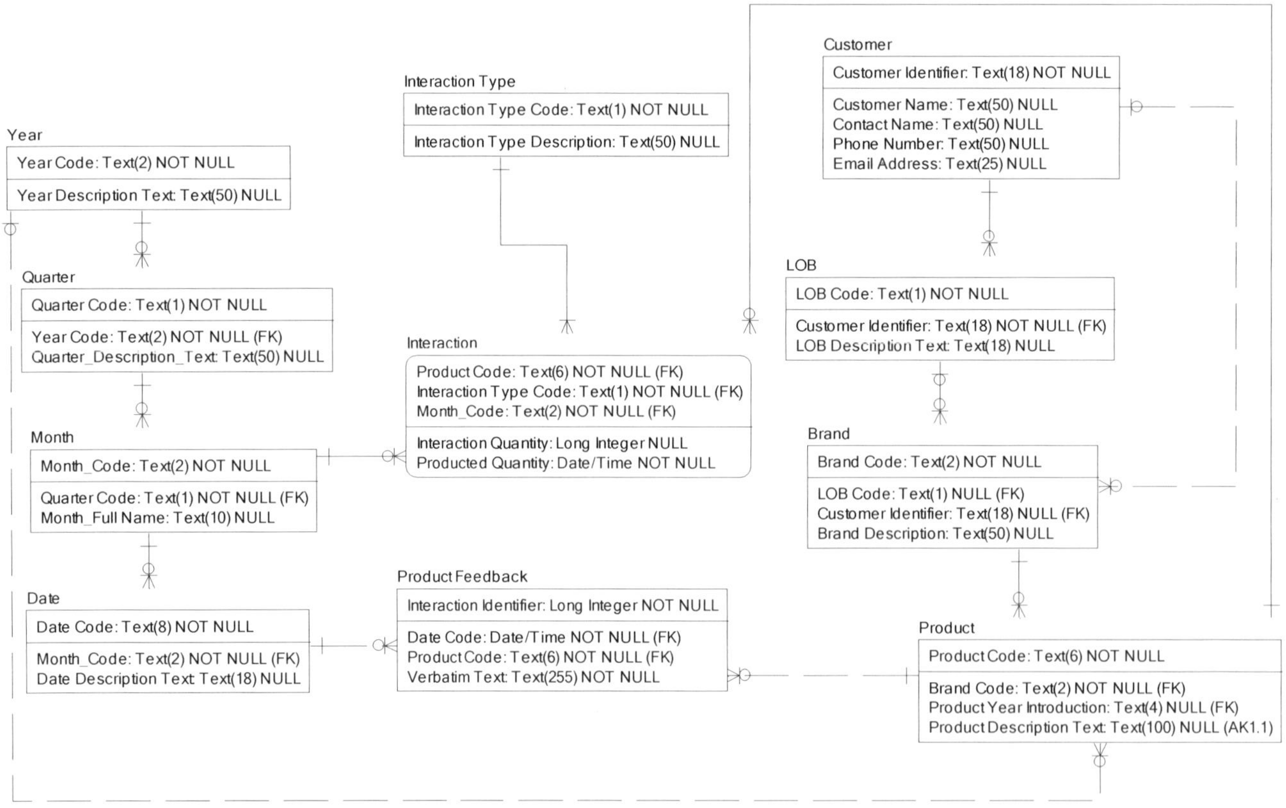

Applying the Data Model Scorecard®

7. How well has the model been arranged for readability?

EXPLANATION

A data model is a communication tool and this category ensures the data model is arranged to make it easy to understand and walk through.

ANTHING YOU WOULD CATCH IN THE MODEL ON THE FACING PAGE FOR THIS CATEGORY?

1.
2.
3.
4.
5.
6.
7.
8.
9.
10.

#	Category	Total score	Model score	%
1	How well do the characteristics of the model support the type of model?	10		
2	How well does the model capture the requirements?	15		
3	How complete is the model?	15		
4	How structurally sound is the model?	15		
5	How well does the model leverage generic structures?	10		
6	How well does the model follow naming standards?	5		
7	How well has the model been arranged for readability?	5		
8	How good are the definitions?	10		
9	How consistent is the model with the enterprise?	5		
10	How well does the metadata match the data?	10		
	TOTAL SCORE	100		

Module 8

Data Model Scorecard® Category #8: Definitions

Category Question: How good are the definitions?

This module is your guide to: Writing clear, complete, and correct definitions

Category overview

How good are the definitions?

Confirms entity and data element definitions are clear, complete, and correct

Put an 'X' in any cell where you are confident your organization has a clear, complete, and correct definition for this term. Can anybody yell Bingo?

B	I	N	G	O
Customer	Product	Account	Prospect	Calendar
Visit	Contract	Department	Credit	Citizen
Site	Order	★	Resource	Service
Employee	Agency	Consumer	Revenue	Case
Organization	Facility	Expense	Project	Event

Category overview

How good are the definitions?

EXPLANATION

This category confirms all definitions are clear, complete, and correct. Clarity means that a reader can understand the meaning of a term by reading the definition only once. Completeness ensures the definition is at the appropriate level of detail, and that it includes all the necessary components such as derivations and examples. Correctness focuses on having a definition that totally matches what the term means, and is consistent with the rest of the business.

PURPOSE

Minimizes doubt that may exist about the contents of data elements and the relationships between entities. Doubts and misinterpretations lead to model ambiguity.

CHALLENGE

You will need to find business people from outside your department or project to validate the definitions. As data governance catches on, this challenge will become easier and easier.

Customer Id

The Customer Identifier is the identifier for the customer
What else can you say about Customer Identifier anyway?
Hmmm...

Customer Id

BACKGROUND

I was showing examples of both complete and incomplete definitions during a recent training class, when I shared the following incomplete definition for a Customer Identifier:

A Customer Identifier is the unique identifier for a Customer.

"What else can you say about Customer Identifier anyway?", a participant asked.

CHALLENGE

What else can you say about Customer Identifier (or any identifier) to add more meaning to its definition?

More about definitions

Importance of definitions

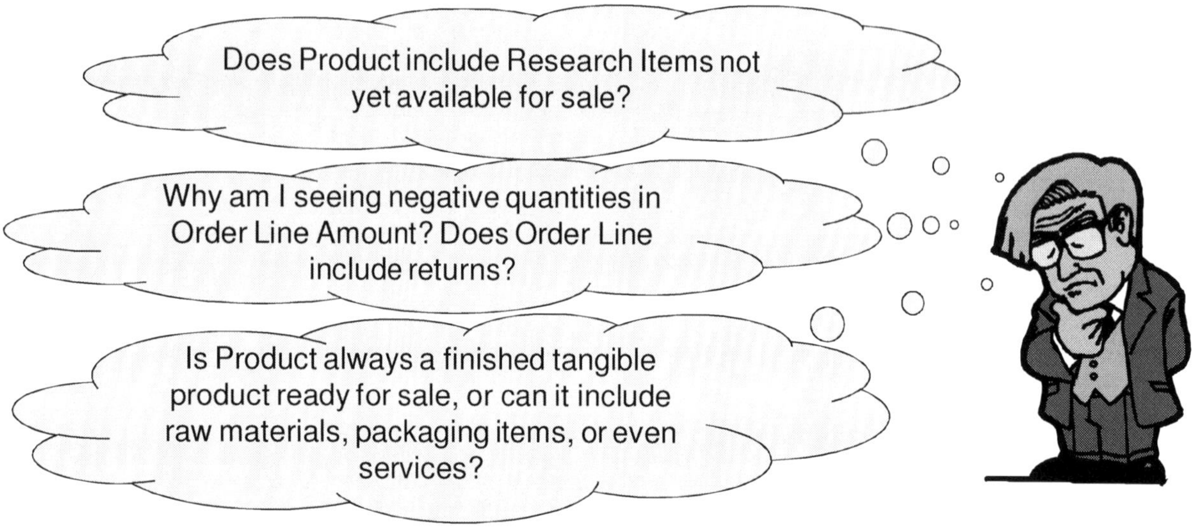

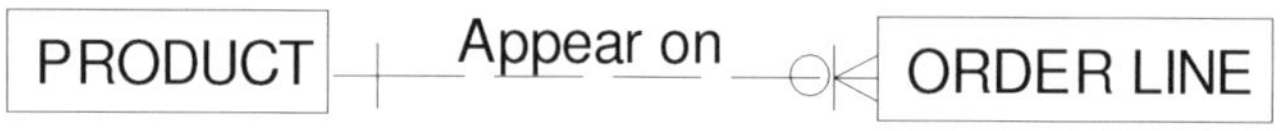

Definitions are important!

- ☐ Assists business and IT with decision making
- ☐ Helps initiate, document and hopefully resolve different perspectives on the same concept
- ☐ Supports data model precision
- ☐ Process of writing definitions could lead to additional rules and data elements

More about definitions

Importance of definitions

ASSISTS BUSINESS AND IT WITH DECISION MAKING

If a business user has a different interpretation of a data element than what was developed, it is easy for poor decisions to be made, compromising the entire application. If a business user would like to know how many products have been ordered each month, for example, imagine the poor judgments that could result if the person expected raw materials to be included with products and they were not, or if he or she assumed that raw materials were not included but they were. IT needs to know which data element to source data from, to use in calculations, or to display to the user. If the definition of *order line* mentions that open orders, canceled orders, and dropped orders are also within the scope of *order line*, this might influence sourcing decisions and database design decisions if space and performance become issues.

HELPS INITIATE, DOCUMENT AND HOPEFULLY RESOLVE DIFFERENT PERSPECTIVES ON THE SAME CONCEPT

Folks in accounting and sales can both agree that Customer is an important concept. But can both groups agree on a common definition? If they can agree, you are a step closer to creating a holistic view of the business.

SUPPORTS DATA MODEL PRECISION

As we can see in the example on the facing page, where each *order line* must be for one and only one *product*, a data model is exact and unambiguous. An *order line* cannot exist without a *product*. However, if the definition of *product* is missing or vague, we have less confidence in the entity and its relationships. Is a *product*, for example, raw materials and intermediate goods, or only a finished item ready for resale? Can we have an order for a service, or must a *product* be a tangible deliverable? The definition is needed to support the *product* entity and its relationship to *order line*.

COULD LEAD TO ADDITIONAL RULES AND DATA ELEMENTS

The analyst is asking lots of questions (or making lots of assumptions) when documenting terms. Much of this information could lead to more concepts that are needed on the design.

More about definitions

Characteristics of a good definition

A Customer is a person or organization who obtains our product for resale. The Customer normally obtains the product through purchase. An example of a customer who does not purchase our product is the Salvation Army, which receives the product for free as a charity organization. A person or organization must have obtained at least one product from us to be considered a Customer. That is, Prospects are not Customers. Also, once a Customer, always a Customer so even Customers that have not obtained anything in 50 years are still considered Customers. The Customer is different than the Consumer, who purchases the product for consumption as opposed to resale.

Examples:
Walmart
Bob's Grocery Store
Military Base 1332

More about definitions

Characteristics of a good definition

BACKGROUND

Despite their importance, definitions tend to be omitted or written with minimal attention to their audience. Therefore, when writing definitions, we need to be aware of three characteristics that lead to a high-quality definition that the audience can understand. Those characteristics are clarity, completeness, and correctness.

CLEAR

Clarity means that a reader can understand the meaning of a term by reading the definition only once. A clear definition does not require the reader to decipher how each sentence should be interpreted. The definition contains what the entity represents, and not what the entity contains or when the entity is used. A good way to make sure your definition is clear is to think about what makes a definition unclear. We need to avoid restating the obvious and using obscure technical terminology and abbreviations in our definitions. Let's say, for example, that the definition of *associate identifier* is "associate identifier" or "the identifier for the associate."

COMPLETE

This category focuses on making sure the definition is at the appropriate level of detail and that it includes all the necessary components, such as derivations, aliases, exceptions, and examples. Having a definition at the appropriate level of detail means that it is not too generic as to provide very little additional value, yet not so specific that it provides value only to an application or department—or that it adds value only at a certain point in time.

CORRECT

This category focuses on having a definition that completely matches what the term means and is consistent with the rest of the business. *Correctness* means that an expert in the field would agree that the term matches the definition. One of the difficulties with this category is that as we define broader terms that cross departments, such as *product*, *customer*, and *employee*, we tend to get more than one accurate definition, depending on who is asked. A good solution to this problem is to use subtypes on your model that contain each of the distinct states of an employee. Through the accurate definition of each subject, every state is captured.

More about definitions

Techniques to write a good definition

See what's available externally

Overly precise

Let's see. I'm not sure if Customer includes prospects. Let me add it to the definition and see what the business says.

Define before name

Is this Insurance Type Code or Line of Business Code? Defining first really helps!

Create a definition template

Provide your team with helpful pointers

The definition of a data object should answer all "what?" questions
The definition should be expressed in *simple complete* sentences
Verbs used in the definition must be in their present tense
Only approved abbreviations and acronyms may be used
Do not define a thing in terms of itself

More about definitions

Techniques to write a good definition

SEE WHAT'S AVAILABLE EXTERNALLY

Bing and Google can make coming up with a definition (or at least a starter definition) very easy. Type "Define:" and then what you would like to define, such as "Define: Student".

OVERLY PRECISE

I know a modeler who will write the initial definition and then have the business user review. In writing the initial definition, she is deliberately overly precise – so precise that she knows the definition is wrong. Than when a business person reviews the definition they correct the one or two sentences that are not accurate and the entire definition is approved. It is easier to correct a sentence than it is to think of it from scratch.

DEFINE BEFORE NAME

A good technique is to define the term before you even name it. If we define the term first, we can create a better name for it after understanding what it is. For example, instead of naming a data element Insurance Type Code, we might name it Insurance Line of Business after first defining and understanding what the data element really means.

CREATE A DEFINITION TEMPLATE

You can provide an easily accessible list of subject area definitions, as well as a list of classword or domain definitions and append these definitions to the definition of the entity or data element so that all the person defining the term needs to do is define the new terms.

PROVIDE YOUR TEAM WITH HELPFUL POINTERS

Here are examples of pointers provided by a large retail organization in their standards documentation:

- The definition of a data object should answer all "what?" questions.
- The definition should be expressed in *simple complete* sentences.
- Verbs used in the definition must be in their present tense.
- Only approved abbreviations acronyms and may be used in the text of definitions.
- Do not define a thing in terms of itself.

Definition differences

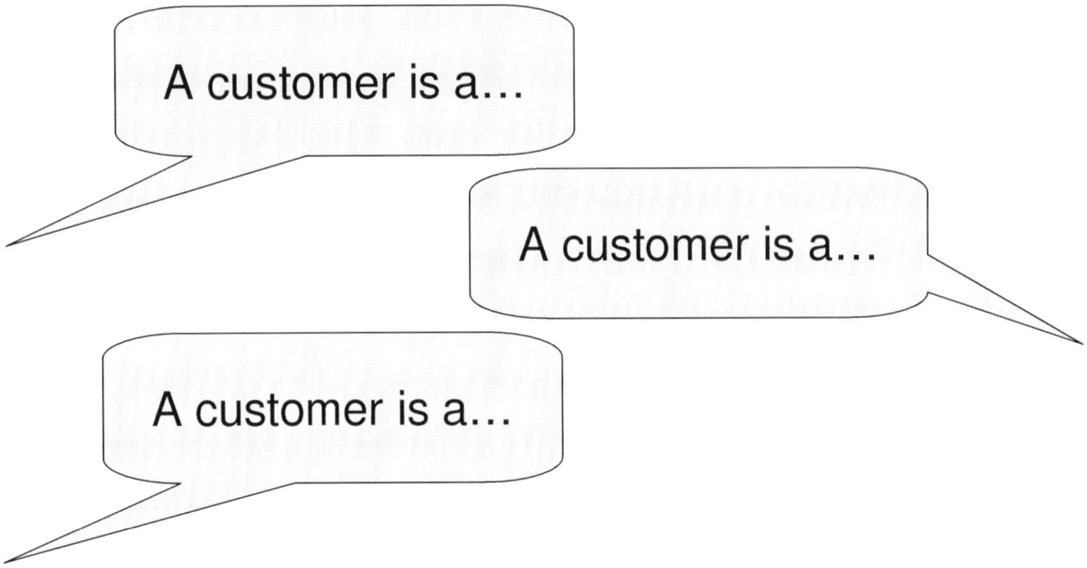

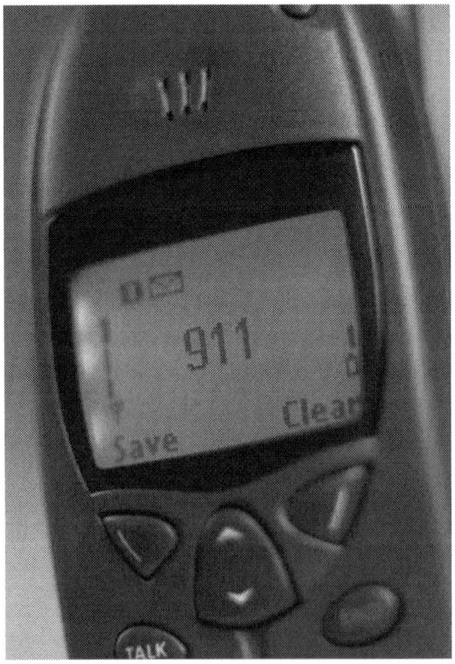

Definition differences

BACKGROUND

Your coworker calls you in the middle of the night with a data modeling emergency. There needs to be a single definition for Customer in the data warehouse, yet he was provided with three different Customer definitions. Each definition was provided by a well-respected business expert and is accurate within that business expert's area.

CHALLENGE

He needs you to recommend a tactic he can use to come up with a definition that satisfies all three business experts. What tactic would you recommend?

PURPOSE

An exercise in integration.

TIPS

Are politics just as important as modeling skills?

Applying the Data Model Scorecard®

Interaction Report for Product BB40 from May 2011

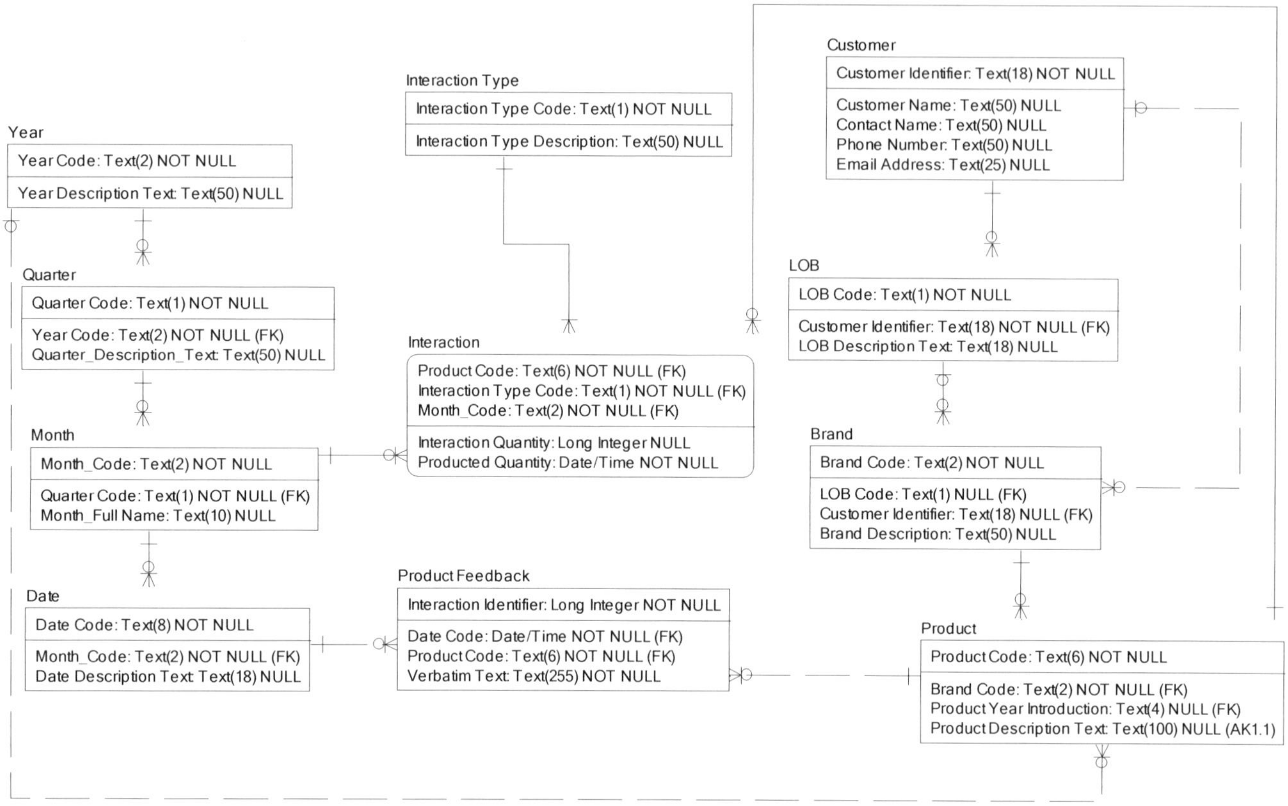

#	Category	Total score	Model score	%
1	How well do the characteristics of the model support the type of model?	10		
2	How well does the model capture the requirements?	15		
3	How complete is the model?	15		
4	How structurally sound is the model?	15		
5	How well does the model leverage generic structures?	10		
6	How well does the model follow naming standards?	5		
7	How well has the model been arranged for readability?	5		
8	How good are the definitions?	10		
9	How consistent is the model with the enterprise?	5		
10	How well does the metadata match the data?	10		
	TOTAL SCORE	100		

Applying the Data Model Scorecard®

8. How good are the definitions?

EXPLANATION

This category confirms all definitions are clear, complete, and correct. Clarity means that a reader can understand the meaning of a term by reading the definition only once. Completeness ensures the definition includes all the necessary components. Correctness focuses on having a definition that totally matches what the term means. The only definitions you were provided with are shown below and on the following pages. How good are these definitions? Review the definitions and give a point score.

Table Name	Column Name	Column Comment
Product Feedback	Interaction Identifier	
	Verbatim Text	The actual comment from the consumer who contacted us, such as "I found something in my product."
	Date Code	The full date in YYYYMMDD format.
	Product Code	The unique way of identifying the product. This is a business natural key.
Date	Date Code	The full date in YYYYMMDD format.
	Date Description Text	
	Month_Code	The code for the month, a number between 01 and 12.
Interaction Type	Interaction Type Code	The code corresponding to whether the interaction with the consumer is a complaint, compliment, or question. Examples: 01 = Complaint 02 = Compliment 03 = Question
	Interaction Type Description	The description corresponding to whether the interaction with the consumer is a complaint, compliment, or question. Examples: 01 = Complaint 02 = Compliment 03 = Question

Table Name	Column Name	Column Comment
Interaction	Interaction Quantity	The number of interactions.
	Producted Quantity	The amount of product produced.
	Product Code	The unique way of identifying the product. This is a business natural key.
	Interaction Type Code	The code corresponding to whether the interaction with the consumer is a complaint, compliment, or question. Examples: 01 = Complaint 02 = Compliment 03 = Question
Month	Month_Code	The code for the month, a number between 01 and 12.
	Month_Full Name	The name for the month.
	Quarter Code	The number 1, 2, 3, or 4 depending on which fourth of the year it is.
Year	Year Code	The four digit code (e.g. 2011) for the period of 365 days (or 366 days in leap years) starting from the first of January, used for reckoning time in ordinary affairs.
	Year Description Text	The text description for the period of 365 days (or 366 days in leap years) starting from the first of January, used for reckoning time in ordinary affairs.
Quarter	Quarter Code	The number 1, 2, 3, or 4 depending on which fourth of the year it is.
	Quarter_Description_ Text	The full description for the quarter of year.
	Year Code	The four digit code (e.g. 2011) for the period of 365 days (or 366 days in leap years) starting from the first of January, used for reckoning time in ordinary affairs.
Customer	Customer Identifier	The identifier for the customer.
	Customer Name	Customer Name.
	Contact Name	The first and last name of the key person to reach at the Customer site. This is usually someone in Consumer Affairs.
	Phone Number	Contact phone number.
	Email Address	Contact email address.

Table Name	Column Name	Column Comment
LOB	LOB Code	The 2 character code corresponding to the line of business. Examples: 01 = Automobiles 02 = Motocycles 03 = Trucks
	LOB Description Text	The description corresponding to the line of business. Examples: 01 = Automobiles 02 = Motocycles 03 = Trucks
	Customer Identifier	The identifier for the customer.
Brand	Brand Code	The American Marketing Association defines a brand as a "name, term, design, symbol, or any other feature that identifies one seller's good or service as distinct from those of other sellers. The legal term for brand is trademark. A brand may identify one item, a family of items, or all items of that seller. If used for the firm as a whole, the preferred term is trade name."
	Brand Description	
	LOB Code	The 2 character code corresponding to the line of business. Examples: 01 = Automobiles 02 = Motocycles 03 = Trucks
	Customer Identifier	The identifier for the customer.
Product	Product Code	The unique way of identifying the product. This is a business natural key.
	Product Description Text	
	Brand Code	The American Marketing Association defines a brand as a "name, term, design, symbol, or any other feature that identifies one seller's good or service as distinct from those of other sellers. The legal term for brand is trademark. A brand may identify one item, a family of items, or all items of that seller. If used for the firm as a whole, the preferred term is trade name."
	Product Year Introduction	The four digit code (e.g. 2011) for the period of 365 days (or 366 days in leap years) starting from the first of January, used for reckoning time in ordinary affairs.

Module 9

Data Model Scorecard® Category #9: Consistency

Category Question: How consistent is the model with the enterprise?

This module is your guide to: Matching the model with the enterprise

Category overview

How consistent is the model with the enterprise?

CONSISTENCY

Confirms the model complements the “Big Picture”

<u>Big Picture sources</u>

Enterprise model (Ideal)

Packaged software (e.g. ERP)

Industry data models

Common thought

Industry consortiums (e.g. SID)

Category overview

How consistent is the model with the enterprise?

EXPLANATION

The structures that appear in the model being reviewed should be consistent in terminology and usage to structures that appear in related data models, and with the enterprise model if one exists. This way there will be consistency across projects.

PURPOSE

Ensures the information is represented in a broad and consistent context, so that one set of terminology and rules can be spoken in the organization.

CHALLENGE

Not all organizations have an enterprise data model. If no enterprise model exists, I look for widely accepted existing models for comparison, ERP models if they are accessible and intelligible, or universal models which are models that are built for a particular industry or function.

EDM overview

EDM definition

An enterprise data model (EDM) is a subject-oriented and integrated data model representing all of the data produced and consumed across an entire organization. Although the EDM needs to be validated by the business, the EDM's primary user is IT. Also known as a corporate model or business model.

Subject-oriented: through the eyes of the CEO
Integrated: all of the data and rules in an organization are depicted once and fit together seamlessly. Single version of the truth, yet maps back to the chaotic real world.

Existing application/functional world	Enterprise view
○ Customer Reference Database creates Customer data ○ Orders Database reads Customer data ○ Marketing Database creates Lead data ○ Consumer Affairs Database changes Consumer data ○ Customer Relations Database changes Customer data ○ Customer Satisfaction Database changes Customer data	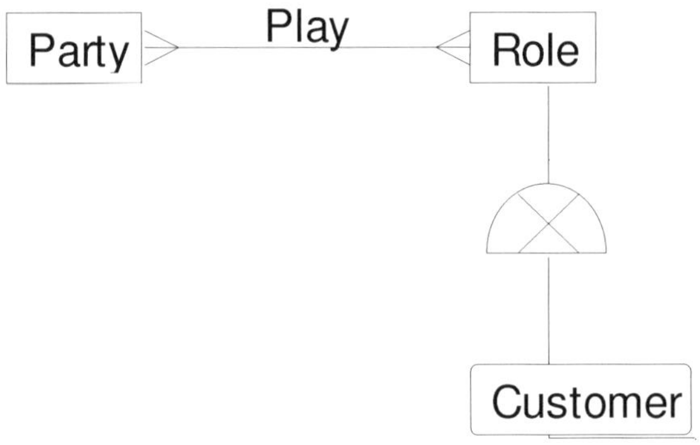 A Party can play many Roles. One of these Roles is Customer.

EDM overview

EDM definition

DEFINITION

An enterprise data model (EDM) is a subject-oriented and integrated data model representing all of the data produced and consumed across an entire organization. Subject-oriented means that the concepts on a data model fit together as the CEO sees the company, as opposed to how individual functional or department heads see their view of the company. There is one Customer entity, one Order entity, etc. Integration goes hand in hand with subject-orientation. Integration means that all of the data and rules in an organization are depicted once and fit together seamlessly. Every data element has a single definition and name. Integration implies that with this single version of the truth comes a mapping back to the chaotic real world. For example, if Customer Last Name lives in 10 applications within an organization, the integrated view would show Customer Last Name only once and capture the mapping back to these 10 applications.

EXAMPLE

In this simplified example, a Party can play many Roles and one of these Roles is a Customer. This is the enterprise view of Customer. Customer exists in many places in the organization however, and this chaos is captured through a mapping back to each of the existing source systems.

Notice some of the issues this mapping raises. An early issue that must be resolved is the terminology issue. Are Customer, Lead, and Consumer the same? If yes, then customer information is created in two distinct systems. Is there redundancy here with a chance of data quality issues? Customer is changed in three distinct systems? If Bob moves to a different address is it being changed consistently across all three systems? All future systems should ideally use the enterprise model as a source. Therefore, they would use the role concept as opposed to a functional view of the world, such as shown through each of the source systems.

EDM BRINGS ORDER

"Data is one of an organization's most valuable assets. All current and future business decisions hinge on data. An EDM is essential for the management of an organization's data resource. The core principle of data management is order; applying order to the vast universe of data. To manage data is to apply order. According to the second law of thermodynamics; the universe and everything in it, continually heads toward chaos; it takes energy to bring order. The same holds true for data, left alone, it continually deteriorates to a state of disorder. It takes concerted effort to keep data in order. An EDM brings order."
Noreen Kendle, Enterprise Data Architect, Delta Airlines

EDM overview

A dimensional EDM?

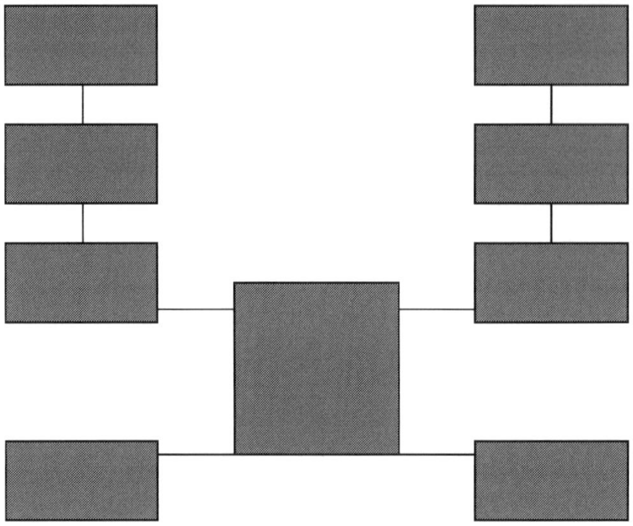

EDM overview

A dimensional EDM?

BACKGROUND

One day a colleague asks you for feedback on an enterprise data model (EDM) she has been tasked with building in partnership with business analysts. The model appears to cover all of the concepts within the organization. The only issue is that the model has been built completely using dimensional structures! There is a Customer dimension, a Product dimension, and many other dimensions. There are financial fact tables, customer satisfaction fact tables, and many other fact tables.

CHALLENGE

Is this right? Can an EDM be dimensional? Why or why not?

EDM overview

Integration is the key!

> Integration is connecting disparate information pieces into a single united whole.

- Very difficult to achieve
- EDM is integrated through mapping

<u>Email integration mapping</u>

Source field	Source table	Source system	Create, read, update, or delete?	Comments	EDM field	EDM table
email	Associate	HR Payroll	Create	Straight map	Electronic Address Txt	ELECTRONIC ADDRESS
e_mail_addr	Vendor	Supplier Contact	Create	Straight map		
company	Consumer	Consumer Contact	Create	90% of time this is the email address and 10% it contains the company name. Search for @ to ensure you have the email address.		

EDM overview

Integration is the key!

EDM IS INTEGRATED

An EDM provides organizations with a single integrated view of their business information. Integration means connecting disparate information pieces into a single united whole. Integration can lead to information consistency.

CHALLENGE

Integration is very difficult for many organizations to achieve, yet it is a prerequisite for most organization-wide initiatives. In fact, according to a recent TDWI Flashpoint, over 69% of organizations surveyed find that integration is a high barrier to new application development. However, if an organization can integrate their data, the rewards are great. Continental Airlines, which in 1994 was ranked lowest by US Department of Transportation metrics, has recently been named the "most admired global airline" by Fortune Magazine. This turnaround time is due to Continental obtaining an integrated view of over 25 of their source systems. This enterprise view has not only boosted customer service, it also has saved Continental over $25 million and brought in over $150 million in additional revenue.

EXAMPLE

To give you a small taste of EDM integration, assume your EDM contains email address (Electronic Address Txt). There are three data elements in this example that map to Electronic Address Txt. Even with such a simple example, you can see some of the complexities such as in resolving the same address that was entered in multiple locations or in parsing out the valid email addresses from the company data element.

JILL DYCHE AND EVAN LEVY ON CUSTOMER DATA INTEGRATION

"Integrated data is increasingly on people's radar, especially management's. Of the information technology (IT) professionals surveyed by Baseline consulting at the end of 2005, over half claimed that their companies lacked a single, authoritative, customer system of record. Ironically, 77 percent of respondents said that their company executives considered having a 'single version of the truth about customers' to be an important issue."

EDM overview

Benefiting from the EDM

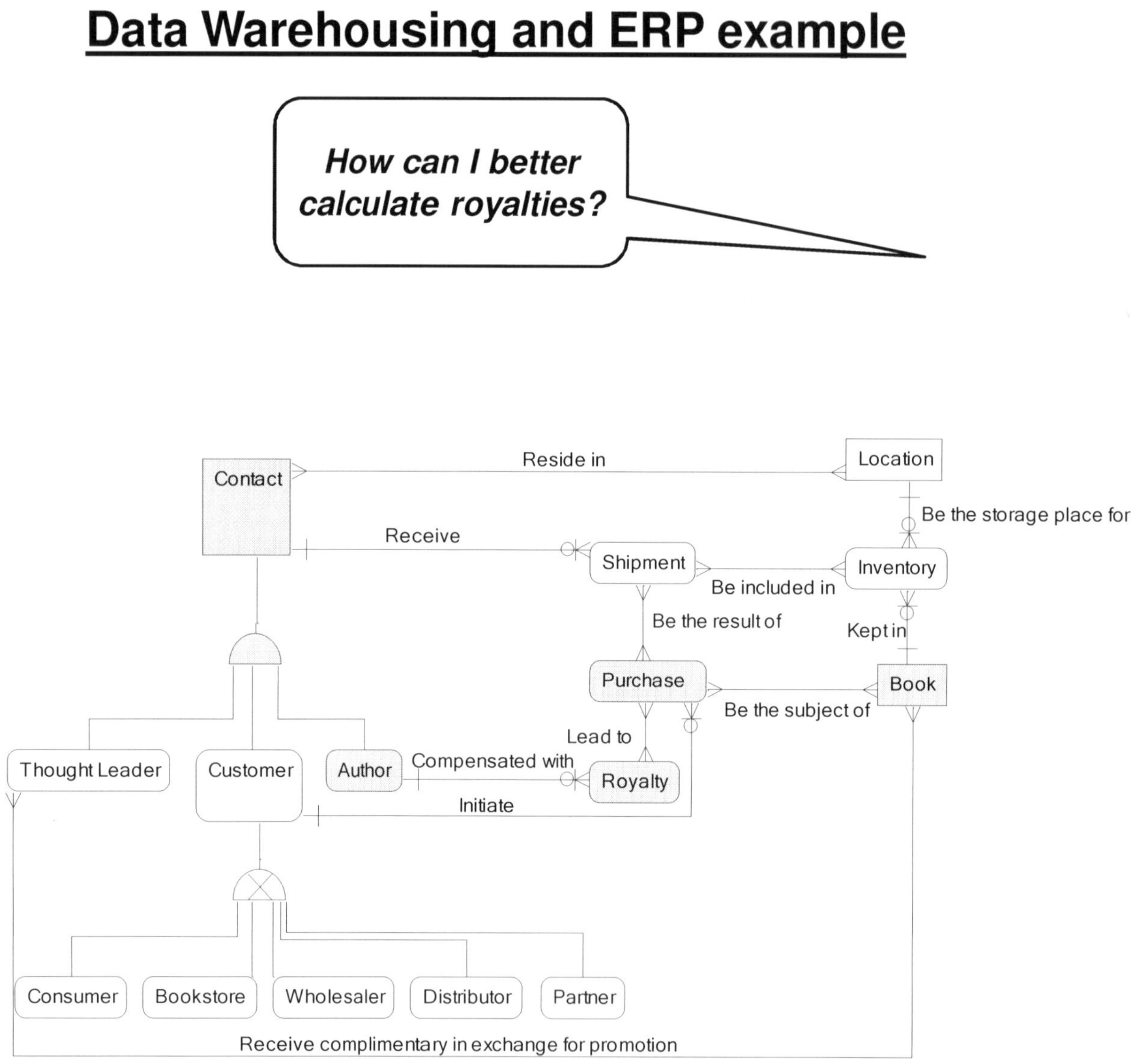

EDM overview

Benefiting from the EDM

AREAS THAT BENEFIT

The EDM along with a mapping back to existing systems offer the greatest benefits for organization-wide initiatives such as enterprise resource planning, master data management, and data warehousing.

ERP

An EDM is a great tool for determining whether a particular ERP package would be a good fit for your organization. ERP vendors should provide some type of model of their system along with definitions, and an analyst can map the ERP system to your EDM to identify any potential data issues prior to investing time and money in the package. Impact analysis is also a frequent use of the EDM for ERP. I participated in a SAP rollout for a global manufacturing company. There were several hundred business and IT employees working very hard to ensure the rollout was a success. However, despite the enormous amount of testing that was done within each of the SAP rollout departments, several unanticipated issues occurred. I built a high level model of part of SAP/R3 for this company to help identify touch points and overlaps within SAP rollouts. It also became a very good communication tool for describing how SAP interacts with other systems and functional areas.

MASTER DATA MANAGEMENT

Master data is all of the data that is shared outside of a single application. Most of the time master data refers to reference data such as Customer and Product, but it can also include event data such as Orders and Credits. An EDM forces a single set of metadata for each data element. This metadata includes a single name, definition, format, domain, and set of business rules. Defining all of this data at an organization level makes master data management possible.

DATA WAREHOUSING

The Data Warehousing Institute defines business intelligence as "The processes, technologies, and tools needed to turn data into information, information into knowledge, and knowledge into plans that drive profitable business actions. Business intelligence encompasses data warehousing, business analytic tools and content knowledge management." The data warehouse is responsible for this first part of the definition: turning data into information. To turn data into information requires both a subject-oriented and integrated view. These are also the two main ingredients of the EDM and therefore the reason the data warehouse needs the EDM.

EDM overview

Top 10 ingredients for success

1. Common agreement on reasons behind building an EDM
2. Correct settings selected
3. Maintenance and use incorporated into methodology
4. Senior manager support
5. Input by those who use and support it (avoid NIH)
6. Input by those considered experts from each area (either broad or depth)
7. Must be developed using standard tools
8. Easily accessible for maintenance and knowledge sharing
9. Tie into organization strategy and mission statement
10. Use their terms

EDM overview

Top 10 ingredients for success

ON THE RIGHT TRACK

1. **Common agreement on reasons behind building an EDM.** Not IT, but business reasons. Most modelers dream of obtaining an enterprise data model. But the dream can become a nightmare if there are no or little business benefits.
2. **Correct settings selected.** Make sure there is a deliberate choice made based on the business reasons.
3. **Maintenance and use incorporated into methodology.** The EDM must outlast fads and budget cuts. I once tied the enterprise effort into our business process framework. I took a slide describing this framework at a high level and superimposed where enterprise data modeling fits on top to create a lasting visual.
4. **Senior manager support.** Not just with talk but by investing resources and money. Both from IT and the business.
5. **Input by those who use and support it (avoid Not Invented Here).** By having the users and the managers of the users have input into building the EDM, not only will you wind up with a higher quality product, but the model will have many supporters.
6. **Input by those considered experts from each area (either broad or depth).** Make them authors of the model.
7. **Must be developed using standard tools.** Tools which many people know or are easy to use.
8. **Easily accessible for maintenance and knowledge sharing.** In one particular case I noticed an EDM I worked on with a university appeared on everyone's wall. A slightly more negative example, in another company nobody knew the EDM even existed because it was just a book in desk drawers.
9. **Tie into organization strategy and mission statement.** In one case, I tied the need for an EDM to 2 of an organization's 10 principles and presented this to the CEO.
10. **Use their terms.** Use the business language. I sometimes use the term 'business model' instead of 'enterprise data model' depending on audience.

Leveraging industry data models

About industry data models

Prebuilt data model that captures how an organization in a particular industry works or should work

<u>Resources</u>

Websites and books

- Data Model Resource Book
- Enterprise Model Patterns
- Databaseanswers.org

Industry consortiums

- National Retail Federation's Association of Retail Technology Standards (ARTS)
- Global Justice XML Data Model
- ACCORD life, annuity and other insurance model
- PPDM/PODS for GEO utilities
- Health Level Seven (HL7) Reference Information Model
- New Generation Operation and Support (NGOSS) Shared Information Data Model (SID)

Vendor models

- Teradata
- IBM
- ADRM

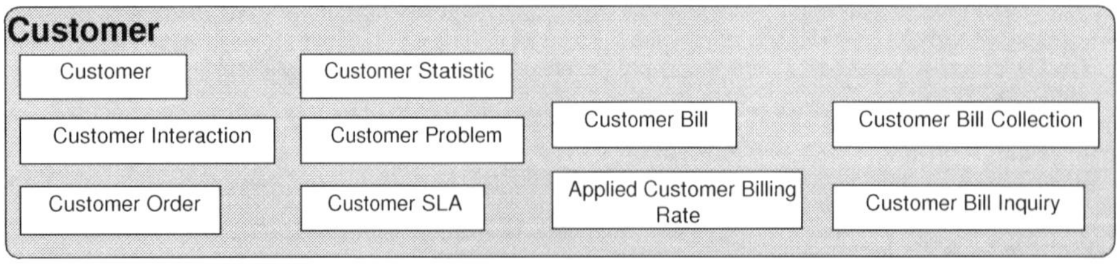

Leveraging industry data models

About industry data models

EXPLANATION

EDMs have been around for over 20 years, yet until recently you would have no choice but to build your EDM from scratch. Today however, instead of reinventing the wheel and modeling structures that have been modeled times before, organizations can leverage industry models. An industry model is a prebuilt data model that captures how an organization in a particular industry works or should work.

COMPETITIVE ADVANTAGE

Use of an industry model is still at its "competitive advantage" stage and not yet at its "competitive necessity" stage. A relatively small number of organizations are using them. For example, in our EDM survey, 18 out of 22 (82%) organizations built their own EDM.

RESOURCES

- **Websites and books.** You can do an online search for terms such as "Enterprise Data Model" or "Insurance Data Model" and see if any of the results can be used. Websites work best when you are planning on building your own EDM and want to supplement it or validate it with existing structures. There are several books on the market that could give your EDM effort a head start. Books are a very inexpensive and at times a very useful source for an EDM. Books written by Len Silverston and David Hay (titles mentioned in the list of references) could shorten the EDM modeling effort. These books provide very flexible reusable structures that you can refine for your business.
- **Industry consortiums.** A number of industries such as telecommunications and healthcare have a consortium that work together on initiatives useful to all of its members. Justice departments also have joined together to produce one common way of looking at justice-related information, called the Global Justice Data Model (JXDM). One of the initiatives many of these consortiums work to complete is an EDM. For example, the telecommunications consortium has the SID (Shared Information Data Model) and healthcare has the HL7 Reference Information Model (RIM).
- **Vendor models.** Vendor models tend to be "on the ground" models that are heavily attributed. In addition, the modelers that build these models have not only heavy modeling experience, but heavy modeling experience within a given industry.

Leveraging industry data models

Use of an industry data model

Ways industry data models are used

- Industry data model is the EDM
- Industry data model is one input to the EDM
- Industry data model is used to identify gaps

Factors that sway an organization towards...

Using an industry data model:

Not using an industry data model:

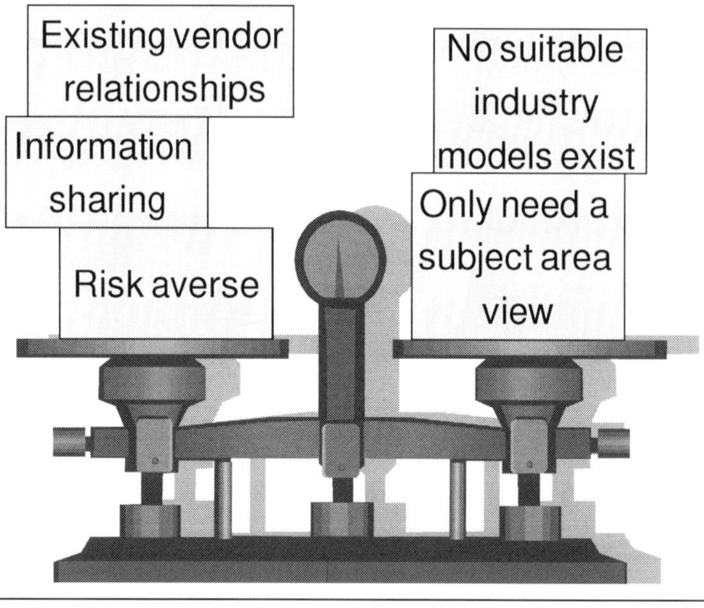

Leveraging industry data models

Use of an industry data model

3 WAYS INDUSTRY DATA MODELS ARE USED

- **Industry data model is the EDM.** Using the industry data model as the EDM means that with the exception of some customization, the organization will completely use the industry data model. Any existing models will need to get mapped into this model.
- **Industry data model is one input to the EDM.** There are many different degrees to which the industry data model can be relied on. It can be the focal point for all of the existing models to map to, or it can be just another model to be used. Each of these models has to be reconciled to create a new model that combines the best of each of the models.
- **Industry data model is used to identify gaps.** This is the least reliance on an industry data model, yet still an important role.

FACTORS THAT SWAY AN ORGANIZATION TOWARDS USING AN INDUSTRY DATA MODEL

- **Risk averse.** What would be the impact if a concept is accidently left off the model or not represented properly?
- **Existing vendor relationships.** If you currently use a lot of existing tools from the same vendor, and already have a strong relationship with that vendor, you might see if they offer any industry models.
- **Information sharing within your industry.** If your business needs to exchange data with other companies within the same industry, an industry model is a good idea.

FACTORS THAT SWAY AN ORGANIZATION TOWARDS NOT USING AN INDUSTRY DATA MODEL

- **Only need a subject area view.** Out of the 18 organizations that built their own EDMs in our survey, 8 of them only needed a subject area view (44%). Subject area models take a relatively short amount of time to create and maintain and therefore the time and money savings of an industry model are minimized.
- **No suitable industry models exist.** There are certain niche industries where no industry model exists and it would be very challenging and time-consuming to customize an industry model to make it work.

Applying the Data Model Scorecard®

Interaction Report for Product BB40 from May 2011

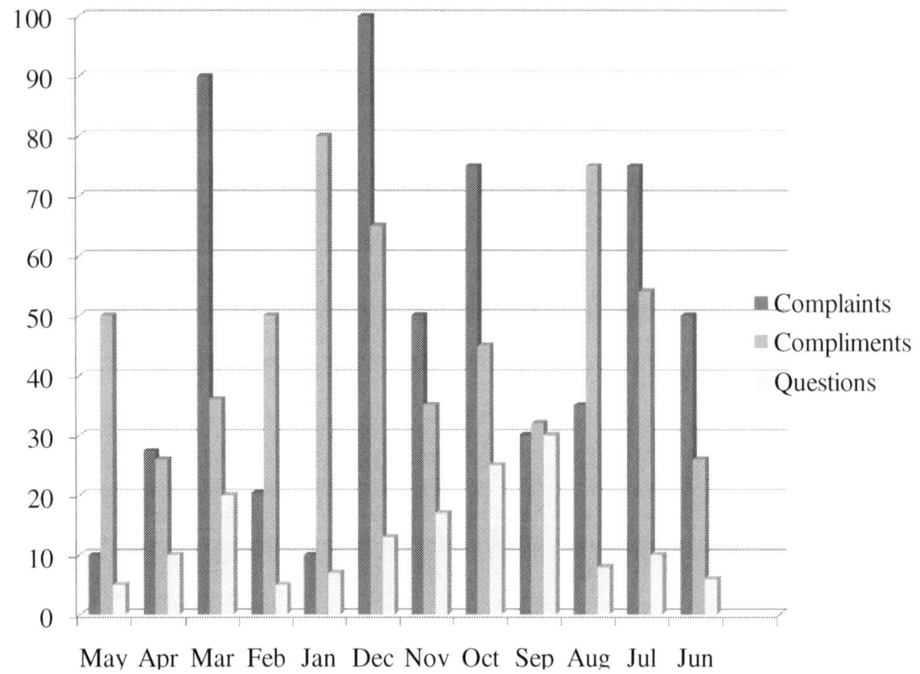

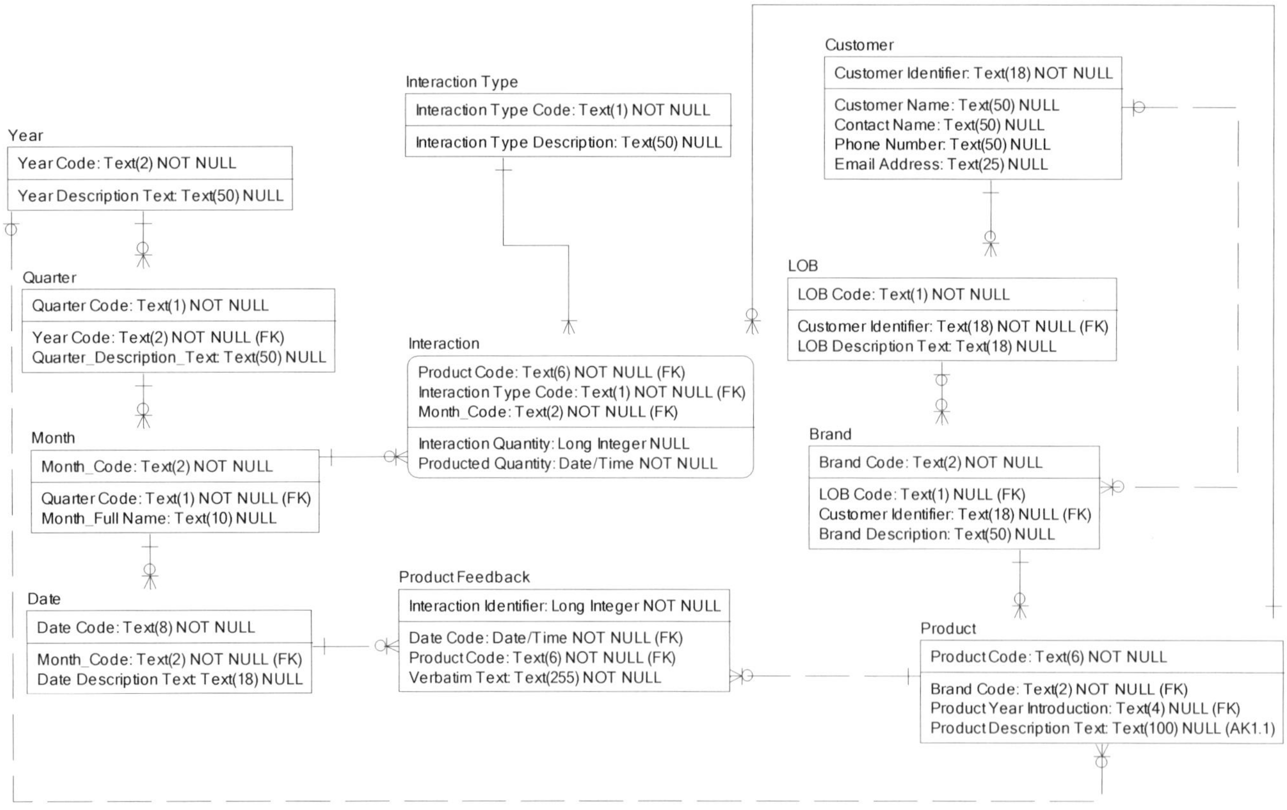

Applying the Data Model Scorecard®

9. How consistent is the model with the enterprise?

EXPLANATION

Confirms the model complements the "big picture". The data model being reviewed should be consistent with the enterprise view.

ANTHING YOU WOULD CATCH IN THE MODEL ON THE FACING PAGE FOR THIS CATEGORY?

1.
2.
3.
4.
5.
6.
7.
8.
9.
10.

#	Category	Total score	Model score	%
1	How well do the characteristics of the model support the type of model?	10		
2	How well does the model capture the requirements?	15		
3	How complete is the model?	15		
4	How structurally sound is the model?	15		
5	How well does the model leverage generic structures?	10		
6	How well does the model follow naming standards?	5		
7	How well has the model been arranged for readability?	5		
8	How good are the definitions?	10		
9	How consistent is the model with the enterprise?	5		
10	How well does the metadata match the data?	10		
	TOTAL SCORE	100		

Module 10

Data Model Scorecard® Category #10: Data

Category Question: How well does the metadata match the data?

This module is your guide to: Comparing the metadata with the data

Category overview

How well does the metadata match the data?

Confirms how well the data elements and their rules match reality

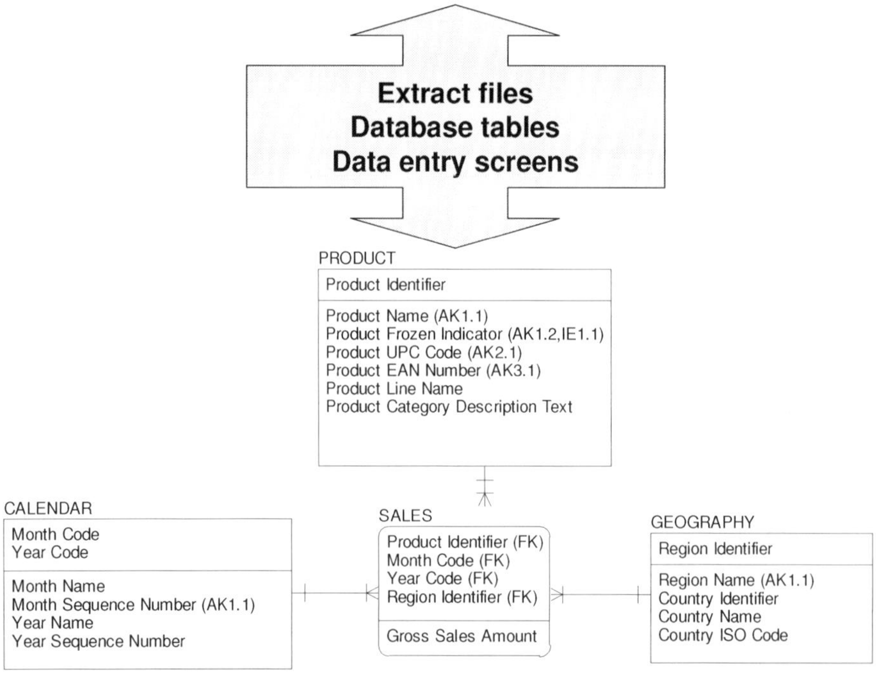

Category overview

How well does the metadata match the data?

EXPLANATION

Confirms how well the data elements and their rules match reality. Does the data element Customer Last Name really contain the customer's last name, for example?

PURPOSE

Ensures the model and the actual data that will be stored within the resulting tables are consistent with each other, so to reduce surprises later on in software development.

CHALLENGE

This might be very difficult to do early in a project's life cycle because data can be difficult to access from the source system before development has begun. However, the earlier the better so you can avoid future surprises which can be much more costly.

WISE WORDS FROM WILLIAM KENT

"An information system is a model of a small, finite subset of the real world. We expect certain correspondences between constructs inside the information system and in the real world. We expect to have one record in the employee file for each person employed by the company. If an employee works in a certain department, we expect to find that department's number in that employee's record....Even these simple expectations run into trouble."

Data Quality Validation Template

Overview

Metadata				Results				Validation (Y / N / ?)				
Name	Definition	Format	Null	First 10-25 distinct values	Percent null	Maximum length	Percent failed lookups	Meaning	Null	Length	Lookup	Comments
PRO_ITEM_REF_DB_ID	The unique identifier generated for a product.	Char(5)	N	12452 33855 85958 37580 38447 38936 33490 48476 38111	0	5	95	Y	Y	Y	?	Are you sure you are doing the lookup properly? Make sure you ignore the last character on each value in this data element when you do the lookup. This last character means something else. Call me if you need more of an explanation.

DQVT is awesome!

- ☐ Documents the accuracy of the metadata
- ☐ Assigns ownership and responsibility to determining if there is a quality issue
- ☐ Highlights problem areas
- ☐ Uncovering complex business logic early

Steps to complete:

1. Copy columns and rows from Family Tree
2. Get access to some data
3. Query data and fill in results section of template
4. Identify the experts and have them validate the results
5. Review their findings
6. Make any necessary changes

Data Quality Validation Template

Overview

EXPLANATION

The spreadsheet on the facing page shows one way of validating data quality early. The Data Quality Validation Template, documents how well the metadata and some of the actual data compares for each data element. This tool contains an expert's opinion of how good or bad the data within each data element actually is.

PURPOSE

- **Documents the accuracy of the metadata**. To make sure that the metadata and data captured side by side is of acceptable quality.
- **Assigns ownership and responsibility to determining if there is a quality issue**. Having the expert's opinions documented, adds more evidence as to whether there is a problem or not.
- **Highlights problem areas**. One of the benefits of any spreadsheet is how easy it can be to highlight information. Cells in a spreadsheet are much easier to find than paragraphs in a long document.
- Uncovering complex business logic early.

STEPS

- **Copy columns and rows from Data Element Family Tree**. This is a simple copy and paste exercise. Try to complete this as early as possible. The earlier you catch a mistake, the more time, money, and frustration you will save early on.
- **Get access to a reasonable amount of data**. Reasonable is defined as at least one week of data for a transaction subject area with lots of daily records, or a month or more for reference subject areas with less records.
- **Run the necessary queries and fill in the results section of the template**. Run simple queries to get a sample set of data, and determine null, format, and lookups. Give linking data elements priority. Linking data elements are those that exist in child tables or interface files and are needed to connect to parent tables.
- **Identify the expert or experts to validate this template and have them review the results**. Usually you can assign validation based on subject area.
- **Review their findings**. This is where we will address any data quality issues that they have raised. The experts should also be in a position to help us resolve these issues. For example, if we are seeing nulls in a not null defined data element, which is right?
- **Make any necessary changes or recommendations**. This is where we will make any updates based on the expert's recommendations.

Applying the Data Model Scorecard®

Interaction Report for Product BB40 from May 2011

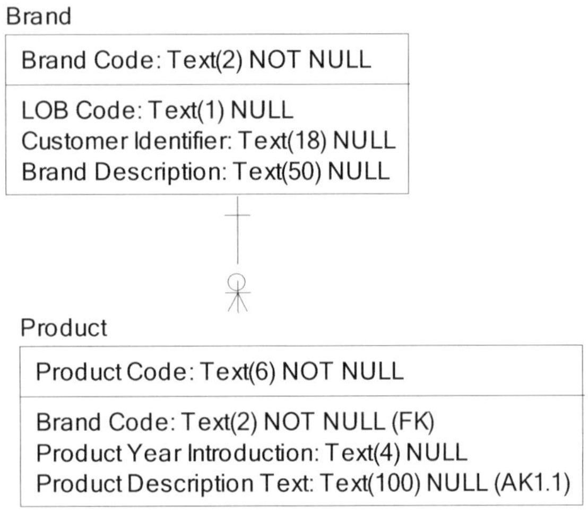

1.

2.

3.

4.

5.

6.

7.

8.

9.

10.

Applying the Data Model Scorecard®

10. How well does the metadata match the data?

EXPLANATION

On the facing page is part of the interaction data model we are reviewing and below are a representative set of data for each of the entities on this model. Anything you would catch on the model in this category? Write the score for this category and from all of the previous categories in the Scorecard below.

Brand

Brand Code	LOB Code	Cust Id	Brand Desc
W1	Q4	391238198	Widgets
	Q4	321912999	
W9		2919128920	Wizards
99			
B3	B2	392191	Warlords

Product

Product Code	**Brand Code**	**Year Introduction**	**Product Desc**
M43431	WI	11	Widget Light
B45328	W1		Widget Heavy
NA		99999	Not Applicable
C21392	B3	2010	Evil Warlords
47	W99	1999	Good Wizards

#	**Category**	**Total score**	**Model score**	%
1	How well do the characteristics of the model support the type of model?	10		
2	How well does the model capture the requirements?	15		
3	How complete is the model?	15		
4	How structurally sound is the model?	15		
5	How well does the model leverage generic structures?	10		
6	How well does the model follow naming standards?	5		
7	How well has the model been arranged for readability?	5		
8	How good are the definitions?	10		
9	How consistent is the model with the enterprise?	5		
10	How well does the metadata match the data?	10		
	TOTAL SCORE	100		

References

Building the Unstructured Data Warehouse, Inmon, W.H., and Krishnan, K.
Technics Publications, LLC, 2007

DAMA Dictionary of Data Management 2nd Edition, DAMA International.
Technics Publications, LLC, 2011

DAMA Guide to the Data Management Body of Knowledge (DAMA-DMBOK), DAMA International.
Technics Publications, LLC, 2009

The Data Modeler's Workbench, Hoberman, S.
John Wiley & Sons, Inc., 2001

Data Modeling Essentials, Third Edition, Simsion G., Witt G.
Morgan Kaufmann Publishers, 2005

Data Modeling Made Simple, 2nd Edition, Hoberman, S.
Technics Publications, LLC, 2009

Data Modeling Made Simple with CA ERwin Data Modeler r8, Burbank, D., Hoberman, S.
Technics Publications, LLC, 2011

Data Modeling for the Business, Hoberman, S., Burbank, D.
Technics Publications, LLC, 2009

Data Modeling Theory and Practice, Simsion, G.
Technics Publications, LLC, 2007

The Data Model Resource Book, Revised Edition, Volume 3, Universal Patterns for Data Modeling, Silverston, L. and Agnew, P.
John Wiley & Sons, Inc., 2009

Data Quality Assessment, Maydanchik, A.
Technics Publications, LLC, 2007

Data Resource Simplexity: How Organizations Choose Data Resource Success or Failure, Brackett, M. Technics Publications, LLC, 2011.

Design Challenge: What is the Enterprise Data Model ROI, Steve Hoberman. DM Review, May 2006

The Enterprise Data Model: A Key Ingredient For Successful Data Warehousing, Kathy Long. The Data Administration Newsletter (www.tdan.com)

The Enterprise Data Model, Noreen Kendle. The Data Administration Newsletter (www.tdan.com)

Enterprise Model Patterns, Hay, David. Technics Publications, LLC, 2011

fruITion: Creating the Ultimate Corporate Strategy for Information Technology, Potts, C. Technics Publications, LLC, 2008

A Guide to the Business Analysis Body of Knowledge® (BABOK® Guide), IIBA, International Institute of Business Analysis, 2009

How Work Gets Done: Business Process Management, Basics and Beyond, Mahal, A. Technics Publications, LLC, 2010

Leveraging the Industry Logical Data Model as your Enterprise Data Model, Hoberman, S. Teradata whitepaper, 2006. (Can be downloaded from www.teradata.com)

recrEAtion: Realizing the Extraordinary Contribution of Your Enterprise Architects, Potts, C. Technics Publications, LLC, 2010

More information on the HL7 Reference Information Model (RIM) can be found at hl7.org.

More information on the SID (Shared Information Data Model) can be found at www.tmforum.org.

More information on the Global Justice XML Data Model can be found at www.it.ojp.gov/jxdm.

More information on the ACORD life, annuity and other insurance model can be found at www.acord.org.

More information on the National Retail Federation (NRF's) Association of Retail Technology Standards (ARTS) can be found at www.nrf-arts.org.

Workshops

Exercises to reinforce skills

Workshop One – BSAM for your org

INSTRUCTIONS Build a Business Subject Area Model of your organization. Write a definition for at least two of the subjects.

TERM	DEFINITION

Workshop One – BSAM for your org

Workshop Two – Modeling Survey Systems

INSTRUCTIONS

A small hotel chain wants to grow, and therefore needs to truly understand consumer feedback and be able to act upon it.

Currently the hotel chain collects consumer feedback using the questionnaire on the facing page, and management briefly examines the stack of completed surveys on a periodic basis looking for areas for improvement. The process is manual and as you can imagine of limited value.

Therefore, management is funding a project to build two applications. One application is a data entry application (called Survey Entry) where administrators will enter the survey results. The second application is a survey analysis reporting application (called Survey Analysis) where users will analyze the Level of Satisfaction ratings for areas for improvement.

You are responsible for eliciting requirements and building the subject area and logical data models for Survey Entry, and the subject area, logical, and physical data models for Survey Analysis. (Note that there is no need to build the physical data model for Survey Entry as management is considering purchasing a package that satisfies all of the business rules in your logical data model.)

Eliciting requirements includes studying the survey form on the facing page and conducting two interviews to arrive at a set of precise and complete business questions. You will scope Survey Analysis with a grain matrix.

Feedback Questionnaire

Please mark X in the appropriate oval ⓧ

JURYS DOYLE HOTELS 2

Gender Male ◯ Female ◯ **Age** 20-30 ◯ 31-45 ◯ 46-60 ◯ 61+ ◯

Are you a Jurys Doyle Priority Guest? Yes ◯ No ◯

Purpose of visit

Business ◯ Mid Week Leisure ◯ Weekend Leisure ◯ Conference in hotel ◯ Conference in city ◯ Tour ◯

Length of stay 1-2 nights ◯ 3-5 nights ◯ 6 nights+ ◯

How many hotel nights have you spent in this city over the last year?

1-5 nights ◯ 6-10 nights ◯ 11-20 nights ◯ 20+ ◯

How many nights have you spent in this hotel over the last year?

1-5 nights ◯ 6-10 nights ◯ 11-20 nights ◯ 20+ ◯

Why did you choose this hotel?

Stayed in this hotel before ◯ Stayed in other Jurys Doyle Hotels/Inns ◯

Company has contracted rates with Jurys Doyle Hotels ◯ Recommended by friend/associate ◯

Recommended by Travel Agent/Tour Operator ◯ Rate offered ◯

How did you make your reservation? Travel Agent ◯ Tour Operator ◯ jurysdoyle.com ◯

bookajurysinn.com ◯ Other website ◯ Jurys Doyle Central Reservations ◯

Nationality Ireland ◯ UK ◯ Continental Europe ◯ USA ◯ Other ◯

Level of satisfaction	Low		Average		High
Friendly and efficient handling of your reservation	◯	◯	◯	◯	◯
Service received at check-out	◯	◯	◯	◯	◯
Overall cleanliness of bedroom and bathroom	◯	◯	◯	◯	◯
How well did the bedroom facilities meet your expectations?	◯	◯	◯	◯	◯
Dinner - variety on wine menu	◯	◯	◯	◯	◯
Breakfast - speed of service	◯	◯	◯	◯	◯
Room Service - quality and presentation of food	◯	◯	◯	◯	◯
How likely are you to stay in other Jurys Doyle Hotels/Jurys Inns based on your experience at this hotel?	◯	◯	◯	◯	◯

Please share any additional comments:

90190

Room No: Date: for office use only

Interview #1: Head of Consumer Affairs

John Jones is the head of Consumer Affairs at Jurys Doyle Hotels. He is our key business user for Survey Analysis. He needs to better understand and track guest feedback.

Interview Question	Response

Interview #2: London Hotel Manager

Bill Barnes is the hotel manager for the Jurys Doyle Hotel based in London. He collects the survey forms and currently submits them to Corporate, to John Jones' attention. Eventually someone on Bill's staff will be entering the contents of the forms into Survey Entry.

Interview Question	Response

Precise and Complete set of Business Questions

Based upon the results of your interviews and the survey form, craft the set of precise and complete business questions needed for Survey Analysis. In the Id column, put a number for each business question from the Head of Consumer Affairs, and put a letter for each business question from the London Hotel Manager.

Id	Precise and Complete Business Question

Grain Matrix

Complete the Grain Matrix below based upon your precise and complete set of business questions and the hotel feedback form.

Survey Analysis Grain Matrix

Survey Entry Subject Area Model

Create a SAM for Survey Entry based upon the interview results and survey questionnaire. Identify the camera settings below.

Survey Entry SAM Camera Settings

Scope	Abstraction	Time	Function
__Dept __Org __Industry	__Bus Clouds __DB Clouds __Ground	__Today __Tomorrow	__Bus __App

Survey Analysis Subject Area Model

Create a SAM for Survey Analysis based upon your completed grain matrix. Identify the camera settings below.

Survey Analysis SAM Camera Settings

Scope	Abstraction	Time	Function
__Dept	__Bus Clouds	__Today	__Bus
__Org	__DB Clouds	__Tomorrow	__App
__Industry	__Ground		

Survey Entry Logical Data Model

Create a LDM for Survey Entry based upon the interview results, survey questionnaire, and Survey Entry CDM. Identify the camera settings below.

Survey Entry LDM Camera Settings

Scope	Abstraction	Time	Function
__Dept	__Bus Clouds	__Today	__Bus
__Org	__DB Clouds	__Tomorrow	__App
__Industry	__Ground		

Survey Analysis Logical Data Model

Create a LDM for Survey Analysis based upon your completed grain matrix, Survey Entry LDM, and Survey Analysis CDM. Identify the camera settings below.

Survey Analysis LDM Camera Settings

Scope	Abstraction	Time	Function
__Dept	__Bus Clouds	__Today	__Bus
__Org	__DB Clouds	__Tomorrow	__App
__Industry	__Ground		

Survey Analysis Physical Data Model

Create a star schema for Survey Analysis based upon your completed LDM above.

Answers

Responses to select exercises

Hierarchy and Network Exercises

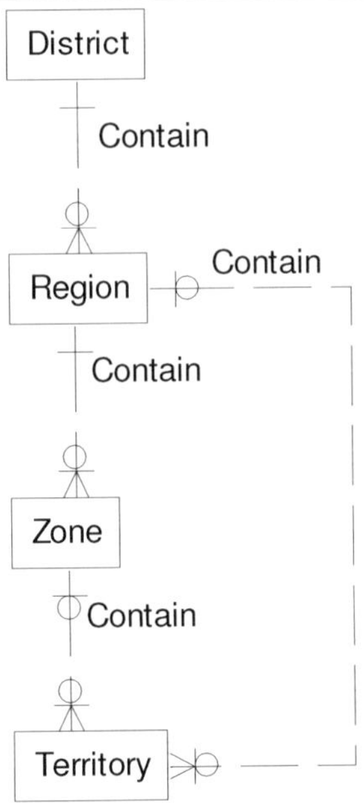

or

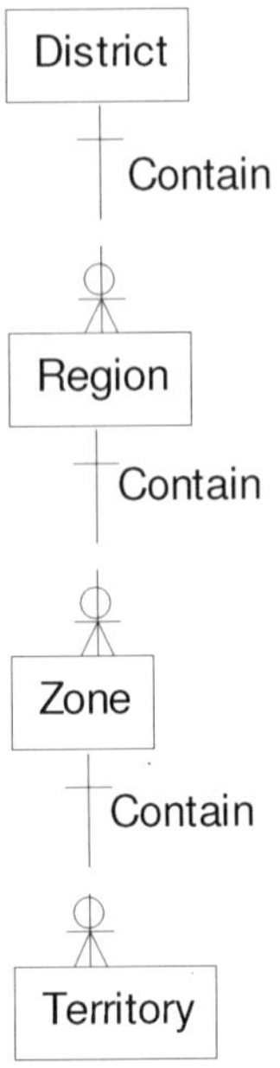

+ 99

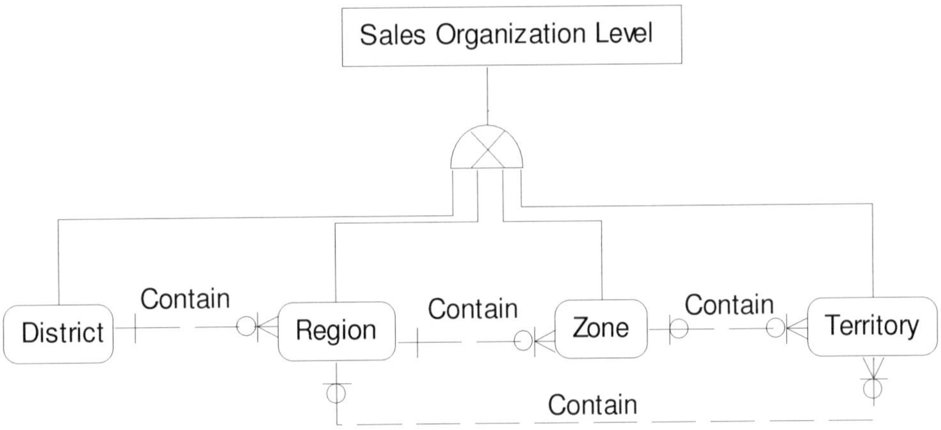

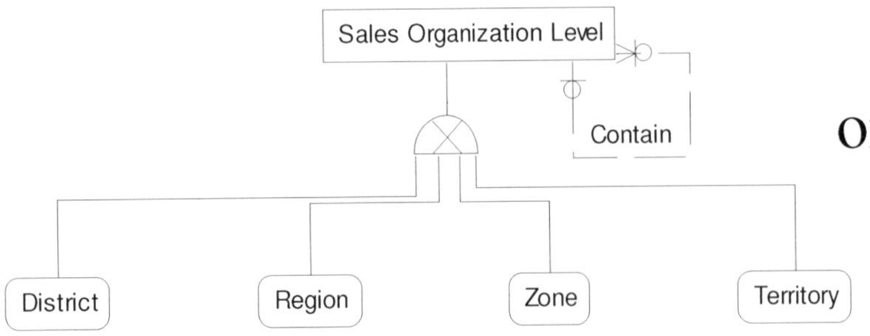

or

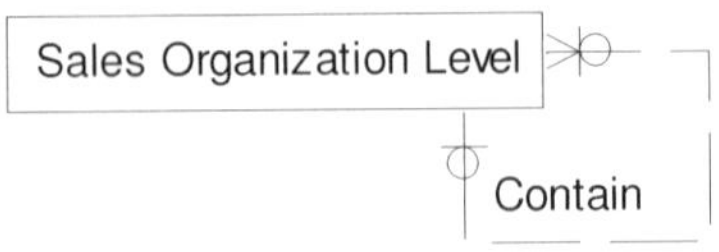

The Corner Office

Option 1:

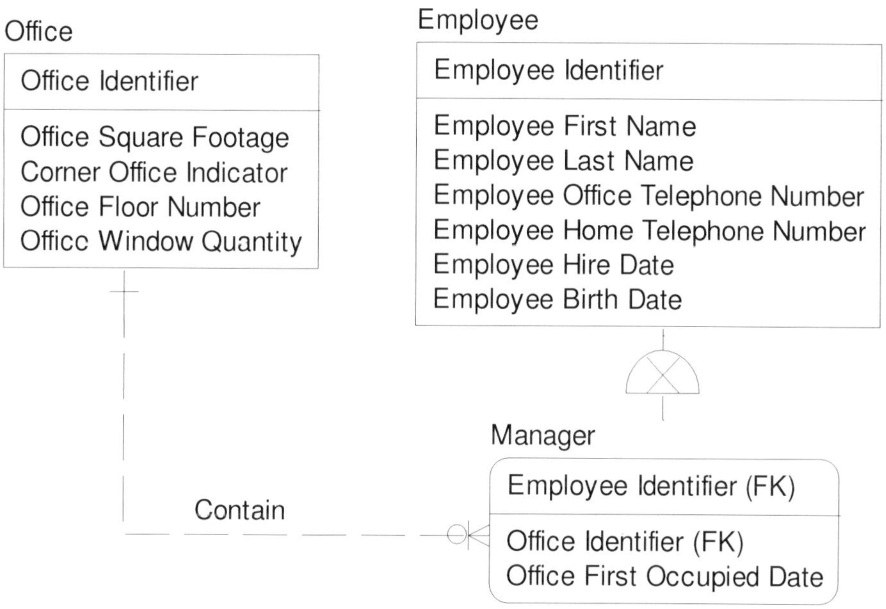

Option 2 (a bit more abstract):

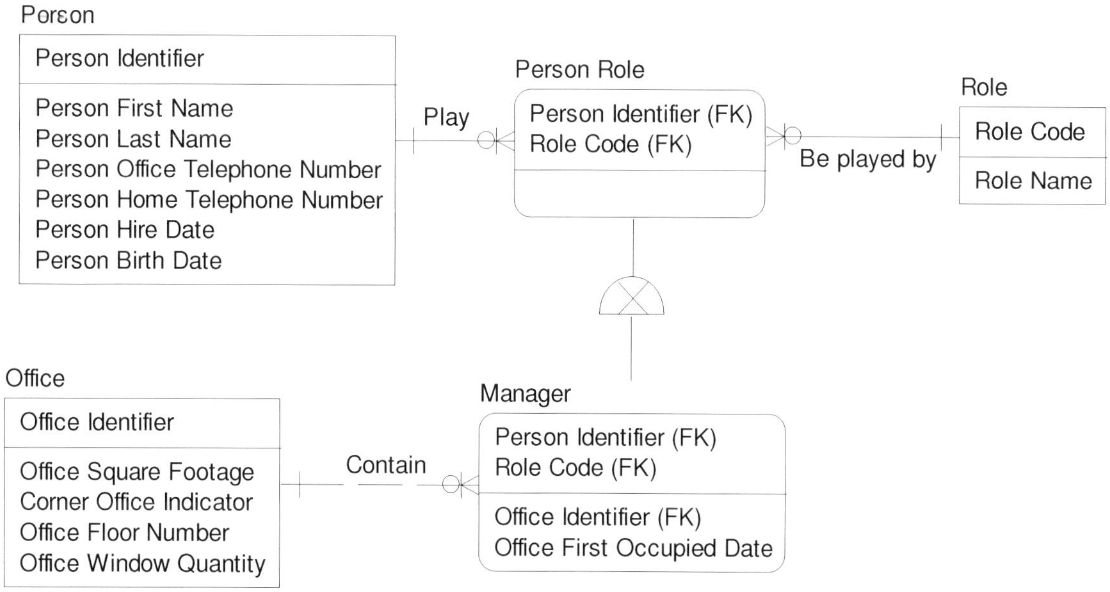

Advanced Normalization Exercises

BCNF exercise

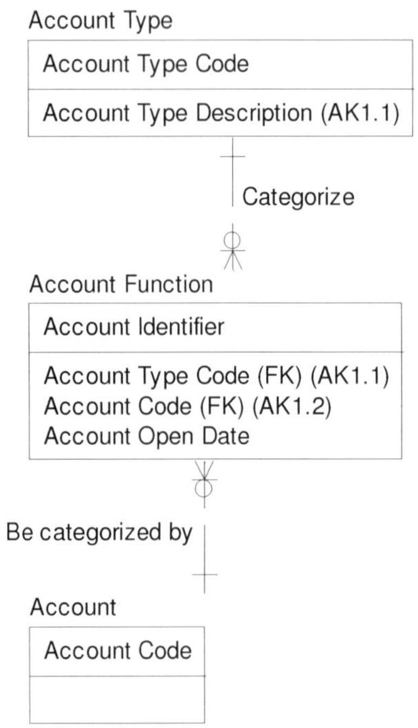

5NF exercise

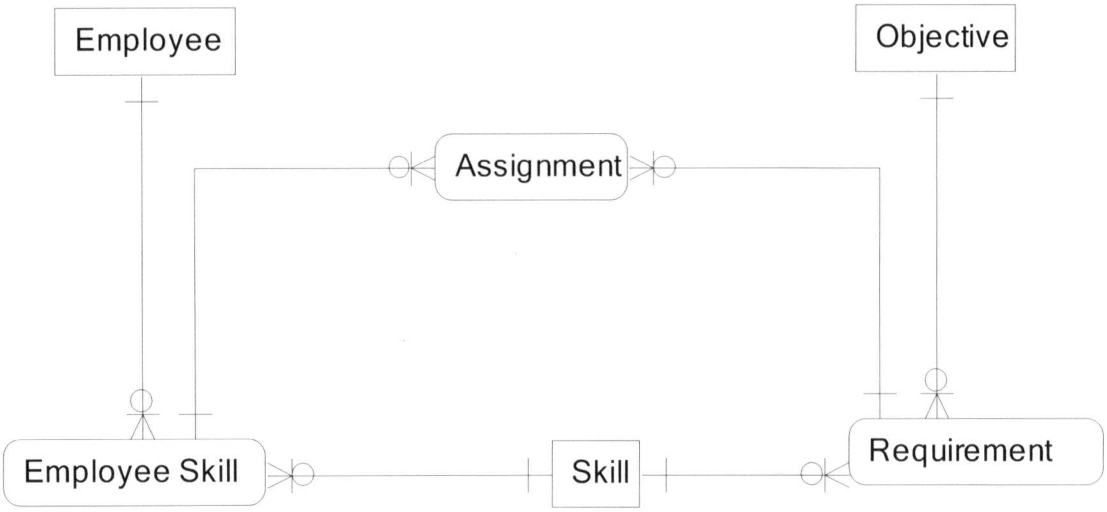

Getting Physical with Subtypes

Rolling down

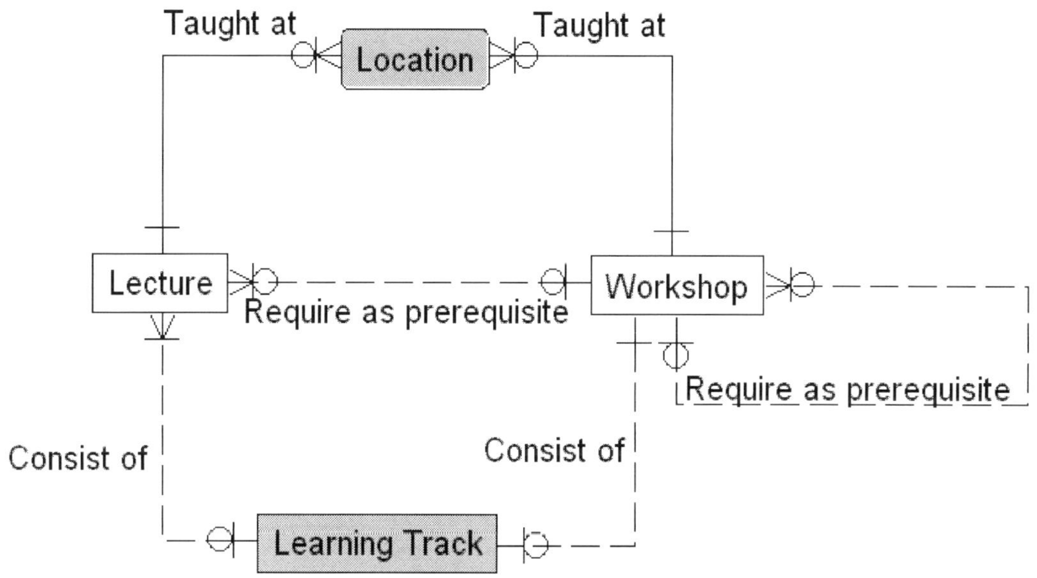

Rolling up

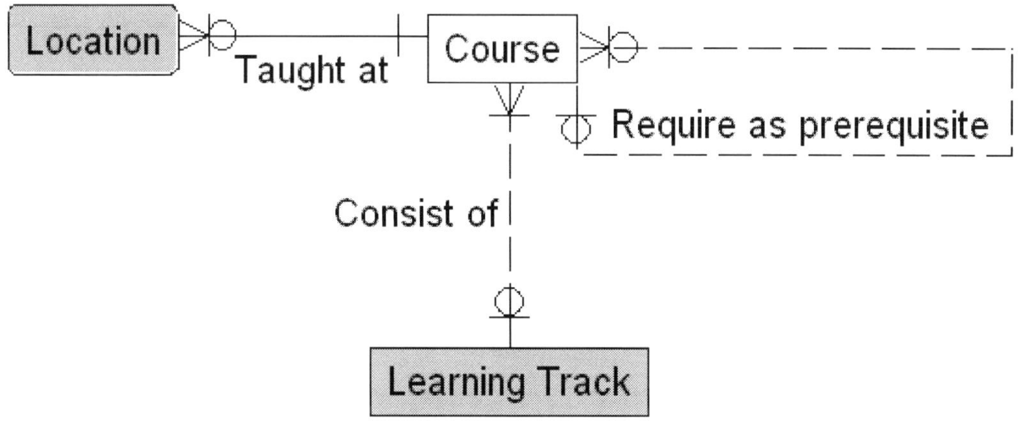

Identity

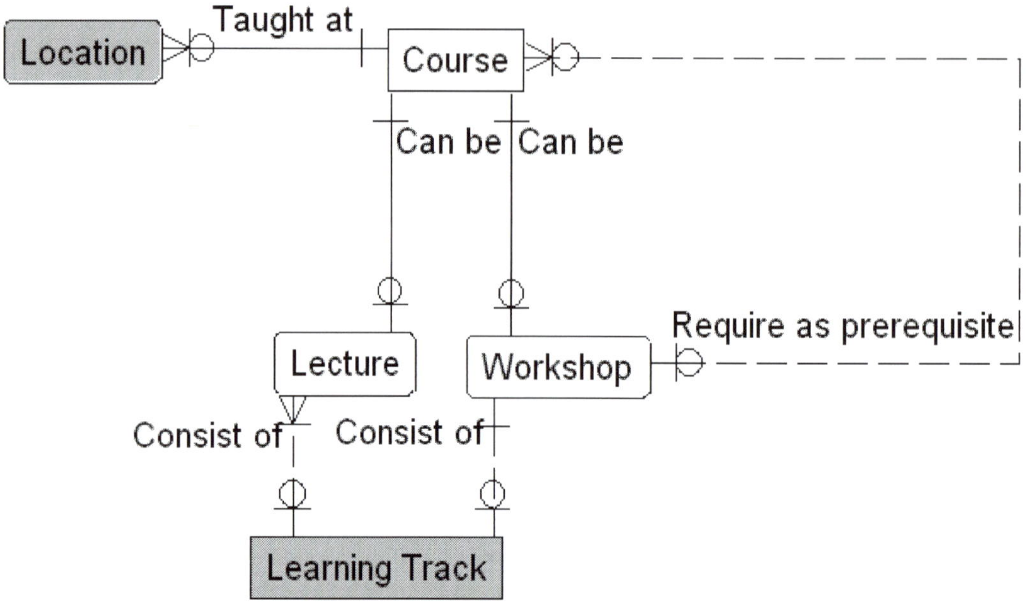

Product Availability

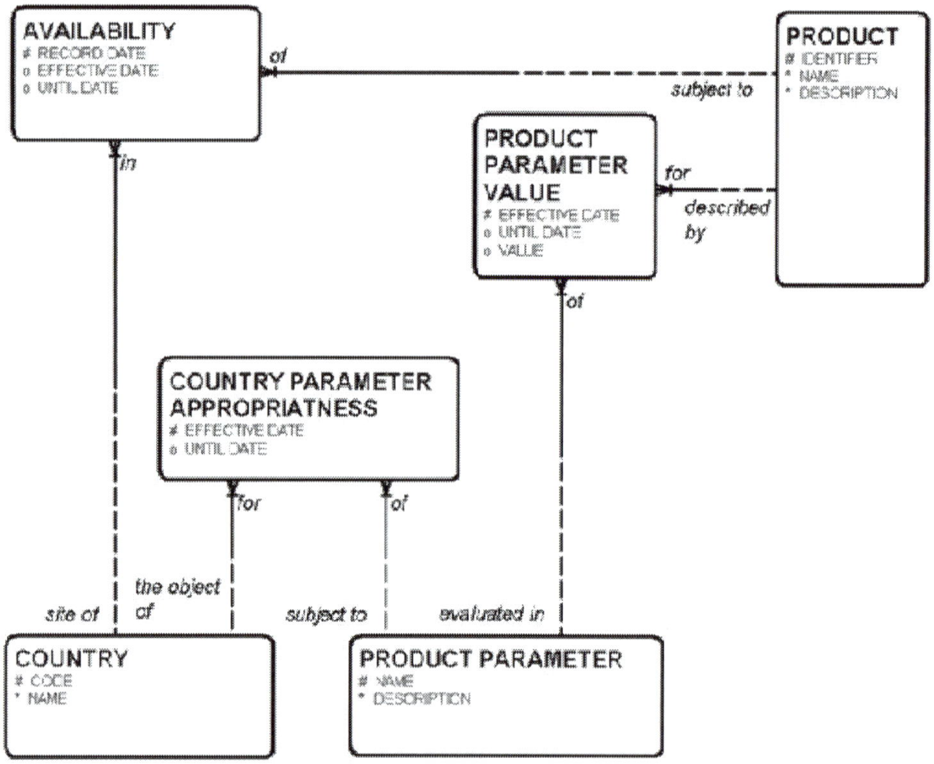

Made in United States
Orlando, FL
10 November 2026

90489287R00254